The World's Greenest Buildings

The World's Greenest Buildings tackles an audacious task. Among the thousands of green buildings out there, which are the best, and how do we know?

Authors Jerry Yudelson and Ulf Meyer examined hundreds of the highest-rated large green buildings from around the world and asked their owners to supply one simple thing: actual performance data, to demonstrate their claims to sustainable operations.

This pivotal book presents:

- an overview of the rating systems and shows "best in class" building performance in North America, Europe, the Middle East, India, China, Australia and the Asia-Pacific region
- practical examples of best practices for greening both new and existing buildings
- a practical reference for how green buildings actually perform at the highest level, one that takes you step-by-step through many different design solutions
- a wealth of exemplary case studies of successful green building projects using actual performance data from which to learn
- interviews with architects, engineers, building owners and developers and industry experts, to provide added insight into the greening process.

This guide uncovers some of the pitfalls that lie ahead for sustainable design, and points the way toward much faster progress in the decade ahead.

Jerry Yudelson is principal of Yudelson Associates, a sustainable design, research and consulting firm located in Tucson, Arizona, www.greenbuildconsult.com and cofounder of the largest green building trade show in the US, *Greenbuild.* The U.S. Green Building Council named him in 2011 to the inaugural class of 34 LEED Fellows, a singular honor.

Ulf Meyer has taught in the U.S. at Kansas State University and the University of Nebraska, where he held the Hyde Chair of Excellence in 2010-2011. He is a partner at Ingenhoven Architects in Düsseldorf, Germany, considered one of the pioneers of sustainable architecture in Europe.

"Addressing the challenges of our time, Yudelson and Meyer identify the true leaders in sustainable building design. Using real performance data, they showcase and compare buildings which combine great design, environmental quality and sustainability, providing the guidance necessary for the next generation of sustainable building design. A must read for every architect and engineer!"

Thomas Auer, Transsolar Climate Engineering, Germany

"This is information we have all been waiting for; while offering a global overview of green buildings, it helps to unlock the truth about the real performance of sustainable commercial architecture."

Steffen Lehmann, School of Art, Architecture and Design,
University of South Australia

"Here, Yudelson and Meyer have identified global design exemplars that integrate architecture and context, economics and social responsibility, performance and aesthetics, demonstrating exciting solutions to meet the challenges of creating a more sustainable world."

Bruce Kuwabara, founding partner, Kuwabara Payne McKenna Blumberg
Architects and design architect for Manitoba Hydro Place, Canada

"Yudelson and Meyer's great achievement is the qualification of the quantitative and the quantification of the qualitative for the ecological commercial typology in architecture."

Martin Despang, School of Architecture, University of Hawaii

The World's Greenest Buildings

Promise versus performance in sustainable design

Jerry Yudelson and Ulf Meyer

FOREWORD
by PROFESSOR ALISON G. KWOK
University of Oregon

LONDON AND NEW YORK

First published in 2013
by Routledge
2 Park Square, Milton Park, Abingdon, OX14 4RN

Simultaneously published in the USA and Canada
by Routledge
711 Third Avenue, New York, NY 10017

Routledge is an imprint of the Taylor & Francis Group, an informa business

British Library Cataloguing in Publication Data
A catalogue record for this book is available from the British Library

Library of Congress Cataloging in Publication Data
Yudelson, Jerry.
The world's greenest buildings : promise versus performance in sustainable design/
Jerry Yudelson and Ulf Meyer.
pages cm
Includes index.
1. Sustainable buildings—Evaluation. 2. Buildings—Performance. I. Meyer, Ulf, 1970–
II. Title.
TH880.Y64 2012
720'.47—dc23 2012019150

ISBN: 978-0-415-60629-5 (pbk)
ISBN: 978-0-203-08216-4 (ebk)

Typeset in Syntax
by Florence Production Ltd, Stoodleigh, Devon, UK
Printed by Ashford Colour Press Ltd, Gosport, Hampshire

Contents

Illustrations

FIGURES

Cover, top: One Shelley Street, Sydney, Australia.
© Brookfield Australia Investments Ltd.
Cover, bottom: Daniel Swarovski Corporation, Männedorf, Switzerland. Photo: Andreas Keller, Altdorf, courtesy of ingenhoven architects.

TABLES

About the Authors

Jerry Yudelson, MS, MBA, PE, LEED Fellow, is the most published author in the green building space, having written twelve previous books since 2005. The US Green Building Council named him in 2011 to the inaugural class of thirty-four LEED Fellows, a singular honor. In 2001, he became one of the ten original national trainers for the LEED system, a position he held for eight years. He is the cofounder of the largest green building trade show in the USA, Greenbuild. Since 2006, Yudelson has been Principal of Yudelson Associates, a sustainable design, research, and consulting firm located in Tucson, Arizona (www.greenbuildconsult.com). He frequently keynotes green building and sustainable cities conferences in the USA and in many countries around the world. He holds civil and environmental engineering degrees from the California Institute of Technology and Harvard University, along with an MBA (with highest honors) from the University of Oregon. He lives in the Sonoran Desert bioregion in Arizona with his wife Jessica and Scottish terrier, Bodhi.

Professor Ulf Meyer, Dipl.-Ing., studied architecture at the Technical University (TU) of Berlin and the Illinois Institute of Technology in Chicago. After his graduation from TU Berlin with a master's degree in 1996, he became an architectural critic and writer for newspapers and magazines from around the world. He has published more than 1,000 articles and ten books, among them the bestselling book *Bauhaus Architecture*, published by Prestel of Munich. In 2001–2002 he worked for Shigeru Ban Architects in Tokyo, Japan, considered one of the pioneering architectural offices in the world for the use of sustainable materials in contemporary architecture. In 2004, Ulf received the prestigious German–American Arthur F. Burns Award and was the guest critic for the *San Francisco Chronicle* in San Francisco, California. Ulf has curated several architectural exhibitions in Germany, China, and the Netherlands. He has lectured at dozens of universities and cultural centers on four continents. He is a partner at Ingenhoven Architects in Düsseldorf, Germany, considered one of the pioneers of sustainable architecture in Europe. Professor Meyer has taught in the USA at Kansas State University and the University of Nebraska, where he held the Hyde Chair of Excellence in 2010–2011. He has traveled extensively in Europe, East Asia, and North America. He lives in Berlin, Germany, with his wife Mao and two young children.

Foreword

Fifteen years ago, if asked the question "What makes a building green?" most professionals in the building industry would have answered, "Bad taste in paint." Today, "green" is clearly identified with having fewer negative effects on the natural environment. Buildings, or rather human uses of buildings, impact the natural environment in a variety of ways, including contributing to anthropogenic climate change, habitat destruction, and pollution of water, air, and soil. To be green, a building must reduce or eliminate these impacts. Running along a scale from the greenish-gray of impact reduction to clear emerald of complete elimination are a wide variety of building practices and a market crowded with the variety certifications, targets, and codes that define what a "green" building is. The ultimate goal of being green is to be sustainable, e.g., to create buildings which either have no impact on or actually improve the inhabitability of the planet. A green building is, therefore, a building that makes progress toward being sustainable.

The appropriate type and pace of movement toward sustainability is defined differently by a number of different certification systems, which more and more require that buildings prove their performance. Most well known in the USA is the LEED system.[1] In terms of energy, LEED establishes performance levels above code minimums. Buildings achieve LEED certification based primarily on their potential and are intended to represent the upper 25 percent of the market in terms of environmental performance. However, LEED is justly criticized for not being based in whole or in part on actual performance. In response, LEED version 3 (begun in 2009) now requires that each project submit actual energy performance data for statistical purposes.

Started in 2005, the 2030 Challenge is a straightforward performance-based challenge to create buildings that drastically reduce energy use.[2] The challenge goal in 2005: 50 percent reduction in carbon emissions from the average building. Every five years, the challenge is increased by 10 percent, meaning that, by 2030, a building meeting this test would be carbon neutral.

The International Living Building Institute launched the Living Building Challenge (LBC) in 2006.[3] The LBC starts with the concept of "triple net zero" where a project generates all of its energy on site with renewable energy systems such as photovoltaics or wind, harvests all of its water from the precipitation that falls on the site, and treats all of the stormwater and sewage so that none leaves the site without being treated. Projects must demonstrate they meet all twenty program requirements by showing a full year of operating data.

Taken together, these ratings systems can present a confusing picture of how to measure green building performance. However, it appears that all rating systems are getting more ambitious and ultimately converging on buildings that have zero-net carbon emissions.

Under its Energy Performance in Buildings Directive, the European Union has required since 2010 that all member countries mandate that building owners provide energy-use data to all prospective renters, tenants and buyers.[4] However, as of the end of 2010, there was still far from universal compliance with this directive, and the EU is in the process of revising its standards to ensure full responsiveness by building owners. Typically, as in the case of the UK, energy-use data is measured against national averages and does not provide adequate methods to compare actual performance against predictions, especially for new buildings.

Predicting how certain levels of carbon-emissions reduction will affect climate change makes it easier to answer the question "How green is green enough?" Clearly, radical reductions in production of greenhouse gases will be necessary even to maintain considerable and dangerous levels of warming. According to climate researchers, to maintain CO_2 levels that would cause 3.6–4.3°F (2.0–2.4°C) in warming, we would have to reduce anthropogenic emissions of greenhouse gases across the board 50–85 percent lower than 2000 levels by 2050. What this number suggests is that emissions reductions must be dramatic and that measuring sustainability by actual building performance is essential to getting the job done.

We cannot judge a building as green unless we know how it performs. This does not require reducing a building merely to a single number such as EUI (energy use intensity or energy usage index), but it must include real data showing energy use, water use, human comfort, and other metrics. There are two primary reasons why post-occupancy verification of green measures is necessary:

1. We won't know if our efforts are working if we don't measure results, leading to wasted effort, money, and time. Green design can only be successful if the process is seen as a cycle moving through design to construction to assessment that improved the next design in the cycle.
2. Designers have become expert at "talking the talk," but if we don't "walk the walk," our clients will begin to see green as just another marketing scheme. Certifying an underperforming building as green understandably leads to cynicism and undermines the massive human effort that must be harnessed if we are to combat climate change and other environmental issues.

Collecting and evaluating building performance information, as Yudelson and Meyer have done for this book, presents many challenges, including privacy concerns, liability, time investment, data availability, and uncertainties about how to interpret the data. On some projects, the building owner who possesses the utility data may not want to share it with others. It is not hard to imagine that after an owner has invested money and time in constructing a "green" building, they might not want to share data that indicates the building is underperforming. Reluctance to share data for underperforming buildings is particularly unfortunate; failed "green" buildings are enormous opportunities for learning.

At other times, measuring building performance may happen or not simply because there is no clear party designated to perform the measurement. Post-occupancy studies take time (and money). Understanding building performance benefits owners, architects, and consultants, but unless there is a clear structure for who will pay for and own the results, collection and evaluation of data may not happen on any given project. A solution to this problem is for project teams to designate a person for this role, at the beginning of the project, as part of initial contract negotiations, whether a consultant, architect, or building manager.

While the only data needed to calculate the gross EUI of a building are utility bills and square footage, the data needed to understand how different building systems are interacting is often unavailable; our sub-metering practices have not caught up with our green innovations. For example, it may be unclear whether good performance in a building is due to lower plug loads or lower lighting loads, if lighting and plug loads are not metered separately. Adding in sub-metering at the project outset would sharpen the tools we have for building performance assessment.

Once data is collected, how is it interpreted? How can this knowledge help to improve design? Though adequate utility and building systems information may be available, the question of why a building is performing in a certain way is often difficult to answer with certainty, or without a large investment in time and effort. Also muddying the interpretation of building performance is human nature. Buildings don't inherently use energy: the occupants and their use of the building do. People with different habits, priorities, comfort levels, or preferences can use a carefully designed building in unanticipated ways. Sub-metering, for example, can separate plug loads from process loads and help in determining whether improvement efforts should focus on occupant behavior or building systems performance.

Understanding the obstacles to collecting and interpreting building data is important but shouldn't distract or discourage building professionals from diving in and attempting to learn from the performance of every building project. The project teams contributing to this book show that these issues can be overcome. Yudelson's and Meyer's effort to collect and document the stories of the world's greenest buildings as measured by performance is essential. Rather than judging these projects on the basis of certification among disparate systems, Yudelson and Meyer compare them against the same yardstick: energy and water performance. These projects represent successful team efforts that, when taken together, define best green building practices worldwide.

Alison G. Kwok
Professor of Architecture
University of Oregon
Eugene, Oregon

Preface

Buildings and building operations account worldwide for about 40 percent of global anthropogenic carbon emissions, including construction, operations, renovation, supply, and maintenance. Consequently, the energy performance of buildings has received growing attention from government, business, and nongovernmental organizations over the past half-decade. Most people realize that global climate change can only be addressed by tackling the issue of energy performance of buildings, as we strive to build and rebuild more sustainable cities. In addition, many people realize that building energy performance can be substantially improved with relatively straightforward design, construction, and operational measures.

At the same time, there is growing appreciation for the extensive benefits offered by green buildings, which include attributes other than energy conservation, such as improved urban design, intelligent location, sustainable site practices, water conservation, materials and resources conservation, and indoor environmental quality.

For the past several years, there has been an ongoing debate about the real performance of green buildings, especially in terms of reductions in energy and water use. In particular, debate has centered on those projects, perhaps 25 percent of the total certified and measured green buildings, shown to be performing *worse* than predicted and, in some cases, worse than conventional buildings (i.e. those built to standard building or energy code requirements).

After all, if a project doesn't deliver substantial savings in energy use and carbon emissions, or in water use (an increasingly important concern worldwide), why call it a "green" building, no matter what its rating might be in a particular sustainable construction scoring system?

More recent research has shown that most LEED-certified US projects are delivering an average of about 35 to 45 percent energy savings, when compared with a baseline determined by the ASHRAE Standard 90.1 (either 2004 or 2007 versions).

Realizing that actual performance is the critical missing information for green building projects, we set out in 2010 to find this information and to put it into a particular context: *the world's greenest buildings.*

Established third-party green building rating systems first came into significant use in the mid-1990s and early 2000s in the USA, Canada, Australia, and the UK. Beginning about 2006, these systems began to gain increasing popularity in these countries, as hundreds, eventually thousands, of projects registered intent to participate in them. The oldest system, promulgated by the UK's Building Research Establishment (BRE), found widespread use primarily in that country, where the top rating was BREEAM Excellent, more recently Outstanding. The second-oldest system, Leadership in Energy and Environmental Design (LEED), developed and promoted by the US Green Building Council and now in use in more than 30,000 nonresidential projects in 130 countries, gives a top rating of Platinum to about 6 percent of total projects certified.

The Australian Green Star system (also used in New Zealand and South Africa) gives a top rating of 6-Star (World Excellence) to a handful of certified projects. Singapore, Japan, Hong Kong, Germany, France, and a handful of other countries created similar green building systems.

LEED was officially adopted (and adapted for local conditions) in Canada and India. However, at this time, LEED is the dominant system in global use. Chapter 3 describes in greater detail several of the more widely used rating systems.

For the authors, the salient fact in the universe of green building rating systems is that they are converging globally around similar issues, similar measurements, and similar weightings of relative importance among a number of environmental attributes, with energy use (and its attendant carbon emissions) as the largest single factor in each system. More than ninety countries have national green building councils (as of year-end 2011), so the issue of how the greenest buildings in the world are performing has become of greater global interest.

In this book, we define the "world's greenest buildings" in the following way. To make its way into this book, a building must satisfy the following conditions:

- have at least 50,000 sq ft (4,500 sq m) of conditioned floor space
- be a nonresidential typology
- be among the highest rated in a recognized national/international rating system (e.g., LEED Platinum)
- be willing to share a full year of energy-use data (and water use where available)[1]
- new construction, with operations beginning after September 30, 2003 (thus representing the sustainable design "state of the art" during the past decade)
- represent "very good to best results" in energy performance, based on local climate and building type (e.g., schools should use less energy than office buildings because of fewer hours of annual operations, whereas laboratories would use considerably more energy than offices because of significant ventilation requirements).

While these conditions are necessarily arbitrary, they do represent a good way to differentiate between projects that are relatively easier to make sustainable (e.g., smaller buildings and homes) and those that require substantially more resources, commitment, and excellence in execution to achieve outstanding green results.

As we proceeded with our research in 2010 and 2011, it became apparent that a number of recent projects (say, those completed after fall 2010) would naturally merit inclusion in this book but would not have a full year of operating data by the end of November 2011, generally our cutoff date for data to be used in this book. As a result, and recognizing that low-energy green design is a rapidly evolving art and practice, we decided to include eight of these projects at the end of the book in Chapter 9, as Projects to Watch.

One final note: we both appreciate good architecture! One of our aims in writing this book is to demonstrate that "über-green building," low energy use, and great architecture are not incompatible. To the contrary, we believe that good-to-great architecture is essential for sustainable design: unattractive buildings will not be as highly valued by owners, occupants, and the public.

We can all argue about defining "good architectural design" but without it the world would be a much poorer place. With it, we can have super green buildings, more each year even with zero-net energy use, that will provide inspiration for the sustainable transformation of the building design and construction industry that we strongly advocate.

We hope that this book represents a way station on the road to a sustainable future, one in which the goal of living lightly on the earth will become increasingly realized through the quintessential human activity: the built environment.

Jerry Yudelson and Ulf Meyer
Tucson, Arizona, USA and Berlin, Germany

Acknowledgments

This book exists because of the dedicated efforts of hundreds of architects, engineers, constructors, owners, developers, and many others who set out over the past decade to create a new world of great green buildings and, despite considerable obstacles, actually succeeded. To these building teams around the world, we all owe our profound gratitude.

We also thank specifically the many architects, engineers, builders, and building owners who responded with case-study information and who cooperated far more than we expected by providing detailed operating data, project information, and building photos. Their contribution is noted in specific case studies throughout the book. Those we interviewed for the book are noted in Appendix A.

We also want to thank our editor at Routledge/Taylor & Francis, Laura Williamson, for championing this book.

Thanks also to those who reviewed the book proposal and offered helpful suggestions along the way and to those who reviewed the manuscript. As always, any errors of omission or commission are ours alone.

There is one person to whom we owe a special acknowledgment; that person is Gretel Hakanson, with whom the senior author has now collaborated on ten books. She was consistently creative, persistent, and reliable in gathering information for this book. She conducted and transcribed many of the interviews for this book, provided initial drafts of many case studies, gathered photos and illustrations along with the required permissions, edited the manuscript, and performed myriad other tasks to see the book through to completion. Without her contribution, this book would not have seen the light of day in any reasonable time frame, or perhaps at all.

We also acknowledge research support from Jaimie Galayda, PhD, who helped us identify the universe of US and Canadian LEED Platinum projects that met our criteria and began the process of contacting building teams for information. We thank Alfonso Ponce of Deloitte France for contributing some of his research on green building rating systems worldwide, along with Meghan Sarkozi, a recent architectural graduate who prepared information describing some of the world's green building rating systems; Francisco J. Alvarado, a graduate student at the University of Arizona, for finding and translating information on a green building project in Chile; and Tim Winstanley, also a graduate student at the University of Arizona, for preparing data for publication. We thank Heidi Ziegler-Voll for the illustrations created especially for the book and for redrawing those that needed it; she is a frequent and imaginative contributor to a number of Yudelson's books.

We also received generous contributions of essays from Alfonso Ponce, Deloitte Real Estate Advisory, Paris, France (Chapter 3); Peter Rumsey, Integral Group, Oakland, California (Chapter 8); and Mark Frankel, New Buildings Institute, Seattle, Washington (Chapter 8).

There is one group of people who are acknowledged in the book, and whose contributions to the book are enormous: the many architectural photographers, architects, and building owners who generously permitted us to use, without fees, the beautiful building and project photos you will see throughout the book. With no real budget for photography, their cooperation was essential to produce this work in the form you see it here. We thank them sincerely for their cooperation.

Finally, we offer profound gratitude to our wives, Jessica Stuart Yudelson and Mao Meyer, for their help and support of this project. A native Japanese speaker, Mao Meyer was helpful in locating and translating information about projects in Japan. As a native German speaker, Ulf Meyer accessed and translated a considerable body of material not easily accessible to a non-German-speaking audience. He also conducted interviews with two leading green German architects, Matthias Sauerbruch and Christoph Ingenhoven.

Jerry Yudelson and Ulf Meyer
Tucson, Arizona, USA and Berlin, Germany

Abbreviations

ABW	activity-based working
ADA	Americans with Disabilities Act
AIA	American Institute of Architects (USA)
ASU	Arizona State University
BD+C	Building Design and Construction (magazine)
BIOCHP	biofuel combined heat and power
BMS	building management system
BRE	Building Research Establishment (UK)
BTU	British Thermal Unit
CBECS	Commercial Building Energy Consumption Survey (published by the US Department of Energy/Energy Information Administration)
CCHP	combined cooling and heating power plant
CDN	Commercial Development Nordic
CFC	chlorofluorocarbon
CFD	computational fluid dynamics
CFM	cubic feet per minute
CHH	Center for Health and Healing
CHP	combined heat and power (plant)
COTE	Committee on the Environment (of the AIA)
Cx	Commissioning
DCV	demand-controlled ventilation
DGNB	Deutsche Gesellschaft für Nachhaltiges Bauen (Germany)
DGU	double-glazed units
DOAS	dedicated outside air system
EEWH	Energy, Ecology, Waste Reduction and Health (Taiwan)
ETFE	ethylene tetrafluoroethylene
EUI	energy use intensity *or* energy use index
FSC	Forest Stewardship Council
GBCA	Green Building Council of Australia
GBCs	Green Building Councils
GHG	greenhouse gases
GRIHA	Green Rating for Integrated Habitat Assessment (India)
GWP	global warming potential
HCFC	hydrochlorofluorocarbons
HP	horsepower
HVAC	heating, ventilation, and air conditioning
kl	kiloliter
kBTU/kBtu	thousands of BTU
KW	kilowatt (power)

kWh	kilowatt-hour (energy)
IAQ	indoor air quality
IDP	integrated design process
IEQ	Indoor Environmental Quality (LEED system)
LCA	life-cycle assessment
$LCCO_2$	life-cycle carbon dioxide
LEED	Leadership in Energy and Environmental Design (from USGBC)
LTES	long-term energy storage
MBR	membrane bioreactor
MEP	mechanical, electrical, and plumbing
NABERS	National Australian Built Environment Rating System
NCKU	National Cheng Kung University (Taiwan)
NLA	net lettable area
NPV	net present value
ODP	ozone depletion potential
PEFC	Programme for the Endorsement of Forest Certification (Switzerland)
RFP	Request for Proposal
RFQ	Request for Qualifications
TCES	Tahoe Center for Environmental Sciences
TES	thermal energy storage
UBC	University of British Columbia (Canada)
UGB	urban growth boundary
USGBC	United States Green Building Council
VAV	variable air volume
VOC	volatile organic compound
ZONE	zero-net energy

Introduction

Form Follows Performance

Ulf Meyer

In the late nineteenth century, the debate in architectural circles revolved around the question whether architecture should use "natural" or "artistic" shapes, whether architecture was "the art of building" or "the art of space making," and whether "form should follow function." It was the German art historian August Schmarsow who finally untied the Gordian knot of this debate: Architectural shapes should neither follow nature nor art, he proclaimed, they are a derivative of performance requirements or expectations. Schmarsow's thinking was about 100 years early. Now, his thinking looks like the hottest thing since sliced bread—or REVIT, to use architecture speak.

Because the situation in the year 2012 is this: Everybody and everything is labeled as "sustainable" or "green," so these adjectives have completely lost any meaning. Regardless of this over-use, their precise meaning is still vague. Architects simply claim to design green buildings and that is it. Are they really green? If so, how and why? These questions barely get raised—let alone answered. Is incompetence or active lying at the base of widespread greenwashing—and which would be worse? Formidable careers in the profession and in academia depend on the lack of curiosity. Contemporary architects can become stars simply by claiming that they make "green" architecture look "sexy" and not "hippie." That makes it acceptable, even desirable in a capitalist mass-consumption society with a short attention span and a guilt complex.

The rating systems of the world first tried to find a common ground for the different endeavors and a way to make them comparable. Whether some have morphed into being more part of the problem than part of the solution, I leave that judgment up to the reader. If the word "sustainable" is passé, then which word do we use? How about "lasting"? Or "solid"? Hmm, less sexy, I admit, but more sustainable than "sustainable" I hope?

Coming from Germany, I was first pleasantly surprised, then shocked, then increasingly angry, when people from all over the world kept telling me how much they admired German building codes and the "advanced German take on sustainability." Who does not like to hear such compliments about their profession back home and who would not be tempted to try to take on the role of a messiah who would spread the teaching of the advanced Germans to the "under-developed Anglo-Saxon world"? Well, I don't.

Because the more I studied and taught the subject the more convinced I became that the no-nonsense things I had known already as a child were more true than anything I have ever heard at any green building conference anywhere in the world: That gray is the new green. We are on the wrong track if we think that we can "make the world a better place," if only our building consumes say 30 percent less energy. But, you may ask, "30 percent of what?" Despite the fact that we as a society do not manage to save energy at large, even if we did, we would still be in trouble. Is being "30 percent less polluting" really not the same as maintaining 70 percent of our clearly unsustainable pollution levels?

I.1 Green building is all about creating green spaces for both people and planet. Photo: G. Löhnert, sol·id·ar planungswerkstatt Berlin.

These relative numbers drive me crazy. It reminds me of the TV commercials for shampoo and skin care. They also claim to make the "hair up to 30 percent softer" or reduce the signs of ageing in our face "by 40 percent." So, should we just continue as if nothing happened? Of course not! But we should resist the temptation to feel good and brag about our little mini-achievements. If the rating systems contribute to the understanding that "green" design needs a big budget or is something that only an elite can achieve, then clearly they contribute to the problem more than to its solution.

Schmarsow knew it already: Performance drives design. Just as a square sailboat will not win the next America's Cup, architecture should "go with the flow" of performance-driven design. During my three years of teaching "sustainable architecture and design" at two different universities in the USA, my most memorable experience happened outside the classroom. My family (wife, daughter, and myself) decided to not buy a car, move downtown, and bike to the grocery shop. Boy, did we earn sympathy! When strangers saw us loading our milk crates onto the bikes, they would approach us with troubled faces, slap on our shoulders, and ask "are you OK?" We thought we were OK, but these things are not. If even in a small college town biking to the market makes a great story for the local newspaper, then clearly something is wrong. My educated academic colleagues of course had more balanced views. They thought that what we did was great and were terribly sorry that they could not do it the same way, because they lived "too far away from downtown." Well, these poor souls! The Communist Party of the USA must have assigned them a faraway suburban home. What I am trying to say is this, and it is very simple: Changes in density, bike paths, public transport, you name it, won't happen without demand—our demand that is. Yours!

Sustainability is not and never should be a matter of technology or gadgets or features. Its success is decided by urban design policy, choice of durable materials, willingness to invest in a building rather than in an electricity bill, and other factors that are way beyond the measures and tools of any rating system. The "age of good intentions" is over and I am happy about that. Now, show me your energy bill from last year and how it is lower than the one from the prior year. And stop slapping my shoulder and feeling sorry for me, please!

Ulf Meyer, Berlin

Part I

Green Building Performance Challenges

Chapters 1–5

1

Green Buildings and the Carbon Challenge

Residential and nonresidential buildings are the single largest source (40–48 percent in the US, 40 percent globally) of global demand for energy and materials that produce by-product greenhouse gases (GHG) from home and building construction, operations, and demolition.[1] Slowing the GHG emissions growth rate and then ultimately reversing it during this century are obviously keys to addressing climate change and keeping global average temperatures from increasing more than 3.6°F (2°C) above pre-industrial levels, which would require atmospheric carbon-dioxide (CO_2) concentrations below about 445 parts per million (ppm). At the current time, global GHG emissions are increasing atmospheric CO_2 concentrations by about 2–3 ppm annually; in 2011, global GHG emissions accounted for 30,400 million (30.4 billion) metric tons, and the atmospheric concentration of CO_2 climbed to 392 ppm.[2] Clearly, a mammoth task awaits those working in the built environment. This book is dedicated to those working at the leading edge of meeting this challenge.

To accomplish this goal of reducing global CO_2 concentrations, the US organization Architecture 2030 issued the 2030 Challenge in 2005, calling for the global building community to adopt the following targets:

- All new buildings, developments and major renovations shall be designed to meet a fossil fuel, GHG-emitting, energy-consumption performance standard in 2010 of 60 percent below the regional (or country) average for that building type.
- At a minimum, an equal amount of existing building area shall be renovated annually to meet a fossil-fuel, GHG-emitting, energy-consumption performance standard in 2010 of 60 percent of the regional (or country) average for that building type.
- The fossil fuel reduction standard for all new buildings and major renovations shall increase to:

  — 70 percent in 2015 (compared with 2005 local averages)
  — 80 percent in 2020
  — 90 percent in 2025
  — 100 percent carbon neutral in 2030 (using no fossil-fuel GHG-emitting energy to operate).[3]

These targets can be accomplished by implementing innovative sustainable design strategies, generating on-site renewable power, and purchasing renewable energy from off-site providers of solar, wind, and biomass energy. This book shows you fifty-seven great green projects with low energy use, some using a variety of solar and wind strategies to get to a zero-net energy building.[4]

2.1 The five-story Forum Chriesbach building, in Dübendorf, Switzerland, uses less than 30 kWh/sq m/year of regulated energy sources. This 92,000-sq-ft office building uses about as much energy each year as two single-family homes. Photo: Eawag – aquatic research.

2 The Issue of Building Performance

Worldwide concern over anthropogenic climate change has accelerated since 2006, and many decision-makers recognize the significant contribution of buildings to global CO_2 and other GHG emissions. If energy use is the source of about 70 percent of GHG emissions and buildings represent 40 to 48 percent of the total energy use,[1] then controlling building energy use and GHG emissions represents about 30 percent of the solution.[2] In fact, a 2007 study by McKinsey showed that reducing building energy use is the *only* large-scale way to reduce GHG emissions that is currently cost-effective (or likely to be so in the near future).[3]

GREEN BUILDINGS AND CLIMATE CHANGE

Green building and energy performance-rating schemes exist in much of the world (as described in Chapter 3), but researchers and practitioners are finding that building performance does not yet match up to the levels needed to avoid catastrophic climate change over the next several decades.[4] In particular, research shows that many high-level green certified buildings in the USA, the UK, and elsewhere are not delivering effective performance in reducing energy use.[5] Even for those projects in the USA that are delivering promised energy savings, the average improvement is about 25–35 percent against the relevant reference standard (ASHRAE 90.1–1999, 2004, and 2007).

However, we already know that reductions in energy use must be far more than 50 percent to get average building energy down to reasonable levels. For example, meeting the 2030 Challenge would require all new buildings by 2020 to use 80 percent less energy than 2005 levels and to be carbon neutral by 2030.[6] Given that most of the design and construction industry has agreed to meet these goals, it's fair to ask, "How well are we doing?"

Since we must control *absolute* GHG emissions from buildings, it's important to know how the *best* buildings in the world are doing in controlling their emissions. That's the purpose of this book.

To understand the status of today's green buildings, one must look at *actual measured performance* over at least 12 months of full-time operations, including both energy and water use. Our research looks also at energy use only in terms of site energy use, even though source (or primary) energy use is the only way to accurately measure induced carbon emissions from building operations. Unfortunately, it's quite common for building teams, particularly in North America, to look only at site energy use and not to look at what it took to generate that energy. Even biomass-fueled boilers and combined heat and power (CHP) systems, nominally carbon neutral, require source energy use, and create carbon emissions, from the activities required to grow, harvest, manufacture, and transport the biomass fuel to the building site.

In the future, building teams will need to employ *normative* design criteria, such as annual electrical consumption (kWh per unit area), fuel consumption, and water use (gallons or liters per occupant or per unit area), for use in building projects that aspire to the highest level of green building certification (see Chapter 8 for the results of the case-study projects). *Without such explicit goals, most designs will fall far short of the needed GHG emission reductions.*

To put it another way, we're looking for buildings that are "positively good, not simply less bad," in architect William McDonough's memorable phrasing, "plus-energy" buildings that actually produce more energy than they consume.[7]

THE PROMISE OF GREEN BUILDINGS

In his book, *Greening Our Built World*, Greg Kats points out the benefits of a major transition to green buildings.[8] He assumes that by 2020 certified green buildings in the USA will represent 95 percent of all new construction and 75 percent of all major retrofits; this scenario would produce a 14 percent reduction in CO_2 from buildings in 2025 vs. 2005 and a net present value (NPV) of green building gains of $650 billion in the USA alone, representing about five to ten times the initial cost premium. Worldwide, it's clear that a movement toward green construction and operations of this magnitude would provide net economic gains of several *trillion* dollars!

This considerable economic potential makes it even more pressing for building owners, designers, and contractors to take seriously the challenge of achieving high levels of building performance. Yudelson's experience in participating as a sustainability consultant in building teams since 2005 revealed that most teams are too preoccupied just with getting a building designed and built within a specified budget to aim at truly high levels of building energy and water performance.

However, it's certainly possible to say that the response of design teams is entirely rational. Given current relatively low energy prices in the USA and other countries, most engineers and architects implicitly limit building energy investments to a three-to five-year payback, which results in investments that achieve 15 to 30 percent improvements over ASHRAE 90.1–2010, the currently applicable standard. The problem is this: aiming at *relative improvements* against a "practical" standard will never deliver the *absolute reductions in carbon emissions* needed from the building sector to combat global warming. After all, Mother Nature doesn't care about relative improvements; she only cares about absolute CO_2 levels in the atmosphere. And Mother Nature is the ultimate arbiter of human activity.

WHERE ARE WE TODAY?

Current building energy assessments used in the USA must rely on 2003 national survey data (Commercial Building Energy Consumption Survey, or CBECS), unfortunately the most recent available, showing average commercial building energy use. As shown in Table 2.1, the average energy use in typical US buildings in 2003, measured at the energy source (i.e. the power plant), amounted to 500 kWh/sq m/year. The ASHRAE 2007 standard represented a *source* energy use of about 280 kWh/sq m/year, while the newer ASHRAE 2010 standard results in a building *source* energy use of about 200 kWh/sq m/year.[9]

Note that the ASHRAE standards (and those used in Germany, for example) are for "regulated" energy use, which includes heating, cooling, hot water, and lighting, but not all "plug" (i.e. computers, printers, etc.) loads, while the CBECS database includes all building energy use. For comparison purposes then, it's important to add in plug loads, which represent about 25–33 percent of total building energy use. Table 2.1 shows some "stretch goals" at which climate design engineers in Germany currently are aiming and achieving, as shown by the case studies in Chapters 7 and 9.[10]

Two things immediately stand out from examining Table 2.1. First, source energy use needs to be reduced dramatically in existing buildings (via retrofit or renovation)—by 80 percent to meet "best in world" new building standards and by 50 percent to meet current new building standards. Second, it's apparent that energy use in new buildings needs to be reduced more than 60 percent versus the newest (2010) ASHRAE 90.1 standard to meet the goals at which the best new German buildings are already aiming (see the KfW Westarkade building case study in Chapter 9).

What is the state of current US design practice? In general, a green building with an EUI (energy use intensity, or annual energy use in thousands of BTU divided by square footage) of 35 to 40 would be considered nearly a state-of-the-art design in the USA, as shown by the NREL/RSF building profiled in Chapters 5 and 7 and by Forum Chriesbach shown in Figure 2.1.[11] That represents a "source" EUI of about 87–100 kBtu/sq ft/year (using a multiplier of 2.5 source/site energy use) or a source energy use of about 300 kWh/sq m/year, about three times Germany's best current design goal. Similar outstanding results exist for a number of European buildings profiled in a previous study, and in those described in Chapter 7, so we know that other

TABLE 2.1

US buildings' average energy use, compared with ASHRAE and German practice[a]

Building type	Source EUI (kBtu/sq ft/year)	Site EUI (kBtu/sq m/year)	Percent electric	Source energy use (kWh/sq m/year)
Office	166	76.3	64	523
K-12 school	153.2	74.7	64	483
Retail store	158.3	72.2	67	499
ASHRAE 2007[b]				375
ASHRAE 2010[c]				267
"Good German Practice"[d]				150
"Best German Practice"[e]				100

a Review of 2003 CBECS Study data, http://info.aia.org/nwsltr_cote.cfm?pagename=cote_a_0703_50percent, accessed September 20, 2010. Note: EUI is in 1,000 Btu/sq ft/year; 100 EUI is equal to (29.3 kWh/100 EUI) x (10.76 sq ft/sq m) = 315 kWh/sq m/year.

b, c Source: Presentation by Terry Townsend, President, ASHRAE, October 21, 2008, "Sustainable Future," using source/site multiplier of 2.5 (e.g., average 40% efficient electric/gas combination).

d, e Personal communication, Thomas Auer, Transsolar, September 2010. Projects are KfW Bankengruppe buildings in Frankfurt, Ostarkade and Westarkade, respectively.

projects can achieve the same results; the results in this book indicate that these lower energy use levels are certainly possible.[12] Also in Chapter 7, we profile a zero-net-energy building in Singapore with a low site energy use, which demonstrates that outstanding results can be achieved even in tropical climates.

Why all this concern about numbers? The bottom line is that current green building scoring systems, by focusing on *relative improvement* against a standard that changes every three years, are misleading in terms of where we need to go to reduce carbon emissions from existing and new buildings.[13] A LEED® Platinum building designed today, even if it achieved all the energy efficiency points in LEED 2009 (representing a 48 percent reduction from ASHRAE 90.1–2007 energy standards), would still represent a source energy use of 187 kWh/sq m/year, well above a state-of-the-art European building.[14]

There is yet another problem with giving credit to percent reduction against a standard that only considers "regulated" energy demands. Non-regulated demands are increasingly important in building operations: "Process energy, plug loads, commercial refrigeration, and other non-regulated energy uses were not included [in the ASHRAE and USGBC standards] because the codes did not establish a baseline for these end uses. In some building types like supermarkets and restaurants, the non-regulated energy use can represent two-thirds of the total. Even in offices and schools; non-regulated energy typically represents approximately one-third of total energy."[15] In addition, one should really focus on total (life-cycle) energy use, eventually even considering embodied energy (*Grauenergie* in German) of building materials, which may add 20 percent to source energy use on a life-cycle basis.[16]

WHAT ABOUT COST?

At this stage in the evolution of building energy design, the best-performing buildings often contain some combination of double façades, thermally active slabs, radiant heating/cooling or ground-source heat pumps, natural ventilation, heat reclaim systems (from exhaust air), and often cogeneration or tri-generation systems, and they typically cost more initially. The harsh reality is that it is virtually impossible to achieve major energy savings in new buildings simply with better windows, lighting controls, demand-control ventilation, and more efficient HVAC systems. One has to either invest more money, or engage in integrated design practices that reduce overall mechanical, electrical, and plumbing system costs while radically improving performance. Some projects have done this, as we show in Chapter 7, but they are few and far between, because most building teams simply don't know how to design, construct, and deliver buildings to get high-performance results.[17]

That's why it's so important that building teams set BSAGs ("big, scary, and audacious goals") at the outset of each project. These BSAGs should challenge the entire team to meet average local costs for the specific building type, while achieving energy use 50 percent or more below the currently prevailing standard while simultaneously enhancing user comfort, health, and productivity. Seen in this way, it's clear that the building owner must bear primary responsibility for choosing the right design and construction team, for charging them with a specific set of BSAGs for the project, and for managing the process to achieve truly integrated design. The importance of the building owner's role is shown in the interviews in Chapter 5 with the owner, engineer, and process consultant for the zero-net-energy Research Support Facility at the US National Renewable Energy Laboratory (NREL RSF) in Golden, Colorado.

In an earlier book, Yudelson investigated how more than twenty building teams actually achieved LEED Platinum certification without spending significantly more money (in some cases, no additional money) using an integrated design process.[18] The conclusion: typically, teams made an early decision (usually in the conceptual design stage) to achieve LEED Platinum status, held an early stage "eco-charrette" (or multiple charrettes) to discuss and plan integrated design options, and engaged with an involved owner who drove the process all the way to a successful completion. Beyond those similarities, there were almost as many approaches as projects. There is no single approach to securing high-performance outcomes. However, the underlying factor is *always* the intention to do so.

IMPLICATIONS FOR BUILDING TEAMS

Consider the implications of these results and the many case studies shown in Chapter 7, and set BSAG goals for your next project. Here are three:

1. The site EUI for building design will be 25–30 (25,000–30,000 Btu/sq ft/year or 79–100 kWh/sq m/year) *before* considering the contributions of on-site or purchased renewable energy.
2. The project will be *carbon neutral* in terms of site energy use, either through on-site renewable power generation, biomass CHP systems, geothermal or geo-exchange systems, or purchased renewable energy.
3. The overall building cost will be equal or close to regional averages for similar building types and sizes.

What could happen if a project set these three goals in stone at the outset of a project?

- Every building-team member would strongly commit to the desired outcome before being selected to participate in the project. This would be similar to the "contract" signed by building teams engaged in integrated project delivery or by using the methods shown in Chapter 5.[19]
- An integrated design process would be essential to the success of the project, and all building teams would need to learn how to make this process work.
- All building teams would begin to learn how to achieve high-performance results on a conventional building budget.

These appear to be worthwhile goals and aspirations, not achievable without a considerable stretch from existing practice. These goals are even a stretch from existing green building practice but are necessary for us all to do our part in the battle to limit global climate change from human activities. That cause is important enough for us "to" say: *If it doesn't perform, it can't be called a green building!*

3 Worldwide Green Building Rating Systems

The most often cited definition of sustainability is human activity conducted in a way that meets "the needs of the present without compromising the ability of future generations to meet their own needs."[1] Sustainability has become an increasingly important business focus across all market sectors in both developed and developing economies owing in part to growing recognition of and sophistication in assessing the real costs of externalities—that is, the negative environmental and social impacts of typical business activities such as manufacturing and selling products, delivery of services, and normal business operations.

Moreover, the business world is changing in response to emerging social and market forces that highly value companies and organizations that consider the effects of their operations, products, and services on the environment and community. The ability to integrate environmental and social responsibility into operations is fast becoming an indicator of good management, decreased risk, and an enhanced reputation. Achieving greater sustainability is becoming an important business driver that helps companies and organizations remain competitive and enhance their reputation among customers, shareholders, suppliers, and employees.

However, while organizations have made progress over the past few decades in addressing their sustainability impacts, sustainability as both a process and objective remains ill-defined. Developing requirements that address an organization's impacts across multiple sustainability-related concepts is necessarily complex. There are many different approaches and a variety of potential answers to difficult questions, such as what indicators to include, how to assign value to specific indicators, and how to assign weights to categories of indicators in one area in relation to others.[2]

Green building certificate programs help market participants ascribe a meaning to compiled attributes of a building. For example, Green Mark provides a national green building standard for Singapore; BREEAM for the UK and EU market; and Green Star for the Australian, New Zealand, and South African markets. The US LEED standard, promulgated in 1998 by the US Green Building Council, is now used in a variety of countries around the world (more than 130 by a recent count). Countries as diverse as Canada and India adopted LEED with modifications, but most LEED projects still certify to the US-based system.

Green building design and rating tools have simplified measuring green design and building outcomes. They successfully provide a widely understood accounting method for assessing a project's environmental attributes. By all reports, their market success results in higher rents, higher occupancy, and subsequent higher asset value.

However, the scope of most of these tools is limited to intrinsic building environmental performance and does not fully integrate the social and economic aspects that constitute the other two pillars of the triple-bottom-line thinking. Moreover, in most cases, the metrics used in these systems are neither consistent nor comparable across the decision-making continuum in the building life-cycle.

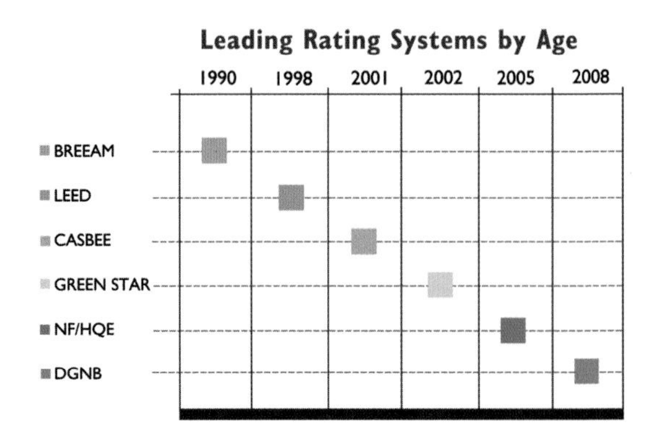

3.1 Leading green building rating systems by date of inception. Source Alfonso Ponce, Deloitte.

GREEN BUILDING COUNCILS (GBCs) AND RATING SYSTEMS

There is a growing appetite for rating methodologies that can be used to assess the environmental performance of human activities. From personal footprint methodologies to the assessment of cities and towns, there's a drive to develop more and better rating systems.

The environmental assessment field has matured remarkably quickly since the introduction of BREEAM in the UK in the early nineties, and the interim period has witnessed a dramatic increase in the number of building environmental assessment systems worldwide. Figure 3.1 shows the evolution of major rating systems around the world since 1990.

However, building environmental assessment systems currently in use in the market were never designed to be used across multiple countries and often have a significantly local flavor, which explains why comparisons are not easy.

A good example of this is what is currently happening (2011) in La Défense, outside of Paris, Europe's first business district, where several buildings are being certified with two or even three different labels, without any coordination on the part of the scheme operators.

This phenomenon is indeed particularly prevalent in France, where no fewer than seven homegrown programs exist, but can also be found in countries where national-scale programs are backed by government such as in China, or in countries where several rating systems exist and confusion among property professionals is high, for example in Italy, Poland, and Spain.

As seemingly absurd as it may seem, dual or cross-certification is also a result of GBCs themselves. A large number of emerging GBCs, particularly in Europe, tend to promote two or even more different rating systems at the same time.

Unfortunately, this approach reinforces the confusion around these tools in the marketplace, even if (when seen from a global perspective) property investors seem to choose between LEED and BREEAM, the only two systems that can claim widespread international acceptance.

EUROPEAN BUILDING ENVIRONMENTAL ASSESSMENT AND CERTIFICATION SYSTEMS

The following review describes the main rating systems used in Europe:

- BREEAM, the BRE Environmental Assessment Method, owned and operated by BRE Global
- NF, Bâtiments tertaires, démarche HQE (Haute Qualité Environnementale; High Environmental Quality), owned by AFNOR and AIMCC and operated by Certivéa
- DGNB, the Germany Sustainable Building Council's assessment method
- LEED, Leadership in Energy and Environmental Design, owned by the US Green Building Council (used in Europe, but described in a subsequent section).

Comparisons between the different rating systems are not straightforward. There is no independent authority collecting data from certification activities, and the level of transparency among the scheme operators is not equal. There's a need for harmonized definitions, data collection methodologies, and independently verified data. Given all these difficulties, the data addressing issues such as certified square footage and total certificates issued by each system are an imperfect indicator of reality.

BUILDING ENVIRONMENTAL ASSESSMENT: THE BEGINNING

The UK's Building Research Establishment created BREEAM in 1990 as a tool to measure the sustainability of new nonresidential buildings. HQE became the French generic methodology six years later. Public authorities at the local level drove the initial stage of development of both BREEAM and HQE. These rating systems originally provided measurement protocols for designers and construction professionals and did not qualify as certification tools. Two sister building research organizations developed them: the BRE, a former UK government organization that carries out research, consultancy and testing for the construction and property sectors in the UK, and the Centre Scientifique et Technique du Bâtiment (CSTB), the BRE's equivalent in France, still a public agency. When the demand shifted from public organizations to the property industry, third-party accredited organizations structured and ran the schemes as certification tools.

Finally, an important means for promotion of these tools in all OECD countries except for France (where such a program does not exist) is the accreditation of professionals who then act as consultants and ambassadors of a given rating system.

EUROPEAN RATING SYSTEMS SPECIFIC REVIEW

Building Research Establishment Environmental Assessment Method (BREEAM)

BREEAM is the world's oldest environmental assessment method and rating system for buildings, with 200,000 buildings (mostly residential) possessing certified BREEAM assessment ratings and more than a million registered for assessment since first launched in 1990. BRE Global is an independent third-party approval body offering certification services to an international market.

The BREEAM assessment tool measures performance against a set of nine benchmarks to evaluate building design, construction, management, and overall use in the future. Some of these benchmarks include energy and water use, health and well-being of the environment, transportation, materials, waste, ecology, and management process. A certified BREEAM assessment points out specific stages of a building's life cycle.[3]

Within each BREEAM section there are numerous environmental attributes for which a project can receive credits. The number of credits for each section are summed and compared to total number of credits available as follows:

$$\text{Section score (\%)} = \frac{\text{total number of points achieved}}{\text{total number of points available}} \times 100$$

The resulting percentage is then weighted as follows:

$$\text{Weighted section score (\%)} = \frac{\text{section score (\%)} \times \text{weighting factor}}{100}$$

These section scores are summed, as well as any innovation credits that have been achieved. This produces the final BREEAM score, which translates to a particular rating level, such as "Outstanding" (above 85 percent) or "Excellent" (above 70 percent). The rating categories and their respective weights are listed in Table 3.1.[4]

TABLE 3.1

BREEAM 2011 sections and weights[a]

Section	Weighting (%)
1. Building/project management	12
2. Health and well-being	15
3. Energy	19
4. Transport	8
5. Water	6
6. Waste	7.5
7. Materials	12.5
8. Land use and ecology	10
9. Pollution	10
Total	**100**
10. Innovation (additional)	10

a www.breeam.org/filelibrary/Technical%20Manuals/SD5073_BREEAM_2011_New_Construction_Technical_Guide_ISSUE_2_0.pdf%20, p. 28, accessed July 23, 2012.

BREEAM can be used as an environmental assessment tool for any type of building, in the UK or internationally. This system can be applied to single units or whole developments, and it can also be tailored for various stages in the life cycle of a building. BREEAM UK is used for both residential and commercial building types. There are standards for new construction, refurbishment, sustainable homes, communities, and operations.[5] In 2011, BRE Global issued a new version, BREEAM 2011, which replaced the 2008 version for new building assessment requirements.

Independent assessors licensed and trained by BRE Global perform BREEAM assessments. For its part, BRE Global is responsible for the technical content of the BREEAM schemes, assessor training, quality assurance, certification of each assessment, and, finally, updating the various BREEAM schemes at regular intervals.

BANKCO

3.2 Located just outside of Paris, EMGP 270 was the first office building certified under France's HQE program. Photo: Javier Urquijo.

Haute Qualité Environnementale (HQE)

The French HQE is an environmental option of the NF brand. HQE takes a multi-criteria approach with targets associated with three different levels:

1. Base: level corresponding to minimum acceptable performance for an operation
2. Performance: level corresponding to good practice
3. High performance: calibrated level relative to maximum performance observed in operations with high environmental quality, while ensuring that "it is still attainable."

The NF/HQE certification scheme is structured around four areas of concern:

1. Site and construction
2. Management
3. Comfort and health
4. Specific targets.

The certification has no ranking system; therefore, comparisons between two NF/HQE certified buildings are not straightforward. The NF/HQE system is the only rating system that does not provide a ranking system but instead gives an *environmental profile*. CASBEE (Japan) and DGNB (Germany) also display the results through *profiles* but in both cases these are complemented by a ranking system. The HQE system identifies fourteen environmental issues and covers two aspects: (1) the building's environmental quality and (2) environmental management of the entire project. The two aspects create linked reference frameworks, with performance criteria in the first and management requirements in the second. This "two-in-one" concept is probably HQE's most original aspect. Fourteen environmental issues are divided into four main areas, the first two having to do with the exterior environment and the second two with the interior.[6]

Deutsche Gesellschaft für Nachhaltiges Bauen (DGNB)

The DGNB system is a framework with detailed specifications and characteristics for conducting a building life-cycle assessment (LCA). The DGNB (German Sustainable Building Council) created and promotes it. DGNB uses benchmarks with two elements (construction and operation) to define the life-cycle environmental performance of buildings. The first element is a fixed value that refers to the construction of the building. It is derived from a German national research project that evaluates "typical" buildings to formulate benchmarks on the basis of average values and an understanding of the relation between a building and its environmental impacts. For this element of the benchmark, values are given in the characteristic documents for each criterion, e.g., 9.4-kg CO_2-eq/sq m of net leasable area per annum for global warming potential (GWP). The second element is a variable part derived from the Energieausweis, the German energy performance certificate. In accordance with the EU's Energy Performance in Buildings Directive, each building has a set benchmark for primary energy demand.

For the purpose of LCA benchmarking, the corresponding final energy demand is multiplied with conversion factors (separately for electric and thermal energy) for each indicator. These factors stem from the national building products database and reflect the electric energy grid mix. The resulting benchmarks ("reference value") for the building's life cycle represent five valuation credits out of a range of one credit (minimum) to ten credits (maximum) and reflect the idea of relation between "state of the art," "best practice," and "still acceptable." Each criterion can be assigned a maximum of ten points, depending on the documented or calculated quality. Three levels of certification (Bronze, Silver, and Gold) reflect the Olympic Games medals, as shown in Figure 3.3.

LEADING GLOBAL RATING SYSTEMS

Leadership in Energy and Environmental Design (LEED)

The United States Green Building Council (USGBC) introduced the LEED Green Building Rating System version 1.0 in 1998 (as a pilot system for evaluation) and version 2.0 (on which the current point structure is still based) in 2000. Since its inception, the system has evolved and expanded and is now considered a leading method of measuring and rating building performance throughout the world, already in use to evaluate projects in more than 130 countries.[7]

By the end of May 2012, LEED certified more than 13,000 non-residential projects, with some 34,000 additional projects registering

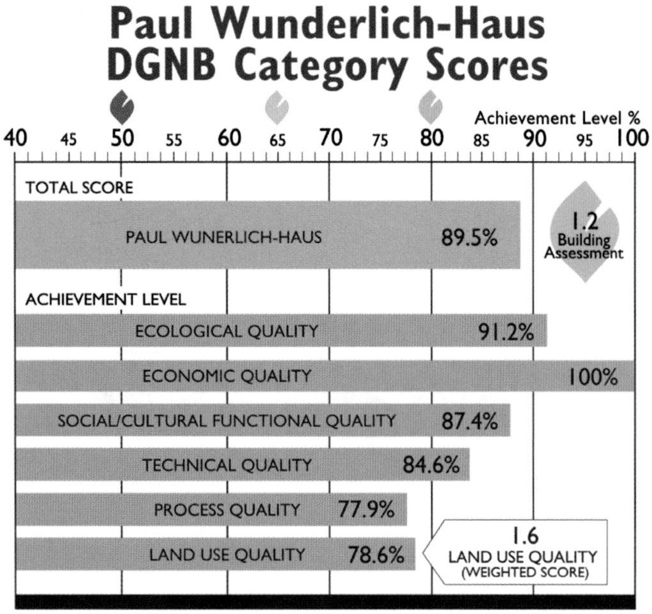

3.3 The DGNB rating system uses the three medal levels of the Olympic Games as the basis for certification.

their intent to pursue future certification.[8] LEED is a system that provides a means for building owners and operators to identify and implement measures for green building design, construction, operations, and maintenance solutions. LEED continues to be developed through an open group of committees representing the building and construction industry as well as NGOs, public agencies, and researchers.

There are nine different rating systems that apply to particular building market segments. The two LEED rating systems that apply to projects considered in this book are:

1 New Construction (NC): Designed to guide and distinguish high-performance commercial and institutional projects (i.e. commercial office buildings, academic buildings, government buildings, hospitals, etc.)
2 Core and Shell (CS): Designed for designers, builders, developers, and new building owners who want to address sustainable design for new core-and-shell office construction. This covers only base building elements such as structure, envelope, and the heating, ventilation, and air conditioning (HVAC) system.

LEEDv4, a multifaceted initiative due out in mid-2013, will streamline these rating systems and increase their capacity for project execution, documentation, and certification. This initiative will update and revise the rating systems, align and re-weight LEED's prerequisites and credits, and strengthen the focus on regional environmental priorities.

LEEDv4 will update eight major environmental attributes that currently define the rating system:

1 Integrated process (IP)
2 Location and transportation (LT)
3 Sustainable sites (SS)
4 Water efficiency (WE)
5 Energy and atmosphere (EA)
6 Materials and resources (MR)
7 Indoor environmental quality (EQ)
8 Performance (PF).

To improve the certification process, LEED reevaluated each of these categories as part of a specific building-type rating system. Each major rating system includes one or more subcategories. For example, as part of the Building Design and Construction (BD+C) rating system, there are eight subcategories to identify a specific building type for LEED certification.

In the BD+C category, the eight subcategories include:

1 New construction
2 Core and shell
3 Data centers
4 Hospitality
5 Retail
6 Schools
7 Warehouses and distribution centers
8 Healthcare.

TABLE 3.2

BEE criteria

Q1	Indoor environment	
Q2	Quality of service	Numerator of BEE
Q3	Outdoor environment on-site	
L1	Energy	
L2	Resources and materials	Denominator of BEE
L3	Off-site environment	

TABLE 3.3

CASBEE grades

CASBEE grade		Ratio
C	(poor)	0.5
B		0.5–1
B+		1–1.5
A		1.5–3
S	(excellent)	> 3

3.4 A LEED Platinum plaque on a building tells everyone about its green building achievements. Photo: Jerry Yudelson.

In this book, we only look at projects certified under the NC and CS categories of the LEED BD+C system.

The most recent update, in 2009, redistributed the available points in the LEED rating systems, using an environmental impact weighting method developed by the US Environmental Protection Agency. In LEEDv4, the update will promote a *whole building approach* to sustainability.

The LEED system awards certification in four categories: Certified, Silver, Gold, and Platinum, with projects that, respectively, acquire 40 percent, 50 percent, 60 percent, and 80 percent of the 100 "core" credit categories and subcategories. For inclusion in this book, we only considered projects that received Platinum ratings and met all other criteria outlined in the Preface.[9] Figure 3.4 shows a LEED Platinum plaque for one of the case-study projects.

Comprehensive Assessment System for Building Environment Efficiency (CASBEE)

Organized in 2001, the Japan GreenBuild Council (JaGBC) and the Japan Sustainable Building Consortium (JSBC) together form the leading authority on sustainable design in Japan. The JaGBC and the JSBC developed the Comprehensive Assessment System for Building Environmental Efficiency (CASBEE), a green building rating system now used in many projects throughout Japan. CASBEE develops procedures to make the assessment both simple and applicable to a wide variety of building types, taking into consideration issues particular to Japan.

The following four basic sustainability criteria are covered by CASBEE:

1 Energy efficiency
2 Resource efficiency
3 Local environment
4 Indoor environment.[10]

The CASBEE system is based on a framework known as the CASBEE family that covers the building life cycle and four assessment tools, covering pre-design, new construction, existing building, and renovation.

The CASBEE system is unique in that it separates construction projects into internal (private property) and external (public property) spaces. The internal space is evaluated on the basis of "improvements in living amenities for the building users," and the external space is evaluated on the basis of reducing "negative aspects of environmental impacts."[11]

The core concept of this rating system is an equation containing an internal or "quality" category in the numerator and an external or "loadings" category in the denominator. The equation is labeled as follows:

$$\text{BEE} = \frac{Q}{L}$$

where BEE = Building Environmental Efficiency, Q = Building Environmental Quality and Performance, and L = Building Environmental Loadings.

TABLE 3.4

GBCA Green Star rating levels

Green Star rating		Points
1 Star		10–19
2 Star		20–29
3 Star		30–44
4 Star	(Best Practice)	45–59
5 Star	(Australian Excellence)	60–74
6 Star	(World Leader)	75+

The four basic criteria listed above are further divided into assessment items that pertain specifically to the numerator (Q) and denominator (L), as shown in Table 3.2. Projects are graded according to the BEE ratio. The higher the Q value and the lower the L value, the more sustainable a building is. For instance, when Q is equal to L, the ratio is 1, which is a CASBEE "B" rating. CASBEE gives buildings grades according to their BEE ratio (Table 3.3). We only considered projects with an "S" rating, a ratio of 3 or higher, for inclusion in this book.

Green Star

Beginning in 2004, the Green Building Council of Australia (GBCA) developed Green Star, a comprehensive and voluntary rating system for evaluating the environmental design and construction of buildings. GBCA developed the Green Star rating system for the property industry to establish a common language and standard for measuring, rating, and assessing green buildings' life-cycle impacts. It recognizes changes in the environment and helps identify and raise awareness of the benefits of green building.[12] The Green Star system used existing green building rating systems such as BREEAM and LEED as a base from which to establish a unique rating system for Australia.[13] Subsequently, both New Zealand and South Africa Green Building Councils adopted the Green Star system for use in their countries.

The Green Star system assesses buildings across nine environmental impact categories:

1 Management
2 Indoor environment quality
3 Energy
4 Transport
5 Water
6 Materials
7 Land use and ecology
8 Emissions
9 Innovation.

Within each of these categories, there are credits that measure various dimensions of environmental performance. A project achieves points when it successfully performs and demonstrates specific actions for each credit. At the end, the project totals the number of credits for each category and calculates a percentage score, then applies Green Star environmental weighting factors. Weighting factors reflect issues of environmental importance for each state or territory of Australia, and thus differ by region. Each category score receives environmental weighting, which balances the inherent weighting that occurs through the differing number of points available in each category. The sum of the weighted category scores, plus any awarded innovation points, determines a project's Green Star rating. Only buildings that achieve a four-star rating and above are certified by the GBCA. The rating levels and their respective scores are listed in Table 3.4. For this book, we only considered projects rated "Six Star," or World Leader.

AUTHOR's NOTE

European examples and overview were contributed by Alfonso Ponce, Deloitte Real Estate Advisory, Paris, France.

Summary

We believe third-party assessment and verification of sustainable building claims is so important that the primary criterion for inclusion of projects in this book is that they have been rated by a recognized third-party scheme. This criterion necessarily excludes great projects with low or zero-net energy use and certainly discriminates against a number of European projects in countries where LEED or BREEAM is just gaining acceptance. But it also excludes projects that simply have not taken the trouble to submit their performance claims to an impartial arbiter or would not furnish operating data for this book. In the future, we hope that all projects will submit themselves to the twin disciplines of documentation and certification, both initially and on a continuing basis.

4

The Business Case for High-Performance Green Buildings

Within a relatively short time period, less than a decade, the business case for green rating new buildings has become the "new normal." Many major national and global property development, real-estate management, and ownership interests, both public, nongovernmental, and private, now consider a LEED (or BREEAM, Green Star, etc.) rating to be an important element of "business as usual." Making the business case is vital to convince executives, those with direct responsibility for managing economic assets to achieve a specified return, to aim at the highest level of green certification. After all, profitability is the key yardstick in business and management; a business that cannot maintain profitability won't be sustainable.

What's the next frontier for green building, beyond LEED Platinum, BREEAM Outstanding, etc.? It might well be zero-net energy (ZONE) buildings.[1] In that case, it's fair to ask, "What is the business case for ZONE buildings?" Here, the focus is only on those buildings that meet the ZONE definition of the Living Building Challenge, i.e. they have no *net* annual energy use and equal or exceed their annual net building energy use with *on-site* renewable energy.[2] It's possible to call a building "zero-net energy" that makes up for energy shortfalls by purchasing green power directly from off-site sources, but that belies the zero-carbon goals of the 2030 Challenge. In Chapters 5 and 7, we show how the NREL RSF building in Colorado, USA, achieved both LEED Platinum and ZONE status.

HOW MUCH EXTRA WOULD A LOW-ENERGY GREEN BUILDING COST?

As most practitioners realize, the key to developing low-energy, super-green buildings is to reduce their energy demand with integrated design, as we show in Chapter 5. An emerging standard for "world class" building performance, as discussed in Chapter 2, is a *source* (or primary) energy use of 100 kWh/sq m/year.[3] This translates to annual *site* EUI goal of about 50 kWh/sq m (16,000 Btu/sq ft/year), assuming a ratio of 2.0 for source to site energy.[4] Reducing the building's energy demand to such a low level will be a great challenge for building teams; however, many leading-edge green buildings in Europe are beginning to aim at this target, such as the KfW Westarkade building in Frankfurt, Germany, profiled in Chapter 9 (p. 229) and the Forum Chriesbach building in Dübendorf, Switzerland, profiled in Chapter 7 (p. 138).[5] Figure 4.1 shows the Zero Energy Building in Singapore with a site EUI of 41 kWh/sq m/year.

To a standard cost for a low-energy building, add the cost of on-site solar to make up this difference. Such systems might add 3 to 5 percent to the building construction cost. To the anticipated objection from building owners—"We can't pay 5 percent more for a ZONE building!"—consider the capital cost reduction that can be achieved by pursuing an integrated design strategy aimed at cutting overall systems and envelope costs (shown in Chapter 5). For example, a 2011 conceptual design study by HOK and the Weidt Group posits that "integrated design on steroids" could produce a 170,000-sq-ft (16,000-sq-m) four-story office building in St. Louis, Missouri, with a site EUI of 22 that would require a 52,000-sq-ft photovoltaic (PV) array and 15,000 sq ft of solar thermal panels to achieve zero-net on-site

4.1 The Zero Energy Building shows what can be done to cut net annual energy use to zero in the tropics. Photo: The Building and Construction Authority of Singapore.

energy use. This approach could produce a zero-net-carbon building with a twelve-year payback for energy-efficiency features going beyond those of a conventional LEED-certified project.[6]

THE MULTIFOLD DIMENSIONS OF THE BUSINESS CASE

The business case for green, low-energy buildings is based on a framework of benefits: economic, financial, risk management, public relations and marketing, and project funding.[7] Table 4.1 lists the wide-ranging benefits of ZONE buildings, which this section examines in some detail. Some benefits accrue directly to the building occupants (in the form of healthier buildings), some to the current property owner or manager, and some to future owners, such as the building's long-term financial and economic performance. However, some key benefits of certified green buildings, specifically those related to improvements in occupant productivity and health (notably daylighting and indoor air quality), will not necessarily be enhanced in a ZONE building, unless they relate specifically to the zero-net-energy or zero-carbon-emissions performance.

TABLE 4.1

Potential business-case benefits of low-energy green buildings

- Utility cost savings for energy and water, typically in the US $2.00–$3.00/sq ft, along with reducing the building's carbon footprint from zero-net-energy (ZONE) use.
- Maintenance cost reductions from commissioning, monitoring, submetering, and other measures to assure proper HVAC system performance.
- In commercial buildings, increased value from higher net operating income (NOI) and better public relations, owing to higher rents and increased occupancy in certified LEED buildings.[a]
- Tax benefits for specific investments in renewable energy and other sustainable technologies, such as those specified in state and federal legislation in the USA since 2005.[b]
- Over the long run, more competitive real-estate holdings for private sector owners especially compared to green-certified newer buildings and others that offer lower energy costs.
- Risk mitigation, especially against future increases in electricity prices (electricity use constitutes 70 percent of typical building energy use).
- Marketing benefits, especially for developers and building owners, but also including NGOs and universities.
- Public relations benefits, especially for developers, building owners, and building management firms.
- Improved recruitment and retention of key employees.
- Higher productivity and morale for tenants and building owners and managers.
- Greater availability of equity funding (such as from institutions engaged in "responsible property investing"), including funding for building sales and for upgrading existing building performance to ZONE standards.
- Demonstration of commitment to sustainability and environmental stewardship, as well as enhancing shared values with key stakeholders.

a See for example, Sofia Dermisi, "Effect of LEED Ratings and Levels on Office Property Assessed and Market Values," *Journal of Sustainable Real Estate (JOSRE)*, **1**, 1, 2009, 23–47; Franz Fuerst and Patrick McAllister, "An Investigation of the Effect of Eco-Labeling on Office Occupancy Rates," *JOSRE*, **1**, 1, 2009, 49–64. See also "Does Green Still Pay Off?" by Norman Miller, CoStar Group, www.costar.com/JOSRE/doesGreenPayOff.aspx, accessed January 2, 2011.

b www.aceee.org/sector/national-policy, "past legislation" tab, accessed January 2, 2011.

Source: Yudelson Associates, 2011

Economic and Financial Benefits

Let's start with the easiest justifications for green buildings: direct economic benefits to the building owner through reduced operating costs and, for commercial properties, induced higher rents, greater occupancy, or higher resale value.

Reduced Operating Costs

With electricity prices rising steadily in many metropolitan areas, making buildings super-green and also energy-efficient makes good business sense. For a small investment in capital cost, green buildings can save on energy operating costs for the lifetime of the building, typically with three to five year paybacks on the initial investment.

Lower Maintenance Costs Through Building Commissioning

More than 120 studies reviewed by US Lawrence Berkeley National Laboratory document that energy-saving new buildings, if properly commissioned, will show continuing savings of 10 to 15 percent in energy costs. Commissioning is an essential quality assurance process for buildings, in which system performance is measured against design intent near the end of construction and into the first year of operations. Commissioned buildings also tend to be much easier to operate and maintain, with marked improvements in building equipment life, thermal comfort, and indoor air quality.[8] In Chapters 5 and 8, we discuss some of the operating problems of high-performance green buildings that virtually mandate "continuous commissioning," at least for the first three years, a process one leading consultant calls "Soft Landings."[9]

Tax Benefits and Other Financial Incentives

Many jurisdictions offer tax benefits for new green buildings or even green building upgrades, including tax credits, tax deductions, property-tax abatements, and even sales tax relief on building products.

Risk Mitigation

Risk in building operations has multiple dimensions: financial, market, and legal, not to mention the risk to the owner's reputation of a poorly performing property. Since it's often hard to increase net operating income from building operations in the short run, mitigating risk exposure also has positive economic benefits.

Meeting Pro-Forma Income Projections

Lower-energy cost buildings tend to be easier to rent and sell, because sophisticated tenants can understand and directly experience their benefits.[10] Obtaining higher rents and increased occupancy for such buildings (compared to similar projects in the same property market) could become an increasingly important risk management benefit of high-performance green or ZONE buildings in the private sector. Indeed, the global property sector is increasingly embracing the Global Real Estate Sustainability Benchmark, as one good way to make these comparisons.[11]

More Competitive Product

It does not require too great a stretch of the imagination to see that buildings with low to zero-net operating costs for energy are likely to be more attractive to a growing group of corporate, public, and individual private tenants who value sustainability, making ZONE buildings more competitive in high-profile real-estate markets.

Benefits to Future Financial Performance

Most private organizations exhibit short-term planning horizons. But many large corporate, nongovernmental, and government owners are long-term businesses and plan to remain in the property business, so they must balance the short-term costs of greening their buildings with the longer-term positive outlook for sustainable buildings. In this context, the long-term reduction in operating costs for green buildings should count as a major benefit, provided that the incremental costs can be financed in a way that is not detrimental to the owner's cash flow.

NEEDED: A CONCERTED, FORTY-YEAR EFFORT

In 2009, a World Business Council for Sustainable Development (WBCSD) report specified how the goal of the United Nations Intergovernmental Panel on Climate Change to reduce world carbon emissions by 77 percent by 2050 might be met with appropriate contributions from the building sector:

- Energy-efficiency projects totaling $150 billion annually could reduce carbon footprints by 40 percent with five-year (or less) discounted payback periods, assuming energy prices around $60 per barrel of oil (they exceeded $80 per barrel in June 2012).
- The study looked at six building markets that produce half the world's GDP and generate two-thirds of global primary energy demand: Brazil, China, Europe, India, Japan, and the USA.
- A further $150 billion annually in energy-efficiency projects, with paybacks between five and ten years, could add another 12 percent in carbon footprint reductions, bringing the total to 52 percent.[12] Other measures recommended by the WBCSD report include:
- tax incentives and subsidies to spur investments and reduce the payback period to less than ten years
- new building codes and inspection procedures focused on energy efficiency
- restructuring the goals of new construction projects, through the planning process, to include integrated ZONE design and carbon emission reduction as a prime requirement.

Beyond these measures, the study calls for major cultural and behavioral shifts, which can be the hardest changes to bring about, but are arguably the most effective in the long run. Getting building occupants to take responsibility for energy use (an issue we discuss in Chapter 8) will be tough, but is achievable with good monitoring, metering, and feedback systems. However, it may be harder to convince owners, architects, and engineers to take responsibility for the performance of systems they create, if they are not otherwise legally required to do so.

Summary

The business case for zero-net energy and high-performance green buildings is solid and will become more apparent worldwide within the next five to ten years. The business case does not rest solely on measurable economic and financial benefits but on many other tangible and intangible benefits, including public relations, marketing, improved employee relations, access to new forms of financing, and increasing a company's "reputational capital" as a sustainable enterprise. The prospect of future worldwide requirements to disclose building performance and carbon emissions will eventually drive the business case toward high-performance green buildings for building owners, developers, operators, and managers.

5
Integrated Sustainable Design for High-Performance Buildings

In the book *Green Building Through Integrated Design*, Yudelson points out that it is difficult, if not impossible to make great strides in green building performance without fully embracing integrated design as a discipline and practice in the building process.[1] An insight from that previous book is that, first of all, integrated design is an iterative process, in which one building-team member or another can take the lead at any given point. Second, it's about finding unique solutions to project-specific problems or design issues, not about simply fitting solutions from previous projects into a new set of shoes. Third, it needs a clear set of goals, such as zero-net energy or LEED Platinum. As we'll see in the case studies later in this book, the best design efforts yield these results as a byproduct of innovative thinking and a willingness to take calculated risks.

Beyond the design team, there is an additional party critical to the success of high-performance projects, namely, the construction team. As more projects start to move toward zero-net energy, zero-carbon, zero-net water, and zero-waste solutions, the architectural and engineering systems and solutions must become more sophisticated and adventurous; however, without active participation and expertise from the general contractor and key subcontractors such as the façade supplier, mechanical, electrical, and controls contractors, these projects are not likely to work nearly as well as designed.

What are the key steps in an integrated sustainable design process? Yudelson identifies six key elements or steps:[2]

1 Make a commitment to integrated design and hire design team members who want to participate in this way of doing things. A key point here is that the building owner or developer also has to commit to the process, which may involve an uncomfortable delegation of decision-making authority to a design-build team, as we will see in the National Renewable Energy Laboratory (NREL) case study in this chapter.
2 Set "stretch" goals for the entire team, such as LEED Platinum, BREEAM Outstanding, Living Building certification, or zero-net energy, and judge the final result from that standpoint.
3 Get the team to commit to zero cost increase (or as close to zero as possible) over a standard budget, so that cost is a consideration from the beginning and that the need to find "cost transfers" or "cost trade-offs" is built into everyone's thinking. In the Genzyme project of Behnisch Architects profiled in Chapter 7, first cost did not increase because a tight building envelope and greater daylighting allowed the designers to significantly reduce the size of the HVAC system. See Figure 5.1.
4 "Front load" the design process with environmental charrettes, site studies, and similar "thinking" time. This gets more difficult if the schedule is compressed but is essential for the process to work.
5 Allow enough time for feedback and revisions before committing to a final design concept. This means that the client supports early-stage studies such as daylighting models and

5.1 At Genzyme, the atrium was a central element in bringing daylighting deep into this cube-shaped building. Photo: Anton Grassl. Courtesy of Behnisch Architekten.

computational fluid dynamics (CFD) models of the airflow around and inside the building and is willing to accept that more money will be spent on such studies during the conceptual and schematic design stages.

6 Everyone has to actively participate. Project team members should not be allowed to fall back into just considering their special interests. For example, this might mean that the electrical engineer who's going to be responsible for lighting design and daylighting integration also has to be concerned with interior designer's choice of paint colors and furniture (that affect internal reflected light), the solar gain through the glazing specified by the architect (for daylighting integration), and other issues that traditionally lie outside the engineer's domain.

THREE GERMAN ARCHITECTS

In this chapter, we chose to interview three well-known German architects whose projects are profiled in Chapter 7, to find out how they successfully employ integrated sustainable design to produce some of the world's greenest buildings. First is Stefan Behnisch, of Behnisch Architects (Stuttgart, Germany and Cambridge, Massachusetts). Behnisch designed the first large LEED Platinum-certified building in the world, the 360,000-sq-ft (33,450-sq-m) Genzyme corporate headquarters in Cambridge, Massachusetts, completed in 2003 and certified in 2004.

Stefan Behnisch Interview[3]

Q: What drives the performance of a building?

A: The performance of a building is closely linked with the prerequisites, the necessities, the purpose, the location, the cultural background, the climatic background, and so on of the place where the building is to be built. And all these prerequisites also influence the form of a building. Most architects perceive this as a contradiction, but actually, it is not.

Q: Does structure influence the form of a building?

A: Definitely; nobody ever questioned that. We have now the new discipline of designing for a more sustainable built environment, which requires a very holistic approach and thus influences definitely the form of buildings. And we are grateful for that, since the newer approaches to architecture are more content-driven and less purely form-driven. So, the prerequisites, the criteria that actually define the performance of the building, or define the request of a certain performance for a building, also inform the architectural language and thus the form of a building.

Q: What came first for Genzyme?

A: At the Genzyme building, the outer form was pretty much given, since a master plan defined the building very strictly. It was our first US project; here in Europe, we try to avoid building floor plates that are wider than 55 ft (16.6 m), for reasons of natural ventilation, natural daylight, and so on. But the master plan and also the necessity of space demanded a deep floor plate, an almost cube-formed building. And so we cut a hole in the building, meaning we gave it an inner atrium with daylight enhancement, which brought light deep into the center of the building. This also went along with the client's requirement to have a highly communicative, sustainable building.

So, one of the first approaches was the atrium. Then we looked at the façades, as we wanted a high-performance façade. External shading, which at that time was not very common in the USA, did lead to roughly 45 percent of the building envelope being a double façade. This double façade was mostly to the south, and it was ventilated to create an almost outside sun-shading device to be efficient. So, the form of the building was determined by the master plan, by the city planning, but also in detail by the requirement for a highly communicative building. The more interesting form at the Genzyme building is definitely the inner form rather than the outer form, so the building, one could say, was designed from the inside out.

Q: How do you make the trade-off between architecture and low-energy goals?

A: There is no trade-off. It is misperception that architects think they can design whatever they want to and then add on technical gimmicks to achieve low-energy goals. Actually, the whole discussion of low-energy consumption, of sustainability, enriches the architectural development. It is not an added aspect; it's a fully integrated aspect from the beginning of the design. Nobody would ever ask the

question, what is the trade-off between structure and architecture? So, it is important to understand that the need for a more integrated design approach between architect and engineers is a medium to lead to a new, *more interesting, content-driven architecture.* And part of this necessity is the aspect of sustainability. To create a more sustainable built environment, we need to take into account the cultural context, the geopolitical context, the topographical context, the social context of the site, the climatic context and so on.

Q: Were there any trade-offs made for Genzyme?
A: There was no trade-off, since Genzyme was from the outset meant to be an experimental, highly communicative, sustainable building. Architecturally, this is what we wanted and also what the client and users wanted. Would we have designed something different, if there wasn't a need for a sustainable building? Yes, we would have designed something different. Would we have designed something different if there was not the requirement for a highly communicative, socially balanced building? Yes, we would have designed something very different.

So, it is very hard in hindsight to think about trade-offs, and, actually, I personally also think it's a mistake, since it makes designing for a more sustainable environment sound like a compromise, and it is not. To keep designing the energy hogs of the past eighty years is compromising our well-being, our environment, and especially our future.

Q: Do you get the engineers involved early enough so that as the form develops during conceptual and schematic design, the energy goals are pursued concurrently?
A: This again is not easy to answer, since I personally think the question should be asked differently. The question should be: "If you include your engineers from the beginning, do they influence the outcome of the design?" Yes, they do. They help us to develop a more informed, more holistic, more human-friendly architecture. And since so many disciplines today are involved in designing good architecture, there are more or less important engineers to be involved, like when designing a concert hall. You would have the acoustical engineers involved from the outset, unless you want to work with technical gimmicks afterwards to compensate for the shortcomings. The same applies to a more sustainable built environment. We need our engineers to actually avoid technical means [that are] applied afterwards to the building. Doing more sustainable and energy-efficient buildings requires 60 percent designing the right architecture with the input of climate engineering, of structural engineering, of building physics, and definitely of natural and artificial lighting engineers. And they are even already involved in working on the first design phases or even in an architectural competition. It is a fully integrated process, a highly collaborative process, and not a one-person creative process.

Q: How do you see the increasing concern over building performance affecting architectural design in the next five years?
A: I do not share this concern, I am absolutely convinced that the more holistic aspect of a more sustainable built environment enriches our architectural abilities, informs the form-finding in a very positive way.

At the beginning of the twentieth century it was almost a miracle to apply Newton's laws and be able to build high towers. And that informed the architecture. That made itself very visible in the appearance of these buildings. A good example is the Eiffel Tower: a brilliant piece of engineering, but also a brilliant piece of architecture. Imagine Paris without the Eiffel Tower. The same applies to the Centre Pompidou in Paris, a brilliant piece of engineering that showed the possibilities of a seemingly highly flexible, high-tech architecture. Did it compromise the architecture? No, it enriched it. Or an even better example, the Olympic facilities in Munich built in the late 1960s, beginning of the 1970s. A brilliant piece of engineering; but also a brilliant piece of architecture, enriched by the art of engineering.

And if we are really willing to accept this challenge, it is possible in the near future to actually enrich our architecture, bring new aspects into the architecture, that help us to develop a new, enriched and more human-friendly kind of architecture. I personally think the days are over when architecture is perceived as an academic art, developed in a clean, unchallenged environment with a felt pen or 6B pencil, by a great master. We should never forget *The Fountainhead* was a book and a movie, but it was never reality.

Christoph Ingenhoven Interview[4]

Christoph Ingenhoven founded Ingenhoven Architects in 1985 at the age of twenty-five. He designed the first large green office building in Europe, the RWE tower in Essen, Germany, in 1995. In this book, his work is represented by the Daniel Swarovski Corporation office near Zürich, Switzerland and by the 1 Bligh tower in Sydney, Australia (Figure 5.2). He is an active and avid proponent of integrated design.

Q: What is your forecast regarding architecture in the future; what functions and designs will be required?

A: Ever since I started my career as an architect I kept in mind the philosophy of sustainability, which in German is referred to as *Nachhaltigkeit*. This term originally means "to protect and restore a forest on long-term basis" and was a familiar idea in German society long before the word "sustainability." In short, an architect should, just as a good forest-keeper would do, aim at an ideal environment where architecture does not decrease the amount of material the Earth has to offer. I give top priority to this philosophy in my projects. As one plans sustainable architecture, the first theme to tackle is the façade. The outer surface has to be minimized, but enough volume must be secured inside to obtain comfortable inner spaces. The bodies of huge creatures such as whales and elephants are deftly designed to fully lower the ratio of the outer surface size to the body volume so that the amount of energy needed to maintain the body temperature can be reduced to the minimum. If we turn our eyes on trees and plants, we will find the opposite phenomenon. Their outer surface is maximized in relation to their volume, because the bigger the surface, the more energy and resources can be gained from the environment such as sun, soil, and atmosphere. Just as the skin is important to living creatures and plants, though different in their functions, so is the outer surface to sustainable architecture.

A buffer area is a device to create an environment that is halfway between an artificial and a natural environment. As to buildings, the required functions of outer surfaces sit halfway between those of animals and plants. While minimizing the energy consumption is a pressing need, it must be designed to let light and air in. Architecture should not excessively shut out the surrounding environment. In an effort to create attractive, though minimized in size, outer surfaces and a luxurious inner environment, I designed winter gardens in the middle of high-rise buildings, as in the RWE building in Essen. I succeeded in increasing the size of "the second skin." For similar purposes I designed winter gardens in a horizontal direction in low-rise buildings such as the Lufthansa Aviation Center (LAC, in Frankfurt) or the new Headquarters of the European Investment Bank (EIB, in Luxembourg). Having such buffer areas, these buildings minimize energy consumption for air-conditioning.

Q: What are your ambitions and directions regarding architectural projects?

A: Architecture should foster innovative ideas. In order to turn huge offices into creative spaces, one needs to design so that numerous informal and unexpected encounters take place. For that purpose I always design big open offices instead of those with rows of rooms, which are still common in German society now. I am aware that an open office has its faults such as "irritant noise" and "psychological burdens of being watched all the time." So the floor plan must be designed for diversity—in horizontal and vertical directions. It is also desirable that spaces other than office rooms—such as corridors—are designed so that workers can meet other workers and enjoy informal communication. Walter Benjamin once said that people gain new experience by being forced to move through the city as "passengers" for a limited period of time. Brilliant and innovative ideas do not sprout in [solitude] or in contacts with the same old folks. Such ideas only come from contact with strangers. That's why I create environments that encourage unexpected encounters. In conventional office buildings, a worker would usually sit next to and work with familiar co-workers. After work he would leave the office through the nearest stairs, go to the parking lot and head home. Such a situation is catastrophic! To avoid such a situation I elaborated on the "passage" setting in the Burda Media Park (Offenburg, Germany), the LAC, and the EIB, so that many unexpected encounters take place there.

I use materials as they are—in their characteristics, texture, and color. For example, I only use reinforced concrete (RC) for structural parts. I simply give a transparent coating to the RC so that anyone can see that the RC is supporting the building. I do not add ornaments. I use glass and steel for roofs and façades, timber for façades and floors—the best-suited material in its right place, with no processing.

5.2 1 Bligh illustrates sustainable urban design in the middle of Sydney.
Photo: H. G. Esch, Hennef. Courtesy of ingenhoven architects + architectus.

But this is not a minimalistic approach. Minimalism is, for me, is a "doctrine" to which people are forced to obey. Of course, Mies van der Rohe impressed me. I was struck by his adoration for minimalism and his approach to bring architecture to the point of absolute abstraction.

But the situation is changing. Architecture today must be given more complex discussion. The pressing issues such as sustainability, global resource limits, and importance of communication enrich as well as complicate the architectural environment. So there is no room to follow Mies's path and get to the point of "absolute abstraction." But as I design, I minimize elements to create a desirable and feasible architecture. What is important in today's architecture is not minimalism, but "clearness"—the concepts must be explicit. For that purpose design must be simple, but should not be oversimplified.

I design simple architecture, one without any unnecessary elements. To reduce elements of architecture in such a way is a rule and a discipline for me, and it takes a lot of effort to do so. But such reduction has its own limits. Once the limit is exceeded, things begin to look complicated. For example, a physicist searches for equations to describe the world. He would find beauty in them. If people would ask him, "What do you mean by beauty in an equation?" he would answer, "its simplicity." But to ordinary people those equations never look simple, and in fact they really are very complicated. The concept of beauty [in physics] would only be gained through the process of pure simplification.

In my case the concept of beauty is more complicated. I think being designed with moderation is more beautiful than mere simplification. For example, the forms of human bodies are not simple. They are not cubicles. But they are beautiful. Human beings are in essence complicated existences, and so is the architecture. Architecture is beautiful for that reason, too. Good architecture contains things that are not indispensable. However, there is nothing that one can remove from it.

It is a necessary complexity. Everything nature creates is very, very beautiful. Architectures built with minimalistic approaches have exceeded the limits with bad intentions and thus reduced what should be retained. But I believe it is possible to design beautiful architecture with moderate simplification.

Matthias Sauerbruch Interview[5]

Sauerbruch Hutton is an architectural practice based in Berlin, Germany. It was founded by Matthias Sauerbruch and Louisa Hutton in 1989. Sauerbruch Hutton's work is recognized in this book by the Federal Environmental Agency (Umweltbundesamt, UBA) in Dessau, Germany and the KfW Westarkade building in Frankfurt, Germany, awarded the "Best Tall Building in the World" honor in 2011 by the Council on Tall Buildings and Urban Habitat.[6] In this interview with Ulf Meyer, Sauerbruch, a pioneer of Green Architecture in Europe, explains why "We are not there yet."

Q: In the realm of "green architecture," many claims are made but few things ever get substantiated or proven. So now I refuse to believe anything and only look at performance data.

A: I understand this sentiment very well. Of our own projects we only have reliable data for the Federal Environmental Agency (FEA). The results were very surprising.

Q: Was it a positive surprise?

A: Unfortunately not. We expected a *primary* energy consumption of 73 kWh/sq m/year, but after the first year, almost twice as much was consumed. We analyzed it and came to the conclusion that there are three reasons:

1. First, simulations work with averages, and weather and seasons can be different from year to year.
2. Secondly, and more importantly, we used innovative technology—and new technology has a tendency not to work. We used a solar thermal cooling plant on the roof, which broke down during the first week. The contractor simply did not know how to install it. A temporary, portable cooling system was used for a while, which had a terrible "footprint."
3. The third thing is user behavior. In residential as well as office buildings, the heating system is designed for redundancies—but here the system was very "tight." Wrong user behavior can easily screw up the whole performance.

Dessau is in the formerly Eastern part of Germany and was under Communist rule: energy was not measured or paid for back then.

5.3 GSW was the first truly green building by Sauerbruch Hutton. Photo: © Annette Kisling. Courtesy of Sauerbruch Hutton.

Often, radiators could not even be switched off. If it got too hot, people would just open the window. Some of that mentality might still be around.

Q: Was the building introduced to the staff properly?

A: Yes, but it is a continuous task, because of the turnover of employees. There is only some "institutional memory." Thankfully, the FEA has a very ambitious staff and management, and the energy consumption was brought down to 85–90 kWh/sq m/year in the meantime. Those numbers are great. *But it took five years to get there.*

Q: Is this the bottom line or can you do even better?

A: We are still aiming for 70 kWh! Certain features work really well such as the geo-exchange (earth) cooling. On a hot summer day when it is 35°C (95°F) outside, the naturally cooled air will only be at around 25°C (77°F).

Q: Has the solar-thermal cooling plant on the roof been fixed in the meantime?

A: Yes, it is working well now. At the KfW Bank building in Frankfurt, we do not have any monitoring data yet. The system there is quite different. We called it a "belt on top of suspenders" system. The building *can* be air-conditioned, but needn't be.

Q: Did you want it that way, or did the client?

A: The client wanted it that way, because our building is an extension to an existing cluster of buildings, all of which are fully air-conditioned. The client wanted the same conditions for all employees. But unlike those older buildings, there is thermal activation of the floor slabs in our new wing, which of course is much more efficient than air-based systems.

Q: If a serious feedback is only available many years after the completion of a building, aren't you as an architect in the role in which you must design new projects before you can learn from the earlier ones? Does this lead to making the same mistakes more than once?

A: The design for the Federal Environmental Agency was our reaction to what we learned at the GSW building in Berlin. We were quite naïve then and had little of our own experience. We designed the building to use less than 50 percent of the energy compared to a mainstream air-conditioned building in an Anglo-Saxon country, say in the City of London. That was easy to do because many buildings there consume 500 kWh/sq m/year and more!

But whether we exceeded that we do not know exactly, unfortunately, because there never was proper monitoring. This was partly because the facility management changed, unfortunately. The building was designed as a headquarters building, but as GSW shrank, the decision was made to partially turn it into a speculative office building with many tenants. Each floor can be divided into a maximum of two suites and each suite has its own control system, so that actual energy consumption can be billed separately—to motivate energy saving by tenants. However, the GSW Corp. was sold (twice) in the meantime, and it is difficult to monitor performance properly.

Q: Tell us about your approach toward an integrated design process. How do you aim at high-level green buildings with low energy use and still do great architecture?

A: There is a biographical aspect to that. Twenty years ago, when we (Sauerbruch and Hutton) still worked in London, there was no mainstream low-energy design in architecture at all. We worked with Arup because they had some experience in that field and also some prototypical simulation tools. At the time, Arup was organized around relatively small groups in which each necessary profession would be represented—such as structural engineering, HVAC, architecture, and so on. People were trained to collaborate. We entered the scene as young architects, and we were lucky to work with Guy Battle and Christopher McCarthy, two very talented engineers. They were very motivated and took on the challenge of green design. Through this experience we were initiated into integrated design; we also learned a lot since and now we can tell our engineers "where to look."

Q: Is it important to "never change a winning team"?

A: It is not always possible. In our projects abroad, in France and Italy, we couldn't always choose our team. In France, for example, the idea of an integrated design is unheard of. The thinking is that the architect should elaborate his design and then hand it over to the

engineer. Since we insisted on a more integrated approach, they set up a meeting during schematic design phase just to do us a favor. But really, the French thought that that was absurd, and it did not change anything.

Q: But if the integrated design approach is so crucial to your projects and you cannot achieve that, how do you guarantee the success of the project?
A: Well, we don't. We started out with an ambitious scheme in France and were unable to realize it. Still, the building turned out beautifully, but technically it is rather conventional. It has a good solar orientation and some effective sun screening at least! But we could have achieved more.

Q: What is your view of the importance of low-energy building design and the relationship of the architect to certification schemes such as DGNB, LEED or BREEAM? Is it a good thing that there are so many different rating systems in the world, or is it time to consolidate?
A: That is hard to say. I guess it makes sense for systems to react to different contexts, such as different climate zones. Also, both LEED and DGNB assume a very high level of comfort for the user and highly developed construction industry. Anyhow, rating systems help to keep "green architecture" alive and provide some comparability between projects. They will lead to another generation of buildings.

INTEGRATED DESIGN: THE IMPORTANCE OF PROCESS CHANGES

There is a saying that one is truly crazy when one expects different outcomes from the same inputs. It works the same way in high-performance green building. In a previous book, Yudelson profiled a fast-track LEED Platinum academic building where one could see several factors at work in a successful integrated design process:[7]

- A strong overriding vision and clear sense that everyone's contribution has value.
- Incredible time pressure; in this particular large project, only twenty-one months elapsed from start of design to occupancy.
- A strong bias toward creating a high-performance design.
- A first-rate team; there is no substitute for expertise when trying to "push the envelope" on sustainable design.
- A determination to create a process for integrated design and to give each specialty the opportunity to participate fully, even in areas where they don't possess particular expertise.
- Sufficient team-building and support of the team leader, so that a seasoned building team can help each other to realize better sustainable design solutions.

Beyond the design team, the contractor's role must also change. No discussion of integrated design would be complete without examining the contractor's role in the process, especially since many high-performance projects are design-build projects (as for example the NREL RSF project described below), which engage the contractor right from the beginning, at the very least to provide pricing and constructability reviews as the design is evolving. In most projects, general contractors coordinate the work of dozens of trades and subcontractors and spend more than 90 percent of the project budget.[8]

Beyond the contractor and designers, a truly integrated design process should include the future operators and occupants of the project, as Matthias Sauerbruch found out in the FEA project. A high-performance green building can't really succeed unless it can be built close to a conventional budget and operated in a sustainable manner by the people who are actually going to be responsible for it.

Each of these integrated design elements came together in the conception, design, construction and operation of the US Government's first major zero-net energy building, the Research Support Facility (RSF) of the National Renewable Energy Laboratory (NREL) in Golden, Colorado, a mile-high (1.6-km) location in the foothills of the Rocky Mountains (Figure 5.4). This project is profiled in Chapter 7, but here we examine its innovative approach to creating a procurement and design process for a major technological leap, within a fixed government budget. To better understand the project (and integrated design process), we interviewed Dave Shelton, with the consulting firm Design Sense; Jeff Baker, Director of Laboratory Operations at NREL, the project owner; and John Andary, who led the building engineering and energy consulting team.

5.4 Creating an integrated design process allowed this project to achieve net zero energy use on a tight budget.
Photo: Dennis Schroeder (NREL Staff Photographer). Courtesy of the DOE and NREL.

CHANGING THE PROCUREMENT PROCESS CHANGES THE DESIGN PARADIGM[9]

In 2007, NREL selected Design Sense as a consultant to put together the acquisition plan and the request for proposal (RFP). Dave Shelton provided the information and perspectives in this section, which has been edited for length.

Design Sense wrote Appendix A of the RFP, which is the conceptual document and has three component parts:

1 Procedures
2 Project program
3 Performance specifications.

Inside the performance specifications are quality-control substantiation elements—elements that the design-build team has to submit to demonstrate compliance with certain programming and performance elements.

The 3PQ Process

Design Sense has a process called 3PQ, which stands for procedures, program, performance, and quality assurance. The procedures section represents who does what, to whom, and when. It has several attributes, but most of them focus around the management of a project.

1 *Procedures*: Oftentimes we think of projects being just design and construction, but there's a whole management and collaboration and coordination that has to be established as well. That's the procedures section.
2 *Program*: There's no mystery there, it's just a project program: the quantitative measure of the scope of the work.
3 *Performance*: The performance specification is the qualitative measure of the program. A program could have six conference rooms to support twelve people in each room. That would be the quantitative measure. Under the qualitative measure, we would go into the criteria for those rooms in terms of lighting levels, acoustic treatments, ventilation, ambient temperature control, IT technology, etc.
4 *Quality Assurance*. The "Q" in 3PQ is basically substantiation: the submittals and requirements of documentation required by the design-builder to be given to the owner, so that the owner can measure with a regular iterative process that the project is being designed and constructed in accordance with the performance criteria.

We create flow diagrams for the 3PQ process. Basically, it starts off at the very beginning before what we call the project definition phase, where we go through a risk and reward analysis. We identify the objectives. It's a 40,000-ft overview.

The second phase we call "procurement model development." Basically we identify what the goal is, the risks associated with that goal, the restrictions to contract methodology. We put all of that together, and that creates a facilitated process of how we structure the procurement. Is it a request for qualifications (RFQ) or request for proposals (RFP) process? As it turns out on the NREL RSF project, they selected three teams [under an RFQ process] and then received their proposals [in response to the subsequent RFP].

Following the RFQ phase we developed the RFP, with all of the little details. On this project, NREL knew a lot about about energy efficiency; there is a building technologies group [at NREL] that understood they could get EUI down to 25,000 BTU/sq ft/year. So we took that information and integrated it into the performance criteria for the competition.

When the RFP was put together, based on submitted qualifications, NREL had reduced the selection to three teams, and then each of those three teams got the RFP in draft form, so they could see the goal of the project. When we put out the final RFP, it was structured with procedures, program, performance criteria, and quality assurance measures, and the objectives and scope of the project with all priorities divided into three groups.

The 3PQ process is an inversion of the traditional acquisition method. In "design–bid–build," owners hire an architect and they put together a defined scope of the work, what the project is in very detailed form, then it's put out to the market to bid on, and various prices come in. Usually the lowest qualified price is the one that's taken. *That's a fixed-scope, variable-price model.* The scope is fixed, but the owner is faced with varying prices.

The Fixed-Price, Variable-Scope Procurement Model

We take that model and we reverse it. We start with a fixed price—in the case of NREL, $63 million—and that doesn't change. In the 3PQ process (it's also called "preferred price priority queue"), for that preferred price of $63 million, here is a queue, or list, of prioritized elements. We work with the owner in a brainstorming exercise where the objectives get written out. Then we arrange them in order of which are required and which are optional.

Any time we start one of these exercises, we found that owners can tell you all kinds of things that they want. But they really only know what they want when they can truly identify what they're willing to give up to get certain other things. That's the idea of prioritization. *In their minds, at the time when NREL prioritized that work, they chose net-zero energy to be great if they could get it, but they weren't willing to give up higher-priority things to get it.*

Those are broad-scale objectives. During the solicitation, when the design-builders had to submit proposals, they had to write a narrative for each of the objectives that they had selected, in terms of what they would provide. *At a fixed price, the design-builder chooses the scope.* They go through that checklist and check off which of those things they're going to achieve. *The program, which is the quantitative measure, prioritized three categories: mission critical, highly desirable and "if possible" criteria.*

Through the architectural program, NREL prioritized various offices and conference rooms. Likewise, the proposers had to check off in their proposal which of the quantitative elements they included. In the end, there is a *fixed-price, variable-scope project,* rather than a fixed-scope, variable-price.

It assures two things. It assures the owner that for their budget, which is finite, they're going to meet their mission-critical goals, the base level of need. *The competition between the design-builders is a competition against scope, not a competition of price.*

Every owner has a different definition of what quality means. Because the owner has a priority queue, they're able to communicate to the competing firms what's important to them. In that regard, I think NREL and the US Department of Energy would say all of the proposals had value. The process also gave them three completely different options. They paid stipends [to the losing teams] because they wanted ownership rights for the two unsuccessful offers.

Design-build is very much a growing trend. I think there's a challenge on the education side. Owners must control the project outcome. This is a different paradigm; it's a complete shift over traditional "design–bid–build," so naturally it takes some education on the owner's part to understand. It takes a little while to understand that the project outcome on the back side can be superior to other delivery methods if you pick the right team and you've got the right criteria put together [on the front side]. It's very much a growing trend. We've done this on more than 100 projects. It works for any kind of project. It's not sensitive to the project type, just the contractual make-up.

The key to this is the understanding that with a procurement model inversion, you've got a fixed price and a variable scope; that scares a lot of owners. Because you must select a team and move forward on a project that is not bound by a set design. When these teams submitted [their proposals], they only completed maybe 10 percent of the design. So that [approach] demands of the owners that they prioritize their scope and objectives properly and that they qualify the teams that are coming in. What you have instead [of a set of plans] are performance metrics that any number of design solutions could satisfy. The RFP doesn't say what something must *be,* it says what something must *do* and the design-builder gets to choose *how* it must be.

Congressional appropriations limited the building construction cost to $63 million, or $259 per square foot. The Congressional appropriations did not include a net-zero building. There was a base scope, and they used some metrics to establish the $63-million price tag for the building. That $63 million didn't have the specific objective of being net-zero energy, which was one of the lowest-rated priorities. Yet NREL accomplished that goal because the design-build team worked collaboratively with the owner and the builder.

Phil Macy [of Haselden Construction] always made a great point. He said that he got out of the way, sat in the corner, and let the energy engineers start the beginnings of the project solution.[10] He knew that one of the owner's big concerns was driving down the energy consumption of the building. Architects don't take a back seat to too many people. [In this project,] to his credit, the architect allowed the energy guys to state what they needed the building to be in order for them to keep energy costs low. That's how the project design took place.

Haselden used what they call "cost transfer." When they took cost out of mechanical and electrical demands on the building, they took that cost savings and put it back in to other architectural features, so they accomplished more of the objectives on the checklist.

Because the owner doesn't state what the solution is, this project puts the designer and builder together with the owner so they can collaboratively work out the solutions for the trade-offs. Here's one of the shocking things they found out about the building afterward: when they brought the energy demand down on the building, all the pumps, fans, duct sizes, and all of that stuff, started reducing in size as well, because the owner managed plug loads so well, there wasn't a need to build heavy-duty air-conditioning systems because the building wasn't heating up.

You've got to get the designer, builder, and the owner all working on it collaboratively, but the box they must work within is the RFP. That establishes performance criteria. It limits the cost to $63 million. It establishes performance specifications relative to acoustics, temperature control, IT, security, interior finishes—everything. So it's a whole-building design concept rather than a prescriptive specification. The owner's protected, because the performance criteria must be met. In this case, it included *all* of the project objectives.

Early on, when the three shortlisted teams started the competition, we brought the three teams together, gave them the draft RFP and asked them two questions: First of all, do you believe that the expectations and the objectives of RFP are clear? Do you understand them? Secondly, do you believe that the project is achievable? By that we mean particularly are the mission-critical objectives achievable? Do you think we can get some of the other objectives and programs—the highly desirable and if possible [objectives]? So it's a dialog with the marketplace.

At the particular point when you've got the shortlist of teams, you've really got to communicate, "we're not trying to 'get you' with anything; we truly want you to pick the scope of the work, and we promise we won't change these performance expectations during the process."

Normally, the design is a trade-off conversation [but] because the goal is to meet the base performance criteria within the $63 million price tag, *there are no change orders in this process by definition.* A change order is traditionally a change to the drawings and specifications in traditional design–bid–build. Here, because the owner doesn't provide drawings and prescriptive specifications [to the contractor], there's nothing to change.

After [it placed the contractor and the architect] under contract, NREL allowed them to develop the preliminary design completely so they could validate that they could do the project within the budget of what they had promised during the selection. They still had risk, because if they bailed out during the development of that preliminary design, they would only get paid 50 cents on the dollar [for their effort]. That two-step process at the front end benefited both sides.

NREL RSF FROM THE OWNER'S PERSPECTIVE[11]

Jeff Baker was the owner's representative for this project. This section is taken from an interview with him and has been edited for length.

For a long time, affordable high-performance buildings were thought to be impossible to do. I think the biggest lesson we learned is that now it's not only possible, but it doesn't require a lot of exotic technologies. It just requires a very focused look at energy and providing the design team the flexibility to make the trade-offs necessary to meet the high-performance goals. The bottom line is, if you [the owner] set up the right goals and get out of the way, you can actually achieve the kind of high performance that we all desire with our buildings today.

We defined twenty-six performance objectives (Table 5.1), which included super energy-efficiency in the form of 50 percent better than ASHRAE 90.1–2007 standards, LEED Platinum, and, of course, the world's most energy-efficient building. We set those goals up front.

In the design-build process, we gave the design teams the flexibility to make the financial, technology, and design trade-offs to achieve those goals. Part and parcel of that was once they won that contract, our obligation was to get out of their way so they could optimize the financial and energy design of the building. That was really key: getting out of the way, being comfortable enough as an owner with our performance objectives.

A lot of folks say [design-build] is giving up control. I don't agree with that. Yes, we had to step back and give [the team] some freedom. But freedom doesn't mean lack of control. If you think about how we define control of the project, the twenty-six performance objectives and the substantiating criteria embodied the control. We knew exactly what we wanted as owner, and we specified it in terms of the performance objectives and substantiation criteria. Once we defined that, we had our control point right there. The second control point was running a

TABLE 5.1

NREL RSF levels of performance requirements[a]

Importance of scope/Objective
Mission critical (3): must be achieved
• LEED Platinum certification
• ENERGY STAR First "Plus"
• Safe work performance/safe design practices
Highly desirable (15): owner believes can be achieved
• Accommodate 800 staff.
• Use less than 25 kBtu/sq ft/year.
• Achieve 50% energy use reduction compared with ASHRAE 90.1–2004.
• Design building for future expansion/addition.
• Honor "future staff" needs in design.
• Design architecturally consistent with site/NREL identity.
• Support NREL culture and amenities.
• Consider ergonomics throughout.
• Design workspaces to be flexible.
• Support future technologies.
• Document process to include in "how to" manual.
• Implement real time public relations campaign.
• Allow secure collaboration with outsiders.
• Implement Building Information Modeling (BIM).
• Achieve substantial completion by June 2010.
"If Possible" (8): valued by owner (even if not achievable)
• Use Zero Net Energy Design.
• Most energy-efficient building in world.
• LEED Platinum "Plus" designation.
• Exceed 50% energy use reduction.
• Develop visual displays of energy efficiency strategies.
• Support public tours of RSF.
• Achieve national/global recognition and awards.
• Support reduced personnel turnover.

a NREL's Source Evaluation Team defined three tiers of performance objectives for a performance-based request for proposals, per the following document: www.nrel.gov/docs/fy12osti/51387.pdf, accessed July 24, 2012.

pretty aggressive selection process to get the right team. Once we did that, we had total control of the project and we handed over the design to our selected team and we gave them the freedom to go ahead and do what they needed to do to achieve the project's goals.

We were always aware of what was going on. In fact, giving credit where credit is due, the building, the way it looks, and the way it operates is due to the design team. That's not ours; it's theirs. However, the building embodies our performance objectives and substantiation criteria.

Phase 1 was done with regular [Congressional] appropriations, money, and the project proceeded as such. We did Phase 2 [an additional wing] with "2009 Recovery Act" moneys, but the really neat thing about the project is what we had learned on Phase 1 was so powerful that we actually took what we had learned and translated that into even better performance in Phase 2.

Specifically, we ended up improving the efficiency of the Phase 2 project, just a year after we concluded Phase 1, by about 17 percent and actually lowered the cost of the building in the process, with what we had learned from Phase 1. With Phase 1, we ended up with one of the world's, if not the world's, most energy-efficient office building. In Phase 2, just one year later, we ended up taking what we learned in Phase 1 and translated that into an efficiency increase with a 5 percent cost reduction.

If owners want to do this and create this kind of extraordinary value that we have created in RSF, they can do it, but they've got to commit [to the process] up front. It's not just assigning a project engineer or project manager. Executive management has to be involved all the way through the process.

[What about payback (return on investment?)] Let's not forget that as an owner, the payback comes every year when you are paying less than half of what you would have paid in utility costs and you have higher productivity because people are happy to be in the building since it's well daylit and a comfortable place to be.

The only way we're going to change the nation is to start doing it this way, one project at a time. Hopefully we can help others do this through the RSF. Two-thirds of all of the buildings that will be occupied in 2030 [in the USA] already exist. So every opportunity we have to do it right [with a new building] is precious.

NREL RSF FROM THE ENERGY ENGINEER'S PERSPECTIVE[12]

John Andary was the chief mechanical engineer for this project. In this section, we interviewed him to get his view on the project. The interview has been edited for length.

One of the most exciting things about the project for me was that, because I was seen as an out-of-town expert, there was a great deal of reliance on me to bring the ideas that would get the design-build team to a point where they could answer the question, "Can we actually design a building this large to be net-zero energy, LEED Platinum, and hit the energy target that NREL had laid out?" That created a great opportunity for my engineering and energy team because, between the time that they hired me to be on the team and the time we had our first three-day charrette in Denver, I had about two and a half weeks to spend in my studio in San Francisco working on what I subsequently called "pre-concept analysis." This consisted of energy modeling; passive design simulations; daylight modeling; analyzing building form, shape, orientation, window-to-wall ratios, floor-to-roof ratios, and envelope construction options; and modeling MEP [mechanical, electrical, plumbing] systems performance, so that I could feel comfortable coming into the very first charrette with some answers in hand. I had to convince myself as well as others [of the answer to the question], how are we going to do this?

It turned out to be a great kick-off to the integrated process that was a little different than most projects, where we develop our goals *at* the eco-charrette, with the owner and the design or design-build team. In this case, NREL already had 300-plus pages of very detailed information about what they wanted and all their goals. This allowed us the pre-analysis time period to take those goals and do some work to figure out how to meet them before we went in and sat down with everybody. In many of these charrettes, a lot of time is taken getting buy-in on the goals of the project and then developing strategies from there. We bypassed a lot of that by having NREL set the goals for us very rigorously and then coming in with numerous vetted solutions that ended up being implemented on the project.

[As a team], we didn't say "how's the integrated design process going to work on this?" It came organically because NREL set up a process that forced it. The fact that it was a design-build delivery and a competition at the beginning and we only had eight weeks to put [the proposal] together, forced a lot of integrated collaboration from the team right off the bat. In retrospect, a lot of the *design* integration came from the acceptance of the solutions that we came in with that first day, such as using radiant slabs for heating and cooling, which forced a certain integration with the structural systems in the building, programming the interiors and other architectural features. The integration of architecture and engineering in that particular building is very seamless. There aren't a lot of components of the architecture that you can eliminate and still have the building work the way it does, and vice versa for the engineering systems. One of the clear results: we delivered the building on a specific budget and on a fast-track schedule. In retrospect, achieving LEED Platinum and the largest net-zero energy building in North America on a fast-track schedule and a fixed budget makes all the more amazing what actually happened. These kinds of constraints can really force design integration to happen, especially around programming, the envelope, and the systems in the building.

Meeting the energy target goal was the most critical aspect of the building design. The scientists at NREL knew that if we hit the EUI target, then the required PV [system] to offset that annual energy use and get to net-zero would be a financially reasonable size.

That's a really interesting part of the story because everybody wants to take a shot at the cost of the project. "What did this building cost?" or "That's fine for the government to spend a bunch of money on the building but I can't do that." They showed in many cases that the building is a market-rate, Class A, build-to-suit office building in the Denver region that wouldn't cost any more than for a developer or any other owner to do a similar-scale building. In my opinion, it's that integration of architecture and engineering in the design that kept it cost-neutral. The [operating] cost per year is half the cost for a [standard] building built to code. It didn't require any more in first costs and you're immediately saving half of the cost of operating the building. The bonus is that it's also a net-zero energy building, measured and verified. This project is truly an exemplary business case model for highly sustainable, net-zero energy buildings.

GETTING BUILDING PERFORMANCE RIGHT: POST-OCCUPANCY EVALUATIONS

What you will see in Chapter 7, in many of the case studies, is that actual operating results differ from predicted results, often by significant amounts, even in high-performance buildings with the best design and construction teams. The NREL RSF case study is in some ways an anomaly because an unusual procurement process and a highly motivated owner served to generate a building where performance of the Phase 1 building is within 1 percent of predictions and to continue on with an immediate successor building (on the same site) where performance exceeded the first building by 17 percent, at 5 percent less cost. What can be done about building performance, especially after the first year, when all commissioning is completed and all warranty obligations are finished?

David Cook, a principal at Haas.Cook.Zemmrich architects in Stuttgart, Germany, expresses a prevailing opinion when he says, "There seems to be a general feeling of 'relief' once a construction project is finished, and there is little enthusiasm for a form of continuous follow-up."[13]

In research for a previous book on European green building approaches,[14] Yudelson found some intriguing approaches that make building performance evaluations and upgrades more readily available to building owners. For this book, we interviewed Adrian Leaman, the UK's leading expert on post-occupancy evaluations, for his assessment of the key issues in building performance evaluation.[15]

Q: What's the biggest problem in green buildings?
A: Unmanageable complexity is the biggest problem of all. Most buildings are too complicated for the people who must run them. There's too much technology that's trying to do too much, there's not enough resources devoted to running the buildings properly, and often designers seem to think that one size fits all. But it doesn't.

Buildings are incredibly context-dependent. The context is increasingly the limited resources that people have to manage and run the building. People know how to design energy-efficient buildings, they know how to do it properly, they've got the technology, but many buildings fail. They intend to be energy-efficient but they're not. Why? It's because they're often too complicated in practice, the users don't understand how to run them, and perhaps they're not that interested [in running them]. To get an energy-efficient building, you need a motivated person somewhere in the system. And of course they can come from the design team or the client, but unfortunately our experience of green buildings is not universally good.

So management is becoming more and more important, and I'm afraid design is becoming less important. Designers will say it's a management problem. Managers will say it's a design problem. Obviously [the problem is] where management meets design; it's the place where the management, design, technology, time, and space go together, and that intersection is ignored. Too much emphasis is given to space, to the physical form of the building, and not enough to the invisibles such as congestion, security, safety, and usability. Things like that are relatively ignored.

Q: What are the characteristics of buildings in which energy use actually comes close to the modeled performance?
A: Meeting user needs quickly so the building responds rapidly to requirements, whatever they are. They can be the facilities manager's requirements in understanding the building management system, or BMS. Or they can be just the ordinary building users' ability to intervene, control, do things for themselves, and not worry the management too much; [in this way] the building is giving them back the ability to control their environment or to leave the space if they want to and not feel inhibited by it or trapped by it.

All of those are characteristics you'll find in a really good building. Of course, a really good building will be energy-efficient and it also will be well managed. You won't get energy efficiency without good management somewhere in the system. With twenty years of work in building performance, we found the same problems over and over again. There are two causes: One is very poor feedback in the construction industry and very poor awareness of the nature of these problems. Second, there is an almost pathological inability to solve these problems.

What we found in particular was that briefing (or programming) is very weak. The people didn't really know what they were trying to achieve in a building. The design often was reasonably good, but when it came to handover, commissioning and after-care, the wheels started falling off the cart, big time!

After-care was very poor, but at the same time, when buildings were handed over, there were intrinsic faults, often very hard to fix, such as embedded software faults in systems (see Chapter 8) and tightness in fabric. Once you've got those problems, you've got them forever.

Q: What is the importance of "Soft Landings" for buildings?

A: The Usable Buildings Trust has just published something called *Soft Landings.* What Soft Landings is all about, is getting buildings to work straight out of the box immediately, so the client doesn't inherit a building with lots of chronic problems that need fixing. The Soft Landings framework is the result of twenty years of post-occupancy evaluations. We actually call them building performance evaluations (BPEs), as we don't like the term "post-occupancy evaluation."

It became clear that we needed something more, an inter-professional collaborative framework, which covered architectural services and all other services, so people picked up the risky things before they actually got built and sorted them out. That's what Soft Landings is about, and the name, Soft Landings, is the opposite of Crash Landings, because many buildings crash land! Soft Landings is all about a feather [floating back down] to Earth and touching lightly and not providing a whole mass of chronic problems. That goes back to the issue of unmanageable complexity—that's where all of the unmanageable problems come from.

A Soft Landing makes sure that whoever commissioned and procured the building gets a building that works. That's the point. The point is to get an energy-efficient building with happy people in it, but one that also makes sense financially. You very rarely find a building that is good at everything including the financial side.

Many green buildings are incredibly self-indulgent. They often have completely over-the-top technologies. They often have what we call "green bling," bejeweled technology that doesn't work properly and which is very hard to run.

[Fortunately] the tide has definitely turned. With green buildings, it's a no-brainer that you've got to monitor them. You've got to look to see whether they're better. As soon as you start monitoring for energy, you might as well start monitoring for everything else: occupant needs and all the other aspects of buildings.

Q: How important are post-occupancy evaluations?

A: It's actually relatively easy to study a building and see how a building works. The real difficult bit is to publish the results in an open and honest way that isn't full of PR and spin and taking out all of the bad news and talking about only the good news. That's the first problem.

The other problem is the feedback loops themselves. You need designers and managers to pick up on the faults and do something about them. If universities do post-occupancy evaluations, the information is published in consultants' reports that might not reach the people that they're supposed to reach, in which case the feedback loops will break down and this knowledge will not get to where it ought to be getting.

We set up the Usable Buildings Trust ten years ago because we wanted to put objective believable information into the public domain that people could learn from. The information that we've managed to put in the public domain is in much demand. But it's unbelievably hard to get the funding for it and to get really good, professional-quality articles published.

Architectural research has always had funding problems anyway, everywhere in the world. But post-occupancy and building performance work tends not to have great funding, because the client is always saying that the architect or designer should pay and the designers are always saying the client should pay. [As a result,] nobody wants to pay for it. The owner thinks, "Why don't they provide this service anyway? Why should I pay for this?"

The Soft Landings [program] makes sure that if you're following the Soft Landings protocol, then that money is earmarked for post-occupancy work, which is then protected from being nibbled away by other cost centers.

Also, the inherit tendency of designers is to want to get on with the next project and to walk away from what they've just done. The designers design; they seem to lack a natural curiosity, an inquisitiveness, about the consequences of what they've done. It's remarkable the extent to which they don't go back and systematically examine the outputs and what has happened. (See Chapter 11, "Afterword".)

A good building is not just a question about having green features; you've got to make them work. The checkbox lists for rating systems tend to do the opposite of what they are trying to do. They make things more complicated, which makes buildings harder to manage, which ultimately introduces a vicious circle which makes things worse rather than better.

Q: What are the keys to a successful BPE?

A: You need an energy survey, which covers both the supply side and the demand side. By that I mean, you not only count how much utilities—gas, electricity, etc.—and renewables are being used by the building but you also break down by use category—heating, lighting, and so on, so you can benchmark where things are going wrong.

A really robust energy analysis is the first component. Second, you need a robust occupancy survey. Our Building Use Studies occupancy survey protocol is widely used throughout the world.

The third thing is that you probably need a good introductory walk-through and interview with the facilities manager at a preliminary stage, so that the surveyors/assessors familiarize themselves with the building and with the good things and the bad things without being too biased. The person doing the analysis should be someone independent from the design team and who has gone "around the block" a few times and understands how buildings work. We (the Probe Study team) added in an airtightness test as well. (The Probe Study is a very famous BPE study that illustrates our ideal of how a BPE should be done.[16])

Q: Are there additional challenges of BPEs and POEs?

A: It's very hard work. People do two things. They underestimate how hard it is to do these studies and write them up. They tend also to collect too much information. It's much better to collect a small amount of information very well than it is to collect a large amount of information badly. People tend to measure too much, and then later they can't make heads or tails of it.

Q: What is the future of BPEs?

A: Soft Landings are the future for us. Because Soft Landings is an approach that is developed from reflecting on the results of BPE surveys and saying, "OK, we've got all of these problems recurring. What are we going to do about it?" The whole point is to improve feedback, improve the buildings, and make people happier and the buildings more environmentally efficient.

A warning: Don't assume that green buildings are all good. People assume that there's some kind of moral and ethical glow that comes off green buildings, that they're somehow better. What we're tending to find is that they're repeating the same mistakes from ten or twenty years ago. I go right back to what we started with—they are too complex and unmanageable. That's the problem. It's not their greenness or their low energy. It's just the sheer difficulty of being able to run the technology in them in an appropriate way.

Summary

It's not possible for building teams to consistently achieve high-performance results without changing the dominant paradigm of architectural design and project procurement. This will be especially true as building owners and developers begin to push teams to deliver zero-net-energy buildings with much lower water use, even to the point of creating regenerative or restorative buildings. To make sure all of this happens, it takes an understanding client, the right design program, an experienced design team, and a process that allows for insight and innovation. But, given that the size of just the US commercial and institutional building market, even in a bad year, exceeds $200 billion, isn't there enough money (and time) to do the right thing, instead of just "doing things right"? In the developed world, there is certainly the design talent, contractors who can build just about any design, product manufacturers who innovate constantly, abundant capital, financiers who can finance just about anything—all the right stuff. Why can't we then build high-performance living buildings—in all of our market sectors—as a profound and beneficial legacy to future generations?[17]

Part II

Case Studies

Chapters 6–8

6.1 Council House 2 in Melbourne's central business district achieved Australia's first Green Star 6-Star "As Built" rating. Photo: Paul Di Nello.

6 Introduction to the Case Studies

Green-building and energy-performance rating schemes are established in much of the world, but what most researchers and practitioners are finding is that building performance does not nearly match up to the level needed to avoid catastrophic climate change over the next several decades. In particular, research has shown many high-level green certified buildings in the USA, UK, and elsewhere are not delivering effective reductions in energy use.

This book provides a review of how far contemporary green buildings have come, based on *actual measured performance* over at least twelve months of operations, including both energy use and water use. Our research for the book reviewed only those buildings rated at the highest level of each national third-party rating system and then selected about fifty buildings from eighteen countries, based primarily on lowest resource consumption, especially lowest energy use per unit area, taking into account the building type. Each building selected is profiled in a case study in Chapter 7, using a common reporting format, although each case study highlights specific design and operational solutions peculiar to that project.

CRITERIA FOR SELECTION

We are specifically interested in high-performance green buildings with contemporary design. For this project, we required that buildings meet the following criteria:

1 rated at the highest level in a third-party rating system, including:

- — LEED Platinum (USA, Canada, China, India, and other countries)
- — BREEAM Excellent/Outstanding (UK)
- — Six-Star Green Star (Australia), such as Council House 2 (Figure 6.1)
- — Green Mark Platinum (Singapore)
- — CASBEE "S" (Japan)
- — DGNB Certificate Gold (Germany)

2 occupied since November 2003 and before June 2011
3 provided at least one year's worth of energy-use data, with water-use data if available
4 new construction, with at least 50,000 sq ft (4,500 sq m) in building area
5 nonresidential use
6 architectural merit, wherever possible.

These are not the only criteria that could be used, but they were necessary to reduce the universe of projects to a manageable number. In excluding smaller projects, we purposefully eliminated from consideration many excellent projects, especially in the USA, that had achieved LEED Platinum status. In limiting ourselves to new construction, we purposefully shied away from dozens of existing buildings that have upgraded their status to LEED Platinum in the USA but that did not face the challenges of design and building to that standard.

In requiring at least one year's worth of energy-use data, we demanded that projects "come clean" about actual use and not rely on modeled projections that often understate energy use in practice. By excluding residential projects, we kept our focus on commercial building typologies, which tend to be much more the same worldwide than residential projects, making global comparisons easier. In limiting our reach to more contemporary projects, we are attempting to profile specific responses to the growing global concerns over the energy use of buildings.

Finally, and perhaps most controversially, we were only interested in the top-rated green projects, thereby excluding many excellent projects that did not reach the top rung. The book's title, *The World's Greenest Buildings*, meant that we had to be serious about excluding projects that were not able to achieve 75 to 80 percent of the available "points" in a given rating system, generally the cutoff point for the highest certification level.[1]

Our purpose was simple: the world needs not only highly energy-efficient and water-efficient projects, but it needs projects that meet all other green criteria. The easiest way to save energy is to build windowless buildings, but that would consign the occupants to unhealthy conditions. The challenge, therefore, is to use all of the techniques of modern design and construction to reach the highest levels of green building performance, while simultaneously making them use much less energy and water than ever, all while producing attractive and humane buildings on reasonable budgets. It is this "trifecta" that we aim to encourage with this book:

1 "max green" building
2 lowest possible resource consumption
3 good to great architectural and urban design quality.

These case studies prove beyond a reasonable doubt that all three are possible. In addition, we argue that all three are essential targets at which designers, builders, and owners must aim.

WHAT'S SPECIAL ABOUT THIS BOOK?

This book is the first we know of to compare building performance among the highest-rated green buildings globally, using actual energy- and water-use data. The analysis of this information provides readers with an understanding of how building performance can be upgraded in future design and construction efforts. The book gives a good overview of the rating systems and shows "best in class" building performance in North and South America, Europe, India, China, Japan, Australia, and the Asia-Pacific region.

Using the case-study data, in Chapter 8 we developed *normative* design criteria, such as annual energy consumption (expressed as kWh per square meter) and water use (expressed as gallons per square foot or liters per square meter), for use by future design and construction projects that aspire to the highest level of green building certification. Since most green building rating systems aim only at *relative improvement*, we felt it essential to provide data on *absolute levels of resource use,* since Nature doesn't care about anything except *actual* levels of water in rivers and lakes and *absolute* levels of GHGs in the atmosphere. Indeed, we need to move our designs from being "less bad" to being "absolutely good." With information from these case studies, we aim to support that mandate.

In addition to energy- and water-use data, this book provides practical contemporary examples of best practices for greening new buildings, useful for architects and engineers, contractors, building owners and managers, and everyone charged with creating, operating, and upgrading the performance of new commercial and institutional buildings.

The book was based on responses to surveys conducted during 2010–2011. For inclusion in the main section of this book, we considered only those projects that met our criteria and provided operating data for at least the first year of operations. To avoid controversy about which countries have the greenest buildings, coupled with the lowest annual energy- and water-use per unit floor area, we tried to balance representation from the Americas, Europe, and Asia–Pacific regions. This approach of course excluded some good candidates from the USA, where more than 500 nonresidential buildings are already LEED Platinum certified (at year-end 2011) and from Continental Europe, where third-party certification is relatively new, but where there are many highly energy-efficient and otherwise "green" buildings.

WHAT'S THE BIGGEST SURPRISE FROM OUR RESEARCH?

The biggest surprise for the authors was how few projects actually have or are willing to share operating data, either because of a lack of interest in the outcomes, concerns about confidentiality of information, divided responsibilities between designers and clients, lack of follow-through by designers in the outcomes of their efforts, or simply our inability to pierce corporate and institutional veils to get information in a timely manner from the right people.

A second surprise was how widely varying the data were: some projects have carefully monitored and recorded their energy use and water use from inception. Others had only utility bills to share with us, and we were forced to do the data analysis. A clear recommendation from this study is that we need common databases for all certified green buildings that allow easy assembly and dissemination of operating data, along with all of the parameters that might influence the data such as percentage occupancy, presence of data centers and laboratories, etc. We also want to express our appreciation for the German and Swiss projects, with their focus on primary (source) energy use, and the UK projects, for a clear focus on carbon emissions from building energy use.

In some cases, energy use reporting only considers "base building" loads (e.g., in Australian multi-tenanted buildings) and neglects "tenant" loads such as lighting and plug loads. In some European projects energy data includes lighting but excludes plug and process loads. Wherever possible, we have made adjustments to reported data to take these discrepancies into account.

In other cases, the lack of publicly accessible databases of green-certified projects hindered our search for projects; this was especially true of the UK's BREEAM system, among others. This paucity of actual operating data tied to specific projects points out the need for more open reporting formats for green buildings' energy and water-use data, reporting that needs to be enforced and implemented by the major organizations such as USGBC, BRE Global, and the Green Building Council of Australia, world leaders in green building rating schemes. To this end, we have included our own modest proposals in Chapter 11.

Chapter 7

Case Studies

In this chapter, we present the world's greenest buildings, in forty-nine case-study profiles. Owing to differences between regional climatic conditions, construction methods, and design techniques, we organized the case studies into three distinct regions: The Americas, Europe, and Asia Pacific. If you don't find your favorite LEED Platinum or equivalent project on this list, it most likely did not meet one criterion (or more) outlined in Chapter 6 or else declined to share data and photos for this book. Within a given region, the projects are listed in alphabetical order first by country, then in alphabetical order within each country. Chapter 8 summarizes the projects' energy and water consumption and discusses key reasons why it is difficult to achieve better performance in most new green buildings. Figures for energy and water use for all case study projects were provided by the project owner, architect, engineer, or consultant, unless otherwise indicated.

THE AMERICAS

Canada

- Charles E. Fipke Centre for Innovative Research, University of British Columbia Okanagan Campus, Kelowna, British Columbia
- Child Development Centre, University of Calgary, Calgary, Alberta
- Manitoba Hydro Place, Winnipeg, Manitoba

Chile

- Transoceánica, Santiago

United States

- 41 Cooper Square, The Cooper Union, New York, New York
- 2000 Tower Oaks Boulevard, Rockville, Maryland
- Biodesign Institute B, Arizona State University, Tempe, Arizona
- Dell Children's Medical Center of Central Texas, Austin, Texas
- Genzyme Center, Cambridge, Massachusetts
- Great River Energy Headquarters, Maple Grove, Minnesota
- Johnson Controls Campus, Glendale, Wisconsin
- Kroon Hall, School of Forestry and Environmental Studies, Yale University, New Haven, Connecticut
- Lewis and Clark State Office Building, Jefferson City, Missouri
- National Renewable Energy Laboratory, Research Support Facility I, Golden, Colorado
- Newark Center for Health Sciences and Technology, Ohlone College, Newark, California
- Oregon Health and Science University, Center for Health and Healing, Portland, Oregon
- Regents Hall of Natural and Mathematical Sciences, St. Olaf College, Northfield, Minnesota
- Tahoe Center for Environmental Sciences, Incline Village, Nevada
- Twelve West, Portland, Oregon

7.1 *Below*: The Fipke Centre at the University of British Columbia, Okanagan Campus will help meet the campus's zero-carbon footprint goal. Photo: Margo Yacheshyn.

7.2 *Right*: The 6,320-sq-m Fipke Centre for Innovative Research achieved five Green Globes, the highest rating. Photo: Margo Yacheshyn.

CHARLES E. FIPKE CENTRE FOR INNOVATIVE RESEARCH, University of British Columbia, Okanagan Campus, Kelowna, British Columbia

Located on the University of British Columbia's Okanagan campus, the Charles E. Fipke Centre for Innovative Research is a 68,000-sq-ft (6,320-sq-m) multi-purpose academic and research facility. It provides office space, classrooms, teaching labs, research labs, and student-support areas. Design goals focused on reflecting generic modular design as well as the ease of converting it into a primary research and teaching facility.

The building structure is cast-in-place concrete for the main floors and structural steel for the entrances and atrium space. Precast panels, brick, and curtain-wall glazing systems were implemented for the exterior skin.

The Fipke Centre achieved five Green Globes, the highest rating, under the Canadian Green Globes Eco-Rating Program.[1] The Green Globes Eco-Rating Program involves a graduated rating system—from one to five Green Globes—designed to recognize buildings that show improved energy and environmental performance.[2] As shown in Table 7.1, the Centre's energy use intensity of 374 kWh/sq m/year is outstanding for a university research laboratory.

"We feel the Green Globes system is an accurate way to assess buildings and their environmental performance," said David Roche, Development Manager for UBC Properties Trust. "The five Green Globes rating that the Fipke Centre has achieved is equivalent to LEED Platinum. To our knowledge, no other lab building in Canada has achieved a rating of either LEED Platinum or five Green Globes."[3]

The University of British Columbia (UBC) is aiming for a campus-wide zero-carbon footprint; the Fipke Centre's groundwater heating and cooling system is a key component in achieving that goal. The system pumps groundwater from beneath the campus, using the water to heat or cool buildings, depending on the season, and then returns the water to the ground. The university expects this system to save more than $100,000 annually campus-wide.[4]

"We're extracting heating and cooling energy from the great Okanagan aquifer upon which half the campus sits," said Aidan Kiernan, Assistant Vice President of Operations. "So this will be the first building on campus that will be heated and cooled using geothermal energy. [It's] likely [that this is] the only campus of its kind

TABLE 7.1

Energy use, September 2010–August 2011

	Annual use	Intensity
Electricity	1,941,433 kWh	307 kWh/sq m
Gas (kWh)	423,667	67.0
Total	**2,365,099**	**374**

Figures for energy and water use for all case-study projects were provided by the project owner, architect, engineer, or consultant, unless otherwise noted.

in North America at this time that will have all of its new buildings on geothermal and all existing buildings retrofitted for geothermal."[5]

Other key sustainability features include:

- high-performance envelope
- radiant slab heating and cooling
- district energy system
- heat reclamation systems
- low-flow fume hoods
- displacement ventilation
- natural and wind-driven ventilation.

"Teaching and research are our top priorities, and the Fipke Centre represents a major expansion in our capacity to excel in both areas," said Doug Owram, Deputy Vice-Chancellor at UBC Okanagan. "This new facility supports learning with state-of-the-art technology and is designed to encourage interaction between students and their professors, and between academic disciplines."[6]

At a glance

Name: Charles E. Fipke Centre for Innovative Research
Location: Kelowna, BC
Size: 68,000 sq ft (6,320 sq m)
Completed: October 2008
Construction Value: CDN$33 million
Distinction: Five Green Globes
Program: Academic research labs, classrooms, theater, animal care facility

Project team

Owner: UBC Properties Trust
Architect: Kasian Architecture Interior Design and Planning
Mechanical Engineer: Cobalt
Electrical Engineer: Falcon

CHILD DEVELOPMENT CENTRE,
University of Calgary, Calgary, Alberta

In 2006, the University of Calgary announced that all new campus buildings would be built to LEED Platinum criteria. Designed by Kasian Architecture Interior Design and Planning, the Child Development Centre (CDC) was the first campus building to receive a LEED Platinum rating from the Canada Green Building Council.

The four-story 125,000-sq-ft (11,612-sq-m) Child Development Centre has one level of underground parking. The building program includes offices, a childcare center, a school, and tenant space for non-university organizations that focus on children with developmental issues.

Upon completion in August 2007, University President Harvey Weingarten said, "The CDC is the flagship of the university's ongoing efforts to make all operations more environmentally sustainable."[7]

LEED Platinum certification, explained Judy MacDougall, Project Architect, "was the primary driver in the design of the building in all respects."[8] Under the LEED-NC Canada system, the CDC received 57 points of a possible 70 and at that time was the highest scoring LEED-certified building in Canada.

Calgary is the largest city in the province of Alberta, located about 65 miles (100 km) east of the Rocky Mountain range. Winters are typically long, cold and dry, while summers are short and moderately warm. Temperatures can be extreme, ranging from –49°F (–45°C) to 97°F (+36°C). Calgary is among the sunniest locations in Canada, with an average 2,400 hours of annual sunshine. Most precipitation occurs during the summer months, with an annual average of 16.2 in (305 mm).

Inside the CDC's main entrance is a lobby and public multipurpose area, connected to a second-floor lounge by a prominent sculptural staircase. This area acts as the building hub, uniting the diverse tenant groups. On the main floor, the west portion houses a university childcare center with space for eighty children and the offices of a community partner. The second, third, and fourth floors are occupied by groups that are focused on research and practice in child development.

Energy

Significant energy savings result from a high-performance design achieved through simple and elegant means. The sustainability features and equipment focus on efficiency, reduced internal demands, low envelope exchanges with the outdoors, heat recovery, and integrated systems. Professor Jim Love undertook the energy engineering, along with his environmental-design graduate students.

"The CDC is the most heavily instrumented building in North America," said Professor Love, at the building's completion. "Nearly everything in this building can be directly monitored, from the boilers to the elevators. This creates an ideal environment for applied research and experiential learning."[9]

The building uses 55 percent less energy and saves about CDN$200,000 annually in energy utility bills, compared to a typical new building built to code.[10] The main level air-handling unit with a high outdoor air fraction (owing to high occupant density) incorporates a heat recovery (enthalpy) wheel, optimizing efficiency of the heating and cooling system. Exhaust air from the upper levels is also routed through this heat-recovery system. Radiant cooling panels along the south perimeter handle higher summer peak loads resulting from solar gain.

The building employs a mechanical fresh-air ventilation system that introduces outside air at low velocity, just below the desired ambient temperature, through low wall diffusers on the main level and an underfloor ventilation system on the upper levels.

Oriented along an east–west long axis, the building minimizes sun penetration. This also results in reduced glare and solar intrusion on the building's east and west sides and reduces cooling loads.

To reduce solar gain, PV panels shade the south façade windows. As both a shading device and energy producer, the PV system produced 52,000 kWh of electricity in 2010, 10 percent of the building's electricity use. The University purchases the remainder of the building's required electricity from a wind-generation facility in Alberta.[11]

Materials

To maximize recycled material content and improve indoor air quality (IAQ), the team carefully considered materials used inside the center.

7.3 *Left*: The CDC is one of the highest-scoring, cold-climate, LEED Platinum buildings in the world. Photo: Kasian Architecture Interior Design and Planning Ltd.

7.4 *Right*: This child-friendly space incorporates natural light and bright finishes to encourage play and spontaneity. Photo: Kasian Architecture Interior Design and Planning Ltd.

- Forest Stewardship Council (FSC) wood accounts for more than 70 percent of the wood in the CDC.
- The roof meets Energy Star requirements, with high reflectivity properties, helping to reduce the urban heat island effect and reducing building cooling costs.
- In the childcare center, rapidly renewable cork is used for floors, combining resilience and low-maintenance requirements.
- Locally produced fly ash, a recycled product and substitute for cement, constituted more than 50 percent of the slab, wall, and footing content.
- The building's exterior was clad in zinc panels, which are highly durable, easy to maintain, and weather slowly in Calgary's dry climate.[12]

Water

The CDC uses 59 percent less potable water than a similar building.[13] An abandoned service pipe from the university's central heating plant was unexpectedly discovered during excavation and was put to use to transport process water to the CDC. This water is used for toilet flushing throughout the center. As a result, the center's overall water use is quite low.

In 2010, this LEED Platinum project realized 66 percent energy savings, confirming it as one of Canada's greenest buildings.

TABLE 7.2

Energy and water use, 2011

	Annual Use	Intensity
Electricity, grid	548,000 kWh	47 kWh/sq m
Electricity, site PV production	52,500 kWh	4.5 kWh/sq m
Natural gas	4,400 GJ[a]	105 kWh/sq m
Total energy use (excluding PV)	**1,817,300 kWh**	**156.5 kWh/sq m**
Potable water[b]	807,000 l (213,000 g)	69 l/sq m 1.7 g/sq ft

a Conversion at 0.277 kWh/MJ; 1000 MJ = 1 GJ.

b Non-potable water from the central plant flushes toilets and is not metered. Water use (primarily potable water for drinking) is about $1/10^{th}$ that of a normal building.

At a glance

Name: Child Development Centre
Location: Calgary, Alberta, Canada
Size: 125,000 sq ft (11,612 sq m), plus one level below-ground parking
Completed: August 2007
Construction Cost: CDN$23 million
PV System Cost: CDN$300,000
Distinction: LEED Canada NC Platinum
Program: Academic, office, childcare center

Project team

Owner: University of Calgary
Architect: Kasian Architecture Interior Design and Planning
Structural Engineer: Read Jones Christsoffersen
MEP Engineer: Wiebe Forest Engineering
General Contractor: Ellis Don Construction

MANITOBA HYDRO PLACE,
Winnipeg, Manitoba

Manitoba Hydro Place proves the feasibility of climate-responsive design even in an extreme climate. The 700,000 sq ft (65,000 sq m), twenty-two-story office tower is located in Winnipeg, Canada, the coldest city in the world with a population over 600,000 and one of the windiest cities in North America.[14] Through a series of elegant, integrated solutions, the LEED Platinum-certified building achieves 66 percent energy savings (compared with a baseline building that would satisfy Canada's Model National Energy Code).

The building serves as the headquarters for Manitoba Hydro, a provincial government-owned electricity and natural-gas utility, the fourth largest in Canada. Prior to this building's completion in September 2009, employees were housed in twelve suburban offices. In choosing a downtown location for a new building hosting 2,000 company employees, Manitoba Hydro acknowledged the importance of investing in Winnipeg's urban revitalization.

Designed by the Integrated Design Consortium of Kuwabara Payne McKenna Blumberg (KPMB) Architects (design architects), Toronto; Smith Carter Architects and Engineers (executive architects); Prairie Architects (advocate architects); and Transsolar (climate engineers), Manitoba Hydro Place breathes new life into the city's "Chicago-scale" urban setting. Perched atop a three-story podium-cum-public mezzanine, angled twin towers are separated by a service core, creating an "A" shape when viewed from above. Accordingly, locals now use the nickname the "Open Book" in referring to the building.[15]

Integrated Design Process

From the project's onset, Manitoba Hydro committed to a high-performance outcome and established a formal integrated design process (IDP). The first task in the IDP is building the integrated team. The team includes key stakeholders and consultants: owner, facilities manager, architects, engineers, cost estimators, and construction managers. The IDP is strongly iterative, based on uncovering hidden relationships and generating new possibilities, and it all starts with clear goals.

For Manitoba Hydro Place, the first IDP session was a team-building exercise and resulted in a three-page project charter that was signed by all team members and the Manitoba Hydro executive. The charter outlined the primary project goals and was used throughout the project to ensure all decisions were in alignment with the goals. The charter contained six goals:

1 *Supportive workplace*: A healthy and effective contemporary office environment for employees that is adaptable to changing technology and workplace environment for present and future needs.
2 *World-class energy efficiency*: Achieve 60 percent greater energy efficiency than the Canadian Model National Energy Code.
3 *Sustainability*: Achieve at least LEED Gold certification.
4 *Signature Architecture*: Design to celebrate Manitoba Hydro's importance to the province and to enhance downtown Winnipeg's image.
5 *Urban Regeneration*: Strengthen and contribute to a sustainable future for Winnipeg's downtown.
6 *Cost*: A cost-effective and sound financial investment.[16]

After the initial goal-setting session, several additional charrettes played an important role in transforming conceptual strategies into integrated systems that met project challenges. An architecturally integrated solar chimney and winter gardens with water features are two unique outcomes of the project's IDP process.

When the team analyzed Winnipeg's climate, they identified prevailing southerly winds (up to 20 mph) and abundant winter sunshine as opportunities. Transsolar, the project's climate engineers, took the lead on developing a hybrid ventilation system that would employ passive wind and solar energies to save energy and reduce electrical lighting requirements.[17]

Although annual daily temperatures seasonally fluctuate between −31°F (−35°C) and 97°F (36°C) in Winnipeg, the city is ranked as the second sunniest year-round in Canada. "It was a shock," Transsolar's Thomas Auer said, to find "that Winnipeg is basically sunny whenever it is cold. We couldn't find a single cold city in the world with so many sunlight-hours, so there is no better location than this for a passive solar design."[18]

Energy and Indoor Air Quality

After the design charrettes, the project team evaluated fifteen schemes to determine the optimal configuration for the building form. Transsolar modeled the best three concepts to analyze thermal

7.5 The twenty-one-story, 690,000-sq-ft Manitoba Hydro Place in Winnipeg, Canada, features European-inspired climate engineering by Transsolar and architecture by Toronto's Kuwabara Payne McKenna Blumberg Architects. Photo: Gerry Kopelow.

7.6 The green roof on top of the podium reduces stormwater runoff, provides insulation, reduces the urban heat island effect, and provides a garden area for employees. Photo: Tom Arban Photography, Inc.

comfort, daylight, and energy consumption. The modeling showed that an "A" shaped tower, open to the south, would maximize southern exposure and passive solar heat gains, while the narrow northern exposure would minimize heat losses in the winter. This tower form would also allow natural ventilation during most of the year.

The façade is a key element in the passive solar design. A glass and aluminum double-glazed curtain wall sits three feet away from the building's interior single-glazed windows, creating a buffer zone that traps heat. Like an extra layer, the buffer zone keeps the building warm in the winter. Even at outdoor temperatures of –22°F (–30°C), space temperature within the buffer zones climb to +68°F (+20°C) owing to solar gain.

What's unique about Manitoba Hydro Place's curtain wall, however, is it also works in the summer to cool the building. The windows on the outer curtain wall open and close automatically based on current weather conditions as determined by two onsite weather stations. This allows venting the double façade and enables natural ventilation, a first among Winnipeg office towers. When outside conditions are appropriate, the BMS sends a message to employees' computers and asks them to open the interior-wall windows. Occupants control the window openings to maintain comfortable indoor temperature and air movement.

The double-skin façade also permits shading devices to be external to the office space yet protected from outside elements. The shade louvers, using real-time weather data, automatically raise, lower, and tilt to trap solar energy in the winter and deflect it away from the building in summer (to prevent overheating).[19] Shades also provide glare control and can be adjusted by all employees with their computers. The glass curtain wall also maximizes daylighting for the interior space.

In collaboration with a narrow, open floor plan, high ceilings, and low-height furnishings, daylight penetrates deep into the office space and reduces artificial lighting demands. Daylight sensors in the light fixtures seamlessly modulate artificial light output to maintain a consistent quality and quantity of light. Low-iron glass makes the curtain wall exceptionally clear and maximizes visual (solar) transmittance and views for employees.

The space between the two office towers contains three stacked, six-story unconditioned winter gardens with southerly orientation. This orientation also uses Winnipeg's prevailing southerly winds for natural ventilation and humidifying or de-humidifying the building, depending on the season. Below the towers, the podium contains a three-story gallery, which provides a sheltered pedestrian route and a public gathering space.

The towers are joined at the pointed top of the "A" by a 380 ft high (115 m) solar chimney that rises from ground level to several stories beyond the roof. The chimney contributes an iconic appearance to the building and is a key element in the passive ventilation system. Through the natural "stack effect," the chimney draws stale exhaust air up and out during the warmer months. At the chimney's top are 632 pipes, enclosed in glass and filled with 17 tons of sand. Functioning as thermal mass, the sand stores summer heat at night to ensure that the cooler night air does not interfere with the natural "stack effect" exhaust of warm air from the building.[20]

In the winter, fans draw air down the chimney to heat-recovery units. The recovered heat from the building's exhaust air is used to warm the underground parking area and preheat incoming cold air.[21] Combining passive solar orientation and using exhaust air for preheating maintains an acceptable ambient interior temperature with reduced energy use.

Located in the space between the towers, the winter gardens function as the building's "lungs." These spaces condition ventilation air prior to drawing it into the six stories adjacent to each winter garden. In winter, fresh air enters the winter gardens through louvers in the south-facing façade. The air is preheated to 41°F (5°C) using exhaust recovery heat and geothermal heat. It is passively heated by the sun to the desired supply air temperature and then dispersed throughout the 73 ft (22 m) high winter garden using warmer air's natural buoyancy.

A water feature that reaches from floor to ceiling within the space helps to humidify the air. Using 280 tensioned Mylar® ribbons, warm water runs down the ribbons and mixes with dry air to improve comfort within the office.[22] The air is then dispersed to the underfloor space for distribution into the office towers.

In summer, warm air enters the winter gardens directly through operable windows. Heat gain is reduced by massive louver shades, which cover the winter garden's entire south face. The water feature dehumidifies air when necessary by cycling cool water at 61°F (16°C) along the strands. The air is subsequently transferred to the underfloor space for each floor.

In the offices, thermal comfort is primarily achieved using thermally active radiant slabs. This is one element of a wider thermal comfort scheme, which carefully manages radiant surface temperatures. The slab temperatures are controlled using heating and cooling loops fed by a geothermal heat-pump system. The closed-loop geothermal system, with 280 geothermal wells drilled 400 ft deep (120 m) beneath the building, is the primary active heating and cooling system, providing about 80 percent of the heating requirement.[23] As main supplier of electrical energy in the province, Manitoba Hydro's clean, carbon-free energy sources (hydro and wind) provide the balance of electricity to the building.

While the building exemplifies Manitoba Hydro's commitment to environmental sustainability, the primary objective was to provide a healthy and comfortable workspace for occupants. The solar chimney, in conjunction with the winter gardens, creates a 100-percent fresh-air environment every day, no matter what the weather outside.[24]

Architect Bruce Kuwabara said that, while sustainability was a priority for Manitoba Hydro, "they also did this for their staff, who are its most valuable asset and who represent the future of a company that wants to stay on the leading edge of its business."[25] Occupants can control their personal environments, using operable windows, task lighting, shading devices, and controllable underfloor air vents in each workstation.

Water

Green roofs on top of the podium provide an important employee amenity. With accessible terraces and planted with native species, green

TABLE 7.3

Energy use, 2011[a]

	Intensity
Total	**112 kWh/sq m**
Base building	86
Tenant plug loads	26

a Bruce Kuwabara, et al. "Manitoba Hydro Place: Integrated Design Process Examplar," http://manitobahydroplace.com/site_documents/PLEAManitobaHydro Abstract%20Final.pdf, accessed January 27, 2012.

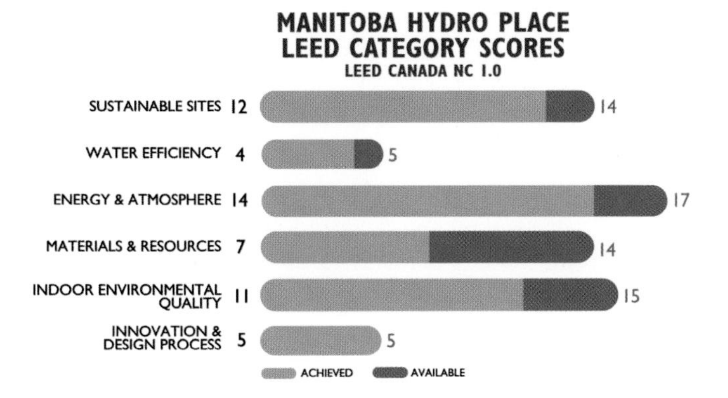

7.7 Manitoba Hydro Place LEED scores.

roof areas offer a garden zone away from street traffic, where occupants can congregate.

When rainfall is not sufficient for irrigation, condensate from mechanical equipment is used. Cisterns located in the parking garage collect excess condensate generated by the mechanical equipment during the summer months. When needed, the reclaimed water is pumped up to the green roof and distributed via an efficient drip irrigation system.[26]

Building Management System

Containing an extensive collection of meters and sensors, including a variety of sub-meters for lighting, plug loads, water heating, HVAC energy, and tenant spaces, a sophisticated BMS monitors internal and external environments to optimize lighting, solar shading, and heating/cooling loads.

The BMS is unique, owing to a very large number of observation points (more than 25,000—more than a major medical complex).[27] This technology enables every individual element within Manitoba Hydro Place to respond in real time to changing weather conditions.[28] Combining high-quality glazing, a narrow floorplate, and advanced lighting fixtures and controls for daylight integration leads to a 65 percent energy savings for office lighting.[29]

With these unique and integrated systems Manitoba Hydro saves more than CDN$1 million annually in energy costs. With a total project cost of CDN$283 million, initial costs were higher than a conventional building, but Manitoba Hydro Place expects to realize a twenty-five-year payback just from energy savings on the incremental investment in efficiency.

Manitoba Hydro Place showcases the idea of a *living building* since it takes maximum advantage of all of the natural assets available on-site—sun and wind—and at the same time responds to current conditions by making automatic adjustments to maintain homeostasis. This project highlights the IDP's multiple benefits; the 66 percent energy saving speaks for itself.

"Manitoba Hydro wanted to demonstrate that you could provide the highest quality of space for our employees while achieving the highest levels of energy efficiency and sustainability cost-effectively. In addition we wanted to integrate these systems into the building form to create signature architecture. The energy features shouldn't look like an add-on to the design," said Tom Akerstream, Energy and Sustainability Advisor for Manitoba Hydro Place.[30]

At a glance

Name: Manitoba Hydro Place
Location: Winnipeg, Manitoba, Canada
Size: 700,000 sq ft (65,000 sq m)
Completed: September 2009
Construction cost: CDN$278 million
Distinction: LEED Canada NC Platinum
Program: Corporate office

Project team

Owner: Manitoba Hydro
Architect: Kuwabara Payne McKenna Blumberg Architects
Executive Architect: Smith Carter Architects and Engineers
Advocate Architect: Prairie Architects
Structural Engineer: Halcrow Yolles
MEP Engineer: AECOM (formerly Earth Tech)
Energy/Climate Engineers: Transsolar Energietechnik
Construction Manager: PCL Constructors Canada Inc.

7.8 *Below*: The Transoceánica building in Santiago is the first building in Chile to achieve a LEED Gold certification. Photo: Guy Wenborne.

7.9 *Right*: Transoceánica uses 75 percent less energy than a typical office building in Chile. Photo: Guy Wenborne.

TRANSOCEÁNICA, Santiago

The Transoceánica building in Santiago, Chile is a 150,000 sq ft (14,000 sq m), LEED Gold-certified commercial office building.[31] The building is long, narrow, and elliptical in shape, maximizing daylight and views. Situated on 183,000 sq ft (about 4 acres/17,000 sq m) of green space, the building includes office space on three levels, two levels of underground parking with a green roof over it, an auditorium, an amphitheater, a cafeteria, and a café. Outside, a park and lagoon surrounding the building act as an artificial wetland with water from a deep well that supports the cooling system for the office.

Rather than employ a typical glass façade and installing traditional air-conditioning, the building was wrapped in a wood screen lattice on its north, east, and west (sun-facing) sides to deflect solar radiation, while allowing natural light into the office space. As a result, Transoceánica only uses one-fourth the energy of a comparable Chilean office.

A project of Empresas Transoceánica, the project design addressed three unique conditions. First, at the owner's request, the building is incorporated into a master plan, which defined the land use and specified the use of curved shapes for each floor, allowing for future site-development possibilities. Second, the building's energy concept emphasized climatic adaptation and required architectural designers to achieve the required sustainability goals. Third, the building site, located near a sports arena, has strict regulations on constructability, land use, and maximum height, forcing the project to be built on a larger-than-normal lot.

The resulting design contains a full-height atrium that opens into two wings. An independent wing along the north houses an auditorium and cafeteria, connected by an exterior canopy that integrates these spaces with the building and the land. The building's narrow shape optimizes solar orientation, favors natural light, provides views to the outdoors from all locations, and provides a careful façade treatment to avoid unwanted heat gain and loss.

The systems incorporate passive design elements such as location, orientation, solar control systems, natural light, renewable materials, and native vegetation from central Chile.

The building is heated and cooled using German-manufactured polypropylene tubing, installed beneath the floor slabs within a plaster layer throughout all office spaces, improving thermal comfort with radiant effects. The heat transfer fluid operates between 61°F (16°C) minimum and 95°F (35°C) maximum. Air renewal takes place using "displacement ventilation," by which fresh outside air is introduced at low speed through the raised floor and rises by convection wherever there are heat-emitting surfaces. It is then retrieved and directed toward the air handler, which precools or preheats the entering air, using a heat recovery system. In addition to the building's internal control unit, the German engineering office responsible for the energy concept monitors the project remotely via the Internet.

A renewable energy source, geothermal energy is incorporated by extracting water from a 248-ft (75-m) well at a constant 54°F (12°C) temperature, which is used to cool air and the fluid in the tubing using heat exchangers, leaving chillers only for circumstances with higher demand and internal heat generation.

TABLE 7.4

Annual electricity and water use

	Annual use	Intensity
Electricity	749,602 kWh	53.7 kWh/sq m
Potable water	4,614 cu m	330 l/sq m

TABLE 7.5

Estimated energy end-use requirements

	%
Lighting	19
Equipment and offices	27
Heating and cooling	32
Other (elevators, pumps)	22

At a glance
Name: Transoceánica
Location: Santiago, Chile
Size: 183,000 sq ft (17,000 sq m) site; 150,700 sq ft (14,000 sq m) gross floor area building (22,600 sq ft/ 2,100 sq m footprint); 143,160 sq ft (13,300 sq m) landscaping and lagoon area; 17,200 sq ft (1,600 sq m) terrace space
Completion: 2010
Cost: Construction: US$1,079/sq m; Site: US$420/sq m
Distinction: LEED-NC Gold
Program: Commercial office building

Project team
Owner and Project Manager: Empresas Transoceánica
Architect: +arquitectos (Brahm, Bonomi, Leturia, Bártolome)
Energy Concept: Bohne Ingenieure
Structural Engineer: Gatica & Jiménez
Construction: Sigro SA

7.10 *Right*: 41 Cooper Square academic center houses the Albert Nerken School of Engineering with additional spaces for the humanities, art, and architecture departments at The Cooper Union in New York City. Photo: © Iwan Baan.

41 COOPER SQUARE,
The Cooper Union, New York, New York

Founded in 1859, The Cooper Union is one of the oldest higher-education facilities in the USA. Founder Peter Cooper believed that education of the highest quality should be as "free as air and water." At this all-honors college, each student admitted to the Cooper Union receives a full-tuition scholarship. Completed in 2009 and originally called the "New Academic Building," 41 Cooper Square became the first academic building in New York City to receive a LEED Platinum certification.[32]

Replacing an aging campus building, 41 Cooper Square houses the School of Art, Architecture, and Engineering. The 175,000-sq-ft (16,258-sq-m) building contains nine above-ground floors and two basements. Classrooms, small engineering laboratories, study lounges, art studio space, and faculty offices populate the first eight above-ground floors. The top floor is dedicated to studio and classroom space. Free public events and exhibitions take place in the ground-floor public art gallery and auditorium.

The lowest basement level contains the school's machine shops and design laboratories, along with most HVAC and other building equipment. The first basement level houses an auditorium, a 198-person-capacity lecture hall, conference rooms, and exhibit space.

Designed by Morphosis Architects, the structure presents a number of unconventional architectural features, including a sculpted mesh façade, full-height sky-lit atrium, aluminum window walls, a four-story central staircase, and sky bridges. The intention behind the overall design was to create an inspiring, interactive space for students and faculty.

"We literally designed out from the core, always keeping in mind that the building should be as strong and innovative as the institution itself," said Thom Mayne of Morphosis Architects.[33]

Connecting the first four floors is the linear Grand Staircase, which is used both for transportation and as a recreational space for students. The higher floors are connected by floating interior sky bridges as well as two standard corner staircases and three elevators.

"Internally, the building is conceived as a vehicle to foster collaboration and cross-disciplinary dialogue among the college's three schools, previously housed in separate buildings," said Mayne. "A vertical piazza—the central space for informal social, intellectual and creative exchange—forms the new academic building's heart. An undulating lattice surrounds a 20-ft wide grand stair which ascends four stories from the ground level through the sky-lit central atrium, which itself extends to the building's full height. This 'vertical piazza' is the building's social heart, providing a place for impromptu and planned meetings, student gatherings, lectures, and the intellectual debate that defines the academic environment."[34]

On top of the Grand Staircase is a student lounge, which overlooks the city and contains a small café as well as naturally lit study areas. To promote both increased physical activity and impromptu meeting opportunities, the design team developed a "skip-stop" vertical circulation strategy, so that most elevators make stops only at the first, fifth, and eighth floors, encouraging people to use the grand staircase and sky bridges. A freight elevator and passenger elevator stop at each floor, both for ADA compliance and moving materials, artwork, and equipment.[35]

In aligning with Cooper Union's mission and values, the floor-to-ceiling atrium and perforated façade allow for physical and visual permeability. "In the spirit of the institution's dedication to free, open, and accessible education, the building itself is symbolically open to the city," said Mayne. "Visual transparencies and accessible public spaces connect the institution to the physical, social and cultural fabric of its urban context. At street level, the transparent façade invites the neighborhood to observe and to take part in the intensity of activity within."[36]

A semitransparent layer of perforated metal panels wraps the exterior window walls. This double-skin system is a key feature of both the building's energy performance and the exterior aesthetic. Operable panels create a continually varying façade while controlling solar gain, providing occupant control, and offering views to the outdoors.[37] In the winter, the panels help to insulate the building, and in the summer, they provide shade.[38]

Recognized as a high-performance building by the US Green Building Council, 41 Cooper Square's sustainability initiatives include:

- Radiant heating and cooling ceiling panels introduce innovative HVAC technology that boosts energy efficiency. This contributes to making the new building 40 percent more energy efficient than a standard academic research building.

TABLE 7.6

2010 performance data

	Annual use	Intensity
Electricity use (kWh)	4,969,600	306 kWh/sq m
Gas use (Therm)	128,862	
Gas use (kWh) @ 29.3 kWh/therm	3,775,657	232 kWh/sq m
Total energy use (kWh)	**8,745,257**	**538 kWh/sq m**

- The full-height atrium enables unique circulation for building occupants, improves air flow, and provides increased interior daylighting.
- Seventy-five percent of the building's regularly occupied spaces are lit by natural daylight.
- A green roof insulates the building, reduces heat island effect, storm-water runoff, and pollutants; harvested water is reused.
- A cogeneration plant provides additional power for the building, recovers waste heat, and effectively cuts energy costs.[39]

The $112 million building was funded in part by New York State, New York City, and alumni donations, identified by nameplates, engravings, and recognition throughout the building.[40]

As an intellectual and cultural center of New York City, Cooper Union wanted to create an iconic building. The school accomplished that goal with 41 Cooper Square and at the same time produced a highly rated green building.

At a glance
Name: 41 Cooper Square
Size: 175,000 sq ft (16,264 sq m)
Completion/Occupancy: June 2009
Cost: $112 million
Distinction: LEED-NC Platinum
Program: Academic and laboratory building with exhibition gallery, auditorium, lounge and multi-purpose space, and retail space.

Project team
Owner: The Cooper Union for the Advancement of Science and Art
Architect: Morphosis Architects
General Contractor: F. J. Sciame

7.11 An undulating lattice envelops a 20-ft-wide grand stair which ascends four stories from the ground level through the sky-lit central atrium, which itself reaches to the full height of the building. Photo: Jerry Yudelson.

7.12 *Top*: Following Vedic architectural principles, 2000 Tower Oaks is oriented perfectly to the cardinal directions: true north, south, east, and west, with the entrance facing east toward the rising sun. Photo: Ron Blunt Photography.

7.13 *Bottom*: The 200,000-sq-ft 2000 Tower Oaks in Rockville, Maryland, was designed using Vedic architecture principles to create an environment that promotes physical and spiritual prosperity. Photo: Ron Blunt Photography.

2000 TOWER OAKS BOULEVARD, Rockville, Maryland

Maharishi Vedic or Maharishi Vastu Architecture is a revival of India's ancient approach to architecture and city planning. It is said to be a complete building science, based on design principles that promote nourishing, life-supporting relationships, through the use of natural materials and the placement, function, and orientation of the building. Introduced in the USA by American practitioners of Transcendental Meditation, Vedic architecture aims to harmonize people, buildings, and land.[41] 2000 Tower Oaks is the largest commercial expression of this approach.[42]

The Tower Companies and Lerner Enterprises, two private real-estate firms and both tenants at 2000 Tower Oaks, developed the 200,000-sq-ft (18,581-sq-m), nine-story project, located 12 miles northwest of the US Capitol. Jeffrey S. Abramson, a partner at family-owned and award-winning The Tower Companies, led the effort to incorporate Vedic principles into 2000 Tower Oaks Boulevard.[43]

"The building went beyond LEED Platinum, beyond green, to become an investment in human capital to enhance productivity and creativity," explained Abramson. "Vedic architecture, in accord with natural law, is the governing intelligence found at the basis of nature's functioning, which upholds life in perfect order. This architecture connects individual life with the extended environment—cosmic life—using principles of building design that mirror nature. This naturally promotes a sense of well being and attunement with nature."[44]

Vedic architecture features several unique elements, incorporated at 2000 Tower Oaks:

- *Orientation*: The building is oriented perfectly to the cardinal directions, true north, south, east, and west, with the building entrance facing east toward the rising sun.[45] (This is contrary to much "green design" thinking, which would orient the long axis of a building east–west, instead of north–south, as in this case.)
- *Proportions*: Nature often mimics the same proportions at different scales, as characterized by fractal geometry. 2000 Tower Oaks Boulevard was constructed according to precise formulas that resonate with the natural world.[46]
- *Centerpoint*: The building has a center of silence or core called a Brahmasthan, a structure replicated in solar systems, cells, and atoms. The activity of the building is arranged around this central core.[47]
- *Vastu fence*: The building is placed within a Vastu, or a fenced terrace surrounding the building, following defined proportions. The fenced terrace extends the coherence of the building into its site.[48]

"All of these points and others combine to create this building's uniqueness," said Abramson. "People don't feel as restricted by time in the building. There is a dynamism here; but rooted in an atmosphere of peace and harmony, there is a sense of rightness and a feeling that you have the wind at your back. People are more innovative, more creative, more willing to let go, more willing to change and collaborate."[49]

TABLE 7.7

Energy and water use, 2010[a]

	Annual use	Intensity
Grid electricity	11,552,053 kBtu 3,385,000 kWh	57.6 kBTU/sq ft 181.8 kWh/sq m
Potable water	2,743,000 g	13.75 g/sq ft

a Energy Star, Statement of Performance, September 21, 2011. Provided by David Borchardt, The Tower Companies, September 28, 2011.

Abramson admits that using Vedic architecture at 2000 Tower Oaks Boulevard had an increased cost premium—about 2 to 3 percent.[50] But, he says, the increased cost more than pays for itself in increased productivity, given that it is about $400 per square foot per year for employee costs in the Washington, DC, area, compared to energy costs, which average $3 to $5 per square foot.[51]

"Human beings respond to space," said Abramson. "That's the cost associated with growing and maintaining your business. It's also the cost with the most variability. I believe this $400 per sq ft cost is an area the real estate developer can address: my job is to help create developments where businesses and people can excel. With Vedic and green buildings, we now have the tools to do so."[52]

2000 Tower Oaks is rated Platinum under the USGBC's LEED Core and Shell (LEED-CS) system. LEED-CS is intended to be complementary to the LEED for Commercial Interiors (LEED-CI) rating system so the entire building would ultimately be certified as if it were fully built out at initial occupancy.[53] And, in fact, the two major tenant spaces in 2000 Tower Oaks, occupied by The Tower Companies and Lerner Enterprises, are LEED-CI Platinum- and Gold-rated, respectively.

2000 Tower Oaks uses an estimated 28 percent less energy than a similar office building, with efficiency features, including:

- an enthalpy wheel that captures energy in heated and cooled air from the building exhaust to preheat or precool incoming air depending on the season
- a frictionless magnetic bearing centrifugal chiller/compressor that consumes 700,000 fewer kilowatt-hours than a typical chiller
- a high-efficiency curtain wall with low-e glass
- a building energy management system that automatically turns off lights at night
- occupancy sensors in shared areas automatically turn off lights when unoccupied[54]
- CO_2 monitors in high-density areas supply fresh air only when occupied.[55]

As a result, only 13 percent of total energy demand arises from space heating and cooling. Because of the generally low building envelope and HVAC energy demands, internal plug loads make up almost one-third of total energy use.[56]

Water-efficiency strategies contribute to a 41 percent reduction in water use. Used for site irrigation, condensate from the air-conditioning system eliminates use of potable water outside the building.[57]

"The purpose of buildings is to house businesses' aspirations," said Abramson. "Therefore, as a developer of the built environment, I have a responsibility to help them get a return on rent and make their workforce more creative and successful. Vedic building design helps to achieve this by elevating environmental responsibility in real estate to its pinnacle performance, going beyond green to create work environments that support success and well being."[58]

At a glance

Name: 2000 Tower Oaks Boulevard
Location: Rockville, Maryland
Completed: Summer 2008
Size: 200,405 sq ft (18,618 sq m), plus 170,000 sq ft (15,794 sq m) of below-grade parking
Cost: Construction $54.3 million, Site $9.3 million
Distinction: LEED-CS Platinum
Program: Corporate office with a café and fitness center

Project team

Owner: The Tower Companies and Lerner Enterprises
Architect: Kishimoto–Gordon–Dalaya Architecture
Construction Management Consultant: Bernie Sanker Associates, Inc.
Maharishi Vastu Architecture: Fortune-Creating Buildings, Jonathan Lipman, AIA
MEP Engineer: TOLK, Inc.
Structural Engineer: Smisloy, Kehnemui & Associates
LEED Consulting and Commissioning: SD Keppler & Associates
Contractor: Whiting-Turner Contracting Company

7.14 *Top*: Building B of the Biodesign Institute at Arizona State University incorporated the lessons learned from Building A to achieve the first LEED Platinum award in Arizona. Photo: Biodesign Institute at Arizona State University.

7.15 *Bottom:* The full-height atrium, centrally located staircases, and glass-walled offices encourage interaction and collaboration. Photo: Biodesign Institute at Arizona State University.

TABLE 7.8

Energy and water use, 2011

	Annual use	Intensity
Energy	25.2 million kWh	927 kWh/sq m
Water	2,587,000 g	14.8 g/sq ft; 602 l/sq m

BIODESIGN INSTITUTE B,
Arizona State University, Tempe, Arizona

Building B at the Biodesign Institute at Arizona State University (ASU) was the first building in Arizona to receive the highest designation for environmentally friendly design and construction: LEED Platinum. The 800,000-sq-ft (74,322-sq-m) master-planned institute currently has two LEED-certified buildings: one Gold (Building A) and the other Platinum (Building B). These two buildings constitute the first two phases of a planned intensive research corridor along the east side of the ASU campus. The two buildings appear as mirror images but were constructed separately and are connected on all levels by sheltered walkways. Together the buildings provide 350,000 sq ft (32,516 sq m) of office and research space. Each building was completed in an eighteen-month span, and the lessons learned from Building A, completed in December 2004, informed the design of the slightly larger Building B, completed in January 2006.

The facilities were designed by architectural firms Gould Evans Associates and Lord, Aeck & Sargent, and built via a joint venture between Sundt Construction and DPR Construction. The institute was designed as not only a state-of-the-art research facility, but also a world-class demonstration of ecological laboratory design. This is apparent through the many sustainable aspects of the building, the site, and the construction process. One of the goals of the institute was to foster a strong connection between the natural environment outdoors and the research occurring indoors.

In the Biodesign Institute, said Trudi Hummel, Principal at Gould Evans, "The idea was for researchers to connect visually from their offices and labs into this amazing natural landscape that's all about the desert. It was a motivational and inspirational aspect of the project."[59] Research offices are oriented to provide Sonoran desert garden views, landscaped with drought-resistant native plants and serving as a natural stormwater management system.

It was important to connect the research not only to the landscape but also to the various research disciplines *within* the building as well. To achieve this, the team limited the building height to four levels, interconnected by a central glazed atrium, to encourage personal interaction among researchers through using stairs rather than elevators. Glass-walled laboratories and office space offer transparent views into the central atrium.[60]

At a glance
Name: The Biodesign Institute B at Arizona State University
Size: 175,000 sq ft (16,264 sq m)
Completion/Occupancy: January 2006
Cost: $78.5 million
Distinction: LEED-NC Platinum
Program: Academic laboratory, offices, conference rooms, atrium, auditorium, public entry lobby, and café

Project team
Owner: Arizona State University
Architect: Gould Evans Associates and Lord, Aeck & Sargent
Civil Engineer: Evans, Kuhun & Associates
Structural Engineer: Paragon Structural Design
MEP Engineer: Newcomb & Boyd
General Contractor: Sundt Construction and DPR Construction

"One of the main goals of the facility was to create an environment where the researchers literally run into each other in their daily work," said Hummel. "The offices are on one side of the daylit atrium and the labs on the other side. There are generous stairwells with large landings and white boards in the corridors to jot down ideas so that there would be opportunities for collaboration among researchers."[61]

Tempe exhibits a hot, arid climate with temperatures reaching or exceeding 100°F (38°C) on average 110 days a year. The area receives scant rainfall, about 8 in (203 mm) per year on average. With the harsh desert climate, mitigating solar gain was a key element in the design strategy. Fixed horizontal aluminum fins provide shading on the exterior for the smaller glazing areas on the south and west façades. Similar exterior shade structures were investigated on the east side as well, but to preserve views to the garden and allow for shading the offices an internal shading system was designed.

"Our concern about the climate control at the Biodesign Institute had to do with the large east façade of glass," said Hummel. "If we had our preference in terms of what was most appropriate for this environment, we would have not oriented the building with the long axis north–south. To understand climate and comfort control for all of those offices on the east façade, we undertook a very detailed energy study."[62]

As a result, the team designed an active, dual internal louver system to control solar gain on the east façade. "The blinds that we ended up using are motorized and located just inside the window system, but are adjustable based on where the sun is," said John Dimmel, with Gould Evans. "They respond to the sun: in the morning they're in a closed position to block the direct east sun, but when the sun moves higher in the sky, they begin to open up, allowing views and daylight."[63]

The biggest energy challenge in lab buildings is flushing the building with fresh air to accommodate the research needs. Fresh air brought in from outside needs to be heated or cooled to the desired inside ambient temperature. In a really hot climate, that requirement creates significant loads on the cooling system.

The Biodesign Institute architects chose an advanced technology system that "controls the valves that control the number of air changes," said Larry Lord, Principal at Lord, Aeck, & Sargent. "We reduced the number of air changes to four per hour. The reason that's possible is that the system has what I call 'sniffers.' It can sense various gases and other contaminants. If it detects a problem, it kicks the air handler back up to 10 to 12 air changes per hour."[64]

A campus central plant supplies chilled water and steam for the mechanical system. The central plant was a major contributor to the LEED Platinum rating. "And that's where the luck came in," said Mike McLeod, Facility Management Director at the Institute. "The entire institute runs off a gas-fired cogeneration plant. We were out of power [on the campus to supply new buildings] so we had to build something [for this project]."[65]

A 167-kW rooftop PV system supplies 2.1 percent of the building's electricity needs and also helped push Building B to a Platinum LEED rating. McLeod said, "Here at Biodesign, we have a 250,000-kWh-annual-output, solar generating system with almost 800 panels."[66]

Minimizing water use and implementing creative reuse strategies were also high priorities for the project. The building harnesses water in a 5,000-gallon (18,927-liter) irrigation water cistern that collects air-conditioning system condensate. Also, building roofs collect rainwater during summer "monsoons" and other rain events and route it via pipes to the drought-resistant native desert landscaping.[67]

"A significant feature that really speaks to good sustainable design practices is the integration of the bioswale in the garden area," said Tamara Shroll with Gould Evans. "It's an integral feature of the way that the landscape is a place of living for the occupants of the building and visitors. It really is a big part of the experience of the site."[68]

After the buildings were open and LEED certified, the Biodesign Institute operation's department implemented a continuous improvement strategy to assess and reduce utility cost by more than 30 percent, generating $1.2 million in annual utility cost savings. These strategies reduced overall energy use by 29 percent.[69] Table 7.8 shows performance data. According to McLeod, in accounting for the high energy use number, the Biodesign Institute's labs are "100 percent wet lab space with a great deal of specialty labs such as Biosafety Level 3s, large lasers, etc. I think Biodesign should be considered as on the very advanced edge of laboratory research and building energy use."[70]

The Biodesign Institute represents a beacon of innovation. The investment has paid off, attracting nationally renowned professors from around the country and helping to start up several companies, garnering substantial grants and sponsoring groundbreaking research.[71]

DELL CHILDREN'S MEDICAL CENTER OF CENTRAL TEXAS, Austin, Texas

Dell Children's Medical Center in Austin, Texas, is part of a 722-acre New Urbanist development on the brownfield site of a former airport. Owned by Seton Healthcare Family, part of Ascension Health and a provider of thirty-one facilities in Central Texas, the center is the first hospital in the world to achieve LEED Platinum certification.

"Being a green hospital has a profound, measurable effect on healing," said Robert Bonar, CEO of Dell Children's Medical Center. "Children are hospitalized in a building that by its very design is far less likely to cause various forms of 'sick building syndrome.' This translates into a better experience for patients and families."[72]

By their nature as a 24/7 operation, with attendant high energy and water demands, regulatory requirements, chemical use, and infection control, healthcare facilities face significant obstacles when trying to implement sustainability protocols.

"Even before the first plans were drawn up, we set our sights on creating a world-class children's hospital. Becoming the first LEED Platinum hospital in the world was definitely part of that," said Bonar. "Our motivation to pursue LEED Platinum was not just environmental. What's good for the environment and good for our neighbors is also good for our patients."[73]

The 169-bed facility is situated on a 32-acre campus. Instead of creating a single 12-story typical hospital building, the architect chose instead to compartmentalize it by department, resulting in an articulated, multi-level building with heights ranging from two to four stories. Seven open-air gardens and courtyards are arranged with the building in a hub-and-spoke configuration, with each garden representing one of the seven bioregions found within Central Texas.[74]

In pursuing LEED certification, the team wanted to make decisions that made sense economically. "We decided that every selection [to meet LEED credits] had to pay back within eight-years," said Alan Bell, Seton's Director of Design and Construction.[75]

A joint project with the local utility, Austin Energy, the 4.5-MW natural gas-fired combined cooling and heating power plant (CHP) provides 100 percent of the hospital's electricity. The exhaust heat from the gas turbine is routed to the heat-recovery generator where it is converted into steam. That steam is used in the plant by an absorption

7.16 The Dell Children's Medical Center uses 10 to 20 percent less energy than other hospital facilities and has lower staff turnover and greater patient satisfaction. Photo: Marc M. Swendner.

7.17 The interior features indigenous materials such as mesquite wood and red sandstone, along with nontoxic paints, adhesives, and carpet. Photo: Marc M. Swendner.

chiller that makes chilled water for building cooling. It's also used to make hot water for use throughout the hospital.[76]

"Because there is an energy plant across the street, one BTU [going] into the energy plant [comes] out at about 0.75 BTUs into the hospital," said Bell. "If we were pulling energy from a coal-fired plant about 70 miles from here, 1 BTU into that plant was about 0.29 BTUs coming into the hospital. So you can see that we avoided a huge loss."[77]

Originally designed to provide daylighting to 60 percent of the building interior, the interior courtyards also assist with ventilation. Acting as the lungs of the building, the courtyards provide fresh air to the many air-handling units throughout the hospital. In place of a single, consolidated, rooftop air-handling unit, the building team "right-sized" individual air handlers for specific zones of the hospital, each with varying needs.[78]

The team also specified four different types of windows based on the unique needs of each façade. Computer models helped determine the ambient exterior light from dawn to dusk, seven days a week, for all four seasons of the year and informed controls of the lighting system to minimize energy use.[79] Figure 7.18 shows the actual versus expected

TABLE 7.9

Energy use, 2011

	Actual	Projected
Energy use (million BTU)	136,162	126,829
Energy use intensity (kBTU/sq ft/year)	287.5	268
Energy use intensity (kWh/sq m/year)	908	846

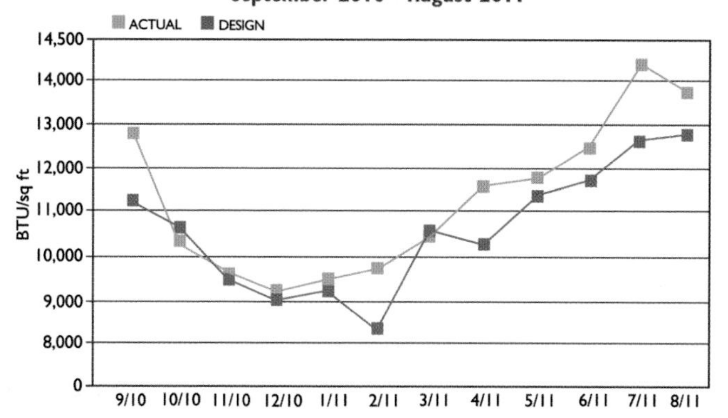

7.18 Dell Children's Medical Center energy use intensity. Data provided by Phillip Risner, Seton, December 22, 2011.

energy use of the hospital in 2010–2011, with very close agreement (only 6 percent more energy use).

If any building should be designed with nontoxic materials, it would certainly be a hospital.[80] "Our business is helping kids get and stay healthy," said Bonar. "How could we look the public in the eye and tell them such if we knew that we had just filled the building with materials that are off-gassing formaldehyde and other harmful products? Building healthy, sustainable buildings is the right thing to do."[81]

It can be challenging for hospitals to achieve significant water conservation, owing to the special need for cleanliness. The building saves 1.7 million gallons (6,435 kl) annually by utilizing low-flow bathroom fixtures and another 1.4 million gallons (5,300 kl) of water a year by using native landscaping. Rainwater is channeled into a stormwater detention pond, which allows it to seep down into the groundwater table.[82]

For the Seton Healthcare Family, the sustainability features go beyond saving energy; they also make good business sense. "And, the fact is, people want to be in healthy buildings," said Bell. "It's easier to recruit medical staff. It's easier to retain staff. And, in this way it makes your facility more competitive in the healthcare market."[83] The average nursing staff turnover rate ranges from 10 to 15 percent nationally, and new hospitals can experience as much as 30 percent turnover during their first year of operation. Dell Children's Medical Center reported a 2.4 percent turnover rate for the first year.[84]

"We had a vision for LEED Platinum from the outset of this project, as we sought to create the optimum environment for our patients as well as our employees," said Phil Risner, Project Manager for Seton. "There was no doubt in our minds that being green had real, positive effects on both the environment and our healthcare delivery capability."[85]

The 473,000-sq-ft (nearly 44,000-sq-m) building cost $137 million to build and is named in honor of Michael and Susan Dell, co-founders of the Dell Foundation, which donated $25 million to kick-start the capital campaign for construction of the center.[86] "The medical center not only boasts state-of-the-art facilities and equipment to better meet the health care needs of Central Texas children," said Susan Dell, "but through its modern design concepts, it is among the most energy efficient and environmentally advanced."[87]

At a glance

Name: Dell Children's Medical Center of Central Texas

Location: Austin, Texas

Size: 473,000 sq ft (43,959 sq m)

Completed: July 2007

Cost: $137 million

Distinction: LEED-NC Platinum

Program: Children's hospital

Project team

Owner: Seton Healthcare Family

Architect: Karlsberger

MEP Engineer: ccrd Partners

LEED Consultant: Center for Maximum Potential Building Systems

Construction Manager: White Construction Company

GENZYME CENTER, Cambridge, Massachusetts

The Genzyme Center is a twelve-story, 350,000-sq-ft (32,500-sq-m) office building in Cambridge, Massachusetts. The project was awarded a LEED Platinum certification in 2004. Naturally, it contains plenty of green features, but extensive daylighting is the most remarkable feature immediately noticed by both visitors and occupants. (The interview in Chapter 5 with architect Stefan Behnisch explains how the daylighting design evolved.)

Genzyme Corporation is an international biotechnology company dedicated to making a major positive impact on the lives of people with serious diseases. The company's products and services are related to rare genetic diseases, multiple sclerosis, cardiovascular disease, and endocrinology.

In 2000, as the company approached its twentieth anniversary, Genzyme decided that the time was right for a new headquarters office, and it wanted a signature building that would be a reflection of its core values. Completed in November 2003, the building provides office space for more than 900 employees.[88]

"Creating a green building—one that sets new standards—is consistent with what we do every day as a corporation," said Henri A. Termeer, Genzyme's former Chairman and Chief Executive Officer, at the grand opening of the building. "Genzyme Center is consistent with our purpose, which is to innovate to create new standards of care for patients with untreatable diseases."[89]

Designed by Behnisch Architects, Genzyme Center uses natural daylighting and transparency to create an optimum working environment for the occupants. Behnisch proposed that the building be designed from the inside out, and the design team carefully studied how Genzyme employees work and interact. The team designed the building around an indoor environment that emphasized natural night, views of the outdoors, and an open communicative environment. Three key concepts reflect the company's values and are the themes for the design: innovation, collaboration, and transparency.[90]

The design team, including the architects, engineers, owner's project manager, and Genzyme employees, followed an IDP, where the entire project team worked together to optimize the building from a holistic perspective. For the Genzyme Center, the design process was dynamic and continually evolved as the team's knowledge of green building practices grew. Because a Platinum rating was the goal, the LEED checklist was used as a guide for making sustainable choices and to maximize the number of points earned by the project.[91]

According to Behnisch Architects, the Genzyme Center is "organized as 'a vertical city' with individual 'dwellings,' public areas and gardens which extend up to the full height of the central atrium. The open staircase forms part of a 'vertical boulevard,' starting at the ground-floor lobby before proceeding upwards through various neighborhoods with open workstations and separate offices."[92] An abundance of open space allows for air circulation and sunlight diffusion and facilitates creativity, interaction, and collaboration among the employees.

"There are all these views. It is communicative," said Christof Jantzen, Partner at Behnisch Architects. "You can wave to your colleague two floors down and across the central space. It is not so much about the details . . . it is a combination of how the elements come together as a whole."[93]

Informed by the interior environment, the building exterior is sheathed entirely in glass, connecting the outside and inside environments and aligning with the company's transparency ethos. Several key employee-friendly features also enhance the connection with the external environment: operable windows, indoor gardens, natural light enhancement systems, and a cafeteria with views of the Charles River and the Boston skyline.[94]

Located in a neighborhood adjacent to the Massachusetts Institute of Technology, the building and site are part of a major urban infill redevelopment project, which is intended to create a mixed community in an area of formerly polluted sites.[95]

One of the building's innovations, which earned it recognition as a top green project from the American Institute of Architects, is the filigreed wide-slab construction system. This technique uses two-inch-thick slabs of pre-stressed, precast concrete which are laid on pillars. Then a concrete reinforcing bar is added, and polystyrene foam is used to fill voids.[96]

This method reduces the amount of concrete used in construction and lessens the weight of the structure. For Genzyme Center, it eliminated 2,552 cu yd (1,951 cu m) of concrete, 386 tons (350 metric tons) of reinforcing steel, and 250,000 sq ft (23,234 sq m) of plywood. Overall, use of the filigreed wide-slab lowered the weight of the building by 25 percent. With less weight, fewer concrete piles were needed, and the number of foundation elements was reduced.

7.19 Completed in 2003, the Genzyme Center in Cambridge, Massachusetts, was one of the first buildings awarded a LEED Platinum certification. Photo: Anton Grassl. Courtesy of Behnisch Architekten.

Concrete remains exposed throughout the building to take advantage of its thermal mass, helping to maintain a comfortable ambient temperature while reducing the mechanical heating and cooling requirements. Filigree concrete-slab construction also contributes to the building's extensive daylighting. It helped create a structure with cantilevered floors situated around a central atrium, allowing for an extensive glass exterior.[97]

The building envelope is a high-performance curtain-wall glazing system with operable windows on all twelve stories. The operable windows are linked to the BMS, which opens on cool summer nights for night-flush cooling. More than 30 percent of the exterior envelope is a ventilated double façade with a four-foot buffer space. In the summer it blocks solar gains and ventilates the heat away before it enters the space, and in the winter it captures solar gains, reducing the heat loss from the façade.[98]

In addition to supplying natural light, the atrium acts as a huge return air duct. Fresh air is introduced to the occupied space by ceiling vents throughout the floor plates or through the operable windows.

7.20 The Genzyme Center is organized as a vertical city, with individual dwellings, public areas, and gardens that extend up to the full height of the central atrium. Photo: Anton Grassl. Courtesy of Behnisch Architekten.

The air then moves into the atrium and up and out via exhaust fans on the ceiling.[99]

Owing to the building design and lighting technologies installed, 100 percent of the regularly occupied workplaces have views to the outdoors, and more than 75 percent receive enough natural light under normal conditions to work without artificial lighting.[100] Innovative technologies such as "U"-shaped blinds, heliostats, reflective ceiling tiles and wall surfaces, metal light distributors, and prismatic chandeliers work together to harvest natural light. Even the reflective pool on the ground floor operates as part of the lighting strategy by reflecting and re-distributing sunlight.[101]

Seven 5 × 5-ft (1.5 × 1.5-m) rotating heliostats (mirrors) on the roof track the sun and direct it into the building through computer-controlled louvers on the atrium skylight. This light is reflected off various surfaces throughout the atrium.[102]

High-gloss, reflection-coated interior vertical blinds in the atrium form a "light wall" that maximizes daylight distribution. The wall is made up of twenty-two polished aluminum panels, and each panel is a series of perforated vertical blades. Also connected to the BMS, the light wall distributes light according to weather conditions.[103]

Hanging in the atrium are 768 prismatic plates arranged as an artistic mobile. The acrylic prisms reflect light and create rainbows that bounce around the building, creating a dynamic interior environment. During daylight hours, the prisms reflect sunlight, and at night they diffuse light and eliminate glare from the interior halogen lights.[104]

The lighting system design is responsible for a 45-percent reduction in the building's annual energy consumption as compared to a conventional building. The design not only reduces the building's peak electrical consumption but also enhances the quality of the working environment.[105] Eighteen interior gardens support high IAQ while increasing occupants' connection to nature.[106]

"Inside, it feels fresher and brighter than outside the building. The light enhancement reduces the glare. Generally, there are certain times of days when you get groggy. But in this building you don't get that afternoon sleepy feeling," said Rick Mattila, Director of Environmental Affairs, Genzyme.[107]

The occupants agree. Administered eighteen months after opening, an occupant survey found that employees felt more comfortable and productive in the new building compared with their prior workspace.

- Seventy-two percent said they felt more alert and productive.
- Eighty-eight percent said having direct views and access to the interior gardens improved their sense of well-being.
- Seventy-five percent said the building's clear glass design increased their sense of connection with colleagues.
- Ninety-two percent said the building increased their sense of pride about Genzyme's commitment to the environment.[108]

The central heating and cooling for the building uses steam from a cogeneration plant two blocks away. This approach reduces energy costs and GHG emissions. The steam drives absorption chillers for summer cooling and is exchanged directly into heat for winter heating. The building is cooled naturally by a "stack effect" as the heat rises up through the atrium and out of the building. The operable windows enhance the airflow and minimize demands on the HVAC system.[109]

A 1,650-sq-ft (153-sq-m) array of roof-mounted PV panels with a peak output of 20 kW produces up to 26,400 kWh annually (a small portion of total energy use). All of the purchased electricity is from certified renewable sources, currently a mix of 10 percent wind, 12 percent landfill gas, 40 percent small hydro, and 38 percent biomass.[110] The facility uses 34 percent less water compared to a similar sized building and saves more than 500,000 gallons (1,893 kl) annually in internal water use.

Genzyme's stormwater system reduces runoff by 25 percent.[111] The 6,000-sq-ft (557-sq-m) green roof filters and absorbs water. Rainwater that falls on other areas of the roof flows into one of four collection tanks, which is used to supplement the water demand for cooling towers and to irrigate the green roof when soil sensors indicate the grass is dry.[112] Stormwater that is not captured and reused is filtered and released to the storm drain system.[113]

Additional sustainable features include:

- recharging station for electric vehicles
- forty preferred parking spaces for carpools
- 50 percent more open space than city requirements
- 100 percent below ground parking to reduce urban heat island effect.[114]

As one of the earliest realized LEED Platinum projects, the Genzyme Center was more expensive than a conventional building, at $140 million (inclusive of furniture, soil remediation, etc.).[115] Approximately $23 million, or 16 percent of the total cost, was attributed to sustainable features.[116] However, forward-thinking companies like Genzyme made sustainable construction a core value long before it became fashionable. From the beginning of the project, the company was confident that over time the premium associated with the sustainability features would be more than compensated for by savings resulting from lower operating costs and increased productivity, including easier recruitment and increased retention of employees. The Genzyme Center certainly accomplished its goal of proving that it's possible to construct an architecturally exciting, beautiful, and employee-friendly building that makes economic, social, and environmental sense.[117]

TABLE 7.10

Energy and water use, 2010

	Annual use	Intensity
Electricity	4,760,460 kWh	149 kWh/sq m
Steam	14.9 million lb = 14,900 million BTU = 4,365,700 kWh	136 kWh/sq m
Total		**285 kWh/sq m**
Solar	26,400 kWh	0.8 kWh/sq m
Potable water	5,404,000 g (41% cooling tower use)	16 g/sq ft 638 l/sq m

At a glance
Name: Genzyme Center
Location: Cambridge, Massachusetts
Size: 344,000 sq ft (32,000 sq m)
Completed: November 2003
Construction cost: $140 million
Distinction: LEED-NC Platinum
Program: Commercial office

Project team
Owner: Bio-Med Realty Trust
Developer: Lyme Properties LLC
Architect: Behnisch & Partner Architects
Electrical Engineer: Buro Happold
General Contractor: Turner Construction Company

GREAT RIVER ENERGY HEADQUARTERS,
Maple Grove, Minnesota

Great River Energy is the second-largest electric power supplier in Minnesota. When the time came for a new headquarters building to accommodate its growing staff, Great River Energy decided that the new building should be a model of energy efficiency and sustainability that would serve as a learning tool for future buildings.[118]

"At Great River Energy, we know the cheapest—and cleanest—kilowatt-hour is the one we don't have to produce," said Great River Energy President and CEO, David Saggau. "So conservation and energy efficiency have become our 'first fuel.'"[119]

Beyond having a high-performing building in energy efficiency, sustainability, and conservation, Great River Energy wanted to do something with energy efficiency that had seldom been done before. They wanted the design of the new building not only to conserve energy but also to contribute to the evolution of green design. "We wanted the building to contribute to the advancement of sustainable green building and be an educational tool for others to see how easily—and relatively inexpensively—these technologies could be applied," said Saggau.[120]

Design Process

Great River Energy engaged Perkins+Will as the design architects and communicated the company's vision for the project. "We wanted our commitment to renewable energy to be visible to even the most casual passerby," said Saggau. "Last but not least, we wanted to dispel the notion that energy efficiency and conservation mean sacrificing beauty, functionality, or practicality. Finally, we wanted our building to be a place people want to visit, and a building that employees love coming to every day."[121]

One of the reasons the project was so successful is because every decision was influenced by a single goal: to build the most energy-efficient structure possible. As an energy company, Great River Energy focused specifically on energy conservation in the design, and it was the top priority that influenced every decision.[122]

An early project goal was Platinum-level LEED certification. "If we can't achieve a Platinum building, who can? If we don't do it, who should?" said Saggau. "An energy company is the one who should build Platinum LEED."[123]

The first step in the project was assembling an internal team that understood vision of the project and the project's three major goals:

1 Drive new construction toward sustainability.
2 Expand environmental stewardship.
3 Achieve LEED Platinum certification.[124]

"We started by assembling a core team that understood what it takes to successfully complete an ambitious project," said Great River Energy's Facilities Manager Mark Lucas. "You need to engage all the disciplines in a way that creates synergies in the project."[125]

Along with an IDP, Perkins+Will utilized a process called "integrated front-end loaded design" that solicited feedback and input from employees throughout the design and construction phases. This process was designed to align with the way Great River Energy conducts business, by valuing everyone's input.[126]

Because employee growth was the motivation for the new building, employee needs guided decisions about the work environment. Before construction began, a group of employees from departments throughout the company toured other LEED-certified corporate offices to learn more about sustainable design.[127]

This process of gathering ongoing employee feedback helped executives to address employee concerns. For example, employees were concerned about a longer commute and the resulting cost increase. In response, a bus route was negotiated with the local transit authority that allowed employees to park at the site of the old office and take a bus to the new office.[128]

Energy Efficiency

Although LEED certification was not an explicit goal when Great River Energy selected the site, the company considered eighteen criteria that would help the building be as efficient as possible. Based on the site's opportunities, Perkins+Will, along with engineers Dunham Associates, identified the opportunities that would drive the building's efficiency: daylight harvesting and lake-source (geothermal) displacement heating and cooling.[129]

To maximize daylight harvesting, the building's long axis runs east–west, orienting most of the glass to face north and south, reducing solar gain on the east and west sides. Narrow floor plates

7.21 About 13 percent of the energy used in the Great River Energy Headquarters building comes from renewable sources, including the 200-kW wind turbine and 72-kW PV system. Photo: Lucie Marusin. Courtesy of Great River Energy.

allow daylight to reach the building's core, reducing the need for artificial lighting. Atriums bring natural light from above into the center of the building. Workstations are designed with lower walls to allow more daylight to reach desk areas, and all offices have a windowed interior wall to receive natural light from the perimeter. Dimming ballasts, motion sensors, smart lighting design, and high-performance window coatings contribute to an estimated 40 percent reduction in lighting energy demand.[130]

One unique and efficient feature is lake-source geothermal heating and cooling, coupled with underfloor displacement ventilation, perhaps the first time these two technologies have been combined.[131]

The system mixes a nontoxic, biodegradable fluid with water and then pumps it through 36 miles (60 km) of plastic piping coiled at the bottom of a 6-acre (2.4-hectare), 32-ft (10-m) deep man-made lake.[132] The system extracts heat from the building in the summer and absorbs warmth from the lake in the winter. Inside the building, seventy heat pumps transfer the heating and cooling to the displacement system. This is the building's primary source of mechanical heating and cooling: there is neither a chiller nor a boiler in the building.[133]

"The geothermal lake system was the most efficient system because the lake water provides cool enough water most, if not all, year to cool the core of the building without refrigeration, owing to the displacement ventilation system's higher supply air temperature," said Dale Holland, Executive Vice President at Dunham.[134]

On an annual basis, about 6 percent of the building's electricity is generated from on-site renewable energy, including an on-site 200-kW wind turbine. Based on the site's wind power study, the

7.22 The narrow floorplate and central atrium allow natural daylight to enter the majority of the workspaces. Photo: Lucie Marusin. Courtesy of Great River Energy.

refurbished turbine was converted to a single-speed machine, trading off better performance at lower wind speeds for reduced performance at higher speeds. The turbine makes a visible statement about Great River Energy's commitment to renewable energy. A 72-kW array of PV panels mounted on the roof and at ground level supplies additional renewable electricity.[135]

Building Management System

A computer-integrated lighting and HVAC system monitors temperature, CO_2 concentrations, occupancy, lighting levels, and equipment levels. The system makes automatic adjustments to artificial lighting, ventilation, and ambient temperature based on weather and interior activities. Lighting increases or decreases depending on the amount of sunlight entering the building. The fresh-air system adjusts as the number of people in a room varies. Localized thermostats communicate with the HVAC system which adjusts as the heating and cooling needs change. These continuous adjustments contribute to the building's 40 percent reduction in energy use.[136]

Water Savings

The plumbing system uses harvested rainwater and low-flow plumbing fixtures to reduce projected water use by more than 74 percent.[137] Rainwater and snow-melt are collected by roof drains, filtered, and stored in a 20,000-gallon (75,700-liter) underground cistern.[138]

The water is filtered in a water-treatment system, using hydrogen peroxide to sanitize the water. The water is then used for toilet and urinal flushing. Low-flow aerators on sinks and showers and low-flow urinals and dual-flush toilets further reduce water use. In 2010, the building used no potable water for toilet flushing and 25 percent less than normal for sinks. By minimizing paved areas, Great River Energy also reduced stormwater runoff by more than 25 percent.[139]

Commissioning and Verification

The Great River Energy team realized that the design process extends beyond construction and occupancy, that the only way to test and optimize building performance is to run the building with the actual occupancy and a year's actual weather, see how it performs, and make adjustments.[140]

Ongoing commissioning, measurement, and verification began in June 2008, two months after occupancy. The measured energy used for heating exceeded original predictions by 3,000 Btu per sq ft (9.5 kWh per sq m), 30 percent more than predictions. This was likely due to complications in calculating, testing, and modeling the unique combination of the lake geothermal and underfloor displacement ventilation systems. Additionally, plug loads and lighting energy use were less than anticipated, reducing internal heat gains and thus increasing winter heating demand.[141]

A two-year ongoing commissioning, measurement, and verification process began with vetting the building's measurement systems. An additional seven-month commissioning cycle resulted in system adjustments that modified the sequence of operation and equipment schedules, recalibrated equipment, and led to other changes that addressed system anomalies. As a result, building energy use incrementally improved to very closely match predicted performance. The result of the commissioning process not only fine-tuned Great River Energy's building but it will also inform future projects using lake geothermal and underfloor displacement systems.[142]

According to CEO David Saggau, it takes a remarkable level of dedication and resilience to finish a project like this and remain true to the original goals. "A project that demonstrates this type of commitment doesn't just happen," said Saggau. "It takes people dedicated to the sustainability of our environment. The vision of our entire team made this incredible building a reality—and it can be seen every time you walk through the doors of this building."[143]

TABLE 7.11

Energy use, May 2011–April 2012

	Annual use	Intensity
Total electricity use	2,866,167 kWh	186 kWh/sq m
PV output	86,619 kWh	N/A
Wind output	113,869 kWh	N/A
Percent renewable energy	7.0%	N/A
Gas*	220,647 kWh	14 kWh/sq m
Total	**3,086,814 kWh**	**200 kWh/sq m**

* The majority of natural gas is used for the snow-melt boiler that keeps the front sidewalk and drive to parking garage clear of ice/snow.

At a glance

Name: Great River Energy Headquarters
Location: Maple Grove, Minnesota
Size: 166,000 sq ft (15,420 sq m)
Completed: April 2008
Cost: $65 million, all inclusive
Distinction: LEED-NC Platinum
Program: Commercial office

Project team

Owner: Great River Energy
Architect and Interior Design: Perkins+Will
Structural Engineer: BKBM Engineers
MEP Engineer: Dunham Associates
Civil Engineer: RLK Kuusisto
General Contractor: McGough

JOHNSON CONTROLS CAMPUS, Glendale, Wisconsin

The Johnson Controls campus in Glendale, Wisconsin, contains the largest concentration of LEED Platinum buildings on one site. The 33-acre complex includes more than 380,000 sq ft (35,300 sq m) of new and renovated office space. The company renovated two existing buildings and constructed two new buildings: all are LEED Platinum certified.[144]

Founded in 1885, Johnson Controls, Inc (JCI) is a "Fortune 500" global company with more than 100,000 employees. The company provides operations and maintenance services for more than 1.5 billion sq ft of building space around the world.

Sustainable operations are nothing new for Johnson Controls. In fact, the company's Brengel Technology Center in Milwaukee was one of the first buildings in the world certified in LEED for New Construction. It later became the first building in the world to receive a Gold certification in the LEED for Existing Buildings program.[145]

The project team implemented a number of sustainable technologies and systems on campus including a geothermal system, solar PV, rainwater harvesting, a green roof, efficient lighting, and a sophisticated BMS. As a result, overall energy use fell by 21 percent, despite the fact that the amount of office space doubled. Potable water use fell by 600,000 gallons annually, from water reuse alone. The use of low-flow fixtures contributed to a total 1.7-million-gallon (6,400 kl) water savings per year.[146]

The campus relies on the earth for heating and cooling. The geothermal system takes advantage of the earth's constant temperature to heat or cool the water used by the HVAC equipment. About 275 wells were drilled for the closed-loop system that supplies water to the heat pumps and chillers in the building. Each well is 300 ft (about 100 m) deep; 180,000 ft (54.5 km) of plastic piping connects the wells to the indoor HVAC equipment.[147]

"Heat pumps reduce winter heating costs by about 29 percent versus current natural gas boilers. We're also using geothermal to remove condenser heat in summer and reduce chiller operating costs by 23 percent," said Debbie Vander Heiden, Johnson Controls' Project Manager.[148]

During the warm season, the geothermal system rejects heat from a centrifugal chiller. The water enters the chiller at a cooler temperature than it would using a conventional cooling-tower system, resulting in a 28 percent decrease in chiller operating costs.[149] During Wisconsin's frigid winters, water circulates through the geothermal system and extracts heat that is stored below the earth's surface. The heat generated by the system's two central heat pumps is enough to heat two buildings and costs about 24 percent less than heat generated by traditional natural gas boilers.[150]

Two PV systems supplement campus energy requirements. A 1,452-panel array supplies about 250 kW of power, and laminated to the roof of one building is 14,000 sq ft (1,300 sq m) of thin-film PV cells that generate about 135 kW.[151]

The lighting at Johnson Controls consumes 0.45 to 0.65 watts per sq ft compared to a national average of 1.5 watts per sq ft. The team designed the lighting to minimize cooling costs while maximizing occupant comfort and productivity. More than seventy skylights harvest natural light, reducing artificial illumination requirements. Window shades automatically adjust based on the varying indoor and outdoor lighting levels.[152] Additional sustainable features include:

- A 12,000-sq-ft (1,115-sq-m) green roof absorbs precipitation, reducing storm-water runoff.
- Low-flow fixtures and dual-flush toilets reduce water use across the campus.
- A cistern captures rainwater, which is used to flush most of the toilets on the campus, reducing water use by 77 percent.
- Stormwater is collected through permeable paving on the parking lots and directed to a detention pond, reducing environmental impact of discharge.
- A solar thermal system supplies more than 30 percent of the hot-water needs for two buildings.[153]

All of the building operations are tied into a JCI building efficiency product, the Metasys BMS. More than 51,000 data points across the campus are monitored from a single point of access. More than twenty building systems, including heating, cooling, and lighting, are integrated with the IT infrastructure.[154]

The management system collects and stores building data, including building-to-building comparisons of energy usage, estimations of GHG emissions, and fault detection diagnostics. Building subsystems are integrated and interact with one another without operator intervention.[155]

TABLE 7.12

Energy use, 2011

	Electricity (kWh)	Gas (therms)	Normalized annual use
Office and assisted space (310,100 sq ft; 28,820 sq m)	4,849,367	84,671	81 kBtu/sq ft; 255 kWh/sq m

TABLE 7.13

Solar production, 2011

	Total	Normalized use (kWh/sq m/year)
Solar electric	423,527 kWh	1.1 kWh/sq m
Solar thermal	2,837 therms, or 83,100 kWh	0.2 kWh/sq m

7.23 Consisting of four buildings, the Johnson Controls, Glendale, Wisconsin, campus represents the largest concentration of LEED Platinum certified buildings on one site. Photo: © John Nienhuis. Courtesy of Johnson Controls, Inc.

As a company that specializes in building operations and maintenance, it makes sense for Johnson Controls to be a leader in building performance. Not only is the Johnson Controls Glendale complex a green corporate campus, but it is also a showcase for the company's building efficiency technologies.

7.24 The campus incorporates a variety of sustainable technologies and systems, including a geothermal system, PV system, and a solar thermal water heating system. Photo: Johnson Controls, Inc.

At a glance

Name: Johnson Controls Headquarters

Location: Glendale, Wisconsin

Size: 384,700 sq ft (35,740 sq m) total on campus

Completed: October 2010

Cost: $73 million

Distinction: LEED-NC Platinum

Program: Commercial office

Project team

Owner: Johnson Controls, Inc.

Architect: Gensler

Mechanical and Plumbing Engineers: Ring & DuChateau

Electrical Engineers: Leady & Petzold

General Contractor: Hunzinger Construction Co.

7.25 The shape of Kroon Hall is reminiscent of a New England barn and cathedral nave. Fifty percent of the wood used in construction was harvested from nearby Yale-owned, sustainably managed forests. Photo: Michael Marsland. Courtesy of Yale University.

KROON HALL, SCHOOL OF FORESTRY AND ENVIRONMENTAL STUDIES, Yale University, New Haven, Connecticut

Founded in 1901, the Yale School of Forestry and Environmental Studies is the oldest professional forestry program in the USA. As the academic programs and research initiatives expanded and students, faculty, and staff grew, the school spread across eight buildings on campus. In the late 1990s, the school decided to construct a building that reflected its mission and values of sustainability.

The 56,467-sq-ft (5,246-sq-m) Kroon Hall, Yale's second LEED Platinum project, contains office space for more than fifty faculty and staff, three classrooms, the 175-seat Burke Auditorium, the Knobloch Environment Center for socializing and study, and the Ordway Learning Center for quiet study.

"Several things led to the success of Kroon Hall, starting with quite a clear and specific client sustainability ambition," said Paul Stoller, Director of Atelier Ten, the environmental consultants for the project. "They asked for LEED Platinum and beyond, which set the tone for the project."[156]

The specific goals of the project included:

- creating an international center for the study of the environment
- transforming a neglected corner of Science Hill into a revitalized gateway
- creating an exemplary academic building for the twenty-first century
- reducing carbon footprint, aiming for carbon neutrality
- achieving the highest LEED certification
- creating educational displays of sustainable design features
- improving collegiality within the school
- enhancing the setting for adjacent existing buildings.[157]

A great team set the stage for success, according to Stoller. Using an extended interview process, the school carefully selected a world-class team, and the owner's project team even traveled to Europe to tour high-performance buildings as part of the selection process. The team of Hopkins Architects, Centerbrook Architects, Arup, Atelier Ten, and Nitsch Engineering won the competition, and they soon were joined by Turner Construction as the general contractor. As a team, they had all done many green buildings before, and the firms had worked together on prior projects.[158]

According to Alan Brewster, former Deputy Dean of the Yale School of Forestry and Environmental Studies, the school's engagement was also critical to the success of the project. "If you, as the ultimate owner and user of the building, really want features of sustainability, then you need to be involved throughout the process," said Brewster. "You don't say, 'We picked the right architect, we have the right contractor. Let's go away and come back later.' You have to be involved throughout the process. That was essential for Kroon Hall in achieving the end result."[159]

The design process was a collaborative effort, and the entire team was involved from the beginning, including the engineers, consultants, and contractor. "The actual design process was collegial," said Stoller. "We all understood that we had to put our best ideas forward constantly and comment on each other's ideas. There was a lot of careful design that went into it. That only could have been possible with a design team that repeatedly tested, shared, critiqued, and tested again our ideas."[160]

The design strategy for the project followed the following guidelines:

- Maximize energy savings through building form and passive solar elements while minimizing the cost of active systems.
- Design a high-performance, energy-efficient building to last more than 100 years.
- Integrate engineering and sustainable features with the architectural design.
- Use materials that age gracefully and endure heavy use: architectural concrete, stone, precast concrete, metals, and timber.
- In addition, design a high-quality contemporary building that responds to Yale's architectural tradition and will inspire its occupants.
- Provide a simple building organization and flexible arrangement of spaces suitable for reconfiguration.
- Knit together the Science Hill community by use of courtyards on the north and south sides of the building. The south courtyard doubles as a green roof over the service node.
- Create a centerpiece for the Yale School of Forestry and Environmental Studies, consolidating its faculty and activities and demonstrating the mission of the school.[161]

The process required compromises from all parties. For example, Hopkins Architects proposed structural stonewalls for the building façades. "It took several rounds of discussion to conclude that, in fact, uninsulated stone walls would be detrimental to the building's energy performance and comfort," explained Stoller.[162]

In addition to the sustainability agenda, one of the overarching project goals was to use strategies that could be replicated on Yale's campus. "We wanted Kroon Hall to be a simple, elegant architectural solution that was pushed hard with good climate-responsive design, so that the systems had less work to do," said Stoller.[163]

The team chose a series of high-performance systems and design strategies that work together. The building uses underfloor air distribution and an air-handling system that recovers heat from exhaust air in the winter, along with ground-source heat pumps. High-efficiency air-handling units and a 100-kW PV array help to lower energy use.[164]

"There was nothing invented for the project per se," said Stoller. "The photovoltaic array is inconspicuous but a fundamental part of the look and feel of the building. It doesn't look like a PV array that was just bolted on. It was very carefully considered, proportioned, and aligned. Part of the iterative design process was in understanding the panel dimensions and clearances, and all of the building proportions took that into account."[165]

Kroon Hall's sustainable solutions include:[166]

- a 218-ft (66-m) long south wall that maximizes solar heat gain in winter and provides natural lighting year-round
- a 100-kW rooftop PV array that provides about 18 percent of the building's electricity
- four solar panels with evacuated tubes filled with glycol on the south-facing wall, which provide the building with hot water

7.26 *Left:* The 100-kW PV system on the roof of Kroon Hall is one of the building's distinguishing features. Photo: Michael Marsland. Courtesy of Yale University.

TABLE 7.14

Energy and water use, 2011

	Annual use	Intensity
Electricity	514,973 kWh	83 kWh/sq m
PV production	95,624 kWh	15.4 kWh
Total energy use	**610,597 kWh**	**98.4 kWh/sq m**
Water use	180,268 g	3.2 g/sq ft 130 l/sq m

- a geothermal energy system that pulls 55°F (13°C) water from four 1,320-ft-deep (400-m-deep) wells in the adjacent Sachem's Wood
- a narrow floor plan (57 ft; 17 m wide) that allows for the penetration of natural light into interior spaces
- interior lighting that responds to occupancy levels and outdoor light
- manually operable windows that encourage natural ventilation
- green construction materials that include "thermally massive" concrete and low-e glass and insulation, water-free urinals, and low-impact paint
- Red Oak paneling that was harvested from Yale–Myers Forest and certified by the Forest Stewardship Council
- Briar Hill sandstone used in the façade was quarried within 500 miles of campus
- a rainwater harvesting system and the Mars cleansing pond.

Stephen Kellert, Professor Emeritus at the Yale School of Forestry and Environmental Studies, was instrumental in pushing the sustainability agenda for the new building. "I think sustainability needs to have embedded within it an understanding of not just energy efficiency, but the need for affirming a positive beneficial relationship with nature within the built environment."[167]

He emphasized: "The majority of our time is spent in the built environment, so connecting to nature and achieving sustainability inside needs to be as much of an objective as it is for the outside landscape. I think connecting to nature is important not just for academic buildings but also for office buildings, manufacturing facilities, and schools."[168]

Kellert cited the third floor as an example of the use of biophilia design principles in Kroon Hall. "It has a great cathedral-like space, an incredible experiential connection to the outside, and it has all of these biophillic elements, from fractal geometry and natural materials to great light and space."[169]

As a result, the third-floor space is much more heavily used than originally predicted. Students occupy the area twenty-four hours a day. "The space is so attractive that people are using it more than what was modeled and, therefore, it uses more energy than originally anticipated, but that's a good thing in a way," said Kellert. "You want your building to be loved and used. But it has had the effect of driving up the energy costs."[170]

Another lesson learned, according to Stoller, Brewster, and Kellert, came from managing the building's operations after completion. The high-performance systems in Kroon are uncommon on campus and require sophisticated management. "There's always a shakedown period for a new facility, but I think it took longer than usual because there was a steep learning curve for a building this sophisticated," said Brewster.[171]

Today the school continues to collect and analyze data on the building's performance, with the following results:

- Kroon is performing 50 percent better than the average US academic building, in terms of energy performance.
- Photovoltaic panels provide up to 18 percent of the building's electricity during the summer and an average of 16 percent year-round.
- LEED Platinum certification awarded in February 2010.

At a glance

Name: Kroon Hall, School of Forestry and Environmental Studies, Yale University
Location: New Haven, Connecticut
Size: 56,467 sq ft (6,206 sq m)
Completion/Occupancy: January 2009
Cost: US$33.5 million
Distinction: LEED-NC Platinum
Program: Academic building with classrooms, offices, meeting rooms, lounges.

Project team

Owner: Yale University
Design Architect: Hopkins Architects
Executive Architect: Centerbrook Architects and Planners
Mechanical Engineer, Structural Engineer, Architectural Lighting and Acoustical Design: Arup
Civil Engineer: Nitsch Engineering
Environmental Consultant: Atelier Ten
General Contractor: Turner Construction Company

7.27 *Right*: The 120,000-sq-ft Lewis and Clark State Office Building showed a 9 percent reduction in staff absenteeism compared to the prior workspace. Photo: Assassi. Courtesy of BNIM.

7.28 *Below*: On the south façade, an exterior overhang blocks heat and glare during the summer while allowing solar heat gain in the cold winter season. Photo: Assassi. Courtesy of BNIM.

LEWIS AND CLARK STATE OFFICE BUILDING, Jefferson City, Missouri

Constructed on the 144-acre (58-hectare) site of the former Jefferson City Correctional Facility, the Lewis and Clark State Office Building reflects the Missouri Department of Natural Resources' (DNR) mission to protect and restore the state's natural resources. Completed in 2005, the building was the first state office building in the USA to achieve a LEED Platinum rating.

Designed by BNIM Architects, the 120,000-sq-ft (11,150-sq-m) office building houses more than 400 DNR employees. The government client challenged the team to design a building that would meet all programmatic criteria while incorporating the highest level of sustainability with no increase in cost over a standard state office building.

Located atop a bluff overlooking the Missouri River, a central, four-story atrium provides a view of the Missouri River valley, creating a visual link between the building and Missouri's natural resources. The project is also part of a mixed-use urban redevelopment project aligned with the state Governor's initiative to revitalize Missouri's urban centers.

An initial early-stage design charrette involving more than 100 people set the tone for sustainable thinking and advanced several large-scale goals for the project. Using a series of subsequent charrettes and constant communication among the integrated design team, the client's resource conservation agenda influenced critical decisions during the early stages of development.

"The client emphasized to us that they wanted to create a very healthy work environment for their employees, and they wanted us to focus on energy efficiency," said Laura Lesniewski, principal at BNIM. "Those two goals, a healthy workplace and energy efficiency, were big drivers for the project. When coupled with the LEED Platinum goal, we were able to focus on doing exemplary site design, fostering water conservation and making healthy material choices."[172]

The building's architecture draws influence from the striated geography of the river's limestone bluffs; it responds to the harsh winter climate through orientation and specialized façade design; and restores the existing habitat through the use of native prairie plants that help to eliminate stormwater runoff from the site.[173]

The team analyzed building aspect ratio (proportion of length to width), to determine the ideal balance between interior flexibility and high environmental performance. Designers determined that a long slender building with an aspect ratio of 5.7:1, with the long axis sited in an east–west direction, had several advantages over more compact buildings:[174]

- Maximizing daylighting potential and reducing operating costs by $50,000 per year.
- Reducing environmental impact (by minimizing lighting loads and blocking unwanted solar gain) and the economic effects of pollutant emissions by $4,125 to $8,259 per year.
- Reducing building construction costs by between $146,436 and $484,536.
- Maximizing LEED certification points and subsequent rating.
- Enhancing the work environment and productivity.

Along with the building form, orientation was critical to achieving the more than 50 percent reduction in energy use. The south façade concrete structural system controls solar gain and glare through vertical fins, horizontal overhangs, and light shelves. The exterior overhangs block heat and glare during the summer, while allowing solar heat gain in the cold winter season. The interior space along the south façade contains reflective-fabric light shelves that distribute sunlight deep into the building.[175]

Early life-cycle cost analyses proved that investing in high-performance glazing would be cost-effective in the long term. As a result of these analyses, the planned perimeter heating system was eliminated, and that cost was invested in improving the building envelope.[176]

Designed by Rumsey Engineers, the HVAC system uses standard equipment applied in intelligent configurations. The overall approach was to use smaller recirculation air handlers in the office areas, with two dedicated 100 percent outside-air handlers supplying conditioned, dry air from the roof.[177]

The building's roof is sloped to an integral gutter, harvesting rainwater to fill an underground, 50,000-gallon (190-kl) cistern, which is then filtered and used for flushing toilets. Water-free urinals and low-flow fixtures further minimize potable water usage. The system conserved 405,000 gallons (1,533 kl) in its first 13 months of occupancy, estimated to be 79 percent of the projected usage of a standard office building.[178]

A 22-kW grid-tied PV system, composed of 168 dark-colored, 128-watt panels, provides 2.5 percent of the building's electricity needs. A solar thermal system provides heating for 42 percent of the building's hot water needs.[179]

TABLE 7.15

Energy and water use, 2008–2010 average

	Annual use	Intensity
Grid-supplied electricity	8,578,100 kBtu/year	71 kBtu/sq ft/year; 222 kWh/sq m/year
Solar PV	216,000 kBtu/year 63,269 kWh/year	1800 Btu/sq ft/year 5.7 kWh/sq m/year
Potable water	223,273 g/year	1.9 g/sq ft/year 75 l/sq m/year

Other load-reducing strategies include local controls for the underfloor air distribution system that allow employees to adjust air flow direction and fan speed for optimum thermal comfort at their workstations; operable windows; and a chilled-water thermal-energy storage tank, which helps extend the "free-cooling" season.[180]

In addition to reduced energy use, there was a nine percent reduction in employee absenteeism during the building's first year of occupancy (compared to the prior workspace). The project also had the lowest construction cost (per square foot) of any Missouri state office building.[181]

At a glance

Name: Lewis and Clark State Office Building
Location: Jefferson City, Missouri
Size: 120,000 sq ft (11,150 sq m)
Completed: March 2005
Cost: $18.1 million including building and site
Distinction: LEED-NC Platinum
Program: Government Office Building

Project team

Owner: State of Missouri, Missouri Department of Natural Resources
Architect and Interior Design: BNIM
Mechanical Design Engineer: Rumsey Engineers
MEP Engineer of Record: Smith & Boucher
Lighting Design: Clanton & Associates
Daylighting Strategies: ENSAR Group Inc.
General Contractor: Professional Contractors and Engineers

NATIONAL RENEWABLE ENERGY LABORATORY, RESEARCH SUPPORT FACILITY I, Golden, Colorado

With its Research Support Facility (RSF) I, the US Department of Energy's (US DOE) National Renewable Energy Laboratory (NREL) aspired to create the largest commercial zero-net energy building in the country (see Chapter 5). At 350,000 sq ft (32,500 sq m), RSF produces as much energy as it uses in a year, making it the world's largest zero-net energy office building. This is especially noteworthy given its location at a high altitude (5,200 ft/1,575 m) in a heating-dominated climate.

Jeff Baker, Director of the Laboratory Operations Office, described the focus as "manic—and I use that word on purpose—but [the] manic focus on energy performance . . . really drove the design and was really the critical factor for us to realize in our strategy. We didn't start off by saying, 'We'll have a nice architecture, and then we're going to think about energy later.'"[182]

The RSF project was completed in two phases. Phase 1, consisting of two wings totaling 222,000 sq ft (20,632 sq m), opened in June 2010. The third wing, Phase 2, opened in December 2011 and increased the total area to 360,000 sq ft (33,457sq m). The 138,000-sq-ft (12,825 sq m) expansion is 17 percent more energy efficient than the original and cost $13 (5 percent) less per sq ft. RSF's average cost for both wings of $254 per sq ft ($2733/sq m) is competitive to standard office buildings in the Denver area.

While building design technologies are important to RSF's extremely low energy use, the key factor in the success of the project was the performance-based design-build acquisition process (described extensively in Chapter 5).

Stantec Consulting designed one of the innovative building systems, the transpired solar collector (TSC) combined with the thermal labyrinth. The TSC (a technology developed NREL in the 1990s), placed on the south face of the building, is corrugated metal sheet siding with punched holes to allow airflow.[183]

The TSC captures and warms outside air in cooler months and stores that air in the thermal labyrinth located under the building. The concrete maze in the building's crawl space acts as a thermal battery. Stored air from the labyrinth is then introduced into the building via an underfloor air distribution system. Overhead radiant heating is provided via each floor slab, to heat the floor below.

7.29 Built on a conventional budget, NREL's RSF I is the largest zero-net energy office building in the USA. Photo: Dennis Schroeder, NREL Staff Photographer. Courtesy of DOE/NREL.

7.30 The annual energy use intensity at NREL RSF I is 35.2 kBTU/sq ft/year, including a data center that serves the entire NREL campus.
Photo: Patrick Cokery (NREL Contract Photographer). Courtesy of DOE/NREL.

By storing cool night air during the summer, the labyrinth, combined with evaporative cooling technology, is also responsible for the 81 percent reduction in RSF's data center power requirements, resulting in an annual cost savings of $320,000. The facility is now a model for other federal agencies following the announcement of the Federal Data Center Consolidation Initiative.[184]

A 1,600-KW PV system made up of more than 1,800 panels helps RSF generate more energy than it uses. To mitigate the up-front costs, NREL and the US DOE partnered with Sun Edison to create a Power Purchase Agreement. Sun Edison financed the PV system and sold the renewable energy credits generated by the system to Colorado's electric utility. At the end of the 20-year agreement, NREL has the option to purchase the system.[185]

Other key high-performance features at RSF include:

- Triple-pane windows with electrochromic features that respond to temperature changes by changing opacity
- Louver system and fixed sunshades that reflect sunlight and control glare
- Operable windows for nighttime precooling (for the following day's occupancy) and occupant control (during mild weather)
- Continuous insulation precast wall panels with integral thermal mass
- Aggressive plug-load control strategies to reduce non-HVAC and lighting loads
- Low-flow plumbing fixtures that reduce potable water use by 57 percent
- Heat recovery systems to return energy in exhaust air back to the incoming air supply
- A web-based irrigation system that irrigates only when soil moisture is low and no rain is expected.

Table 7.16 shows the distribution of energy uses, with the data center contributing more than one-third of annual energy use.

TABLE 7.16

Annual energy use distribution by end use, Phase 1[a]

	%	kBtu/sq ft
Data center	35	12.11
Space heating	24	8.58
Office plug loads	22	7.87
Lights	6	2.07
Ventilation fans	5	1.88
Domestic hot water	3	0.90
Space cooling	3	0.85
Pumps	1	0.48
Data center fans	1	0.20
Data center cooling	0	0.02
Exterior lights	0	0.12
Task lights	0	0.10
Total (kBtu/sq ft)	**100**	**35.4**
Total (kWh/sq m)		**111**

a "NREL's Research Support Facility: An Energy Performance Update," October 2011, www.nrel.gov/sustainable_nrel/pdfs/rsf_operations_10–2011.pdf, accessed October 8, 2011.

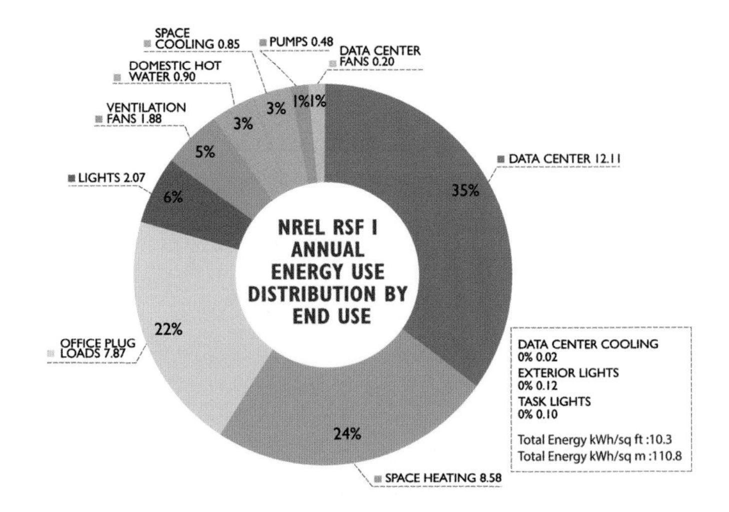

7.31 NREL RSF annual energy use distribution by end use. Source: *NREL's Research Support Facility: An Energy Performance Update*, October 2011, www.nrel.gov/sustainable_nrel/pdfs/rsf_operations_10–2011.pdf, accessed October 8, 2011.

Operating Data[186]

Building gross floor area: 222,000 sq ft (20,632 sq m) for initial Phase 1; 360,000 sq ft (33,457 sq m) total.

Number of occupants: 1,325 (plus sixty visitors averaged daily)

Percentage of workspaces with daylight: 100

Percentage of the building that can be ventilated or cooled with operable windows: 67

Potable water used, indoors and outdoors: 791,202 gallons (2,995 kl) per year

Annual EUI: 35.4 kBTU/sq ft (112 kWh/sq m), including the site-wide data center

Total energy savings vs. standard building: 46 percent

Annual PV production: Approximately 32,800 kWh/month (2.73 million kWh/year)

At a glance

Name: Research Support Facility, National Renewable Energy Laboratory

Location: Golden, Colorado

Completed: Phase 1, June 2010; Phase 2, December 2011

Cost: $91.4 million construction cost ($254/sq ft)

Distinction: LEED-NC Platinum

Program: Government research facility, offices

Project team

Owner: US Department of Energy National Renewable Energy Laboratory

Architect, Interior Designer, Landscape Architect: RNL

MEP Engineer, Sustainability Consultant: Stantec Consulting

General Contractor: Haselden Construction

7.32 *Below*: The campus design at Ohlone College features low-water-using hardscape and landscape. Photo: © Robert Canfield Photography.

NEWARK CENTER FOR HEALTH SCIENCES AND TECHNOLOGY, Ohlone College, Newark, California

Initially the new campus building was going to be a copy of its original strip-mall location in nearby Fremont, California. But when a new college president, Douglas Treadway, took over, he insisted that the building prioritize sustainability principles throughout the design, construction, and operation phases. This would offer several advantages to the college: it would signal a commitment to sustainability, give a boost to a new environmental studies program, and reduce energy costs.

"A college's purpose isn't just to distribute content. Our purpose is to develop knowledge workers," said Treadway. "Once you look at it that way, then you shift the paradigm. You start asking, what kinds of environments are conducive to learning and discussion? Then you start thinking about the built environment."[188]

Designed by architects Perkins+Will, the Newark Center for Health Sciences and Technology is a state-of-the-art research and teaching facility that houses laboratories, classrooms, offices, a library, and an exercise center. The Center serves 3,500 students in the academic areas of health sciences and technology. Built on a former brownfield site adjacent to San Francisco Bay, the 130,000-sq-ft (12,077-sq-m), two-story building was completed in January 2008 and received a LEED Platinum certification.

"Number one, the most important key to reaching Platinum certification was the partnership between the architect and the builder. We didn't start out with green [certification] as a goal," said Treadway. "However, [Perkins+Will] were very motivated to push everything and come back to us and offer suggestions. They would ask us, 'How about if you did this? Could you do this and would you see the value of it, not just for LEED but on the face of it?'"[189]

Two wings, one for health sciences and the other for technology, come together around a campus green. Located in a natural transition zone between land and sea, where fresh and salt water merge, the Center is an "estuary for learning." For Perkins+Will, the estuary was a metaphor for the coupling of technological advancement within an ecologically sustainable environment.[190]

The roof, a combination of metal and membrane, extends over the edge of the building, serving as a rain screen and passive sunshade. Glass curtain wall and storefront, cement plaster, glass fiber-reinforced concrete, and metal elements make up the exterior.[191] "We used the architecture to support the alternative-energy systems [as] part of the environmental studies curriculum," said Perkins+Will architect Susan Seastone.[192]

The engineering (MEP) consultant, Michael Lucas, created several energy models to determine the best combination of sustainable features. The models evaluated the pros and cons of six different options, each considering performance and cost. The result was an "energy cocktail" of horizontal-bore geothermal heating and cooling with 26 miles (41.8 km) of underground coils; 35,000 sq ft (3,252 sq m) of PV; and two 16-ft-diameter (4.8-m) energy recovery enthalpy wheels.[193]

The US Department of Energy promotes geothermal systems as one of the most energy efficient and environmentally friendly systems available today. At the Newark Center, the geothermal system supplies the HVAC needs of the entire campus. The ground-coupled, water-source heat-pump system capitalizes on both the proximity to the Bay and also the soil's high thermal conductivity, owing to the high water table. The tidal action of the Bay further enhances the heat exchange, as it constantly exchanges the moisture content in the geothermal field. The naturally stable temperatures below ground, usually 58°F to 62°F (14°C to 17°C), efficiently remove or add heat via water circulated to the heat pump units located in the building, which use these ambient temperatures to provide space heating or cooling.[194]

In lieu of operable windows, architect Perkins+Will along with Alfa Tech and Ohlone College ultimately compromised by sealing the windows and instead choosing enthalpy wheels, which flush the class and lab spaces with fresh air, greatly improving indoor air quality. The synergy between the enthalpy wheel systems and the heat pump systems causes an overall reduction in compressor run time and therefore energy use. In fact, this saves up to 25 percent of the costs for cooling and heating.[195]

Enthalpy wheels are housed within 20-ft (6-m) square steel boxes and handle 52,000 cu ft (1,472 cu m) of air per minute, tripling the amount of fresh air required by California building codes. "It feels as if all the windows are open," said MEP design principal Michael Lucas, even though they are not operable.[196] The system also filters the outdoor air twice before it enters the school interior.[197]

More than 70 percent of the building space contains laboratories and classrooms, which require large volumes of air flow. Lab air is typically exhausted directly to outdoors, resulting in significant energy

7.33 *Left*: A 450-kW (peak) PV system covers four rooftops with 35,000-sq-ft of solar panels. Photo: © Robert Canfield Photography.

loss. However, at Newark Center, where the materials used and stored in the labs are not hazardous or toxic, the enthalpy wheels recover up to 90 percent of the energy in the exhaust air.

Enthalpy wheels are most effective located at the center of a building. They also take up a lot of space, require a lot of ductwork and are therefore challenging for architects to incorporate into their buildings. "Perkins+Will did a great job," said Michael Lucas. "As a matter of fact, they made circular windows, like portholes, on two sides of the building so students and faculty can actually look through the windows and see the wheels rotating."[198]

A PV system generates more than 50 percent of the building's energy needs.[199] Covering 35,000 sq ft (3,251 sq m) of roof area, 1,585 rooftop panels generate more than 450 kW (peak) AC power. In the first year of operation, the solar array generated 710,000 kWh of clean power, creating four months of net-zero energy consumption on campus. Purchased power was only 31 percent of total use, and annual energy savings were $134,082, compared with a similar building designed to current California building standards.[200]

At the entrance to the building, students and visitors can see animated displays of the solar PV system, geothermal, and enthalpy wheel systems, providing an educational tool. The displays show how each system works, along with real-time temperatures of water and air, as well as how much energy is recovered or saved in real time. Along with a public website, the display shows a continuous reading of how much solar power the system produces, the total power generated to date, and carbon emissions reductions.

In its first year of operation, the Newark Center's net energy consumption was 15,310 Btu per sq ft (48,253 kWh/sq m), with a cost of $0.48 per sq ft ($5.16/sq m) per year. This amount is significantly less than a standard building and 87 percent less than the federal Energy Star standard for a typical higher-education building.[201]

The total project cost was $58 million, or $365 per sq ft. The HVAC system had a $478,000 premium, which translates into a 5.25-year simple payback (compared to rooftop units with chilled/hot water coils and a conventional chiller plant). The cost of the PV array was approximately $3.9 million, with a payback of approximately nineteen years.[202] In this case, the design team worked with Ohlone College to secure funds through private donations and California's state solar rebate program.[203]

TABLE 7.17

Energy and water use, 2011

	Annual use	Intensity
Total energy use	**1,235,810 kWh**	**9.5 kWh/sq ft** **102 kWh/sq m** (including PV contribution)
Electricity (purchased)	469,656 kWh	3.6 kWh/sq ft
PV	710,000 kWh	5.5 kWh/sq ft
Natural gas	1,910 therms[a] 55,963 kWh	0.4 kWh/sq ft
Water	1.37 million gallons	10.4 gal/sq ft 425 l/sq m

a Guy Esberg, 2010, "Dispelling the Cost Myth", *High Performance Buildings*, Winter, pp. 30–42.

Treadway said that any additional cost incurred to create such an innovative learning community is well worth it. "I've been able to show people that when you cut back a bit on building size, and build more for quality and durability, when you're more concerned for the students' well being, ergonomics, and sustainability, you can pay the additional cost by retaining just two or three percent of the students who would've dropped out. Build that way, and you're always going to get dividends."[204]

At a glance

Name: Newark Center for Health Sciences and Technology, Ohlone College
Location: Newark, California
Size: 130,000 sq ft (12,000 sq m)
Electricity Use: 48.5 kWh/sq m/year net of PV
Completion/Occupancy: January 2008
Cost: $58 million
Distinction: LEED-NC Platinum
Program: Academic building for community (two-year) college with laboratories, classrooms, offices, a library, and common areas.

Project team

Owner: Ohlone Community College District
Architect: Perkins+Will
MEP Engineer: Alfa Tech Cambridge Group
General Contractor: Turner Construction

OREGON HEALTH AND SCIENCE UNIVERSITY, CENTER FOR HEALTH AND HEALING, Portland, Oregon

Located on a brownfield redevelopment site in Portland's emerging South Waterfront neighborhood, the Oregon Health and Science University Center for Health and Healing (CHH) combines cutting-edge health and wellness technology with environmentally responsible building design.

Credit for the success of the sixteen-story, 410,000-sq-ft (38,090-sq-m) building goes to early collaboration among the project team. An IDP, begun in 2003, allowed the design team to conceive the project holistically, producing far-reaching environmental efficiencies and cost savings. Analyzing how individual systems could perform double-duty and be "right-sized," with the option of future expandability, allowed this high-performance building to be constructed without excessive cost premiums for sustainable features.

With 600 staff and 4,500 visitors per week, CHH is a busy place, requiring a complex HVAC systems approach. The program includes laboratories, surgery suites, medical offices, research and education spaces, a comprehensive health and wellness center with a swimming pool, retail spaces, a café, a pharmacy, underground parking, and a public atrium. The Portland Aerial Tram connects the site to OHSU's main Marquam Hill campus located at a 500-ft higher elevation and a mile distant.

At the project outset, developer Gerding Edlen Development challenged the engineering design team to reduce capital costs for mechanical systems by 25 percent while still outperforming the Oregon energy code (based at the time on ASHRAE 90.1–1999) by 60 percent.[205] A two-day eco-charrette added further goals including capturing and reusing 100 percent of rainwater, treating 100 percent of wastewater on site, and reducing potable water use by 50 percent.[206]

As a result of responding successfully to these ambitious "stretch" goals, CHH received a LEED for New Construction (LEED-NC) v. 2.0 Platinum rating. Although the initial goal was to achieve LEED Silver,[207] CHH was ultimately awarded 55 points out of a possible 69,[208] earning the highest rating for a medical and research facility at the time. Upon reaching full occupancy and certification in 2006, it was also the largest building in the world to achieve LEED Platinum recognition and among the first "build to suit," developer-driven projects to achieve this award.

To successfully meet the developer's demanding goals, engaging all of the stakeholders early in the process was necessary. "Everyone is under the spotlight, not just the architects," said Dennis Wilde, then a principal at Gerding Edlen Development. "Both the MEP engineering consultant and general contractor must feel invested in the outcome from the beginning; neither can take a 'sit back and wait' attitude. And commissioning agents and building facilities managers must be involved early."[209]

Financially, the building was created through a public/private partnership between the Oregon Health Sciences University Center, Portland's largest employer, and OHSU Medical Group, a separate nonprofit comprising the campus medical staff.[210] The total project cost was $145.4 million,[211] with a net cost premium for the sustainability features of 1.3 percent, a testament to the success of the IDP.[212] Tax credits and incentives saved more than $3 million of the initial $30 million mechanical, electrical, and plumbing (MEP) systems budget.[213]

By using strategies such as return-air plenums instead of ducts, precooling the building through "night flushing," and reducing the size of air-handling units owing to a more efficient building envelope, the engineering team was able to reduce the capital budget for MEP systems further by $4.5 million, or 15 percent of the initial budget, while still achieving ambitious performance goals.[214] Daylighting models and a detailed energy model informed the placement of sunshades and stair tower ventilation that helped to reduce estimated cooling loads and downsize the mechanical system by 30 tons (360,000 Btu/hour or 105 kW).

Instead of designing for maximum future loads, Interface Engineering (the MEP engineer) sized for planned initial use, with the ability to expand if needed. A portion of the resulting savings was re-invested in other architectural and environmental features.[215] In this way, the building was able to incorporate high-cost systems such as green roofs, photovoltaics, and on-site sewage treatment without adding to the capital cost, decreasing operating costs and increasing building value.[216] The reinvestment measures, along with the increased efficiency building systems, translated to a $660,000 (about $1.60 per sq ft, or $17.22 sq m) reduction in estimated annual operating costs.[217]

Additional equipment savings were found by strategies such as combining garage ventilation fans with atrium smoke-evacuation fans, using a timed egress analysis of the atrium to justify reducing the size

7.34 The 410,000 sq ft Oregon Health and Science University's Center for Health and Healing accommodates 600 staff and 4,500 visitors per week. Photo: Jerry Yudelson.

of the smoke exhaust fans and specifying chilled beams for radiant cooling to reduce the length of ventilation ducts.[218] As an added benefit, reduction of mechanical space needed for the HVAC system recaptured an additional 10,000 sq ft (929 sq m) for programmatic use.[219]

The team chose displacement ventilation for treatment rooms and offices because it is both energy-efficient and minimizes recirculation of contaminants.[220] In this system, cool air drops along the wall from the high point of an interior wall at relatively low speeds in a "waterfall effect" and spreads out along the floor.[221] As bodies and equipment heat the air, it rises but remains cool enough for occupant comfort. The air enters at about 60°F (16°C) and rises to 78°F (26°C) as it exits the other side of the room near the ceiling.[222] This results in a more comfortable room with less air movement and less energy use. Displacement ventilation reduces fan energy use by two-thirds and eliminates the typical, but inefficient system of reheating incoming cool air at each terminal.[223]

A December 2010 post-occupancy evaluation showed that the building is performing slightly better than its design target. An initial post-occupancy evaluation in 2008 resulted in implementation of measures to improve energy conservation.[224] Additionally, the building's systems were recommissioned, the project implemented a measurement and verification program, and the owner secured a LEED-EBOM Platinum Certification for building operations.[225] Also, major alterations were made to the controls of the 300-kW micro-turbine (cogeneration) system, responding to a discrepancy in measured heat recovery from the system compared with initial projections.[226]

OHSU's energy savings are 61 percent below Oregon Energy Code and 50 percent below ASHRAE Standard 90.1–2004.[227] Overall electrical energy use, 30 percent less than predicted by the LEED baseline model, is supplied from three sources: 72 percent is purchased energy, 27 percent is produced by the microturbines in the central heating and cooling plant, and less than 1 percent comes from 60 kW of building-integrated PV on top of sunshades along the top twelve stories of the south façade.[228]

Gas consumption by the micro-cogeneration plant and the building is 18 percent less than predicted by the baseline model. The verification analysis suggests that this is due to the higher than anticipated equipment plug loads, which add heat to the space, reducing the need for supplemental heat in the cooler months.[229]

Achieving high-efficiency levels required scrutiny of every aspect of the building's energy use. That scrutiny began at the start of the design process when the design team analyzed temperature, rainfall, groundwater temperatures, and levels, along with wind-flow data, to identify climate loads, evaluate passive energy resources, and explore integrated design strategies.[230]

"The sun is going to shine, the wind is going to blow, and it's going to rain. These things are going to happen and you might as well take advantage of them," said Kyle Anderson, lead designer for GBD Architects.[231]

As a result, the team developed forty-two distinct strategies for energy efficiency.[232] Perhaps the most innovative is the giant solar air heater on the top fifteenth and sixteenth floors of the building's south façade. About 6,000 sq ft (558 sq m) of low-iron glass was placed 48 in (122 cm) outside the skin and sealed tightly. As air rises between the façade and the glass, sunlight heats it. The warm air then moves through air-handling units across a heat exchanger and preheats

7.35 Photovoltaics on the south façade double as sunshades, reducing HVAC system size. Photo: Jerry Yudelson.

water for domestic use such as hand-washing.[233] This is the country's largest site-built solar air heater. It also provides some passive solar heat gain for those two floors during cooler months.

A CHP (combined heat and power) plant using five 60-kW micro-turbines provides heat and power to the building; the turbines achieve 78 percent energy conversion efficiency, compared to conventional electric power plants that achieve about 32 percent efficiency. Waste heat from the turbine exhaust is converted to hot water, which is used to preheat tap and shower water, to supply hot water demand in the thermo-active first-floor slab, and to heat the health-club swimming pool inside the building.[234]

CHH uses passive and active chilled beam systems, which not only provide substantial energy savings but also reduce the load on HVAC system. The chilled beam system allowed the HVAC system to be more than three times smaller than a traditional forced-air ventilation approach for cooling, saving considerable money.[235]

Located west of the Cascade mountain range, Portland's climate is relatively mild, allowing the team to take advantage of natural ventilation and the use of outside air for cooling much of the year. CHH employs low-velocity night-flush cooling, using outside air, which lasts until one hour before daily occupancy begins.[236]

Sunshades topped with solar panels were integrated into the building's south-facing exterior to shield the interior space from direct sunlight and lower the HVAC system requirements for cooling. The sunshades themselves also provide a surface for PV panels.[237]

The rainwater/groundwater reclamation system is another example of building systems integration. The system services six building requirements: it provides water for flushing toilets and urinals, the cooling tower, the radiant heating and cooling system, the green roof, the micro-turbine power generator, and exterior irrigation.[238] The system also detains stormwater, reducing the load on the city stormwater collection infrastructure.[239] An on-site blackwater treatment system treats and recycles up to 35,000 gallons (132 kl) of sewage daily,[240] completely eliminating the need to convey sewage from the site.[241] In 2011, the project generated an average of about 21,000 gallons per day. This figure includes weekend days, however, when flows average only about 8,000 gallons. Weekday sewage generation, especially in the summer months, sometimes can approach the system's treatment capacity.

Seventy-five percent of the CHH's potable water use is provided by onsite reclaimed water, reducing water demand by 56 percent compared to a similar building. Avoiding the high cost of the city's wastewater and stormwater connection fees and system-usage charges, combined with a third-party "build/own/operate" approach to the on-site sewage-treatment facility, created enough savings to reduce the net cost of the water-harvesting system to nearly zero.[242]

A cistern stores collected rainwater for fire suppression, detains stormwater to prevent overload of the municipal storm sewer system, collects rainwater for recycling to decrease the need for municipal potable water, and provides a free source of cool water to the radiant floor slabs.[243] A 20,000-sq-ft (1,858-sq-m) green roof covers 50 percent of the total roof area and contributes to the goal of retaining 100 percent of rainwater on site.[244]

The Energy Trust of Oregon reports that the building set a record for the most strategies integrated into a facility. However, one of the lessons learned from the CHH project focused on the complexity of the building's technical features. "The complexity of the systems leads to an elongated commissioning process and also creates more potential for problems and 'domino effects' when one part of the system breaks down," said Dennis Wilde.[245] For example, the green roof and landscape required more water than anticipated, leaving the water level in the cistern too low at times to create enough pressure to flush the toilets. As a result, the City imposed a penalty for the accelerated demand for permits for a backup system.[246]

Wilde said that future buildings should be smarter and simpler; one of the design members said, in hindsight, "next time the goal should be to accomplish the same results with half the stuff."[247] The lead engineer on the project, Andy Frichtl, gave these "lessons learned" from the design and operation of the building:

Plug loads were underestimated and caused less heat recovery to be needed. These are hard to predict but we are now more careful and less conservative in our predictions.

Make allowances for projects to be much more successful than you think initially. In the case of CHH, the daily occupant count was originally predicted to be 1,000, but because of its success, there is nearly twice that number, causing added energy and water consumption as well as sewage effluent. This required us to add a filter section to the on-site sewage treatment plant right away to keep up with demand. The additional treated water is available to adjacent buildings for non-potable use but no one yet uses this valuable resource.[248]

For energy strategies with large energy savings such as the group of six micro-turbines, continuous commissioning (Cx) is required to ensure they continue to operate as intended. In this case, the microturbine controls were changed after the initial commissioning process and nobody knew about it until after the completion of the post-occupancy evaluation.

This last observation illustrates points made by Adrian Leaman in Chapter 5, that building designers need to remain engaged with a project for three years after it opens, to stay on top of how it's actually operating.

TABLE 7.18

Energy and water use, 2011

	Energy use, July 2010–June 2011	Intensity
Total (includes PV)	**17,888,490 kWh**	**469 kWh/sq m**
Electricity (purchased)	7,195,200 kWh	59,896 Btu/sq ft 189 kWh/sq m
Natural gas[a]	364,962 therms 10,693,386 kWh	89,015 Btu/sq ft 281 kWh/sq m
PV annual production	45,111 kWh	375 Btu/sq ft 1.2 kWh/sq m
Potable water (purchased)	4,618,900 g 17,482 kl	11.3 g/sq ft 459 l/sq m
Non-potable water (from recycled water supply)[b]	6,661,646 g 25,214 kl 4,809,168 g from MBR and 1,852,478 g rainwater and graywater	16.2 g/sq ft 662 l/sq m
Total water use		**1,121 l/sq m**

a In 2011, adjustments made to the prioritization of the microturbines in 2011 increased overall efficiency resulting in slightly higher purchased electricity and considerably lower purchased natural gas. The overall, result was a higher efficiency PSF.

b Note that overall water consumption has remained relatively flat although the project has been able to use about an additional million gallons per year from the onsite reuse system than expected.

At a glance
Name: OHSU Center for Health and Healing
Location: Portland, Oregon
Size: 410,000 sq ft (38,090 sq m)
Completed: October 2006
Cost: US$145.4 million
Distinction: LEED-NC Platinum, LEED-EBOM Platinum
Program: Mixed-use facility for wellness, medical research, clinics, surgery, classrooms, ground-floor retail, underground parking

Project team
Owner: Rimco, LLC (OHSU and OHSU Medical Group)
Developer: Gerding Edlen Development
Architect and Interior Designer: GBD Architects Inc.
Structural Engineer: KPFF Consulting Engineers
Civil Engineer: OTAK
MEP Engineer: Interface Engineering, Inc.
General Contractor: Hoffman Construction

7.36 *Right*: Large glazed areas use fritted glass to allow "aggressive daylighting" while cutting down unwanted solar heat gain, reducing the need for artificial lighting. Photo: St. Olaf College.

7.37 *Far Right*: Regents Hall of Natural and Mathematical Sciences is a 190,000-sq-ft academic laboratory in Northfield, Minnesota, on the campus of St. Olaf College, a private liberal arts college. Photo: St. Olaf College.

REGENTS HALL OF NATURAL AND MATHEMATICAL SCIENCES, St. Olaf College, Northfield, Minnesota

Regents Hall of Natural and Mathematical Sciences is a 190,000-sq-ft (17,700-sq-m) academic laboratory in Northfield, Minnesota, on the campus of St. Olaf College, a private liberal arts college. The LEED Platinum-certified facility is perhaps the most prominent expression of the college's twenty-three-year-old sustainability agenda. The design adhered to the College's Sustainable Design Guidelines and to principles of lean construction, an approach that maximizes usefulness while minimizing waste.

Replacing a forty-year-old science building, Regents Hall is divided into east and west wings joined by an atrium. The interior is organized according to areas of study and research interests rather than traditional disciplines such as chemistry and biology.

"We designed the building so we could support an innovative science program without imposing a huge operating cost increase on the overall college budget," said Pete Sandberg, Assistant Vice President for Facilities. "We try to operate with as few BTUs per square foot and as little carbon footprint as possible. Our goal is stewardship of the resources that families have committed to their children's educations."[249]

Regents Hall emphasizes green chemistry, a growing movement that seeks to minimize the amount of hazardous chemical waste produced from laboratory experiments. Experiments at St. Olaf replace toxic substances with water-based and nontoxic chemicals, which are more efficient and generate less waste.[250]

As a result, the building requires only half as many fume hoods as traditional chemistry laboratories and produces only half the amount of exhaust (conditioned) air that requires fresh-air make-up. In addition, student researchers found equipment suppliers and then selected hoods that could perform with 40 percent lower airflow than conventional fume hoods, with equal effectiveness.[251]

Due to the nature of laboratory buildings, managing IAQ is an energy-intensive process. In Regents Hall, the air-distribution system contains several energy-saving features: a heat-recovery loop, a "cascade" air system, and a low-flow, variable-air-volume (VAV) fume-hood exhaust system.

Instead of immediately discharging exhaust air from the building, all of the exhaust air is routed through a heat exchanger. A glycol heat-recovery loop recovers heat from the laboratory-fume-hood exhaust-air stream. A standard heat-exchange coil is located in the laboratory exhaust manifold upstream of the exhaust fans, and a similar coil is strategically located in the air-handling unit. Energy is transferred from the warm exhaust air to the glycol loop and transported to the air handling unit coil where it is used to preheat the outside air coming into the unit.[252]

The second feature, a cascade air system, is an efficient way to provide the high air exchange rate required for the laboratories. Fresh air is introduced to the system through the louvers in the northeast wall of each wing. The air drops to the lower-level mechanical room where it is warmed by the reclaimed heat from the lab exhaust.[253]

Because many spaces need to be cooled most of the year—people, lighting, and equipment generate a lot of the heat—the HVAC system distributes air to the building supply ducts at 55°F (13°C). Even during very cold weather, for most of the year incoming air is only heated to 55°F. If additional heat is required, a reheat coil on the VAV boxes will reheat the air when it reaches the space.[254]

TABLE 7.19

Energy and water use, 2010

	Annual use	Intensity
Steam	1,149,170 kWh	6.04 kWh/sq ft
Electricity (62% less than predicted)	2,208,508	11.43
Total	**3,357,678 kWh**	**188 kWh/sq m**
Water use (2011)	970,001 g	5.1 g/sq ft 208 l/sq m

For perimeter heating, when necessary, hot-water radiant panels that are suspended at the horizontal mullion provide heat and double as reflective light shelves. Light bounces off them to the ceiling and through clerestory-like windows above the office and seminar room doors.[255]

Table 7.19 shows the actual monthly electricity consumption for the first two complete fiscal years of operation. All electricity use is supplied by an on-campus, 1,650-kW Vestas V-82 wind turbine. Excess wind-generated electricity more than offsets the small increase in campus gas load attributed to the building, as well as a small increase in electricity use at the central chilling plant.

Energy efficiency is enhanced by corridor lighting equipped with occupancy sensors, as are faculty and staff offices. In offices, occupancy sensors turn on light switches and wake up VAV boxes from a setback setting. When the space is unoccupied for fifteen minutes, everything shuts off. Most motors over one horsepower are on variable-frequency drives.

As a result of the energy-saving features, Regents Hall is performing better than anticipated. "We added 190,400 square feet (17,658 sq m) of technical space, and the base energy model for the building initially predicted more than 8-million kWh would be consumed annually if designed and constructed just to meet code requirements," said Sandberg. "The aggressive energy-conservation design changed the model to predict 4.88-million kWh energy use, and we actually operated the first 12 months using only 2.17-million kWh."[256] This energy use is quite low, considering that St. Olaf is located in an extreme climate with 8,100 (F) combined heating and cooling degree-days.

Reduced energy usage results in an estimated annual utility savings of $452,600 compared to a standard building. Energy produced by the St. Olaf wind turbine, estimated at 5.7 million kWh annually, contributes to an additional $167,400 reduction in energy costs. In Regents' first full year of operation, the entire campus consumed 6 percent less energy (per sq ft) than in the previous five years. From a base in 2001, the campus-wide heating-energy intensity dropped by 11 percent in 2010, even with the addition of energy-intensive spaces for art and science.[257]

A rooftop rainwater collection system provides water for the campus greenhouse. A green roof, planted with low-maintenance sedums, cacti, grasses, and columbines, reduces stormwater runoff, filters CO_2 out of the air, and removes pollutants out of rainwater. Water that does not infiltrate is captured and released in a waterfall that cascades 15 ft into a stream next to the building, which travels to stormwater basins below the building,[258] where it undergoes further treatment before discharge.[259]

Inside the building, all of the purchased wood was certified by the Forest Stewardship Council. Much of the wood for furniture in the building was handcrafted in the St. Olaf carpenter shop using lumber milled from trees on the construction site.[260]

"We're operating at one-third of the predicted costs," Sanberg said. "Ten years ago, we started developing our own sustainable design guidelines and made them part of our design and construction contracts. Regents Hall is the building we would have built even if LEED didn't exist. It's that important to St. Olaf to provide the best teaching environment it can."[261]

At a glance

Name: Regents Hall, St Olaf College

Location: Northfield, Minnesota

Size: 190,400 gross sq ft (17,689 sq m)

Completed: August 2008

Cost: $63 million

Distinction: LEED-NC Platinum

Program: College chemistry laboratories, conference room, classrooms

Project team

Owner: St. Olaf College

Architect/Engineer: Holabird & Root Architects and Engineers, Weidt Group

Contractor: Oscar J. Boldt Construction

7.38 Located in Incline Village, Nevada, the Tahoe Center is a 45,000 sq ft facility which houses research programs of three universities that focus on understanding the unique ecology of 6,225-ft (1,900-m) elevation Lake Tahoe. Photo: Collaborative Design Studio.

TAHOE CENTER FOR ENVIRONMENTAL SCIENCES, Incline Village, Nevada

The Tahoe Center for Environmental Sciences (TCES) is the result of a unique partnership between a private college and a state university. Sierra Nevada College and the University of California at Davis (UC Davis) are both focused on studying and preserving the Lake Tahoe watershed, which straddles the border of California and Nevada. Both needed a new building. Sierra Nevada College, a small liberal-arts college with 20 acres of forestland on the shores of Lake Tahoe, needed additional funds. UC Davis, which had completed a fundraising drive for a new high-tech laboratory, needed a location. The two institutions combined their resources and built a jointly owned laboratory facility.

"Normally, people would say that getting a California university and a Nevada private college to work out a joint occupancy agreement on property in Nevada, and getting $9.6 million of California money into a building in Nevada, would be impossible," said Jim Steinmann,

7.39 Along with light shelves, the full-height atrium draws daylight deep into the building. Photo: Collaborative Design Studio.

Sierra Nevada College Trustee and Tahoe Center Project Manager. "But it turned out to be the easiest thing to do, because both parties wanted it to work."[262]

The 47,000-sq-ft (4,366-sq-m), three-story building serves two main functions: (1) an academic laboratory and classrooms for Sierra Nevada College and (2) a research laboratory for the UC Davis Tahoe Environmental Research Center.

According to project architect Todd Lankenau, the design goals incorporated all of the building needs "into a tight building shell with height and footprint restrictions with the greatest level of efficiency possible."[263]

Laboratory buildings are notorious for their high energy use. "That was really one of our biggest challenges," said Lankenau. "A laboratory, just by its nature, is a very energy consumptive building. Although we devised numerous innovative strategies to reduce energy consumption, had it been any other type of building it would've been much easier."[264]

Proper ventilation is the first priority in laboratory design. To meet safety requirements, 100 percent outside air ventilation is required. To reduce energy consumption, project engineer Peter Rumsey designed a series of systems that decoupled the heating and cooling functions from the ventilation and humidity systems, a divergence from traditional lab design. At TCES, the air-handling system provides ventilation air only to the laboratory and offices, while heating and cooling are provided separately, cutting energy use dramatically.[265]

At 6,300 ft (1,920 m), TCES is one of the highest-elevation laboratory buildings in the USA, and it was designed to take advantage of local climatic conditions. Incline Village has a mild climate with large nighttime temperature swings. During warmer months, night flushing precools interior air and concrete thermal mass, which reduces the cooling load throughout the next day.[266]

All of the building's cooling needs are met without the use of a chiller. "We can cool the building without the use of any compressor-based cooling," said Lankenau. "There are no chillers, but instead, there are two 25,000-gallon [95,000-l] underground chilled water storage tanks and a cooling tower for direct evaporative cooling, which is used only at night to produce chilled water. This system also uses chilled beams, low-flow displacement ventilation, radiant floor heating, and overhead radiant heating and cooling panels."[267]

Active chilled beams are connected to primary air-supply ducts and distribute cool air through diffusers in the ceiling. "One of the outstanding characteristics of this building is the number of different systems it uses and the way they interact to achieve excellent energy efficiency while delivering optimal comfort and safety for students, researchers and other users," said Peter Rumsey. "We're particularly happy that the laboratory was the first in the US to use chilled beams, as this technology presents excellent energy-saving potential for labs."[268]

TABLE 7.20
Energy use, 2010

	Annual use	Intensity
Utility electricity	261,440 kWh	5.6 kWh/sq ft
Cogeneration electricity	127,672	2.7
Photovoltaics	30,169	0.6
Gas (to boiler)	31,273	0.7
Total	**450,554**	**9.6 kWh/sq m** **103 kWh/sq m**

The building generates electricity on-site in two ways: cogeneration and solar electric. Both increase energy efficiency while decreasing emissions. The cogeneration plant produces a substantial amount of the building's power (about 30 percent) while recapturing the building's waste heat, which then is used for domestic hot water and snowmelt systems.[269]

A roof-mounted solar PV system produces less than 1 percent of the building's power demand. Nine hundred solar panels make up the 31.5-kW system; their sloped glass surfaces immediately shed snow to maximize energy production.[270]

Along with natural ventilation, daylighting contributes to occupant comfort and the indoor environmental quality of the building. "The atrium in the center is skylit which allows for indirect light into all of the offices and circulation spaces around it," said Lankenau. "It's almost like a donut shape, with office spaces on the outside. Because of the center atrium, natural light enters the office spaces and the labs from both the inside and the outside. We also used light shelves to bounce the light back off the ceilings to a greater depth within the space. We designed the lighting so it's tied to photocells. It automatically adjusts lighting levels as it senses the natural light levels in the spaces."[271]

Other sustainable features at TCES include:

- a rainwater storage system which harvests and purifies water for toilet flushing
- low-flow plumbing fixtures, dual-flush toilets, water-free urinals
- structural concrete with 25 percent fly-ash content.[272]

Sustainability was always a project goal, but the initial goal was to achieve a LEED Silver rating. "Our goal was this: if there was ever a choice between good design practice and attaining a LEED credit, we would always choose the good design practice. We would never design something just to attain a LEED credit," said Lankenau.[273]

"We had reached a stage in the project where we were at Silver without really pushing the envelope at all. We hadn't done anything special. We decided to set Platinum as our goal and see what good design features we could work into the building that would be still cost-effective, to achieve that goal."[274]

Instead of designing things and making additions just to achieve credits, the team focused on efficiency and refinements. "Our thinking was that, since we're so close on so many of the credits, if we refine the design toward what is a good design, that's even better," said Lankenau. "We did that by continually going back and refining things. An example of that is the ductwork. Every time there's an elbow in ductwork, it creates a static pressure drop, which makes the fan work a little bit harder, which in turn consumes additional power. We went through a whole exercise of looking at the mechanical system in the building and eliminating every conceivable elbow that wasn't necessary. We reached the goal of Platinum merely by going to that level of detail."[275]

That strategy proved effective in terms of both the rating and the economics. Jim Steinmann of Sierra Nevada College: "We were able to achieve a LEED Platinum certification in a laboratory building, on a site which receives 200 in (508 cm) of snow a year, at 6,300 ft (1,920 m) above sea level, while working with one of the strictest regulatory agencies in the country, for only $1.1 million [$23.50/sq ft] beyond what we would have spent for a LEED Silver building."[276]

At a glance
Name: Tahoe Center for Environmental Sciences
Location: Incline Village, Nevada
Size: 47,000 sq ft (4,366 sq m)
Completed: August 2006
Construction cost: US$25 million
Distinction: LEED-NC Platinum
Program: Academic Laboratory and Classrooms

Project team
Owner: Sierra Nevada College and UC Davis
Architect: Collaborative Design Studio
Structural engineer: John A. Martin & Associates of NV
Mechanical engineer: Rumsey Engineers, Inc.
Contractor: Turner Construction Company

TWELVE WEST, Portland, Oregon

Twelve West is a twenty-three-story mixed-use building in Portland, Oregon. Designed and partially occupied by ZGF Architects LLP (ZGF), the project achieved two LEED Platinum ratings and exceeds the 2030 Challenge benchmarks for 2009 with a 50 percent reduction in both energy and water use. Twelve West includes many sustainability features but it is known to locals as "that wind-turbine building," owing to the four rooftop turbines.[277]

Named a "Top Ten" green project in 2010 by the American Institute of Architects' (AIA) Committee on the Environment (COTE), the building earned two LEED Platinum certifications, one under LEED's New Construction scheme and the other under the LEED for Commercial Interiors for ZGF's office space.

The building uses the Pacific Northwest's abundant natural resources—wood, concrete, and a mild climate—to create an open, daylit space designed to foster connection between the occupants. John Breshears, an architect at ZGF, said the new workspace is "light-filled, not glare-y, spacious, and comfortable. Conversations and interactions are happening now that wouldn't have happened in our old, cramped space. And that's changing how we do our jobs."[278]

Having completed more than forty LEED buildings across the USA, ZGF was an early leader in adopting sustainable design.[279] Upon outgrowing their former offices in a nineteenth-century warehouse-style building in Old Town Portland, the firm decided that it was time to move.[280]

"We wanted to be on a site that would help revitalize a re-emerging neighborhood," said Eugene Sandoval, ZGF Partner and lead designer for the project. "That brings with it the responsibility to achieve a balance between life and work, which is the whole idea of mixed use. We also wanted to combine rental housing with an architectural office and retail—and do it well as a 'hybrid' building."[281]

The site was formerly an underused 20,000-sq-ft (1,858-sq-m) surface parking area with a derelict one-story building.[282] Today, the building is an anchor for Portland's up-and-coming West End neighborhood.[283]

On the first floor, double-story retail spaces with large street-level windows share space with the building's office and residential lobbies. From the main lobby, a steel and wood staircase hovers suspended above the floor and leads to ZGF's reception area. ZGF's offices occupy Floors 2–5 in an open floor layout. The spacious, light-filled office features custom-designed workstations, thirteen conference rooms, a library, model shop, six balconies, and two outdoor decks. Reflecting the building's connection to the Pacific Northwest, wood is used throughout: floors, paneling, stair treads, and doors.[284]

On the upper seventeen floors are the "Indigo @ Twelve West" apartments, with 273 units ranging from 541 to 2,125 sq ft (50 to 197 sq m) including penthouse homes on three floors. To maximize natural light, living spaces are oriented along a floor-to-ceiling glass curtain wall. Design and materials optimize daylight with exposed concrete, operable windows, balconies, and natural ventilation. There are low-flow plumbing fixtures and Energy Star appliances in each unit. Shared amenities include a twenty-one-seat screening theater, a workout room, a 700-sq-ft (65-sq-m) glass-walled rooftop room with a fireplace, and a rooftop deck with fire pits and barbecues.[285]

"Its architecture is contemporary—and stunning—and yet the design of the skin and how they put the different components of the building together is equally exciting to me, both for the exterior and

7.40 *Far Left*: Twelve West serves not only as an anchor in a rapidly transforming urban neighborhood, but also as demonstration project to inform future sustainable building design. Photo: © Timothy Hursley.

7.41 *Left*: The four floors of street-level entry feature a "suspended" staircase, hung with stainless steel cables, that leads to the building's second floor and ZGF Architect's main office reception. Photo: © Nick Merrick, Hedrich Blessing.

interior. Twelve West is a pioneering project within an emerging neighborhood," said project developer Mark Edlen.[286]

Pre-Design

The project's success can be attributed largely to the design process. An office-wide "culture charrette" asked ZGF employees questions such as: How do we increase interaction and make the most of public space? How can the office foster further innovation? Feedback led to design-team brainstorming and collaboration on ways to improve overall productivity and work quality, which informed the overall scheme.[287] Having dual roles as both the client and the architect, ZGF selected a group of employees—diverse in gender, longevity, job function, and personality—to work with the design team as the client.[288]

The dual-role relationship was not without its challenges. "There were definitely too many chefs in the kitchen," said Breshears. The in-house "client" team got to participate in the creative exploration process usually reserved for outside clients.[289]

Through a series of design charrettes, the project team outlined important project goals, including:

- create a structure that unites the live, work, learn, and play components of the building
- construct a transparent building—inviting and active—that connects the building's inhabitants to the urban landscape, while taking advantage of natural light
- accommodate exterior gardens and terraces for areas of interaction and respite
- integrate advanced and symbiotic sustainable building systems to promote resource conservation
- design residences for lease that maximize space, light, and views and include luxurious amenities along with energy savings.[290]

Initially, Glumac (the MEP engineer) generated seventy different energy and carbon reduction strategies for the building, which were later narrowed to twenty-five possible solutions. Energy modeling was

TABLE 7.21

Twelve West energy use comparisons, energy use index (EUI)

	Actual use (2009–2010)	Modeled use	Building code	CBECS (2003)	2030 Challenge (2009)	2030 Challenge (2010)
EUI (kBTU/sq ft/year)	43.7	33.8	73.5	98.7	49.4	39.5
EUI (kWh/sq m/year)	138	107	232	311	156	125
Comparison of actual with benchmarks	29% greater than modeled	–	40% less	56% less	11% less	11% greater

performed continuously throughout the design process to inform system choices.[291] An invaluable tool throughout the development was a detailed matrix, which evaluated the proposed energy-efficiency strategies' energy savings, carbon reduction, cost, savings payback, and interaction with each other.[292]

"Historically, energy analysis happens separately from design development," said Leonard Klein, a Glumac principal. "For this project, we deviated from the tried and true stacks of detailed energy analyses by simplifying everything into an 11-by-17 spreadsheet that summarized all the pros and cons, energy requirements, carbon reduction impact, and overall construction cost."[293]

This tool was the basis for selecting underfloor air and chilled beams within the building and instrumental for reaching LEED Platinum and 2030 Challenge targets.[294] ZGF, Glumac, and the developer, Gerding Edlen Development, joined the 2030 Challenge and adopted its performance targets for Twelve West.[295]

Glazing

While a glass façade contributes to transparency, lots of exterior glass doesn't usually bode well for a building's energy performance. "We wanted the building to be an urban catalyst, to show 24-hour life on the street, which means a lot of glass. We also want this to be a paragon of sustainable performance," said Breshears. However, "those two don't always go together."[296]

With highly glazed, vertical bands, the façade has "shadow-box" panels behind, giving the appearance of transparency, but with a solid wall's energy performance.[297] A local company, Benson Industries, built the façade for Twelve West using operable windows. "There are about 373 reasons not to do operable windows," Breshears says. "There's one reason to do them: Occupants like them."[298] All major spaces contain at least one operable window. A light well provides access to natural light within the office area where external glazing is not feasible.[299]

Wind

On the building's roof sits the building's most high-profile feature: four 45-ft (13.7-m) wind turbines. This installation is the first turbine array on an urban high-rise in North America and functions as a key element of the building's role as a "living laboratory." According to Wilde, the turbines "are just a bit of frosting on the cake,"[300] producing about 10,000–12,000 kWh per year, around 1 percent of electrical demand for the office floors.[301]

The team found it feasible to place wind turbines on top of a residential-office building. "The real world performance of the turbine array is stellar in terms of noise and vibration," said Craig Briscoe, formerly an architect with ZGF. "You never know if you've been really successful acoustically until you get to measure the actual sound and vibration with those subjective but sensitive instruments that we call 'occupants.'"[302]

Another source of renewable energy at Twelve West is a 1,360-sq-ft (126.3-sq-m) array of flat-plate solar hot-water collectors that offset the building's natural-gas use for water heating by 24 percent, supplying hot water for showers, hand washing, and kitchen use.[303]

Energy Use

For space heating and cooling, the building relies on night flushing (an easy choice in Portland's temperate climate), chilled beams, and thermal mass. Made possible via the operable windows and specialized multiple-fan-array technology, night flushing is essential to building performance, especially on the office floors. Combined with natural ventilation, the underfloor air system provides most office cooling. Using less energy than a conventional HVAC system, adjustable floor-mounted diffusers deliver cool air to occupied zones at each workstation.

On hot days, passive chilled beams located around the perimeter provide additional cooling. The beams bring 55°F (13°C) water into the building and cool the space through natural convection. Passive chilled beams save energy over conventional systems by absorbing heat with water (not air) and by providing comfort and recirculating air without using fan energy.[304]

Table 7.21 compares actual energy use in 2010 with other indices, including the modeled use, Oregon Energy Code requirements, US averages from the last comprehensive survey (2003, CBECS), and the 2030 Challenge's requirements, as estimated for 2009 and 2010.

In over twelve months beginning in September 2009, actual energy use was 29 percent greater than predicted, for a variety of reasons still under investigation. However, actual use was 40 percent less than a standard building built to Oregon energy code and 56 percent below

TABLE 7.22

Energy and water use, October 2009–September 2010

	Total (BTU)	Intensity (BTU/sq ft)	Intensity (kWh/sq ft)
Electricity	8,827,966	20,641	6.0
Chilled water	4,929,204	11,525	3.4
Gas	4,947,680	11,569	3.4
Total energy use	**18,704,850**	**43,735**	**12.8 (138 kWh/sq m)**

the average for similar buildings based on the CBECS 2003 detailed national survey. Comparing this building to the 2030 Challenge, which seeks carbon-neutral buildings in the USA by 2030 and prescribes a pathway to get there, Twelve West uses 11 percent less energy than the 2009 level, but 11 percent more energy than the 2010 requirement.

Water

Water conservation at Twelve West employs several strategies, augmented by rainwater harvesting and reuse. Low-flow and dual-flush fixtures used throughout the building reduce water use by more than 44 percent compared to similar buildings.[306] Native species make up exterior landscape plants and require little to no irrigation, reducing outdoor water-use by 84 percent. The building's 6,000-sq-ft (550-sq-m) green roof diverts and cleans rainwater while reducing the roof temperature in the summer.[307]

Rainwater is harvested and reused to meet all irrigation needs and about 90 percent of office toilet-flushing requirements. Along with cooling-tower condensate, rainwater is collected and stored in a 50,000-gallon (189 kl) storage tank located in the underground garage. A portion is also stored in an on-site fire-suppression storage tank for use during drier months. Reusing rainwater and condensate saves more than 285,000 gallons (1,079 kl) of potable water annually and reduces flow of stormwater leaving the site.[308]

An efficient, healthy building for residents and employees, Twelve West also stands out as a strong urban design and community-building gesture, reflecting ZGF's design ethos and functioning as a living laboratory that will inform future sustainable building designs.

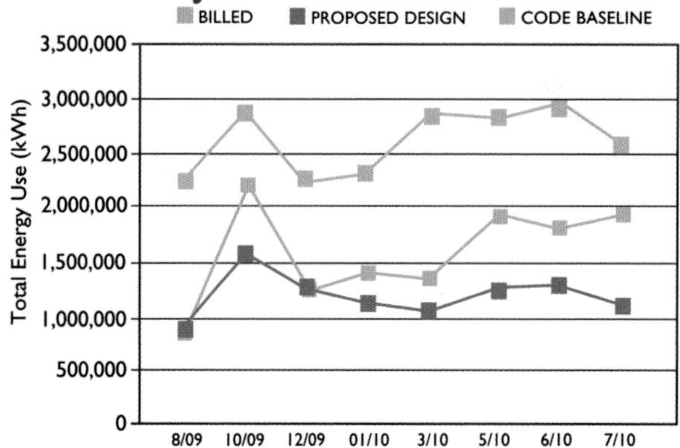

7.42 Actual versus projected energy use at Twelve West. Source: Mitchell Dec, Glumac, March 22, 2011.

At a glance

Name: Twelve West

Location: Portland, Oregon

Size: 427,681 sq ft (39,747 sq m)

Completed: July 2009

Construction cost: $138 million

Distinction: LEED-NC Platinum, LEED-CI Platinum

Program: Commercial office, multi-unit residential, retail, restaurant

Project team

Owners: Gerding Edlen Development, Downtown Development Corp., ZGF Architects LLP

Architect: ZGF Architects LLP

MEP engineer: Glumac

Structural engineer: KPFF Consulting Engineers

General contractor: Hoffman Construction

EUROPE

European projects are arranged by country, then in alphabetical order. In the case of European green buildings, we looked first to LEED Platinum, BREEAM Excellent or Outstanding, or DGNB Gold, then to other certifications. In the case of BREEAM, the lack of a publicly accessible data base meant that we had to identify BREEAM Outstanding projects using the Internet, then attempt to contact owners and design teams, which proved surprisingly difficult, perhaps owing to the lack of a strong connection between the BRE Global group (the BREEAM certifier) and the UK Green Building Council, a gap not found in other countries. We strongly urge the BRE Global team (and, in fact, all green building certification groups) to make its database of certified projects more accessible to researchers, along with contact information for the project teams.

EUROPE

Czech Republic

- CSOB Headquarters, Prague

Finland

- Lintulahti, Helsinki

France

- EMGP 270, Aubervilliers

Germany

- Federal Environmental Agency, Dessau
- Heinrich Böll Foundation, Berlin
- SOLON Corporate Headquarters, Berlin
- ThyssenKrupp Quartier, Essen
- Paul Wunderlich-Haus, Eberswalde, Brandenburg

Ireland

- SAP, Galway

The Netherlands

- TNT Express Headquarters (TNT Centre), Hoofddorp

Sweden

- Hagaporten 3, Stockholm

Switzerland

- Eawag Forum Chriesbach, Dübendorf
- Daniel Swarovski Corporation, Männedorf

United Kingdom

- 3 Assembly Square, Cardiff, Wales
- The Suttie Centre for Teaching and Learning in Healthcare, University of Aberdeen, Aberdeen, Scotland

CSOB Headquarters, Prague

What once served as a dumping ground for hazardous waste is now the site of one of the greenest buildings in the Czech Republic. CSOB, a commercial bank, member of KBC Group, decided to consolidate its headquarters offices in southwest Prague, an area of the city that had not been redeveloped since it was destroyed during World War II. The former brownfield site is now home to the first LEED Gold certified building in the country.

Prior to moving into the new headquarters building, the CSOB Group occupied several buildings in Prague's old town. Pavel Kavanek, Chairman and CEO of CSOB, explained one of the main reasons for moving the bank's offices, "So far, we have been scattered in various buildings in the center of Prague, so a lot of colleagues knew each other more from telephone calls than personally. At last, we will be closer to each other in the new headquarters. It is an important incentive for corporate culture of the entire CSOB Group."[1]

More than 2,500 bank employees are located in one of the largest office buildings in the country.[2] In addition to offices and workspaces, the five-story 900,000-sq-ft (82,392-sq-m) building contains a public bank branch, a café, a medical center, post office, hairdresser, dry cleaners, and a flower shop. Public, shared, and amenity spaces comprise 35 percent of the net built area.[3] Located in Radlice, in Prague, the new building spurred urban redevelopment and stimulated local economic development in the area.[4]

Designed by Czech architect Josef Pleskot, the building combines sustainability and efficiency with sense of place and occupant comfort.[5] "Thanks to its energy-saving design, the use of natural materials and its sensitive setting in the landscape, [the building] contributes to the development and revival of the central part of Radlice," said Pleskot. "People should learn also that purely purpose-built office buildings may be interesting from the architectonic point of view and be environment-friendly."[6]

Sense of Place

Integration into the surrounding urban and natural environment was an important component of the project. Landscaping elements include new trees in the area. The protection of open space aims to restrict excessive development. The grounds surrounding the new headquarters are open to the public and provide green open space for local residents.[7]

The building itself incorporates the natural character of the Radlice area by restricting vertical dimensions to five stories, with nearly half the site set aside for public use. Existing trees were preserved and local species of trees were planted on the site and in the nearby forest park. The project provides six landscaped roof gardens, 193,000 sq ft (18,000 sq m) of lawn, and 7,000 shrubs, including climbing plants that cover sections of the façade.[8]

Occupant Comfort

Employees need a moment to stop and relax, according to CSOB, "The architectural concept emphasizes harmony and a pleasant work environment. The main motive is openness, but many natural 'obstructions' like plants and cabinets are used to make the place friendlier."[9] On-site employee amenities, abundant natural light, views to the outdoors, and the ability to adjust task lighting and local ambient temperature also enhance occupant comfort.

Sustainability

The CSOB headquarters building set new standards for sustainable strategies and energy-efficiency in the Czech Republic. Prior to construction, the brownfield site was cleaned up by treating contaminated soil. More than 75 percent of building waste was diverted from disposal, including 353,000 cu ft (10,000 cu m) of concrete from prior structures that was crushed and reused on site. Fifty-five metric tons of contaminated wooden railway cars, which could not be reused, were disposed of at a hazardous waste facility.[10]

With underground parking for 125 bicycles, the building is directly above the Radlická metro station, about ten minutes' ride from central Prague. By request of city officials, redevelopment of the metro station was included in the CSOB project.[11]

Energy Efficiency

At about the same latitude as Frankfurt and Paris, Prague's climate requires little cooling (primarily heating energy use), with moderate summer temperatures and low humidity. The building's energy-efficient design features daylighting, passive solar design, green roofs, and natural ventilation.

The long façades of building are oriented to minimize eastern and western exposure. This reduces cooling loads and provides passive solar

7.43 Once a brownfield site, for its new headquarters building CSOB redeveloped an area that was destroyed during World War II.
Photo: CSOB.

gains during winter months. With a 70 percent glazing ratio, each level contains floor-to-ceiling glazing with direct views to the outdoors. An automated external Venetian blind system prevents glare and minimizes solar gains on the east, south and west façades.[12]

The HVAC system uses a combination displacement ventilation system with perimeter fan coils for heating and cooling. Three high-efficiency natural-gas condensing boilers serve as the primary active heating system. The distribution system is a variable-speed, low-temperature hydronic system with a flow temperature that automatically adjusts in response to the current weather conditions, enhancing to the system's efficiency.[13]

Integrated with the HVAC controls, the operable windows provide free cooling when conditions permit. When additional cooling is needed, rooftop air-cooled chillers supply chilled water to the air-handling units and fan coils for space cooling. The team chose an air-cooled chiller over a more efficient water-cooler chiller, based on Prague's moderate summer climate combined with the building's integrated passive design strategies.[14]

The annual EUI for the entire building is estimated at about 58,000 BTU/sq ft (183 kWh/sq m) in the above-grade conditioned areas. The building uses 30 percent less energy compared to a baseline standard (ASHRAE Standard 90.1–2004) and consumes 8,000 BTU per sq ft (25 kWh/sq m) of natural gas for heating, which is low, considering Prague's cold winters. The building also houses the bank's computer servers. These are responsible for 30 percent of the building energy consumption and push up the energy use intensity by at least 10,000 BTU per sq ft (32 kWh/sq m).[15]

To ensure that the building's energy-efficient features were used as designed, building managers provided employee training before occupancy to explain the building operations system and local controls.[16]

7.44 Water-efficient landscaping has reduced outdoor water consumption by over 50 percent. Photo: CSOB.

TABLE 7.23

Energy and water use, 2011[a]

	Annual use	Intensity
Electricity	12,482,410 KWh	152 kWh/sq m
Gas	236,536 cu m	31.9[b]
Total		**184**
Potable water	26,760 cu m	325 L/sq m

a Figures for energy and water consumption for all case-study projects were provided by the project owner, architect, engineer, or consultant, unless otherwise indicated.

b 11.13 kWh/cu m of natural gas.

Water Efficiency

More than 41 percent of the total roof area is planted.[17] Low-growing vegetation, trees, and shrubs are planted on the roof in a 5-ft (1.6-m) layer of soil. The green roof and climbing plants on the façade improve the heat-insulation properties of the building and reduce the urban heat island effect.[18] Roof gardens are watered by an automatic rainwater-collection system, which stores water in underground reservoirs for use during dry periods.[19]

"Friendly" is not a word that is typically used to describe commercial office buildings. However, that was architect Josef Pleskot's original vision for the CSOB headquarters: a building welcoming and friendly for its users, the bank's employees, and friendly toward its surroundings. As first LEED-certified building in the Czech Republic, the CSOB headquarters is the model for future "friendly" buildings in the country.

At a glance

Name: CSOB Headquarters

Size: 886,860 sq ft (82,392 sq m) (+ 237,732 sq ft/22,086 sq m below ground)

Completion/Occupancy: April 2007

Cost: US$107 million/CZK 2.95 billion

Distinction: LEED-NC Gold

Program: Corporate office building, data center, cafés, below-ground parking, medical office, retail.

Project team

Owner: KBC

Architect: AP Atelier

MEP and structural engineer: VPU Deco

General contractor: Skanska Czech Republic

LINTULAHTI, Helsinki

Located about one mile from Helsinki's city center, Lintulahti was the first office building in Finland to receive a LEED Platinum certification. A project of Skanska Finland, Lintulahti was certified as a LEED for Core and Shell building and is now nearly fully occupied. The building is also registered with the European Union's Green Building Programme, which requires all new green buildings to consume at least 25 percent less energy than standard buildings.

The eight-story, 137,125-sq-ft (12,744-sq-m) building, with a 28,234-sq-ft (2,624-sq-m) garage, was constructed on a formerly

7.45 Built on the site of a former brownfield, Lintulahti anchors a redevelopment project to regenerate Helsinki's eastern harbor. Photo: Anders Portman and Kuvio Oy. Courtesy of Skanska Finland.

7.46 The 10,700-sq-m Lintulahti building was the first project in Finland to receive a LEED Platinum certification. Photo: Voitto Niemelä. Courtesy of Skanska Finland.

contaminated brownfield site. Lintulahti is located within Helsinki's Eastern Harbor redevelopment area. Neighboring projects include the redevelopment of a power plant and a coal-storage area. The design team chose a red brick façade that blends in with the revived industrial architectural style of the surrounding area.[20]

On each floor there is workspace of about 14,600 sq ft (1,360 sq m) that accommodates up to 100 workstations. Building facilities include a main reception area, restaurant and conference rooms on the ground floor, and two levels of underground parking.[21]

The Lintulahti building is part of an energy-efficient office block that is supplied with renewable electricity and efficient district heating and cooling. At Lintulahti, district heating is provided by a cogeneration heat and electricity plant. District cooling is generated by either absorption chillers or from seawater from the harbor.[22]

The base building consumes 87 kWh/sq m of electricity for heating and cooling annually, better than the original projections of 120 kWh/sq m, more than 25 percent below the Finnish maximum electrical energy consumption requirement, and 21 percent below a

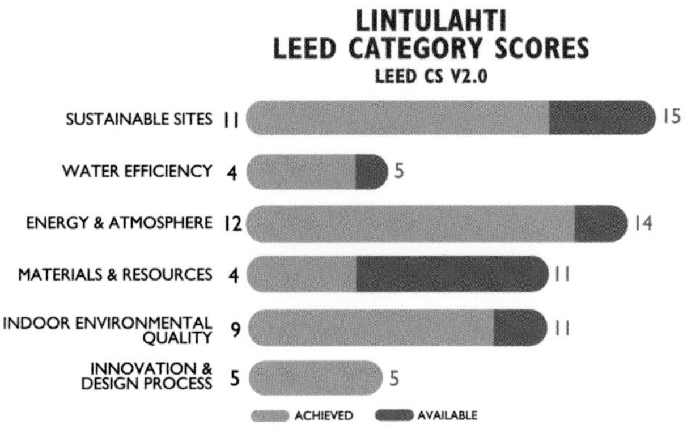

7.47 Lintulahti LEED category scores.

TABLE 7.24

Energy and water use (base building and tenant use), 2010–2011[a]

	Annual use	Intensity (based on 12,744 sq m)
Electricity	1,105,856 kWh	86.8 kWh/sq m
District heating (normalized)	1,136,300 kWh	89.2 kWh/sq m
District cooling	502,500 kWh	39.4 kWh/sq m
Total energy use	**2,744,656 kWh**	**213 kWh/sq m**
Water	2,813 cu m	221 l/sq m

a "Energy Consumption Report: May 2011," June 20, 2011, supplied by Anu Korhonen, Halton Group Ltd., from a report by Talonrakennus Oy/M&E Services, July 6, 2011.

typical building. The well-insulated building envelope is twice as airtight as building codes require. The windows' U-value is 20 percent less than required by Finnish building regulations, and their low-e coating reduces heat loss but allows solar heat gain during the long winter season.[23]

The windows are equipped with adjustable sunshades to reduce solar gain during warm sunny days and minimize the need for cooling. The ventilation system can be controlled by occupancy sensors to ensure optimal operation. Operable windows allow fresh-air ventilation and cooling from outdoor air, and heat-recovery units with an efficiency of around 75 percent are used in the office floors, to preheat incoming air with exhaust air. All of the timber used on the project was certified by the Programme for the Endorsement of Forest Certification.[24]

The development was designed to reduce the urban heat island effect in central Helsinki by reducing the extent of paved dark surfacing. To meet this goal, the building's parking area is located underground and the grounds are covered with vegetation or light-colored reflective paving.[25]

At a glance

Name: Lintulahti
Location: Helsinki, Finland
Completion: Summer 2009
Size: 137,125 sq ft (12,744 sq m) office space plus a 28,234-sq-ft (2,624-sq-m) garage
Cost: £19 million, about $29.5 million
Distinction: LEED-CS Platinum
Program: Corporate office building

Project team

Owner: Skanska Commercial Development Finland
Architect: Gullichsen Vormala Architects
Mechanical engineering: Pöyry Building Services
Indoor climate: Halton Group Ltd.

EMGP 270, Aubervilliers

Located just outside of Paris in the town of Aubervilliers, EMGP 270 is a project of Icade, a French property investment firm, and the EMGP Real Estate Company. Opened in September 2005, the 107,000-sq-ft (10,000-sq-m) building is certified under France's HQE program (see Chapter 3).

"In the City of Light, Parisians can see the vivid spectrum of light emanating from nearby Aubervilliers," wrote Frank Hovorka, then the Program Director at Icade. "EMGP 270 is not only beautiful, but also provides a comfortable office working environment and sustainability as the first private commercial building certified under the HQE Offices program."[26]

Designed by the Paris-based architectural firm Brenac and Gonzalez, EMGP 270 rises seven stories above ground, with a two-story underground garage. A trapezoidal base contains ground-floor retail and serves as a platform for a six-story triangular-shaped tower. Each of the three façades varies according the street characteristics.

Located in a former industrial zone, the brick façade pays tribute to its common heritage. The brick walls come alive with 600 dynamically colored windows, varying in width and depth, in a palette of twelve colors. The range of colors and volumes is further accentuated at night by the colorful lighting display.[27]

"The color and light movement produces a distinct visual identification, visible from nearby Paris," wrote Havorka. "By day, the windows appear to diffract light. By night, each window is colored with light in five sequences."[28]

To ensure the health and well-being of 450 occupants, the building used a "health book" to specify all the building materials with the

7.48 Located in a Paris suburb, the 10,000-sq-m EMGP 270 is the first commercial office building certified under France's HQE program. Photo: Javier Urquijo.

7.49 To ensure the health and well-being of the 450 occupants, EMGP 270 has a "health book" that specifies the composition and location of all building materials. Photo: Jacques Le Goff. Courtesy of Ademe.

composition and location of each. Employees may also, by means of remote control, manage the atmosphere inside the building: light, heat, ventilation, position of the blinds, etc.[29]

Key high-performance features include:

- triple-glazed windows to enhance daylighting and reduce street noise
- north-oriented entrance for glazed side without air conditioning
- chilled-beam radiant space cooling
- workspaces with direct daylight access
- office space with user-adjustable air diffusers, temperature controls, and artificial light dimmers
- motor-controlled blinds with automatic control based on solar heat gain
- 47,500-gallon (180-kl) rainwater storage tank
- dual-flow toilet flush systems (0.8 gallon/3 liter and 1.6 gallon/6 liter) that use harvested rainwater
- airflow recycled by triple filters in two air-handling units before it is redirected to occupied spaces
- BMS with metering by component (with seventy-five sub-meters for energy).[30]

Lessons Learned

EMGP 270's energy consumption for heating and cooling, ventilation, hot water, lighting, and plug loads, at 228 kWh/sq m annually, is significantly less than a typical office building in France (380 kWh). However, the originally projected energy use was 120 KWh per square meter. One cause for the discrepancy is the fact that one of the tenants (a newspaper) occupies the building twenty-four hours a day, seven days a week, which leads to significantly more energy use than the originally projected occupancy of five days a week for ten hours a day.[31]

Additionally, the occupants are not using the heating and cooling system as designed. The team based the building's energy-use predictions around a 7°C temperature fluctuation with temperatures ranging from 66°F (19°C) in the winter up to 79°F (26°C) in the summer. However, the temperature is set to 71.6°F (22°C) in both summer and winter. Studies show that had the building been occupied and operated as predicted, it would meet energy-use projections.[32]

TABLE 7.25

Energy use, 2007[a]

	Annual use	Intensity
HVAC	1,295,238 kWh	130 kWh/sq m
Lighting	202,299	20
Individual electrical sockets (plug loads)	360,389	36
Miscellaneous	418,286	42
Total	**2,276,210 kWh**	**228 kWh/sq m**

Note: Miscellaneous includes the consumption of 900 sq m of shops and a restaurant on the ground floor, elevators, parking garage and façade lighting and small equipment.

a Frank Hovorka 2008, "Coloring Paris", *High Performing Buildings*, Summer, 2010. www.hpbmagazine.com/images/stories/articles/coloring%20Paris%20Nights.pdf (accessed November 9, 2011).

At a glance

Name: EMGP 270
Location: Aubervilliers, France
Completed: June 2005
Size: 107,639 sq ft (10,000 sq m)
Cost: €16.2 million ($24.9 million)
Distinction: HQE Office
Program: Commercial office building

Project team

Owner: ICADE/EMGP
Architect: Brenac & Gonzales
Project Manager: Meunier
Mechanical Engineer: Igeni, Thor Engineering
Structural Engineer: SCYNA 4

GERMANY

FEDERAL ENVIRONMENTAL AGENCY, Dessau

The Federal Environmental Agency (Umweltbundesamt) in Dessau does not resemble a typical government office building. The exterior is clad with polychromatic panels, while its serpent shape loops back on itself to surround a covered atrium. Completed in May 2005, this 428,263-sq-ft (39,800-sq-m) building is not only architecturally unique; it's also one of the highest performing office buildings in Germany.

Iconic buildings are not unprecedented in Dessau. The legendary Bauhaus was built there in 1925–1926 after it moved from Weimar. The Bauhaus remains an international icon of design and technology.[33] After the city was destroyed during World War II, most of Dessau was rebuilt in the concrete-slab style typical of the time and went on to become an industrial city of East Germany.

Founded in 1974, the Federal Environmental Agency is Germany's central authority on environmental matters. The Agency employs economists, chemists, biologists, and legal experts who work together to find solutions to environmental problems.[34] Formerly based in Berlin, the Federal Environmental Agency chose Dessau for a new headquarters building in an effort to revitalize the city, then saddled with a high unemployment rate.[35]

Designed by Berlin-based architects Sauerbruch Hutton, the building's façade is primarily responsible for its iconic image (see the interview in Chapter 5 with Matthias Sauerbruch). Horizontal strips of Bavarian larch wood cover the parapet and lintel areas. The glass panels between the window strips alternate between transparent and colored areas. The surrounding site inspired the colors used, with thirty-three separate shades. Nearest to the park, the panels are varying shades of green. Panels near an old brick factory, which is now the library, are dark red, lavender, and purple hues. Ochre, orange, and red-toned panels adorn the eastern façade, which faces a nineteenth-century residential neighborhood. The main building includes a café, auditorium, information center, and library.[36]

The four-story main building consists of a 1,520-ft (460-m) long, snake-shaped loop that serves as the office wing for the Agency's 800 employees. This floor plan reduces exterior wall space that would otherwise be exposed to the elements and favors gently curving corridors.

The ends of the loop converge at a large serrated glazed wall which serves as the main entrance. The forum, which is just behind the main entrance, is a crescent-shaped space that links the offices and public areas together. The covered atrium, located in the center of the loop, is a neatly landscaped area. Bridges cross the atrium at three points to connect the surrounding offices. Each employee has a private office with a window and the offices facing the atrium are the most sought-after.[37]

The Agency wished to create an ecological building with high standards of energy efficiency and renewable resource use.[38] The building's sustainable strategies include geothermal heat, solar thermal collectors, PV panels, and natural ventilation. Renewable energy supplies 9 percent of the building's energy requirements. As a result of its green measures and energy performance, the building was awarded a DGNB Gold certificate (the highest level) from the German Sustainable Building Council.[39]

The main building is a poured-in-place concrete frame with a flat-slab construction supported by two rows of edge columns. The exposed concrete ceiling provides thermal mass to hold heat and cold at the appropriate times of the year. The interior ceilings remain uncovered because ducts for electricity, data, and other cables are integrated into channels under the floor.[40]

Fitted with a glazed sawtooth roof, the atrium plays a key role in maintaining a comfortable indoor ambient temperature. During the cold months, the temperature in the atrium is about 22°F (12°C) warmer than the outdoors, which helps minimize heat loss from the offices. The atrium assists the building's natural ventilation in the warm months.[41]

A 2,475-sq-ft (230-sq-m), 32-kWp PV system is integrated into the glazing of the sawtooth roof above the forum and provides sun protection as well as power for the building. An additional 4,575 sq ft (425 sq m) of PV with 68 kWp output was installed in 2010. On the roof of the main building, 2,325 sq ft (216 sq m) of vacuum-tube heat-pipe solar collectors harness solar energy to help cool the building's server room, print office, and lecture theater, via an absorption chiller.[42] The chiller cools water to around 44°F (7°C). The chilled water is then transferred to a series of pipes that cools air which is blown across the pipes and into the rooms.

The building is mainly heated using a geothermal heat exchanger, the building's most significant energy-saving feature. The system contains about 5 km (three miles) of underground pipes and is the

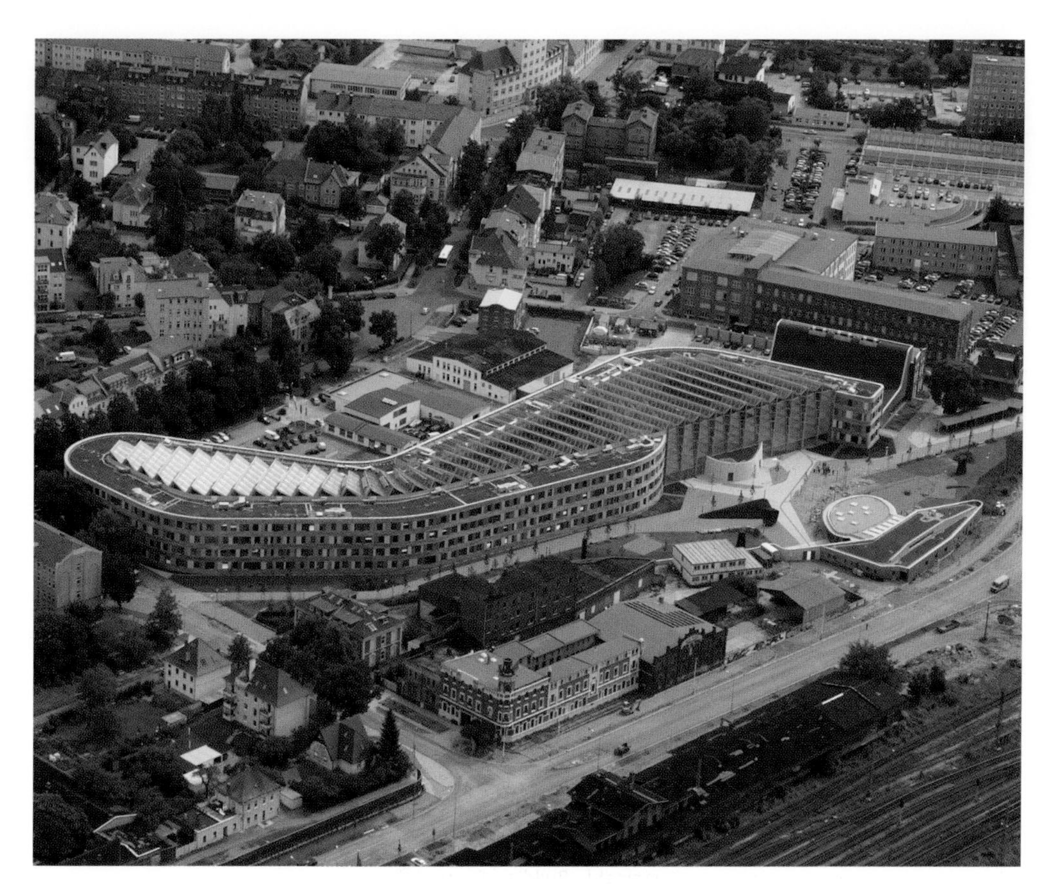

7.50 The Federal Environmental Agency headquarters in Dessau has a 110-m snake-shaped loop that reduces exterior wall space and creates gently curving corridors inside. Photo: © bitterbredt.de. Courtesy of Sauerbruch Hutton.

world's largest geothermal heat exchanger.[43] When the outdoor temperature is particularly high or low, the supply air to the offices is conditioned in the earth-to-air heat exchanger. The air intake and exhaust systems for the office area include heat recovery equipment with a recovery efficiency of 74 percent.[44]

In winter, heat is distributed throughout the offices through panel radiators with thermostat valves. The atrium and forum are not heated or fed with supply air in winter as they are not part of the insulated building envelope.[45]

In lieu of air-conditioning, the building is cooled using natural

TABLE 7.26

Annual energy and water use, 2007–2008[a]

	Goal	Intensity (2007)[b]	Intensity (2008)[c]
Electricity	15.9 kWh/sq m	27.5 kWh/sq m	22.9 kWh/sq m
Cooling (electricity)	2.0	(3.9)	(3.6)
Cooling (thermal)	3.5	(3.0)	(7.2)
Heating	44.7	63.1	62.8
Total site end-use energy	**66.1**	**90.6**	**85.7**
Primary energy	82.0	113.1	99.7

a Bundesinstitut für Bau-, Stadt- und Raumforschung (BBSR), April 10, 2009, "Abschlussbericht: Part A and Part C," 117–07–10–04–2009.

b Ibid., Part C, p. 111, Table C 1.3.

c Ibid., Part C, p. 112, Table C 1.4.

7.51 With a glazed sawtooth roof, the atrium helps to minimize heat loss from the offices and provides natural ventilation in the warm months. Photo: © Annette Kisling. Courtesy of Sauerbruch Hutton.

ventilation with operable windows and natural convection. In summer, all offices are mechanically fed with supply air conditioned in the earth-to-air heat exchanger. Natural night-flush ventilation removes heat that accumulates during daytime operations. A "thermal chimney" effect in the atrium draws air from the overflow openings in the corridors, which then exits the building.[46]

After the building was put into service, the owner identified a number of areas for optimization. For example, the building management adjusted the operating times for air-conditioning systems to account for actual occupancy. Additionally, the interaction between heat-recovery systems and the earth-to-air heat exchanger was optimized.

With these and other measures, the planned target energy-use values moved closer in 2008 to predicted levels, as seen in Table 7.26. Targeted primary energy levels were still nearly 22 percent greater than estimated originally.[47] Still, the primary energy use was below the "absolute best practices" goal of 100 kWh/sq m/year. For that balance, the energy demand/consumption for the processes of heating, lighting, ventilation, cooling, and domestic hot water were taken into account. Furthermore, the target value from the planning phase contains the use of a CHP generator fired with biogas which has not been erected. Due to the expansion of the PV system, the primary energy consumption is now even closer to the target value.

The Federal Environmental Agency building in Dessau exemplifies an architecturally iconic building that is also highly energy conserving.

At a glance

Name: Federal Environmental Agency
Location: Dessau, Germany
Size: 446,000 sq ft (41,000 sq m)
Completed: May 2005
Construction Cost: €68 million
Distinction: DGNB Gold
Program: Government office building

Project team

Owner: Federal Republic of Germany
Architect: Sauerbruch Hutton
Structural Engineer: Krebs & Kiefer
Energy and Environmental Engineer: Zibell Willner & Partner

7.52 The Heinrich Böll Foundation office has an annual site energy consumption of 98 kWh/sq m, less than half of Germany's code-mandated maximum. Photo: Jan Bitter.

HEINRICH BÖLL FOUNDATION, Berlin

In Germany each political party has a "political foundation" or "think tank." For the Green Party, it is the Heinrich Böll Foundation, named after a famous German writer and winner of the Nobel Prize for Literature. Their new headquarters building in downtown Berlin contains a conference center for 300 people and offices for the foundation's 200 employees.

The foundation gave the architects, E2A from Switzerland, the task of designing a landmark building that reflects the green values for which the Böll Foundation stands. The client's priority was to meet the highest ecological building standards in a cost-efficient design.

The building stands in a city park close to the Bundestag in Berlin-Mitte and occupies a small footprint, to preserve the largest possible open area. To meet the project's tight budget, the offices were simply

7.53 The 3,971-sq-m Heinrich Böll Foundation building contains a conference center for 300 people and offices for the foundation's 190 employees. Photo: Jan Bitter.

stacked. While the project's tight budget dictated a simple layout, the second floor was developed as the showcase of the building. This level, the *piano nobile* ("noble floor"), houses the convention center and cantilevers over the park below. From the interior, this *piano nobile* offers unobstructed views to the surroundings.

To assist in saving on fittings, furnishings, and materials, the architectural approach became an economic concept: everything that could be saved in the offices could be spent on the *piano nobile*. To create an efficient energy concept, the designers implemented only "little but innovative" technology. The building insulation is very efficient, with triple glazing. The energy concept depends on individual controls to allow users to regulate interior temperatures.

The building shows that ambitious architecture meeting both high environmental standards and strict economic targets is feasible. Careful oversight of the design ensured that ecological standards were met not only for daily energy consumption but also for the production of materials, technical systems, and equipment.

Energy Concept

The energy concept was developed by the Zürich engineering firm Basler & Hofmann and follows three basic principles:

1 Employ intelligent systems with minimal equipment to save resources and reduce installation and operating costs.

TABLE 7.27

Energy and water use, 2011

	Annual use	Intensity
Water	**4,742 kl**	**681 l/sq m/year**
Heat	255,351 kWh	36.6 kWh/sq m
Electricity	425,778 kWh	61.1 kWh/sq m
Total Energy	**681,129 kWh**	**97.8 kWh/sq m**

2 Energy is not lost until it leaves the building. Waste heat is recycled, using heat rejected by the data center servers.
3 Ventilation and cooling are as natural as possible and give users maximum control.

This concept puts the building in the ecological vanguard. As a result, the building uses only 37 kWh/sq m of site energy annually (based on gross floor area), undercutting the legal maximum in Germany by more than half.[49] A PV system on the roof provides an annual energy yield of 53,000 kWh.

The central atrium acts as a lung: using natural ventilation keeps work environments pleasant. The heating and cooling systems employ cooled water in the summer and reuse heat rejected from the computer network servers that would otherwise be wasted in winter.

In many office buildings, occupants are left to the mercy of technology. At this new head office, however, staff can decide the degree of ventilation and cooling for themselves.

Here, water alone is used for cooling, not air-conditioning equipment. Outlet slits ("trickle vents") run at window-sill level along the glazing in every office. The sill casing houses high-performance heat exchangers, through which water, at a temperature of 68°F (20°C), circulates in summer. A small ventilator inside ensures that cooled air is distributed throughout the rooms. Even when the temperature outside exceeds 86°F (30°C), the room temperature does not rise above 77°F (25°C).

The water for cooling comes from an adiabatic re-cooler in the basement. The re-cooler has cooling fins, with normal tap water sprayed on them. The energy used when it evaporates is drawn out of the fins, reducing the temperature of the coolant water inside to 68°F (20°C). The cooled water is then ready to circulate through the under-sill heat exchangers once more.

The system also makes effective use of recovered heat from computer network servers, which are kept in cool racks that remove heat from the equipment as does a refrigerator. This integrates the servers with the building services system and makes the waste heat available. Water flows into the cool racks at a temperature of 70°F (21°C), where it is warmed by the servers to 86°F (30°C). It is then fed into the heating system and circulated through the offices to keep them warm in winter. In summer, the servers also are cooled by an adiabatic re-cooler. For this concept, the Böll Foundation received a "Green CIO Award" in recognition of innovative projects that improve the energy efficiency of IT systems.

Keeping the air inside the building fresh requires a regular intake of outside air. Many modern office buildings function only with costly ventilation systems. The Böll Foundation building, in contrast, opted for using natural ventilation, in which the atrium works like a lung. In summer, the internal courtyard ventilates naturally through the open roof of the atrium. In winter, when the roof is closed, a ventilation system coupled with heat exchangers maintains a flow of fresh air into the atrium. This extracts heat from the exhaust air and uses it to warm the incoming supply air. The office spaces and internal corridors can be opened up to the atrium, creating a cross-current to provide the interiors with fresh air. Thanks to the atrium, this occurs without much of the heat loss that would otherwise be experienced in winter.

In this way, the Böll Foundation building demonstrates that when architecture, façade, and building services are closely coordinated during design, primary energy consumption can be reduced to a minimum. This energy balance takes into account not only the energy consumed in daily operation but also the embodied energy needed to produce the technical systems and equipment.

At a glance

Completion: May 2008
Construction: 2007–2008
Site Area: 22,700 sq ft (2,106 sq m)
Building Footprint: 13,600 sq ft (1,263 sq m)
Net Lettable Area: 43,000 sq ft (3,971 sq m)
Gross Building Area: 75,000 sq ft (6,968 sq m)
Building Cost: €12.5 million
Distinction: DNGB Gold

Project team

Owner: Heinrich Böll Foundation, Berlin
Architect: E2A Eckert Eckert Architekten, Zürich
Engineer: Basler & Hofmann Ingenieure und Planer, Zürich

SOLON CORPORATE HEADQUARTERS, Berlin

As an innovative company for the production of renewable energy, Solon is committed to sustainability and thus wanted an avant-garde "green" building for its new headquarters building in Berlin. Solon wants not only its products, but also its manufacturing to contribute to environmental well-being and climate protection. Thus the new headquarters was intended to serve as a showcase for high-quality architecture and green design. Completed in 2008, the building cost €47 (US$66) million. The work force consists of 320 people in the administrative wing and another 340 in the manufacturing section.

Founded in 1996, Solon is a German solar-energy company that produces solar modules, with subsidiaries in Italy, the USA, and Germany. In 2009, Solon's production capacity for solar modules was 435 (peak) Megawatts (MWp), and it actually produced 132 MWp. In 2011, it was one of the largest producers in Europe and employed 900 people.[50]

The Solon corporate headquarters is based on the concept of a "refined building shell," with interwoven interiors and exteriors. The high-tech envelope contains considerable insulation and high-quality, durable materials. The interior spaces are minimally enclosed, allowing for maximum flexibility. Electric cables and ventilation ducts remain unclad and exposed.

The building contains manufacturing as well as administration, because "one needs the other." The Solon plant in the western part of the site consists of a large rectangular hall (with 203,437 sq ft/ 18,900 sq m of floor space) with some administration offices and conference rooms along its southwestern side. The Solon administration building (which offers 89,340 sq ft/8,300 sq m of floor space), situated to the east, lets the sun travel around it during the course of the day, making optimal use of natural daylight. Between these two wings is the main entrance with a large glass atrium. From this atrium several inner "streets" lead to the various departments.

An exterior clad in corten steel lends the building a raw, unfinished touch. Three bridges connect the administration and the manufacturing wings. The glass, steel, and wood façades help create an open, inviting atmosphere.

The architects closely collaborated with the "energy designers." Their goal was to reduce energy consumption and CO_2 emissions by 25 percent compared to conventional office buildings in Germany. The high-performance façade and climate-engineering solutions helped reach this goal. The façade is made of wooden frames that contain both fixed floor-to-ceiling glass elements and operable highly insulated panels with integrated radiators and acoustic panels.

7.54 Solon's sloping roof supports a 210-kW PV system. Photo: © Myrzik and Jarisch. Courtesy of Solon SE.

The concrete slabs are thermally activated (with water tubes) and the windows have triple glazing for excellent thermal insulation. To protect the building from excess heat in summer, outer sunscreens and solar glass are used. The windows are operable for natural ventilation. Green courtyards allow for natural daylight and prevent excess heat in summer (via shading), thus reducing the energy used for cooling. All IT and building technology uses an innovative control system, making traditional switches redundant. Employees can regulate daylight, heating, and light by means of computer-aided touch-screen panels according to their needs.

In addition to the building controls, there is a flexible energy supply at each desk using "energy shuttles." These are batteries on wheels, powered by the building's PV system, that each employee gets filled in the morning and can see his or her energy consumption during the course of a day. They contain electric sockets for laptops and cell phones. For a thorough monitoring of the project, data are gathered from more than 10,000 points, also with more than 250 energy meters.

At a glance

Project: Solon Corporate Headquarters with integrated manufacturing plant
Address: Berlin-Adlershof
Client: Solon SE
Architect: Schulte Frohlinde Architekten
Construction Period: 2007–2008
Site: 360,064 sq ft (33,451 sq m)
Gross Floor Area: 352,141 sq ft (32,715 sq m)
Net Floor Area: 244,846 sq ft (22,747 sq m)
Distinction: DNGB Gold

TABLE 7.28

Energy use, 2009[a]

	Intensity	Intensity
Annual energy demand intensity (Office + production facility)		
Electricity	41.9 kWh/sq m	13,300 Btu/sq ft
Heating (from Biogas)	67.3	21,300
Total demand	109	34,600
Annual renewable energy supply intensity		
Electricity from PV on site	9.2	2,900
Electricity from CHP plant	71.3	22,600
Heat from CHP plant	148	47,000
Total supply	**229 kWh/sq m**	**72,500 Btu/sq ft**
Total exported (electricity)	38.6 kWh/sq m	12,200 Btu/sq ft
Total exported (heat)	80.7 kWh/sq m	25,600 Btu/sq ft

a M. Norbert Fisch, Stefan Pesser, Henrik Langehein, 2011, "Pushing the Envelope," *High Performing Buildings*, Spring, p. 49.

7.55 The glass atrium between the production facilities and the administration building serves as the main entrance to the 10,000-sq-m headquarters for Solon. Photo: © Myrzik and Jarisch. Courtesy of Solon SE.

7.56 *Below*: Offices with full-height glazing overlook the atrium, and suspended bridges link departments. Photo: © JSWD Architekten and Chaix & Morel et Associés.

7.57 *Right*: The 29,000-sq-m ThyssenKrupp headquarters building in Essen houses 500 of the company's 177,000 employees. Photo: © Christian Richters.

THYSSENKRUPP QUARTIER, Essen

The history of the city of Essen and the Krupp Corporation are heavily intertwined: At its peak, the company controlled almost 30 percent of the city's area. After World War II, the destruction of the Krupp Steel Factory had left behind a large wasteland in Essen. In 1999, Thyssen, another German steelmaker, merged with its biggest competitor to form ThyssenKrupp. The global conglomerate today employs 170,000 people across eighty countries. In 2006 it decided to build a campus to house its employees in its "spiritual home." The ThyssenKrupp Quartier is a high-tech, highly literal expression of the company's identity. After the merger, the combined company was headquartered in Düsseldorf, but the new corporate headquarters returns the company to its roots. In 2010, the new ThyssenKrupp Quartier, designed by JSWD Architekten of Köln (Cologne) and Chaix & Morel et Associés from Paris, was inaugurated.

The ten buildings planned for the campus (four new buildings have been erected so far) are part of an even larger urban design scheme called the "Krupp-ribbon" that will run west of downtown Essen on 550 acres (223 hectares) and will offer places to work, play, and relax. At the center of the new corporate campus and situated at the northern end of a large (64,582-sq-ft/6,000-sq-m) water basin, a thirteen-story, 164-ft (50-m) tall office tower, called "Q1," forms the central landmark. Built to house 500 employees, the building looks as if it was made of two large L-shapes hugging a large central atrium between them. Its 7,535-sq-ft (700-sq-m) glass façade on the north and south, creating a floating space between inside and outside, was designed by Werner Sobek, a famous German architect and engineer. Bridges span across the atrium for horizontal circulation. The campus is DGNB Gold-rated, which is the highest level in the German rating system.

The two big glass façades have ninety-six windows each, held in place by a fine steel cable structure. The façades in front of the office have slim steel profiles and operable vertical lamellas. The same set of elements shapes the entire campus. Together with a highly effective waste-heat recovery system, this geothermally heated structure uses 30 percent less energy than a standard building. Overall energy consumption is about 150 kWh/sq m/year.

The cluster of buildings is linked by repeating forms: the buildings are arranged around a landscaped campus with "Q1" as its centerpiece. Q1 is a 164-ft (50-m) cube, created by wrapping L-shaped volumes around a recessed glass wall. Separating these volumes by propping them on steel columns breaks the bulk, and the voids they create on the third and tenth floors are used for balconies.

The structure is dominated by 12-ft-high (3.6-m) steel sunshades on the exterior, which cover 86,000 sq ft (8,000 sq m) of the façade, designed specifically for the project. They are fixed on a central vertical frame and open and close depending on the sun's rays, reflecting light into the offices. The towering central atrium defines the internal space, with offices arranged either side of the void. Offices overlooking the atrium feature full-height glazing.

The façade is made of three layers: the thermal and spatial enclosure, made of glass; the inner, a textile for glare protection; and the outer, a sunscreen. Together with the geothermal plant, an efficient heat-recovery and thermal activation of the concrete floor slabs, they make for an energy-efficient sustainable building. The sunscreen is made of horizontal stainless-steel lamellas that are fixed to a vertical axis.

Controlled with the help of 1,280 electric motors, all elements take on one of these settings:

- closed (parallel to the glass façade)
- moving with the sun (variable and perpendicular to the sun)
- open (the horizontal lamellas move perpendicular to the glass façade).

The differentiation into trapezoid, triangular, and rectangular elements creates a façade that follows the sun. It was custom designed for the project and protects the building from overheating and also reflects daylight into the interiors. The architects specified vertical sunscreens in the shape of horizontal lamellas fixed to two concentric drive shafts. The matt underside of the lamella was designed after research at the Fraunhofer Institute for Solar Energy Systems that considered reflection, shadow, daylight, glare, and heat protection. Unpleasant "light gaps" were avoided. The façade elements can be moved even in wind speeds as high as 42 miles/hour (70 km/hour).

At a glance

Distinction: DGNB Gold

Energy Consumption: 150 kWh/sq m/year

Client: ThyssenKrupp AG, Essen

Architect: JSWD Architekten, Köln with Chaix & Morel et Associés, Paris

Overall Planning: ECE Projektmanagement GmbH & Co. KG, Hamburg

Completed: 2010

Site Area: 42 acres (17 hectares) total

7.58 Paul Wunderlich-Haus contains the world's largest collection of works by artist Paul Wunderlich, Eberswalde's most famous artist.
Photo: Martin Duckek. Courtesy of Ulm/GAP Berlin.

PAUL WUNDERLICH-HAUS, Eberswalde, Brandenburg

Eberswalde is a small town in the state of Brandenburg in northeast Germany. The German chancellor, Angela Merkel, would not usually visit a place like this, but she went to Eberswalde in 2007 for the inauguration of "Germany's most modern ecological service and administration center."[51] The name Wunderlich-Haus derives from the fact that the building also contains the world's largest collection of artist Paul Wunderlich's work. Located on the local market square and designed by GAP Architects from Berlin, the building is the seat of the county government.

About 500 people work in the building. The administration wing contains 204,500 sq ft (19,000 sq m) for offices, with the remaining 26,900 sq ft (2,500 sq m) for restaurants, services, and shops. The zero-emission building uses geothermal heat, vacuum-based insulation, and natural ventilation which is directed out over the green courtyard. An internal weather station measures temperature, rain, and wind and sends demands to the building systems. In summer, at nighttime the windows open automatically. The geothermal heating and cooling system, connected to heat pumps, comes from a depth of only 33 ft (10 m) below the building through 593 of the 850 piles that were drilled into the ground for stability reasons. During the winter, groundwater has a constant temperature of 50°F (10°C) and is used for heating. In summer, the system uses the same cold groundwater for cooling. The building closes an urban "wound" from WWII in the

7.59 The 21,500-sq-m Paul Wunderlich-Haus consists of four three- to four-story blocks with glass-covered courtyards. Photo: Martin Duckek. Courtesy of Ulm/GAP Berlin.

historic city center. Because trees had grown on the vacant site and people had gotten accustomed to the greenery, the client wanted the new building to be environmentally friendly.

There are four three- to four-story blocks with glass-covered courtyards. The goal was to keep primary energy consumption at or below 100 kWh/sq m/year. It was awarded First Prize and was part of the Program for Low Energy Building (EnOB) of the National Ministry of Economics and Technology of Germany. While the offices are located in the upper floors, the plenary hall, a museum, and 32,292 sq ft (3,000 sq m) of shops are at grade level. The shape, glazing, sunscreening, façades, and thermal mass were designed to combine low energy use with high user comfort. The design quality, the prominent site, low maintenance cost, and a good indoor climate were intended to motivate the building's users. However, the system was designed for a room temperature of 68°F (20°C), but it turned out that users preferred 72°F (22°C) in winter, so energy use for heating was higher than expected.

In each of the four buildings, an atrium acts as a thermal buffer. The façades are made of wooden sandwich panels with cellulose filling. Exposed concrete surfaces act as thermal mass. All windows consist

TABLE 7.29

Energy and water use, 2007–2010[a]

	Final (site) intensity, 2010 (kWh/sq m/year), estimated	Final (site) intensity, 2007 (kWh/sq m/year), calculated	Primary energy intensity, 2010 (kWh/sq m/year), adjusted for gross to net floor area[b]
Lighting	10	12	33
Heating	12	6	17
Cooling	4	3	8
HVAC drives (motors)	6	4	12
Fan energy	5	5	14
Hot water	1	1	4
Total auxiliary energy	10	10	30
Total energy	**48**	**41**	**88**
Water use	121 l/sq m		

a Günter Löhnert, Andreas Dalkowski and Sabine Dorn, et al. "Paul-Wunderlich-Haus: Von Der Bedarfsplanung Bis Zur Betriebsoptimierung: Eine Neue Mitte Für Eberswalde" ("Paul Wunderlich Haus: From Requirements Planning Through Operations Optimization: A New Center For Eberswalde"), *Xia Intelligente Architektur*, 76, July 2011, pp. 24–35. Ratio of primary (source) to site energy for electricity is given at 3 to 1 for this site. Thermal uses are reduced from primary to site use by a ratio of 2 to 1.

b http://iisbe.org/iisbe/sbc2k8/teams/SBC08_world/SBC08_Germany/SBC08_Germany_OFFICE_Paul_WundHaus.pdf, accessed January 27, 2012. Note that this list of energy end uses does not include plug loads, elevators, etc.

of triple glazing. A heat-recovery system recycles 80 percent of the energy used for warming. Narrow office wings promote natural cross-ventilation. Occupancy sensors detect if people are in the rooms and switch off the lights if there are no users in the area. The project's central square, the Pavillonplatz, was adorned with some of Wunderlich's sculptures.

In 2009, a 120-kWp PV plant with a total surface area of 6,888 sq ft (640 sq m) was placed on the building's south façade and the roof of the nearby parking garage. The façades have outer sunscreens and glare protection inside. The mix of daylight and artificial light can be adjusted on each employee's computer. The sunscreens are split so that daylight can still penetrate the depth of the rooms, even if the lower portion is shut.

The energy performance of the building was monitored by Dr. Tobias Häusler of the Technical University of Cottbus in 2009 and 2010. Every five minutes, data were collected from 300 points throughout the building and stored in a data base.

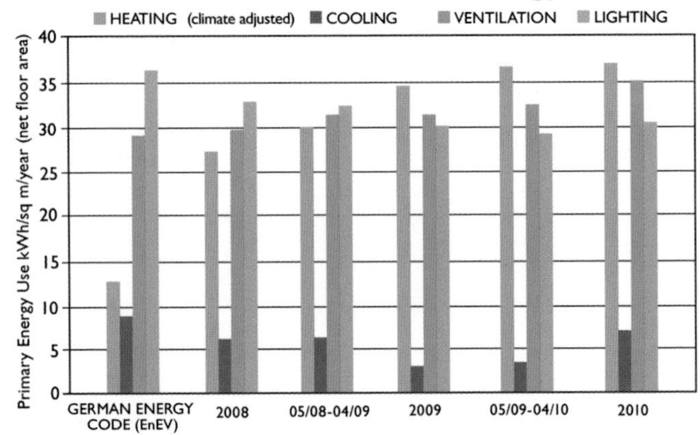

7.60 Paul Wunderlich-Haus energy use. Source: Günter Löhnert, Andreas Dalkowski and Sabine Dorn, et al., "Paul-Wunderlich-Haus: Von Der Bedarfsplanung Bis Zur Betriebsoptimierung: Eine Neue Mitte Für Eberswalde [Paul Wunderlich Haus: From Requirements Planning through Operations Optimization: A New Center for Eberswalde]," *Xia: Intelligente Architectur*, 76, July 2011, pp. 24–35.

At a glance

Client: Barnim Kreis (County), State of Brandenburg

Architect: GAP, Berlin

Gross Floor Area: 236,800 sq ft (22,000 sq m)

Completion: 2007

Cost: €23.9 million

Distinction: DNGB Gold

7.61 The SAP building in Galway was designed to optimize daylight penetration in Galway's cloudy climate. Photo: © Michael Moran/ottoarchive.com.

SAP, Galway

In early 2005, SAP, makers of business-management software, held a design competition for a building in Galway that would serve as the firm's new call center. However, SAP had not yet selected the site. In an effort to procure the lowest price for their new building, inclusive of the land, SAP held two separate competitions: one for the design and one for the site.

There were five sites under consideration, each at about the same latitude and longitude. The winning architectural firm designed a building that focused on energy optimization that could fit into any one of the sites. The new building is located near the Galway airport in a suburban business park; it is practical, but not utilitarian, and prioritizes energy performance.

"For the design of office buildings and many other building types where functionality is a primary concern, once you know where on Planet Earth (from a latitude and longitude point of view) the building is going to go, you can design the building completely based on climatic conditions and functional requirements," said architect Merritt Bucholz of Bucholz McEvoy Architects, Dublin. "You may not design an art gallery this way for example, but on the other hand, if you want a low-energy office building, it's a pretty good [method] because the building is defined by its functionality both in terms of environment and economic feasibility. In this case, it was financially very advantageous to do it this way."[52]

SAP's goals for the building included a balanced environment for employee comfort and a space that used a reduced amount of energy from non-renewable resources. The design-build contract required a simple approach to the main structural frame, while maximizing transparency. The building's form started with concrete-frame in-situ columns and beams with precast slabs, all of which are exposed within and outside of the building. On the exterior, the concrete frame is filled in with cedar panels, windows and a brise-soleil.[53]

7.62 In the winter, waste heat is recycled and used to warm the incoming air via heat exchangers that are built into the façade. Photo: © Michael Moran/ottoarchive.com.

Light is one of the most important requirements for a project in western Ireland's cloudy climate. The building form optimizes daylight penetration. Windows on the east and west façades span floor to ceiling, and the vertical cedar brise-soleil helps to control solar gain. The office space is located in two three-story, 180-ft (55-m) long blocks, which are connected by an atrium. The office façades are oriented toward east and west to maximize daylighting and views to the outdoors.[54]

Although the building is filled with natural light during the day, the artificial lighting system plays a central role in the energy strategy because the building is occupied eighteen hours a day. "The lighting installation within the office areas is managed and controlled via a lighting control system that applies a series of scenes throughout the day," said Ian Carroll of IN2 Engineering Design Partnership. "The scenes devised by the lighting consultant are intended to create differing effects at different times of the day, raising and lowering the intensity and color tone of the artificial lighting, which in turn allows the output of the luminaires to be reduced, with a reduction in input electrical usage."[55]

Located between the two office blocks, the atrium is the exhaust air engine for the building. The atrium takes advantage of Galway's prevailing southwest winds and eliminates the need for mechanical exhaust systems. The semi-conditioned atrium is heated by spillover air from the offices and naturally ventilated through top and bottom openings. The structure of the atrium roof, a herringbone pattern with timber beams, shades the internal façades of the offices.[56]

"This has been completely driven by what I would call a highly technological approach to the environmental strategies," said Bucholz. "In this building, there's an architecture where form follows environment, and this is a pretty good example of it."[57]

A relatively young international staff of about 800 covers three shifts, occupying the building from 7 a.m. to 1 a.m. With a density of 65 sq ft (6 sq m) per person, the demands for both ventilation and cooling are high. The internal electrical loads are about 4.3 W/sq ft (46 W/sq m). Per-person fresh air supply rates in this high-density building are about 18 cu ft/minute (30 cu m/hour) to remove air pollutants and maintain a low CO_2 concentration.[58]

Ventilation and heating are controlled primarily by the exterior vertical louvers. Each louver block is equipped with an automatic

operable vent, which is controlled, together with the heating system, by the BMS. Inside the office space, the exposed thermal ceiling mass is cooled at night by cross-ventilation and buffers the internal and external heat gains during the day. The natural cooling potential of the nighttime lower-temperature ambient air is stored in the ceiling mass and used the next day.[59] Operable windows are also a key part of the ventilation strategy, and, at the same time, they encourage occupants to participate in the building's energy-saving goals.

Located on the west coast of Ireland, Galway has a mild, wet climate. Supplying heat in office buildings is a very simple problem in the country according to Bucholz, as the outdoor temperature rarely goes below 32°F (0°C). The biggest issue concerning heating (particularly in a building with high envelope integrity) is managing the heat that's generated inside the building by people, lights, and computers.[60]

In the wintertime, that heat is recycled and used to warm the incoming air via heat exchangers built into the façade. One hundred fan units are integrated into the louvers and controlled by the BMS. They mix fresh ambient air with the return air to supply 57°F to 64°F (14°C to 18°C) air to the workspaces. The building is equipped with two standard condensing gas boilers that supply additional heat when necessary. In the summertime, the fan units bring cool air into the building during the night flush.[61]

For 2009 and 2010, average energy use in this eighteen-hour-per-day, seven days-per-week facility was 168 kWh/sq m, which is an excellent result, given the cool climate, intensive computer and lighting energy use, and a duty cycle nearly twice that of a typical office building.

Architect Bucholz described the integrated design process for SAP Galway:[62]

The building's form derives almost completely from the environmental performance [criteria] taken together with the building's intended function. The decision to use environmental performance and climate as the primary "context" for the building stems from the fact that there were five potential sites for the building. The building therefore had to fit and be viable in any of five different sites. Given that the architects had to design the building without really knowing exactly which site was going to be chosen, they ranked the constraints such that environmental performance was the primary consideration. The latitude and longitude of each of the sites was the primary context for the building. In a way, that's why the building doesn't align with the road.

That means, for example, the orientation of the building, the width, depth, and height of the office accommodation box, the decision to have the atrium (the ventilation lung), the "exhaling" space for building, the exposed concrete slab, the design of the façade, daylighting, and so on, were studied very much from the environmental strategy viewpoint.

The area in which the low-energy goals were engaged with the architecture was at the level of the building's intended use. The function of the building is a service and support center for a software product. One of the big constraints was that the employees' role in controlling their internal environment was restricted. Normally in low-energy buildings, I work [directly] with the people who are going to use the building. It's kind of like treating it as if it was their house, so they feel comfortable opening the windows and operating the building in the same way that they feel comfortable about operating their homes. This approach tunes them into what's going on around them. In this manner, a building's inhabitants are less likely to develop an "entitlement" attitude toward using the building, where the building automatically performs, as if it were empty or somehow not intended for humans. Making people feel like participants and, above all, in control of their environment, is an important aspect of building design.

In this case it was hard to do that in every respect because of the nature of the work going on in the building. The building's users serve several time zones from Eastern Europe to the West Coast of the USA and parts of South and Central America. The building has a very long workday. The nature of the work is highly controlled, and therefore the level of automation in the building for the natural ventilation systems had to be higher than it would be in a building where the employees were engaged with operating the environmental controls. That constraint led to the development of a decentralized heat-recovery unit which was built into the façade bays. This unit essentially recovers warm air from inside the office space and uses this air to warm the cooler outdoor air. To accommodate these units, the façade is composed of vertical vision-glass panels and vertical cedar louvers at 5-ft (1.5-m) intervals. The cedar vertical louvers are divided into three sections; in the top third is the heat-recovery device, in the middle third is a vent that users can open themselves for comfort control, and in the bottom third is the radiator. Looking from the outside, behind each vertical louver bay there's an orange panel on the bottom third, and the rest of it looks like a louver from the outside.

Essentially, the shape of the building was something that the architects worked very closely with the engineers on from the very beginning of the project. Even in the conceptual design phase, the environmental engineers, Transsolar, worked with the architects, evaluating and testing their conceptual sketches and helping them understand which strategies were best from an energy performance point of view.

Heating is a very simple issue in Ireland because ambient temperatures aren't that low. In the wintertime, it rarely goes below 32°F (0°C). In the summertime, it rarely goes over 65°F (18° C). The average temperature is in the high 40s, both in the winter and in the summer, pretty much interchangeably. In essence, a standard hot-water heating system with conventional radiators is heating the place, but it is not used during much of the year.

Annually, the biggest source of heat gain is from people, lights, and computers. With high envelope integrity (meaning the façade is very airtight), the biggest heating load is the heat generated inside the building. It is recycled to heat the air introduced from the outside with heat exchangers that are built into the façade. In low-energy buildings, Bucholz works with the building fabric, with opening sections in the building's façade, and with the different types of occupants within the building. In this case, the building's occupants speak a variety of languages, come from all over the world, and have very different ideas about comfort. According to Bucholz, Scandinavians start complaining when the temperatures rise above 65°F (18°C), whereas Brazilians don't mind if the temperature is 75°F (24°C). These cultural differences, in terms of how people perceive temperature, have a big impact on the strategies that a designer might employ during different times of the year to make everyone comfortable.

Lessons Learned

"Most of what we learned has to do with what happens after the building is handed over to the client and they start using it," said Bucholz. "There's a process by which new buildings must be seasonally commissioned and brought into balance with the natural environment on one hand and with the use of the building on the other."[63]

The building is meeting its energy consumption targets, and occupants report satisfaction with the space. However, there were a few initial operational issues. Quickly rising temperatures in the summertime, for example, required the facilities team to install blinds on the windows and manually open vents to increase airflow.[64]

"The reality is that until you've been in a building for the four seasons, it's only then you truly know how the building works," said David Myers, of construction and property consultancy Gardiner & Theobald, which provided surveying services. "The expectation seems to be you walk into the building and it's all working perfectly on day one."[65]

Bucholz agrees but believes that human interaction is essential for today's high-performance buildings. "Environments are something people create, not something they're given. We cannot take this thing for granted; environment, temperature, climate. We cannot say, 'OK, I expect this to happen with no action from me,' nor can we say buildings are automatically functioning environments; there is an important reciprocity at work between form and use in the best low energy architecture. People have to engage with an environment that engages them."[66]

TABLE 7.30

Energy and water use, 2009/2010 average

	Annual use	Intensity
Electricity	580,125 kWh	96.7 kWh/sq m
Gas[a]	429,296 kWh	71.5 kWh/sq m
Total	**1,009,421 kWh**	**168 kWh/sq m**
Water use (8/09–8/11)	8179 kl	681 l/sq m/year

Note: Building use is 18 hours per day.

a Conversion at 7.08 l/kWh for LPG, www.carbontrust.co.uk/cut-carbon-reduce-costs/calculate/carbon-footprinting/pages/conversion-factors.aspx, accessed January 12, 2012.

At a glance

Name: SAP Galway

Location: Galway, Ireland

Size: 64,583 sq ft (6,000 sq m)

Program: Corporate office

Project team

Owner: SAP Ireland

Architect: Bucholz McEvoy

Climate Engineer: Transsolar

TNT EXPRESS HEADQUARTERS (TNT CENTRE), Hoofddorp

According to Architect Paul de Ruiter, the priority of this energy-positive building is "connectivity, comfort and health of the building's users."[67] The new headquarters of Dutch courier giant TNT Express is the beginning of a new era in truly sustainable Dutch corporate buildings. The building's sustainability was recognized by both the LEED Platinum certification and the Dutch GreenCalc+ system with a score of 1,005 points. TNT Express is the first zero-emissions freight company in the world. The company's "Planet Me" environmental program was the point of departure for the TNT Centre, which aims to improve the carbon-emissions efficiency of all TNT's activities. Before the construction of the new TNT Centre, TNT's buildings were responsible for 20 percent of the company's CO_2 emissions. The new building, with five office floors containing more than 600 workplaces, is emission-free. According to the company, the design reduces commuting, lowers operational costs, improves its reputation, increases staff commitment, and creates modern, efficient workplaces.

The "Green Team"

TNT started its search for a "landlord" in 2007. The developers, OVG Real Estate and Triodos Bank, responded to TNT's initiative. In 2008, TNT (number one on the Dow Jones Sustainability Index), Triodos (the most sustainable bank), and OVG (the most sustainable developer) formed a "green team," also involving the engineer and

7.63 The TNT Centre comprises two six-story volumes. Stepped terraces connect the bottom three floors, and bridges link the top three floors. Photo: Alexander Berge.

contractor. Contractually, OVG and Triodos Bank entered into a long-term relationship with TNT as a client, to guarantee meeting sustainability objectives. An innovative contract set out design, build, finance, maintain, and operate components, all based on sustainable performances. The contract's long-term approach required an integral approach to the design, as the only way the consortium could guarantee all sustainability outcomes. A green lease contract was drawn up as a performance contract, in which the consortium and TNT laid down agreements for achieving the building's energy-saving and environmental objectives. OVG set up its own energy company, the Green Machine, to supply energy to TNT at a fixed fee per square meter, a performance contract unique for the Netherlands.

Ratings

The TNT Centre achieved among the highest GreenCalc+ scores in the Netherlands (1,005 points). It also received a Dutch A+++ energy label and a LEED for Core and Shell Platinum certificate. GreenCalc+ is a tool to chart the sustainability of a building. The GreenCalc+ environmental index shows at a glance whether a building is sustainable. Buildings that score 750 points or more achieve the highest energy label category: A+++.

Architecture

The 185,680-sq-ft (17,250-sq-m) building is open and transparent, with a U-shaped main volume of six floors surrounding an atrium. This atrium forms the central space and functions as the primary meeting area. The building backs on to the water zone with a walking trail on the Geniedijk (a dike that circumnavigates the city). The open "front" and entrance faces the future office park of Beukenhorst-Zuid in Hoofddorp (Amsterdam area).

On the design's west side (the Geniedijk), stepped terraces connect the bottom three floors of the two volumes, and connecting bridges link the top three floors. The connections also form places for users to meet. On the east side (the Taurusavenue) both main volumes are connected by a third, suspended volume.

The orientation of the atrium within the building allows daylight to penetrate in the best way. The atrium and entrance are closely connected; the stepped terraces invite users to walk up to the other floors and to meet up with each other on the conference floor (reducing elevator use). The design includes smart sun blinds, natural ventilation, heat recovery from ventilation exhaust air, energy-efficient equipment and lighting, and thermal energy storage. The north façade is glazed; the south façade is half-closed to prevent it from becoming too hot in summer. Daylight can come into the atrium via slatted blinds. The atrium ensures that workplaces also enjoy daylight from inside.

The TNT Centre is transparent with its orientation and layout defined by the site, the urban setting, and the landscape. In the urban planning, logistics, and social sense, connectivity is a key concept for sustainability. Sustainability lies not just in the choice of materials, energy-efficient practices, carbon emissions reduction, healthy indoor climate, and flexibility in future use. A connective building enhances social interaction; it connects people and promotes professional and social contact. This is embodied by meeting places in the atrium that make this area the heart of the Centre. Staff can meet here and receive clients at a coffee corner, with opportunities to sit and talk in areas ranging from open to enclosed, from formal to informal, from large to small.

An imposing staircase links the ground floor to the terraces on the upper floors. On the five upper floors, there is room for activity-related workplaces and office space for the executive board. There is no fixed arrangement for each desk. Departments are allocated areas, which means they can expand and contract without any structural alterations. The changeover to flexible workplaces throughout the entire building reduces the floor area needed for the workplaces by 30 percent, saving considerable money in construction.

Open workplaces are combined with concentration workplaces, which also serve for small meetings. Both open and closed workplaces are designed for excellent acoustical performance. Between these closed meeting rooms, there is an area for open and informal consultation and meeting up. The atmosphere is that of a lounge, thanks to a large coffee corner with sofas, armchairs, and *ad hoc* workplaces. This is where department presentations are given and birthdays are celebrated. Connectivity was the guiding principle for the design. How is this focus on people put into practice? One way is to offer users all kinds of facilities that contribute to making work more enjoyable, combining comfort, communication, and cooperation. Stairs in the atrium, stepped terracing, and linking bridges all effectively encourage meeting up. Daylight penetrates deeply through the building due to the atrium and the glass façade, which faces the sun. Smart sun blinds,

7.64 The TNT Centre in Hoofddorp is LEED Platinum and Dutch Greencalc+ rated with an A+++ energy label. Photo: Alexander Berge.

zero-emissions materials, and natural ventilation (staff can open the windows themselves) provide a pleasant and healthy indoor climate. Despite the volume and the openness of the design, the interior is peaceful, almost hushed.

Interior Design

The selection of restrained colors—gray, white, and beige—give substance to the ambiance, as does the recurrent use of the basic materials. Interior designer Odette Ex said, "I love simple, sustainable materials, mainly because of their purity and authenticity. But to delve so deeply into their origins, environmental impact, life cycle, transport, and all other aspects was a revelation." [68]

Green Features

The Green Machine provides the TNT Centre with green power using second-generation biological waste. Periodic surpluses go into the power grid, while periodic shortfalls supplied by the grid. Excess heat produced by the BIOCHP and LTES systems is used to heat other buildings in the immediate vicinity. The private energy supply ensures that little energy is required from other sources. Any energy still necessary is generated sustainably by the building itself. Thermal energy storage in the water-bearing layers in the ground takes care of this. Summer's stored heat is used in the winter to heat the building; winter's stored cold cools it in the summer.

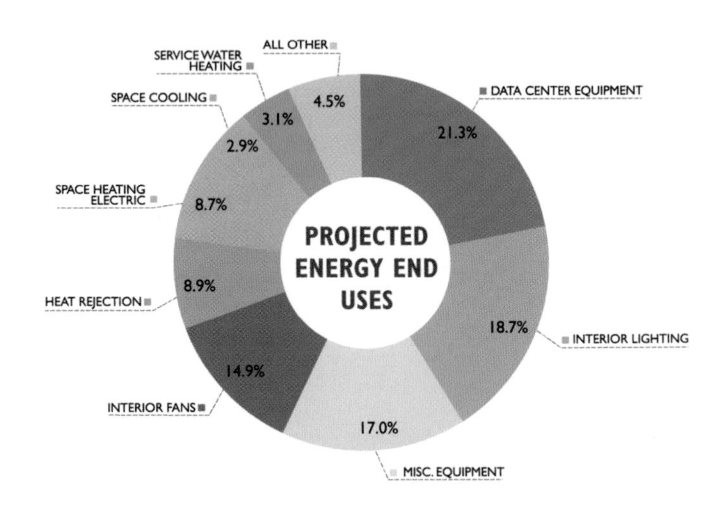

7.65 TNT Centre energy use. Based on the LEED credit submittal template, furnished by TNT Centre.

The TNT building is energy-positive, i.e. it produces more energy than it consumes. The Green Machine shares its surplus heat with the neighboring buildings occupied by Asics Europe and Schneider Electric. TNT's central energy-generation system comprises a long-term energy storage (LTES) system, a biofuel combined heat and power (BIOCHP) plant, and solar panels to produce electricity.

This noteworthy project contains the following significant sustainable features:

- 100 percent sustainable energy generated on site
- energy-positive building; surplus green energy is shared with neighbors
- building design 60 percent more energy-efficient than Dutch building law
- anticipated productivity rise of 1.5 percent, owing to healthy indoor climate
- 10 percent decrease in total cost of ownership, from reduced operating costs
- thermal energy storage (TES) with heat pump
- BIOCHP plant from biological waste
- electrical charging locations for cars and minibuses
- innovative sun blinds to optimize daylight access to building
- a healthy, fresh, and daylit indoor climate for every employee
- atrium provides interaction, energy-efficiency, and an open ambiance
- flexible work floor layout, making building suitable for future multi-tenant occupancy.

Energy and Water Use

- Total energy use (all from renewable biodiesel fuel): 1,968,200 kWh = 31 kBTU/sq ft (97.8 kWh/sq m) (includes parking garage); actual office building EUI is higher (at a calculated 114 kWh/sq m)[69] because nearly 30 percent of the space is parking garage, with a very low energy use intensity.[70]
- Electricity is supplied by 300-kW combined heat and power (CHP) plant using biodiesel and about 0.2 percent by solar panels.[71]
- Annual water use: 2,900 cu m = 4.1 gallons/sq ft (168 l/sq m)

At a glance
Owner: TNT Express
Program: Sustainable office building with parking garage
Distinction: LEED-CS Platinum
GreenCalc+ Score: 1,005 points
Energy Label: A+++
Occupancy: March 2007
Gross Floor Area: 185,680 sq ft (17,250 sq m) (not including parking garage)

Project team
Developer: Triodos–OVG Green Offices BV
Owner: Green Office ICV
Architect: Paul de Ruiter
Interior Design: Ex Interiors
Contractor: Boele & van Eesteren BV (Volker Wessels Group)
Installer: Kropman Installatietechniek
Building Services Consultant: Deerns Raadgevende Ingenieurs BV and Arup
Structural Consultant: Van Rossum Raadgevende Ingenieurs BV
Sustainability (GreenCalc+) Consultant: DGMR
Sustainability (LEED) Consultant: B & R Adviseurs voor Duurzaamheid
Building Physics and Fire-Safety Consultant: DGMR

SWEDEN

7.66 The Hagaporten 3 building in Stockholm has an energy use intensity of 135 kWh/sq m/year and is registered with EU's Green Building Programme. Photo: Åke E:son Lindman.

HAGAPORTEN 3, Stockholm

Hagaporten 3 is an office building in Stockholm certified under the Swedish Miljöbyggnad Green Building rating system. Skanska, an international development and construction company, completed Hagaporten 3 in October 2008. Skanska Sweden built the US$130-million project for Skanska Commercial Development Nordic (CDN), which will lease office space to external tenants. Hagaporten 3 comprises six above-ground office floors and an entrance level, which includes conference facilities and a restaurant. The building contains 323,000 sq ft (30,000 sq m) of office space and 215,000 sq ft (20,000 sq m) of underground parking for 550 vehicles.[72]

The building was CDN's first project to be registered with the European Union's Green Building Programme, a voluntary initiative aimed at improving the energy efficiency of nonresidential buildings in Europe. The project redeveloped an underused piece of land and advances sustainable urban planning. Design and construction choices were made from a life-cycle perspective; the project minimized environmental impacts during construction. The project also contributed toward CDN's energy-savings goals and raised awareness of more sustainable buildings and construction through the EU's Green Building Programme.[73]

The building is fuelled in part by renewable energy, sits under a green roof, and has a healthy indoor environment for the occupants. Hagaporten 3 was designed to promote social interaction and develop solidarity among employees. The office floors consist of an outer ring of open-plan office space and an inner ring with meeting rooms and communal space, located around a "light" garden at the center of the building. Communal areas in the inner ring are designed to encourage spontaneous meetings and casual social interaction. Office spaces in the outer ring are separated from communal areas to create a feeling of privacy, although the offices are open to facilitate employee collaboration.[74]

Each floor can be occupied by a single company, or many smaller companies with individual tenant entrances, and the office spaces are designed to allow tenants to customize and create their own unique space identity. The interior design also enables easy rebuilding to meet the future needs of tenants. The ventilation system, which circulates large volumes of air throughout the building, enables the future expansion of the building without a significant upgrade to the existing system.[75]

The use of natural light, high-quality ventilation, nontoxic construction materials, acoustic insulation, and minimal levels of electromagnetic radiation all contribute to a healthy working environment. Glass façades and the inner light garden at the center of the building allow natural light into the building and to all workstations. The ventilation system far exceeds the air-exchange requirements of the Swedish building code.[76]

Inside the building, materials with low-toxicity ensure the total VOC (volatile organic compound) levels are less than 200 micrograms/cu m, compared to the Swedish standard of 300 micrograms/cu m. The flooring and ceiling were manufactured with natural materials and

7.67 *Left*: About 30,000 sq m of office space surround a "light garden" in the center of Hagaporten 3. Photo: Äke E:son Lindman.

TABLE 7.31

Energy use, 2010[a]

	Annual use[b]	Intensity
Cooling	540,000 kWh	18 kWh/sq m
Heating	1,290,000	43
Service Power	510,000	17
Total Base Building	2,340,000	78
Tenant Power	1,710,000	57
Total Energy Use	**4,050,000**	**135 kWh/sq m**

a Skanska, Hagaporten 3 Energy Use. PDF supplied by Jonas Gräslund on September 23, 2011.

b Maija Virta (ed.), in "HVAC in Sustainable Office Buildings," REHVA Guidebook No. 16, Brussels, 2012, p. 93.

wood oils. Low-VOC paints, approved by the Swedish Asthma and Allergy Association, minimize indoor pollution and adverse impacts on human health.[77]

The use of potentially hazardous construction materials was restricted, and every material was checked against Skanska Sweden's chemical rules and the BASTA system, an agreement within the Swedish construction industry to phase out substances hazardous to the environment and human health. As a consequence of BASTA compliance, the project used non-halogen lighting containing minimal mercury and specified non-bromide flame retardants throughout.[78]

The walls, windows, and glass façades are designed to reduce external noise disturbance from the nearby highway. Electrical junction boxes were intentionally separated from regularly occupied areas to ensure that electromagnetic radiation does not exceed 10 volts per meter.[79]

Hagaporten 3 consumes 25 percent less energy than conventional office buildings in Sweden, reducing operating costs for tenants and raising the market value of the property. Space efficiency in Hagaporten 3 averages 160 sq ft (15 sq m) per employee, which creates further value for tenant companies.[80]

Hagaporten 3 consumes 12.5 kWh/sq ft (135 kWh/sq m) of energy for heating, cooling, and operational electricity annually, with tenant lighting and power demand constituting about 45 percent of total energy use.[81] The ventilation system is equipped with a low-speed, high-efficiency air-handling unit, a surplus-heat storage system, and an efficient heat-recovery system that recycles approximately 70 percent of the heat energy from outgoing air. (Additionally, the building is heated and cooled by district heating and cooling systems, which are more efficient than building-specific systems.)

The windows are highly insulated to minimize heat loss during cold weather and are tinted to reflect approximately 85 percent of radiation from the sun and to reduce solar heat gain during summer operation. Energy-efficient elevators and low-energy lighting were installed, and occupancy sensors control lighting in spaces not regularly occupied. Energy supplied to Hagaporten 3 produces 4.5 kg/sq m of CO_2 annually, about half the amount created by the average office building in Sweden.[82]

The electricity and district heating and cooling supplied to Hagaporten 3 are environmentally certified and sourced from renewable energy sources. The building is supplied with 100 percent hydroelectric power. District heating is generated from treated wastewater and hot-water boilers, which are primarily fueled by wood briquettes and pine oil. District cooling is generated from chillers and cool water from the Baltic Sea.[83]

The building has a drought-resistant sedum green roof, which reduces runoff during wet weather by absorbing water. The roof also provides additional insulation, creates wildlife habitat, absorbs atmospheric pollution, and extends the life span of the roof by protecting the roof surface from UV light.[84]

According to the company, "Skanska is determined to be the world's leading green project developer and contractor." With high-performance projects around the world, Hagaporten 3 is just one of Skanska's projects in Sweden. Skanska believes that, "The striking architecture and energy efficient nature of Hagaporten 3 may strengthen a tenant company's brand."[85]

At a glance

Name: Hagaporten 3

Location: Stockholm, Sweden

Size: 323,000 sq ft (30,000 sq m)

Completed: October 2008

Cost: US$130 million

Distinction: Miljöbyggnad Green Building Gold level and EU Green Building Programme

Program: Commercial office

Project team

Owner: Skanska Commercial Development Nordic

7.68 *Right*: The 92,000-sq-ft Eawag Forum Chriesbach in Dübendorf uses 75 percent of the energy of a typical office building.
Photo: Eawag – aquatic research.

EAWAG FORUM CHRIESBACH, Dübendorf

Forum Chriesbach, a 92,000-sq-ft (8,533-sq-m), five-story office building in Dübendorf, Switzerland, uses only as much energy as a typical residence, even though it is forty times larger. Occupied by Eawag, the Swiss Federal Institute of Aquatic Science and Technology, the building was designed to be a place for researchers and scientists to learn, study, teach, and, most importantly, collaborate.

Eawag is an international research institute committed to the ecological, economic, and socially responsible management of water. Naturally, one of the Institute's objectives for its new building was to incorporate the best water-management practices. The building is named after the Chriesbach stream, which flows to the north of the building. *Bach* is German for brook or stream, and a *forum* is a meeting place for discussion. Thus, the name "Forum Chriesbach" not only signifies the location of the building but is also a fitting name for a collaborative knowledge center focused on water science.[87]

Eawag is concerned not only with water, but with all natural resources. Additional requirements for the new building included:

- Energy, materials, land, and funds should be handled frugally.
- Energy use must be minimized.
- Renewable energy sources must be utilized.
- Room temperatures should be 66°F (19°C) minimum and 79°F (26°C) maximum.
- Rainwater must be collected and used.
- Urine must be collected separately from wastewater and solids.
- The site must be landscaped as naturally and integrated with the Chriesbach as appropriately as possible.[88]

When planning the building, the construction techniques and technology selected pushed available systems to their limits. For example, the building uses only one-third of the energy of a conventional building, and the office areas are not conditioned by conventional HVAC systems. Rainwater is used for flushing toilets, and a sophisticated sanitation system was installed with urine-separating NoMix toilets.[89]

Designed by Bob Gysin + Partner (BGP Architects), the interior of Forum Chriesbach is organized into various functional zones, grouped around a full-height atrium. Cantilevered conference pods hover over the atrium. The main 2-m-wide staircase and transparent wall partitions link the building together and turn the atrium into a spatially expansive experience.[90]

"We laid out the interior spaces around a large, five-story atrium which functions as a village square where presentations, exhibits and events can be held," said Gysin. "This community space is open, flanked at each floor by glass parapet walls. In fact, a great many partitions throughout the building are in glass, which gives the interior its great transparency. So from the lobby you can see into the offices and meeting rooms, practically through the whole building. Orientation in the lobby is instant; you understand the building immediately. You can see the stairs leading to the corridors, leading to the offices around three sides of every floor. You can see who is there and who is not, who is in a meeting room, who is talking together in the corridors. And the corridors are three times as wide as normal corridors—we conceived them as places for communicating. Spontaneous, informal conversations are vital to the activities that go on in this building. The researchers like their informal meetings, and they feel comfortable in the building."[91]

In addition to providing office space for 150 employees, the floor plan includes a lecture hall for 140 people, seminar rooms, meeting rooms, contact areas on four floors with desks and seating areas, a joint library, and a staff café. "Researchers don't like to work in open-plan offices, so we gave them small offices for a maximum of four people," said Gysin.[92] Instead, the corridors between the atrium and offices are designed to be collaborative spaces with seating for spontaneous meetings.

The building interior is designed for flexible room configurations. "The term 'sustainability' has become a bit of a vogue word in recent years. But if you consider it seriously, it would mean that things we make quickly might not necessarily be the best in the long run," said Gysin. "A sustainable building is surely one that serves its purpose for a long time. In this age, in which no building type remains unchanged over the centuries, architecture should possess flexibility. Materials that are appropriate for a building designed to last a century are different from those for a building design to last only 20 years. But in either case, the materials must be suitable for recycling, or even better, up-cycling."[93]

The architectural scheme is based on the principle of "saving

energy rather than paying to generate it" and resulted in a low-energy building.[94] The sustainability strategy consists of three primary systems that are highly integrated and serve multiple functions:

- A multi-layered, super-insulated, light-modulating building envelope that incorporates emergency egress externally.
- A highly efficient HVAC system that relies on multiple passive energy sources.
- A full-height atrium that unites interior spaces, transmits daylight, and helps control the indoor climate.[95]

One of the goals of the project was to align with the vision of the 2,000-Watt Society, an initiative of the Swiss Federal Institute of Technology. The initiative advocates the reduction of each person's consumption to 2,000 watts, or 17,520 kWh annually.[96] According to the 2,000-watt program, energy consumption in office buildings should be limited to 600 watts per capita, or 5,256 kWh per person per year.[97]

Envelope

The box-like shape of the building may be traditional but the shimmering aqua façade is not. The appearance of the façade changes with the weather, time of day, and season. Composed of 1,232 blue glass louvers, the façade is a visual reference to the main concern of the institute—water—but is also a major contributor to the building's performance. Each of the glass panels is 9 ft 3 in (2.8 m) high, 3 ft 4 in (1 m) wide and nearly an inch (24 mm) thick. Each is laminated from two sheets of glass, one of which is light blue with a transparent dot-screen (frit) pattern. Considering Dübendorf's climate, the team tested varying shades of blue and sizes of frits to find an ideal amount of transparency for both daylighting and thermal gain.[98]

The active louvers surround the building like a second skin and adjust automatically to optimize temperature and lighting conditions while minimizing energy use. In synchrony, the motor-driven louvers rotate on a vertical axis in five-degree increments following the daily movement of the sun based on data from the building's weather station. In the winter, the louvers usually remain parallel to the sun's rays to allow for maximum solar gain. In the summer, panels angle to block direct sunlight while allowing daylight to penetrate the building.[99]

Atrium

The interior is divided into two climate zones: the comfort zone and buffer zone. Comprising offices, meeting rooms, and other work areas, the comfort zone is mechanically ventilated, with the temperature actively maintained at a comfortable level. The buffer zone, comprising the atrium as well as the adjacent corridors on each floor, has no permanent ventilation or direct temperature control. The design allows for greater fluctuation in temperature in the buffer zones. To allow this, the zones are separated by insulated glass partitions.[100]

7.69 Forum Chriesbach's interior spaces surround a large, five-story atrium featuring artwork inspired by a water molecule. Photo: © Eawag – aquatic research.

In winter, the building uses energy to heat the offices and other permanently used rooms, but not the circulation spaces in the buffer zone. The atrium is not only warmed by the sun but via the well-insulated comfort zone that surrounds it on three sides. It maintains a comfortable temperature year-round with almost no added energy.[101] According to a detailed study of the building, "the atrium plays decisive role in determining the temperature regime of the whole building."[102]

In summer, the building is cooled using night-flush ventilation. The atrium windows open to flush out the warm air and provide cross-ventilation. Motorized windows on both sides of workspaces—the exterior windows and corridor partitions—open to allow warm air to exit via the atrium and outside cool air to enter the offices. The incoming air cools the thermal mass (the interior concrete floors), which provides cooling throughout the day. The only energy used in the cooling process is the weather station, the control system, and the motorized windows.[103]

HVAC

With the exception of the ground floor (café, library, and reception area) the building is not mechanically heated with a typical (Swiss) hydronic radiant system. External (solar, geothermal) gains and internal loads (people, lighting, computers, and other equipment) generate enough heat to maintain a pleasant ambient temperature.[104]

A forced-air system uses geothermal, solar, and recovered energy to provide supplemental heating and cooling. A series of seventy-eight plastic ducts draw fresh air into the earth where it is preheated in winter. The air is then directed through the server room to pick up additional heat while cooling the computers. A heat exchanger extracts the heat, and the warm fresh air is distributed to the rooms within the comfort zone via insulated ceiling ducts. If additional heat is required, a 3,170-gallon (12,000 liter) thermal storage tank captures heat from the kitchen appliances and rooftop solar vacuum-tube collectors (which also supply service hot water).[105]

The PV installation on the roof provides 70,000 kWh of electricity annually, about one-third of the building's energy consumption (not including the computer servers). The solar thermal installation produces about 25,000 kWh annually, equal to the site's heating demand from the local area heating network.[106]

With a measured primary (source) energy demand of 98 kWh/sq m/year, the building is significantly below the required Swiss federal Minergie-P standard of 141 kWh/sq m/year.[107] Developed in 2001, Minergie-P is a more stringent specification, based on the Passiv Haus concept that originated in Germany to designate ultra-low-energy buildings.[108]

Water

Water is the main topic of research at Forum Chriesbach, and so of course the building incorporates an innovative water-management strategy. In fact, one building system is a component of current research. In addition to water-free urinals, the restrooms utilize NoMix toilets, which separate urine and feces. Urine is collected and drained into local storage tanks for research purposes. Men's and women's urine is even stored separately, to study the differences. Separate

TABLE 7.32

Annual energy and water use, 2007[a]

	Annual use (kWh)	Intensity	Primary Energy Intensity with servers and solar
Heating from network	63,971 kWh	7.5 kWh/sq m	7.5 kWh/sq m
Space cooling from network (excl. servers)	124	0.0	0.0
Gas for kitchen/cooling from network	14,000	1.6	1.6
Domestic hot water and heat losses	32,700	3.8	3.8
Electricity (excl. servers)	266,000	31.2	71.4
Embodied energy (Grauenergie)[b]		—	28.6
Server electricity (allocated to building)	43,000	5.1	11.5
Total site energy use	**419,795 kWh**	**49.2 kWh/sq m**	**98 kWh/sq m**
Add: solar thermal	26,439	3.1	3.1
Waste Heat Recovery			1.9
Net primary energy demand			**103 kWh/sq m**
Solar PV & thermal			23
Water use	**1,300 kl**	**152 l/sq m**	

a B. Lehmann, et al., op.cit.

b Based on 37.6 average life-span of building components, B. Lehmann, Ibid.

treatment of urine reduces loads on wastewater-treatment plants and makes solids treatment easier. Eawag scientists study practical uses for substances found in urine and test various urine-handling technologies for future widespread use.[109]

Collecting and reusing rainwater on the roof of Forum Chriesbach reduces potable water demand. Captured water is used for toilet flushing. Potable water is only used for preparing meals in the staff café, filling the water fountains, and hand washing.[110]

Adjacent to the building, a rain garden stores rainwater harvested from the green roof. The garden is also a triple-chamber biological system that conditions the water for use in toilet flushing. Eawag researchers are also studying new processes for treatment and purification of rainwater.[111]

Forum Chriesbach proves that a high-performing building is possible through innovative and progressive approaches using conventional materials and existing technologies. At a cost of 29.5 million Swiss francs (US$32 million[112], or $348/sq ft), similar to conventional Swiss offices of the same size, the building was also financially practical, especially considering the reduced operating costs.

Some may say that the architecture and technology at Forum Chriesbach tests the limits of what's possible, but Gysin disagrees. "Actually, there are no limits; at the most there are limit ranges. In geography, the transition from mountains to steppe to desert is fluid. On my first trip to Italy when I was 16, I looked intently out the train window to notice the change between Switzerland and Italy, but everything looked exactly the same on both sides of the border. Limits are artificially defined. This room [we are in] might have clearly defined limits, but as soon as we are outside this building, we talk about intermediate spaces and if we look up toward the heavens, space has no limits. We set our own limits ourselves."[113]

At a glance

Name: Eawag Forum Chriesbach
Location: Dübendorf, Switzerland
Size: 91,850 sq ft (8,533 sq m)
Completed: September 2006
Construction Cost: CHF 29.5 million
Program: Office building
Vacuum-Tube Heat Pipe-Type Solar Collectors: 538sq ft (50 sq m)
PV Power Plant: 77 kWp

Project team

Owner: Eawag, Swiss Federal Institute of Aquatic Science and Technology and Empa, Materials Science and Technology
Architect: Bob Gysin + Partner BGP
Energy and Mechanical Engineer: 3-Plan Haustechnik AG
Architecture and Energy Engineer: EK Energiekonzepte AG
Engineering and Design: Henauer Gugler AG
Electrical Engineer: Büchler + Partner AG
General Contractor: Implenia General Contracting Ltd.

DANIEL SWAROVSKI CORPORATION, Männedorf[114]

The Swarovski Corporation built its new headquarters building 12 miles (20 km) south of Zürich on the eastern shore of Lake Zürich. The office building for some 450 employees of the famous crystal manufacturer was designed by ingenhoven architects' international branch office in Männedorf, Switzerland. The transparent, all-glass façade resembles a crystal. The marvelous view over Lake Zürich was key for the orientation of the horseshoe shape of the building and the design of its façades. The building frames the view over the lake and the Alps. It was inaugurated in 2010.

Swarovski and its glistening crystals, with their "poetry of precision," fascinate people. This quality had to be reflected in the architecture. The attractive views shaped the design. The building's curved form allows for great views from anywhere within the building through floor-to-ceiling glass façades. The design goal was to support teamwork using high-quality open, transparent workplaces that are flexible and reversible. The upper floors contain an open office

7.70 The new Swarovski headquarters in Zürich houses 450 employees of the famous crystal manufacturer. Photo: Andreas Keller, Altdorf. Courtesy of ingenhoven architects.

7.71 The marvelous view over Lake Zürich was key for the orientation of the horseshoe shape of the building and the design of its façades. Photo: H. G. Esch, Hennef.
Courtesy of ingenhoven architects.

landscape with a close visual relationship to the actual landscape. The design supports informal as well as formal communication and a healthy lifestyle.

The design aims for ecologically sustainable, economic technology, providing a great climate and creative atmosphere in which to work. Underneath the raised upper floors, the ground-level floor contains the foyer with lounge, a restaurant, conference rooms, and workshops. Short paths of communication were designed to improve the workflow. The building is designed to fit in well with the surrounding site, while the transparency of the façade lends some lightness to the building. The garden terraces visually connect to the nearby vineyards, meadows, and orchards. The entry plaza is a welcoming gesture for visitors, employees, and clients. All materials and surfaces were chosen for good comfort and good acoustics. The largely open office floor plans maintain a balance between open group areas and more protected individual workrooms with transparent partition walls for highly concentrated work. There are wardrobes and "technik points" (with printers and copy machines) throughout each floor as well as so-called communication islands.

The water of the nearby Lake Zürich is used for heating in winter and cooling in summer, sharply reducing the energy used in and for the building. The building is one of the first at Lake Zürich to use lake water for heating and cooling, and the system is designed to supply a second building on site. Together with the façade, the building services, and the thermoactive systems, the building exceeds the requirements of the Swiss Minergie standard. The design also exceeds all other Swiss requirements for airtightness, daylighting, thermal insulation, high-quality glazing, and controlled ventilation. The heat pumps and the control system together use less than 25 percent of the energy they help save. The system is constantly assessed, and its function has improved over the first two years of operation. To complete the sustainability aims, the garbage in the building is separated, there are public bus lines and a commuter rail station nearby for workers, and the building materials were chosen for easy recyclability.

A detail was developed for the double-skin façade that allows natural ventilation of the offices. The inner façade has floor-to-ceiling triple glazing with a special gas filling. It comes in elements of 8.9 ft (2.70 m) in width and is self-supporting, not requiring any further vertical structure. Integrated into the ceiling there are electrically operated louvers that can open and close for natural ventilation. They alternate between air intake for the floor above and exhaust for the floor below (with a width of 4.45 ft [1.35 m]). For sun and glare protection there are moveable louvers (with a depth of 6 in [150 mm]). To protect the building against noise and storms there is an outer glass layer (VSG security glass), with natural ventilation in between. Filigreed steel brackets hold the outer glass layer at the top and bottom. The outer façade can be opened for cleaning and maintenance. Curved perforated aluminum sheets close the gaps between floors. The metal sunscreen outside the inner façade contains extra-wide lamellas to let in sunlight, while allowing for great views.

Light-reflecting white materials in the interiors bring daylight into the depths of the building. The lighting controls combine direct and indirect light and offer complete flexibility of the office layout. To improve acoustics, absorbing surfaces (tab-silent acoustic absorbers) were placed in cut-outs in the concrete floor slabs. They also are thermally conductive. This way, the ceiling can be used for the acoustic concept without compromising the thermal activation of the slabs.

TABLE 7.33

Energy and water use, October 2010–September 2011

	Annual use	Intensity
Electricity: heating, cooling and hot water	176,210 kWh	14.0 kWh/sq m
Electricity: lights	165,600	13.1
Electricity: pumps, fans, controls	136,900	10.8
Electricity: plug loads and computer server	459,500	36.4
Total energy use	**938.200 kWh**	**74.3 kWh/sq m**
Water use	5,720 kl	453 l/sq m

At a glance

Site: 92,096 sq ft (8,556 sq m)
Total floor area: 206,667 sq ft gross (19,200 sq m)
Conditioned area: 135,40 sq ft (12,620 sq m)
Capacity: 450 work places, 158 parking spaces, 30 bicycle parking places
Cost: CHF 61 million (US$57 million)
Construction: January 2009–July 2010

Project team

Client: Swarovski Immobilien AG
Architecture: ingenhoven architects international branch office, Männedorf, Switzerland
Structural Engineering/Façade: Werner Sobek, Stuttgart, Germany
Energy Concept: Thomas Baumgartner und Partner, Dübendorf, Switzerland
HVAC: Grünberg und Partner, Zürich, Switzerland
Building Physics: Mühlebach und Partner, Wiesendangen, Switzerland
Building Services: Bühler & Scherler AG, St. Gallen, Switzerland
Lighting (Artificial and Daylight): Tropp Lighting Design, Weilheim, Germany
Fire Protection: BPK Brandschutz Planung Klingsch, Düsseldorf, Germany

7.72 At 3 Assembly Square, more than 30 percent of the total building energy is supplied by renewables or low carbon-emission sources, including a biomass boiler. Photo: Martin Hopkins Partnership.

3 ASSEMBLY SQUARE, Cardiff, Wales

Located on the waterfront in Cardiff, Wales, 3 Assembly Square is a six-story, 66,000-sq-ft (6,132-sq-m) speculative office building. Situated near the Welsh Assembly Government building and close to the Wales Millennium Centre opera house, the building is part of the Cardiff Waterside master plan.

Completed in June 2009, the project received a BREEAM Excellent rating from the UK's Building Research Establishment (BRE).[115] The development was managed by Knight Frank and designed by Scott Brownrigg, in conjunction with Arup engineers. All in all, the building reduced its carbon footprint 31 percent below UK building regulations in terms of energy consumption.[116] The high-performance design at 3 Assembly Square includes biomass-fueled boilers, efficient and well-controlled lighting, as well as an active chilled-beam cooling system with exposed thermal mass.[117]

"The team used the BREEAM tool as a methodology to measure our success in terms of reaching our environmental goals for this project," said Paul Webber, a director at Arup. "It became a real focus

7.73 The 22-m-high atrium offers views to Cardiff Bay. Photo: Martin Hopkins Partnership.

for the whole team including the client. The success of this team approach is illustrated by the project gaining BREEAM Excellent well in advance of practical completion."[118]

Key project objectives were:

- creating prime office accommodations within the Cardiff Waterside development
- achieving BREEAM Excellent status without compromising commercial viability
- maximizing the beneficial use of the site
- providing an end product that would meet tenant requirements
- ensuring the project will be "future-proofed" for performance in terms of investment as well as income return
- utilizing the setting's unique resources and attributes, e.g., using sunlight and the sea views to enhance the quality of the office environment
- enhancing the built environment around Cardiff Bay.[119]

Combined with the rain-screen cladding, flat roofs give the building a contemporary appearance. Coated aluminum windows, aluminum shading, and timber spandrel panels provide visual interest. The structural frame is concrete, which was left exposed to provide thermal mass to assist the environmental cooling systems. A bayside curtain wall opens out to the views from the building.[120]

The 72-ft (22-m) high atrium features a staircase and elevators designed as a single sculptural form and an art installation celebrating

TABLE 7.34

Predicted energy use (full occupancy)[a]

	Annual use	Intensity (net area)	Intensity (net area)
Electricity	934,335 kWh	14.2 kWh/sq ft	
Biomass	341,250	5.2	
Total	**1,275,585**	**19.4**	**209**
UK Good Practice Benchmark[b]	2,630,880	39.5	425
Estimated reduction in energy use	51%		

a Knight Frank consultants, "Energy Performance Analysis," June 7, 2011. Based on the building being fully let (leased). The biomass (wood) boiler is considered carbon-neutral in the UK.

b Ibid., at p. 5.

TABLE 7.35

Actual energy use, 2010 (30% occupied)

	Total energy use	Intensity (net area)	Intensity (net area)
Electricity	674,070 kWh	10.2	
Gas	84,633	1.3	
Biomass (wood) boiler	47.3 tonne (metric) 236,689 kWh[a]	3.6	
Total	**995,392 kWh**	**15.1 kWh/sq ft**	**163 kWh/sq m**

a At 18,000 MJ/tonne and 0.278 kWh/MJ, www.biofuelsb2b.com/usefulinfo.php?page=Eerg, accessed November 22, 2011.

the local coal-mining tradition, in which 3,000 pieces of coal hang from vertical steel wires. The space and location of the artwork were specifically designed to encourage the general public to come into the building, and this access prompted numerous requests from the public to use the atrium for private functions. Glazed elevators are designed within an open shaft in the atrium offering panoramic views of Cardiff Bay. Each floor is designed as a barrier-free open space for maximum flexibility and maximum daylight.[121]

Meeting the project's sustainability and eco-friendly criteria required innovation in materials, engineering solutions, and future-management plans.[122] During the early stages of the project, a series of multidisciplinary meetings identified the optimum solutions to achieve the quality of design required by the client, the environmental credentials, and an office building that would be readily leasable and that would provide future-proofing against any environmental obsolescence.[123]

As a result, the team chose chilled beams for cooling. To support the chilled-beam strategy, the team selected a flat-slab concrete frame with exposed soffits. This allowed for a reduction of total building height while maintaining a floor-to-ceiling height of 10 ft (3 m). The exposed concrete soffit has a tight tolerance and needs no skim coat. The concrete mass helps maintain a comfortable and fairly constant ambient temperature during the day. To minimize the need for casting a large number of conduits and services into the concrete, the active chilled beams serve several functions including cooling, heating, lighting, and fire control.[124]

Three Assembly Square is heated using a biomass boiler system, further reducing the building's carbon emissions. Mechanical ventilation and cooling are provided via active chilled beams located on all floors, which contributes to flexibility in a multi-tenant commercial building.[125]

Nearly 25 percent of the total building energy will be supplied by renewables or low-carbon-emission sources, including the biomass boiler. This will also help to reduce the operating costs of the building. All spaces in the building are separately metered, which will allow separate tenants to closely monitor their own energy use.[126] The full-height glazed atrium is naturally ventilated and provides excellent views over Cardiff Bay. A rainwater harvesting system and low-flow fixtures contribute to water conservation.[127]

"Despite current economic conditions, there remains a flight to quality buildings amongst tenants," said Ben Bolton, with Cooke and Arkwright, a joint agent for the project. "With its waterfront location, easy accessibility and great amenities, 3 Assembly Square offers the best Grade A space available in the Welsh capital at the moment, and we're confident it'll continue to attract businesses and organizations looking to make a statement [about environmental responsibility]."[128]

At a glance

Name: 3 Assembly Square
Location: Cardiff Bay, Wales
Size: 66,000 sq ft (6,132 sq m) net leasable area; 81,346 sq ft (7,560 sq m) gross internal area[129]
Cost: £13 million (US $19.5 million)
Completion: June 2009
Distinction: BREEAM Excellent (Score: 75.52 percent)
Program: Commercial office

Project team

Owner: Cardiff Bay Partnership
Asset and Development Manager: Knight Frank
Architect: Scott Brownrigg
Mechanical, Electrical, Structural Engineer: Arup
Project Manager: Michael Edwards & Associates
Contractor: BAM Construction Ltd.

THE SUTTIE CENTRE FOR TEACHING AND LEARNING IN HEALTHCARE, University of Aberdeen, Aberdeen, Scotland

The Suttie Centre for Teaching and Learning in Healthcare is located on the University of Aberdeen Foresterhill Campus in Aberdeen. A joint project of the National Health Service Clinical Skills Training and the University of Aberdeen's Department of Anatomy, the Suttie Centre serves as a medical education and clinical teaching center.

The building objectives as outlined by Aberdeen University included:[130]

- becoming the most significant healthcare-related education center in the north of Scotland
- providing a focus for teaching and learning, an attractive place to learn, study, meet colleagues, and hold meetings
- a light and airy ambience; elegant, timeless, and fresh
- complying with the complexities of anatomy education, which is licensed by the Scottish Government.

Completed in June 2009, the 70,000-sq-ft (6,500-sq-m), five-story building is configured in a doughnut shape with a 220-seat lecture theater at ground level. Designed by the Edinburgh office of London-based Bennetts Associates Architects, the project features a centrally located atrium that provides daylighting and a social focus to the building. Two cores with elevators, stairs, and restrooms are located

7.74 *Above*: The Suttie Centre for Teaching and Learning in Healthcare is a 6,500-sq-m, five-story building on the University of Aberdeen campus in Aberdeen, Scotland. Photo: © Keith Hunter.

7.75 *Right*: Two full-sized figures composed of MRI scans and a light work based on the Hippocratic Oath are suspended in the central atrium. Photo: © Keith Hunter.

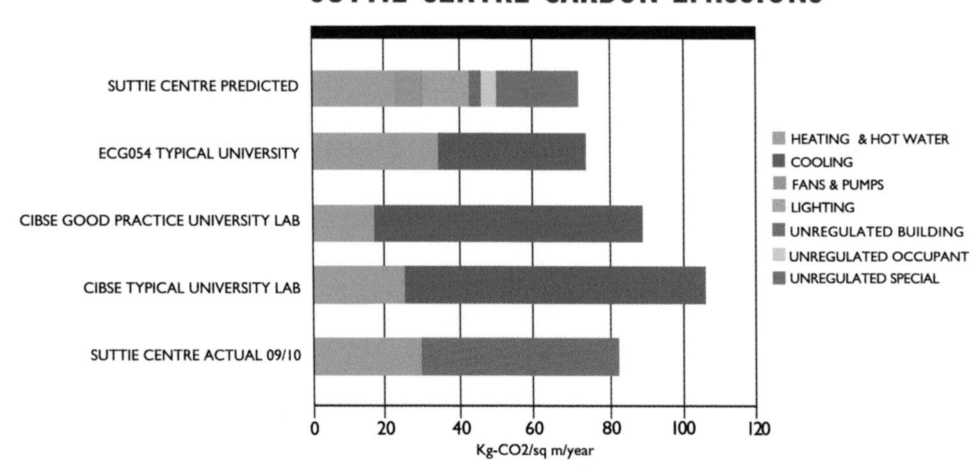

7.76 Suttie Centre carbon emissions, compared with other standards. CIBSE standards are from The Chartered Institution of Building Services Engineers, a UK organization, ECG 054 is a UK national standard for "Energy efficiency in further and higher education," dating from 1997. Source: Bennetts Associates Architects.

on the north and south sides of the atrium. Laboratories and teaching spaces occupy the east and west sides. The communal areas feature historic artifacts and medical-themed, commissioned artworks. Two full-sized figures composed of MRI scans and a light work based on the Hippocratic Oath are suspended in the atrium space.[131]

"Externally, the project's scale and materials remain sensitive to the site's context whilst also giving the building a distinct architectural identity that befits its specialized function and role within the University," according to Bennetts Associates Architects. "The use of sustainable, western red cedar cladding on the façade both complements and contrasts the grey Aberdeen granite of the surrounding buildings, allowing the institution to appear as a visual anchor that responds to and enhances its context. The envelope of the Suttie Centre is animated further with metal walkways and timber solar shading which adds depth to the façade and contributes to the project's impressive green credentials."[132]

The project achieved a BREEAM Bespoke (Custom) Excellent rating with a score of 76.2 percent, the highest score in the Bespoke category in 2008. "Bennetts has come full circle," said John Miller, a former director at Bennetts Associates. "Ten years ago we talked about environmental sustainability. Six years ago we started to make briefs more holistic—trying to add in social and economic aims as well as environmental ones. But three or four years ago we felt that it was a little trite for architects to talk about economic and social benefits when they were so hard to measure, and that maybe we should return to the environmental issues where we can set out to demonstrate the benefits."[133]

The high-performance approach for the Suttie Centre concentrated on passive design first, before turning to active engineering. The exposed concrete structure is part of the architectural expression of the building and at the same time the thermal mass helps regulate temperatures in the building. The building relies primarily on natural ventilation. Perimeter spaces are naturally ventilated via the operable windows. Cool air enters the windows, is warmed from the activities of the building, and then rises and is released through the atrium.[134]

The mechanical ventilation system incorporates high efficiency thermal heat recovery wheels, which remove heat from the exhaust air that would normally leave the building. The system transfers it to the supply air, preconditioning incoming air in the cool months. This reduces demand on the central plant's boiler.[135]

In the northeast of Scotland, heat loss is a common concern, both through air leakages and poor insulation integrity. To minimize heat loss, the team designed the façades to be elegant, simple, robust, and technically proficient. The building exceeds the original air-tightness target by 33 percent. "Do one window well and repeat it, and design simple sequencing and sealing plans," said Miller. The building's annual operational carbon emissions are 72.7 kg CO_2/sq m compared to 99 kg CO_2/sq m, the typical emissions output for university laboratory buildings. Emissions were reduced further with the introduction of a biomass CHP.[136]

A 60:40 solid-to-glass ratio was selected for the skin. The integrity of the building's insulation was assessed using thermal imaging surveys, which were carried out during and after construction. The independent testing company, IRT Surveys, said the building was "one of the best buildings we have ever surveyed."[137]

Thermal modeling also influenced the design of the solar shading on the south and west façades to optimize natural light, views, and solar heat gain. The solar shading consists of both timber louvers and open metal floors. The modeling also informed the optimum pitch of the louver blades, the size, quantity, and spacing.[138]

Other high-performance features of the Suttie Centre are listed below.

- A green roof planted with sedum covers the fourth floor and reduces rainwater runoff and increases biodiversity.
- The cedar cladding was procured from a source approved by Programme for the Endorsement of Forest Certification (PEFC).
- All other wood is from Forest Stewardship Council-approved sources.
- A rainwater-harvesting system collects, treats and recycles rainwater to flush toilets; low-flow fixtures further reduce potable water use.
- A low-temperature hot-water system provides hot water to serve perimeter heating.
- Natural ventilation and mechanical ventilation systems contribute to high indoor air quality.
- A campus-wide, biomass-powered, CHP plant provides a heat source and low carbon power to the building.[139]

"The Centre showcases the ability of the University to develop buildings where environmental concerns are given high priority throughout the procurement process," said Angus Donaldson, Director of Estates (Facilities). "From the reduction of energy demands to the use of systems which maximize natural energy resources, the design elements of this center set a high benchmark for future construction projects undertaken by the University."[140]

Energy Use

72.7 kg-CO_2e/sq m, energy use calculated as all electric: 169 kWh/sq m/year.[141]

At a glance

Name: The Suttie Centre for Teaching and Learning in Healthcare
Location: Aberdeen, Scotland
Size: 70,000 sq ft (6,500 sq m)
Completed: June 2009
Cost: £13.8 million
Distinction: BREEAM Award
Program: Academic medical building

Project team

Owner: University of Aberdeen
Architect: Bennetts Associates Architects
Structural Engineer: SKM Anthony Hunt
Services Engineer: K J Tait
Quality Surveyor: Thomas and Adamson
Contractor: Mansell Construction Services Ltd.

ASIA PACIFIC REGION

High-performance green building projects in the Asia Pacific region present different issues in locating and assessing environmental performance. Australia is highly organized, with a rating system (Green Star) nearly ten years old and nearly 500 projects already certified. Japan's CASBEE system, also more than ten years old, has certified about 100 projects. Language issues also presented difficulties in accessing project data, but this was offset by the help of Mao Meyer, a native Japanese speaker. Singapore's Building and Construction Authority helped find projects in that country. India adopted LEED but to date has certified relatively few large projects at the Platinum level, although that situation is changing quickly.

China presented considerable difficulties, primarily because of language, but we did locate a few LEED Platinum projects for this chapter and for Chapter 9, "Projects to Watch," which were willing to share data and photos. We are quite impressed with the green-building movement in China and expect it to be a major global player within the next five years.

In all cases, we diligently attempted to locate projects and, using a network of contacts throughout the region, to identify owners or consultants who could help access project data. That this vast and dynamic region is still under-represented in this book attests to some of the difficulties researchers have in accessing information from government, NGOs, universities, and the private sector.

ASIA PACIFIC

Australia

- 2 Victoria Avenue, Perth
- Council House 2, Melbourne
- One Shelley Street, Sydney
- The Gauge, Melbourne
- Workplace6, Sydney

China

- Vanke Center, Shenzhen

India

- Suzlon One Earth, Pune, Maharashtra

Japan

- Epson Innovation Center, Nagano Prefecture
- Honda, Wako, Saitama Prefecture
- Kansai Electric Power Company Headquarters, Osaka
- Keio University Hiyoshi Campus Fourth Building, Yokohama
- Nissan Global Headquarters, Yokohama

Singapore

- School of Art, Design and Media, Nanyang Technological University
- Zero Energy Building, Building and Construction Authority, Braddell Road Campus

Taiwan

- Magic School of Green Technology, National Cheng Kung University, Tainan City

7.77 2 Victoria Avenue uses 50 percent less energy and produces half of the carbon emissions of a typical office building in Perth. Photo: Stockland.

2 VICTORIA AVENUE, Perth

Located in Perth's central business district, 2 Victoria Avenue is a 77,340-sq-ft (7,185-sq-m), four-story, Class-A office building. Designed by Woodhead Architects, the contemporary and innovative glass and burnt-orange metal façade represents the building's most prominent design feature.

The western façade is fully shaded by automatic operable louvers that respond to the sun's movement throughout the day. Individual louver bays respond independently depending on shade created by adjacent trees and buildings, providing movement and visual interest across the building's front façade. The building entrance is located behind a louvered façade. Visitors approaching the building pass through a sheltered area behind the façade, which provides protection from prevailing southwesterly winds.[1]

A simple rectangular floor plate with cores located along the perimeter offers maximum flexibility for a modern office building. The floor plate is wrapped in a contemporary curtain-wall system, which maximizes the views into the building and allows occupants to have

7.78 A high-quality indoor environment, natural daylight, and visual connection to the outdoors contribute to high occupant satisfaction at 2 Victoria Avenue. Photo: Stockland.

views to the outdoors. All floor space is at most 41 ft (12.5 m) from a perimeter window to maximize natural light.[2]

Owned and managed by Stockland, 2 Victoria Avenue was designed to be a benchmark for new sustainable office developments. Located adjacent to Stockland's thirteen-story Durack Center, 2 Victoria Avenue is the company's highest-rated certified green building. The project was the first in Western Australia to receive a 6-Star Green Star Office "Design" v2 rating from the Green Building Council of Australia (GBCA).[3]

The building was also the first in Western Australia to commit to a 5-star energy rating from NABERS (National Australian Built Environment Rating System), a program that assesses buildings on a 0–5-star rating scale based on measured operational impacts in categories such as energy, water, waste, and indoor environment. NABERS is a national initiative administered and managed by the New South Wales (state) government.[4]

Active chilled beams provide most base building air-conditioning in the occupied spaces. Tenant-installed air-conditioning units are used as a secondary source, where necessary, in such places as computer, server, and high-occupancy rooms. The chilled-beam system cools specified zones using ceiling-mounted cooling coils connected to the chilled water loop. The system circulates chilled water around the ceiling space to each chilled beam as opposed to circulating air via ductwork, using conventional VAV systems.[5]

A floor-by-floor air-handling arrangement provides air to the active chilled beams with eight air-handling units per floor. This allows tenants with differing working hours and thermal comfort levels to operate air-conditioning for their area within a floor without having to turn on systems for the entire building.[6]

The building's graywater recycling system was decommissioned during a short period of vacancy and tenant fit-out and was re-commissioned after building occupancy.[7] Wastewater from sinks is collected via a gravity-fed system and is then discharged into a treatment plant located in the basement. After treatment, the water is then pumped to a graywater holding tank on the roof. From here, the treated water is supplied to restroom cisterns located throughout the building and used for toilet flushing.[8]

Upon occupancy, building staff and facilities management received comprehensive training during a twelve-month building "tuning" period. Training included topics such as optimizing energy efficiency, building operational features, control systems, and specific energy and environmental features.[9]

Recognizing that sustainable design, by definition, is a long-term endeavor, design-team decisions throughout the project were based on projected life-cycle costs rather than initial capital outlay. With its energy- and water-efficient design attributes, the building is expected to save approximately AUD$85,000 per year in operating costs compared with an average building.

TABLE 7.36

Energy and water use, 2011 (excluding tenant electricity use)[a]

	Annual use	Intensity
Total (with tenant use)	**565,853 kWh (700,853)**	**78.8 kWh/sq m (97.6)**
Electricity	405,723	47.6
Tenant electricity use estimate (add 33%)	135,000	18.8
Gas	556,211 MJ 157,281 kWh	13.6
Diesel	275 l[b] 2,849 kWh	0.4
Water	5,209 kl	725 l/sq m

a Figures for energy and water consumption for all case study projects were provided by the project owner, architect engineer, or consultant, unless otherwise noted.
b @ 37.3 MJ/L; 10,258 MJ = 2,849 kWh

At a glance
Name: 2 Victoria Avenue
Location: Perth, Western Australia
Size: 77,340 sq ft (7,185 sq m)
Completed: 2009
Distinction: 6-Star Green Star Office "Design" (Score: 75), 5-Star Green Star Office "As Built", 5-Star Green Star Interiors
Program: Commercial office

Project team
Owner: Stockland Trust Limited
Architect: Woodhead
Structural/Civil Engineer: Arup
MEP Engineer: AECOM
General Contractor: Diploma Construction

COUNCIL HOUSE 2, Melbourne

Owned and occupied by the City of Melbourne, Council House 2 (CH2) is part of the city's ambitious plan to be carbon neutral by 2020. Built on an existing city building's former parking lot, the 135,000-sq-ft (12,536-sq-m) building provides some remarkable green features in Melbourne's central business district and achieved the country's first 6-Star Green Star Office "As Built" rating.

An innovative cooling strategy, solar thermal and PV systems, an indoor air-quality scheme, as well as reduced lighting levels, represent some features that contribute to the potential for over 80 percent reduction in energy use and GHG emissions compared to the neighboring council building.[10] The use of more energy-intensive computers reduced the building's GHG savings, compared with modeled predictions. In operation since October 2006, the building produces about 50 percent fewer GHG emissions when compared to similar office buildings.[11] There are many innovative strategies in CH2, but it's their integration that makes this building's story memorable.

The initial project goal was to achieve a Green Star 5-Star minimum rating, with 6-Star as the system's highest possible rating.[12] The Green Star Office "Design" tool pilot rating system became available during CH2's design development stage, and the City worked closely with the GBCA to fine-tune the program before GBCA released version 1.0 into the marketplace.[13] CH2 received a 6-Star rating under Green Star Office "Design" with 80 points (75 is the threshold for a 6-Star rating) and a 6-Star rating under Green Star Office "As Built" with 78 points.[14]

Design began in 2002 with a three-week charrette that included all project consultants and stakeholders. The charrette process cost AUD$170,000 that, while significant, resulted in cutting the design time by six months.[15] During the charrette process, the team designed the majority of the building envelope, the interior layout, and the environmental systems.[16] According to the project-design report, "The key lesson from the charrette process is that significant innovations can come from getting all consultants on a project together early on to discuss the project and pool their ideas."[17]

Not only were most issues resolved during the charrette process, "those that came up afterwards were resolved based on the same trust and cooperative intention which had been built up in the charrette process," the report stated.[18]

Melbourne City Council Architect Mick Pearce worked with the architectural firm DesignInc. Pearce is a biomimicry proponent—using nature's processes as inspiration for design and is well known for the Eastgate office building in Harare, Zimbabwe, a structure that mimics an African termite mound's cooling system, an early biomimicry example in architectural design. Following the approach in Pearce's previous projects, natural systems inspired CH2. Thermal mass and natural air movement mimic a termite mound's cooling aspects.[19] Like lotus flower petals, CH2 opens and closes with the sun. The recycled-wood louvers, mounted on the west façade—the building's distinguishing feature when viewed from the street—open and close to control solar gain.[20]

Similar to the way a tree's branches shrink in size from bottom to top, CH2's windows get smaller as they rise toward the top, allowing more light in on the bottom floors where there is less available light from the street. Biomimcry aside, the building's integrated cooling system is perhaps its most innovative feature. Engineers Lincolne Scott developed a cooling system that combines common sense and emerging technology along with available site resources.

Melbourne, a city on the southeast coast, is known for its capricious weather conditions. Snowfall is rare, but gales from the Southern Ocean, severe thunderstorms, and sudden temperature drops are not uncommon. A robust cooling system is necessary as summer daytime temperatures can reach 115°F (46°C).

Instead of using air to cool the building, as in most conventional buildings, CH2 uses passively cooled water—a decision that was a major breakthrough during the charrette process.[21] At night, windows on the north and south façades automatically open to allow cooler air to remove built-up heat and to cool the 7.1-in (180-mm) thick, precast concrete ceilings.[22] Sensors close the windows in conditions of high wind, rain, or high external temperatures.[23] Studies predicted that the night purge alone could be responsible for reducing air-conditioning loads by up to 14 percent in the summer.[24]

The night purge process utilizes the building's vaulted, concrete ceilings as a key component of its success. Bonacci, the structural engineer, developed a structural system that addressed complex demands: gravity, light, air, people, heat, services, and energy.[25] The night purge and concrete mass combination is an effective strategy largely owing to Melbourne's unique climatic conditions.[26] Through

7.79 Five shower towers—transparent polycarbonate shafts on the southern façade—precool water for the cooling systems.
Courtesy of: DesignInc Architects, Melbourne.

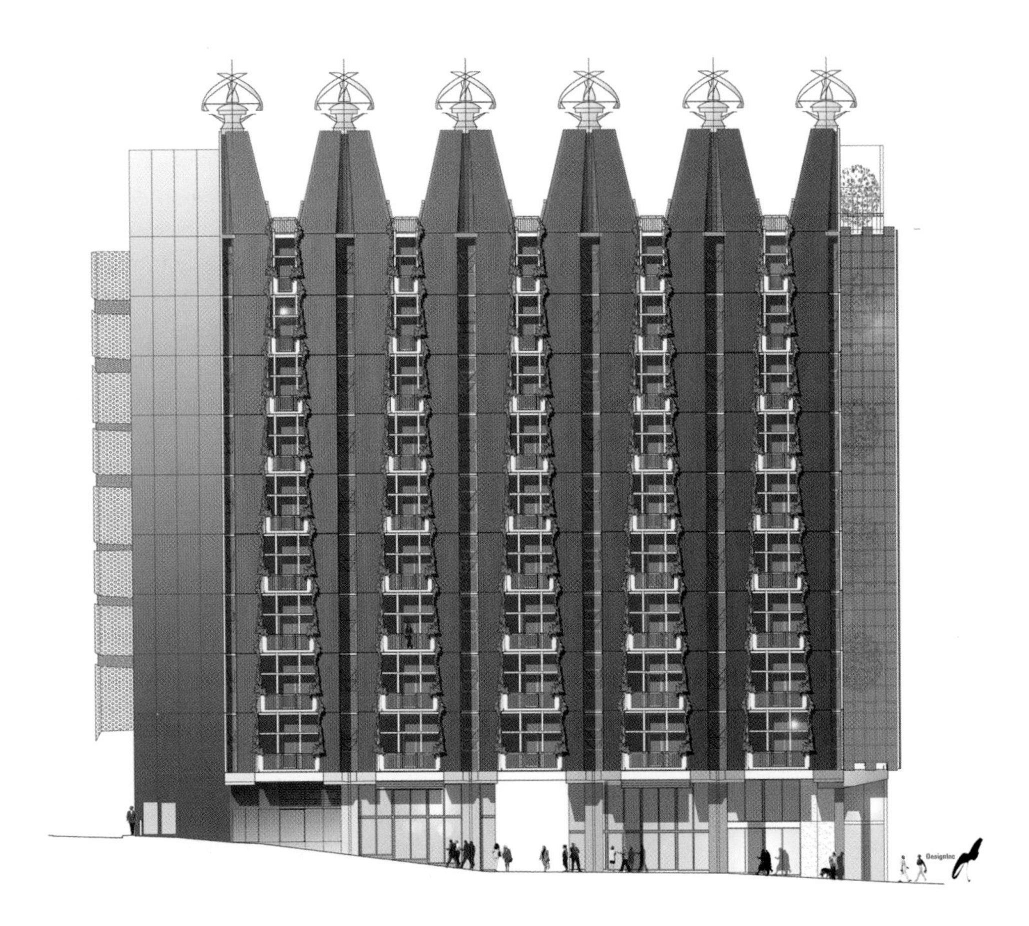

passive thermal design principles, the cool concrete ceiling absorbs heat, lowering the ambient temperature.[27]

In the afternoon, when the building needs additional cooling, chilled water travels through ceiling beams to supplement the radiant cooling system. Five shower towers—transparent polycarbonate shafts on the southern façade—precool water for the cooling systems.[28] As the water circulates through the system, it falls 56 ft (17 m) down the towers. Air is also sucked in at the same time, and both air and water are cooled by evaporation.[29] This air then cools the ground-floor retail and office spaces.[30]

By the time the water reaches the tanks in the basement, it is 55–59°F (13–15°C). Inside the tanks are thousands of grapefruit-sized balls that contain a phase-change material that freezes at 15°C.[31] Water for the phase-change tanks is also provided by the cooling towers and chillers. Then as water is needed for cooling, it passes over the balls, melting them and cooling the water.[32] This is often referred to as the building's "battery."[33] The cooled water travels to the radiant ceiling panels on each floor, and the process starts all over again with the water recirculating through the shower towers. [34]

The greatest cost-saving feature is the IAQ system. By far, employee salaries and benefits represent building operations' most expensive element, and most buildings fail to adequately consider occupant comfort, health, or productivity. For commercial buildings, employee costs are about ten to twenty times greater than rent, which is in turn about ten times greater than energy.[35] Even a 1-percent gain in worker productivity can offset an entire annual energy bill in most

7.80 As water falls down the 17-m-high shower towers, air is sucked in, and both air and water are cooled by evaporation. The air then cools the retail and ground-floor spaces. Courtesy of: DesignInc Architects, Melbourne.

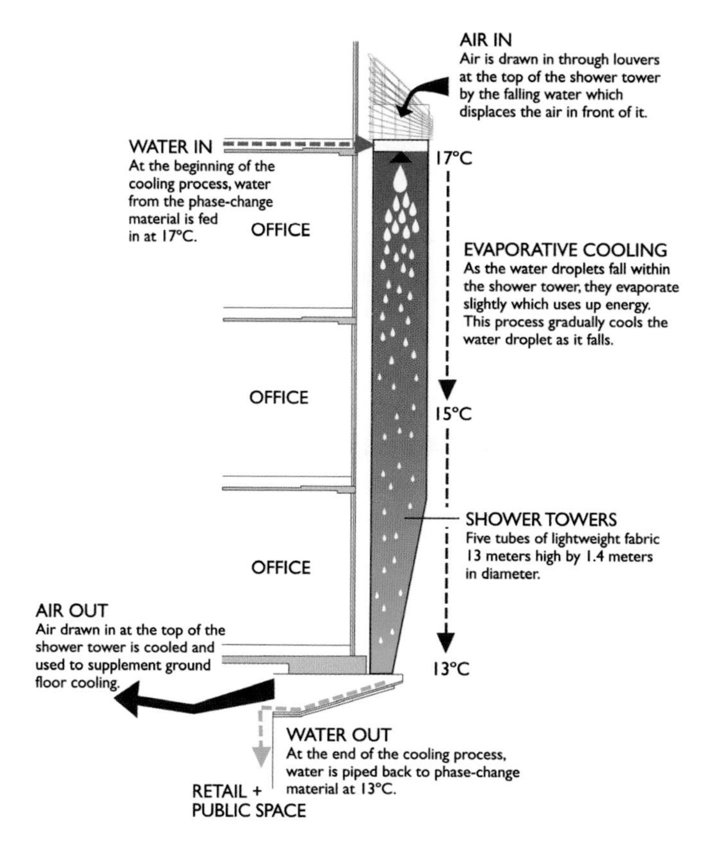

commercial office buildings.[36] Many studies link higher productivity to a building's green features.[37]

CH2 houses more than 500 full-time city-government employees on nine office floors.[38] The City recognized that when employees are healthier, the result is less absenteeism along with increased productivity. Occupant health and well-being are greatly influenced by IAQ. In CH2, there are two complete air changes per hour, three times more than Australia's minimum standard building code.[39]

Fresh air drawn from the roof travels down through ducts in the south perimeter walls and under each floor.[40] The 64°F (18°C) fresh air rises up through individually controllable vents on the floors, displacing warmer air.[41] As computers and people heat it up, the warm air rises and then exits through slots in the concrete ceiling.[42]

In a typical office building, fresh air and conditioned air are mixed with stale air already in the space. In CH2, no air is reconditioned or recirculated; it has a 100-percent fresh-air system.[43] Employees at CH2 exhibited a 10.9 percent improvement in productivity and well-being, compared to the prior city building.[44] This improvement is equivalent to more than AUD$1 million in annual savings to the Council.[45]

Along with IAQ, occupant comfort is increased if people can control their environment.[46] Design-phase research showed that people find radiant heating and cooling the most comfortable, which led to the decision to use the chilled ceiling panels.[47] Hydronic heating panels are located below floor level in the access floor space. In addition, each floor vent can be adjusted to control temperature in the cubicle space.[48] Indoor plants constitute part of the IAQ strategy, with one plant for every occupant.[49]

Along with passive design, chilled beams, phase-change materials, and night purging, CH2's energy strategy includes micro-cogeneration, solar thermal hot water, PV to power the louvers, low-energy fittings, natural light, flat-screen monitors, and a BMS that brings it all together.[50] Successful integration of these disparate systems required collaboration from all team members from the concept stage through to final design.

A natural gas-fueled cogeneration system provides 40 percent of the building's electricity.[51] The CHP system also satisfies 40 percent of the building's heating or cooling requirements from the plant's waste heat.[52]

The 280-sq-ft (26-sq-m) PV system produces about 3.5 kWh daily.[53] A 517-sq-ft (48-sq-m), roof-mounted solar thermal array, supplemented by a gas boiler, provides 60 percent of the building's hot water needs.[54]

Daylighting is less than expected, partly due to the 70-ft (21-m.) wide floor plate designed to limit solar gain in this warm climate.[55] Individual workstations reside in the building's center, leaving the daylit areas for meeting rooms and common areas.[56] Natural light enters through floor-to-ceiling windows. Artificial lighting from T5 lamps is set to 150 lux (14 foot-candles or 0.25 w/sq m), less than half the light level of traditional buildings, and is controlled by switching and daylight sensors.[57] The design did not use operable windows, in part to meet Class A level national commercial building standards.[58]

CH2's high-performance achievements are listed below.

- A 150 percent increase in the fresh-air-rate (compared to the Australian Standard 1668.2–1991 requirement) promotes healthy indoor environment.
- Ventilation systems provide 100 percent outside air with no recirculation to keep CO_2 levels low.
- 90 percent of the net lettable area (NLA) can control thermal comfort (air supply, temperature) individually.
- Sub-metering is installed for all substantive base building uses.
- Metering is installed for all major water uses and includes BMS integration with leak detection.
- Cooling systems use 90 percent non-potable water.[59]

Before initial occupancy, all employees participated in a two-hour building workshop to educate occupants about the new building. The focus centered on the protocols associated with an open floor plan, with no enclosed offices and meeting rooms. The workshop also explained the radiant heating and cooling system's operation.[60]

TABLE 7.37

Energy and water use, December 16, 2010–December 15, 2011

	Annual use	Intensity
Electricity	967,668 kWh	77.2 kWh/sq m
Gas	4,772,777 MJ (1,325,771 kWh)	106
Solar PV and thermal	2,377	0.2
Total energy use (base building)	**2,295,816 kWh**	**183 kWh/sq m**
Potable water (entire building)	7,417 kl (1,959,364 g)	592 l/sq m (14.5 g/sq ft)

One year after occupancy, 260 employees taking a post-occupant survey gave compliments overall with considerable unsolicited praise. Most criticism had to do with noise levels, uncomfortably high afternoon temperatures, and lighting. Occupant comfort conditions rated good or very good, with few exceptions. Interestingly, comfort, productivity, and noise scores varied by floor, and employees on less densely occupied floors reported higher satisfaction levels. Employees said, "CH2 makes them feel healthier; they are relatively more productive at work; and the building provides a strong image of environmental intent."[61]

The total project cost for CH2 was AUD$77.14 million, with an estimated ten-year payback on the cost of additional green features, stemming from reduced energy and water costs.[62] However, the extra AUD$11 million for environmental and IAQ features is projected to pay back in fewer than ten years, based solely on the increase in employee productivity along with energy and water savings.[63] Generating significantly fewer GHG emissions than its sister government building, CH2 stands out as one of the greenest buildings in the Southern Hemisphere.

At a glance
Name: Council House 2
Location: Melbourne, Australia
Size: 134,940 sq ft (12,536 sq m)
Completed: October 2006
Cost: AUD$77.14 million
Distinction: 6-Star Green Star Office "Design" (Score: 80) and 6-Star Green Star Office "As Built" (Score: 78)
Program: Government office building

Project team
Owner: Melbourne City Council
Architect: Melbourne City Council & DesignInc
Structural Engineer: Bonacci Group
MEP Engineer: Lincolne Scott
General Contractor: Hansen Yuncken

ONE SHELLEY STREET, Sydney

One Shelley Street is a 355,000-sq-ft (33,000-sq-m) commercial office building located in Sydney. Owned by Brookfield and constructed by Brookfield Multiplex, the 6-Star Green Star Office "Design" v2 and 6-Star Green Star Office "As Built" v2 building was completed in February 2009 in collaboration with the building's sole tenant, Macquarie Group. The building comprises 24,750 sq ft (2,300 sq m) of retail on the ground level, five levels of underground parking, ten levels of office accommodation, and a central atrium.

The completion of One Shelley Street also marked the completion of Brookfield's nine-year redevelopment of the King Street Wharf precinct. King Street Wharf is a neighborhood in the Sydney central business district that provides a waterfront location with varied uses: commercial office space, residential, retail, and restaurants.

The sole office tenant, Macquarie Group's Banking and Financial Services group, was the driving force behind bringing a new way of working to One Shelley Street, called activity-based working (ABW). ABW is a program that challenges more traditional ways of working by seeking to empower workers with the ability to choose a work setting that is most aligned to their particular needs for each day. Each floor also features a themed community space, effectively a shared break-out area, accommodating up to 100 employees. A central staircase winds its way through the atrium connecting the different work zones, contributing to the focus on transparency, light, and space. The atrium contains twenty-six cantilevered, cube-shaped meeting rooms that project over the atrium, with seating options ranging from traditional tables and chairs to more casual built-in benches.[64]

ABW is a relatively new concept promoted by Dutch consultant Veldhoen & Co. Through ABW, space efficiency is also improved in comparison to a traditional office environment; the same workforce can be accommodated in approximately 20 percent less total space.

At One Shelley Street, employees are encouraged to reduce paper use. Mail is scanned and distributed electronically, decreasing the need for file storage. "Follow-me" printing is used throughout the building; many meeting spaces are set up with wireless presenter technology for ease of sharing documents; and the building is fully wireless, supporting the mobility of staff who all work from laptops.

"One Shelley Street is testimony to Brookfield's commitment to owning and developing prime office assets with strong focus on sustainability and shows that we work to incorporate sustainable practices from design through to construction and the ongoing operation of the finished building," said Kurt Wilkinson, Chief Operating Officer of Brookfield Office Properties Australia.

Designed by architects Fitzpatrick + Partners, the building's glass façade is wrapped with a diagonal steel grid—a diagrid—making it one of Sydney's most recognizable buildings. This exoskeleton eliminates the need for perimeter columns by minimizing the top-end weight and distributing weight through the exterior walls, allowing maximum flexibility for interior floor layouts. The steel diagrid's pattern consists of repeating 20-sq-ft (6-sq-m) parallelograms.[65] The ability to enter the building by walking between the ground level diagrids is an intentional design feature that involves occupants in the building's structural elements.[66]

For this project, Built Ecology produced a detailed design brief before the design consultants even started.[67] The design brief was based on a large modeling, benchmarking, and targeting exercise, which virtually defined what the building would become, before many other consultants were engaged. This brief defined systems, materials, and energy expectations and represented a 200-page version of the "Owner's Project Requirements," an essential first step for design and eventual building commissioning.

A holistic set of sustainable design features, innovative use of technology, and forward thinking work practices contribute to a reduction in overall energy use by 50 percent.[68] High-performance components include: passive chilled beams, 100 percent fresh outside air with no recycling or heat recovery, CO_2 monitoring for fresh-air ventilation, energy monitoring, high-performance glass, extensive daylighting, low-flow fixtures, and provision for rainwater harvesting.

Instead of water-intensive cooling towers, One Shelley Street uses water from Sydney Harbour for heat rejection. A passive chilled beam system circulates cool air throughout the office space via pipes in ceiling spaces containing medium-temperature chilled water supplied at 59°F (15°C). The chilled water plant is split into low and medium temperature chillers with more than 60 to 70 percent of cooling provided by the more efficient medium-temperature chillers. Low-temperature chilled water is used for dehumidification when required. The system rejects heat from the condenser water and returns it to the harbor via a series of titanium heat exchangers. Compared to conventional

7.81 *Below*: A defining aesthetic element, the external diagonal steel grid structure wraps all the way around the glass façade and maximizes the interior space flexibility. Photo: © Brookfield Australia Investments Ltd.

7.82 *Right*: The interior design of One Shelley Street supports activity-based working, where employees may choose a different work environment each day. Photo: © Brookfield Australia Investments Ltd.

air-conditioning systems, passive chilled beam systems use approximately 30 percent less electricity. A single-pass air system provides 100 percent fresh air, resulting in higher IAQ.[69]

Natural daylight serves 80 percent of the floor plan.[70] In the entryway and atrium space, the lighting designers applied LED technology in original ways. The goal was to maintain lighting power density at less than 2 W/sq m while providing 100 lux, and to secure an overall power density under 9 W/sq m. The result exceeded these targets, achieving 1.58 W/sq m per 100 lux with overall power density just over 5 W/sq m.[71]

Donn Salisbury, with Lincolne Scott engineers and Vision Design, the lighting designers, noted that, "If we typically spend more time in our workplaces than any other environment, why not make them exciting and fun? The tricky bit is making this happen in an efficient

way, both in cost and energy. Emerging technologies have taken us so far over the last decade and will keep accelerating at an alarming rate, but knowing their purpose and using them in ways that work is critical to successful design. The architecture transforms what could have been just another office building into an engaging, community-inspired working environment. The lighting design then had to follow their lead by providing an atmosphere that works with the structure's openness and the external environment's vast influence."[72]

With a 6-Star Green Star Office "Design" v2 rating from the GBCA—the highest rating available—Brookfield's One Shelley Street achieved "World Leadership" in the high-performance building realm. "By backing up the Design rating with a 6-Star Green Star 'As Built' v2 rating, Brookfield confirmed that the sustainable design intentions were implemented during the construction process," said Romilly Madew, Chief Executive at GBCA.[73]

Other key high-performance features at One Shelley Street are listed below.

- Significant energy uses are separately metered to facilitate ongoing management of energy consumption. (This is a major requirement to progress from the "Design" rating to the "As Built" top Green Star rating.)
- Landscape irrigation uses 90 percent less potable water (compared to traditional landscapes).
- The ventilation system supplies more than twice the fresh-air circulation volume required by Australian standards.
- CO_2 monitors linked to the BMS keep the floors supplied with fresh air as needed.
- Dual pipe work was installed for future gray and blackwater recycling.
- Public artwork doubles as exhaust systems.
- PVC use was reduced by more than 60 percent.
- Siphonic piping system reduces stormwater runoff.[74]

Occupancy Evaluation

An independent, comparable, and comprehensive pre- and post-occupancy evaluation and indoor environment quality (IEQ) study was undertaken in collaboration with Brookfield Multiplex and Macquarie Group by University of New South Wales and University of Technology, Sydney. The study draws on data from a benchmark occupant survey, focus groups, site visits, and interviews with key stakeholders. The survey results indicate that One Shelley Street occupants are in the top 3 percent of the Australian benchmark for satisfaction, comfort, and overall performance.[75]

TABLE 7.38

Energy use, June 2011–May 2012

	Annual use	Intensity
Electricity (base building)	2,957,972 kWh	96.2 kWh/sq m
Gas (tenant)	1,773,733	57.7
Gas (base building)	197,794	6.4
Total	**4,929,499 kWh**	**160 kWh/sq m**

TABLE 7.39

Predicted energy use

	Annual use	Intensity
Electricity (base building)	1,927,717 kWh	62.7 kWh/sq m
Electricity (tenant, no prediction)	1,773,733	57.7
Gas	228,434	7.4
Total	**3,929,884 kWh**	**128 kWh/sq m**

Energy Use

One Shelley Street was designed to achieve a NABERS energy base building rating of 4.5 stars with predicted potential to achieve five stars. Tables 7.38 and 7.39 compare actual energy use and modeled (predicted) energy use. The building uses about two-thirds more energy than predicted, which can be attributed to the extended operating hours. Nevertheless, the actual energy use is still an excellent result and well within the range of other world-class large modern office buildings.

An energy monitoring report was prepared in October 2011 by the consulting firm AECOM, which states:

The results above show a significant discrepancy between the [engineer's] simulation results and actual building performance, though energy use appears to be closing this gap. Continued reduction in 2011 year-to-date gas and electricity use has provided the best result so far despite a reduction in the number of rated operating hours. It is evident that re-commissioning and programming of certain [physical] plant, starting in May 2010, has contributed to the decrease in energy use. The building's ability to achieve its potential is primarily hampered by the continuous operation of the Harbour Heat Rejection Pumps.[76]

Water Use

Water use in the building, for the twelve months ending April 2011, is in line with Australian best practices for large offices, in our experience.[77]

Water use (whole building): 3,965,918 gallons (15,011 kl)
Water use intensity: 11.9 gallons/sq ft (490 l/sq m)

Lessons Learned

One Shelley Street needed to be designed and constructed within the base footprint of a previously planned residential development; the previous scheme was built to ground-floor slab level when the program shifted from residential to commercial. The new commercial development had to transfer its loads through the existing structure, without any loss of basement amenity. This was a huge challenge for the design and construction team, but one that was well executed.[78]

Early contractor and tenant involvement and collaboration were keys to the successful delivery and operation of the building.

As a result, most services at One Shelley Street are located in the basement rather than in a rooftop plant. The need for ground-level exhaust led to an innovative solution: commissioned public art pieces double as exhaust risers.

Actual energy use was 67 percent more than the modeled use, as shown in the tables. Energy-efficiency upgrades through April 2012 are expected to reduce use by about 5.6 percent, but energy use will still be greater than modeled by 57 percent. A detailed consultant's report shows that there is a need for large, complex modern office buildings to receive "continuous commissioning," at least for the first two to three years of operation. Chapter 5 highlights this issue in discussing the need for post-occupancy evaluations.

At a glance

Name: One Shelley Street
Location: Sydney, New South Wales, Australia
Completion: February 2009
Size: 355,000 sq ft (33,000 sq m)
Distinction: 6-Star Green Star Office "Design" and 6-Star Green Star Office "As Built"
Program: Corporate Office

Project team

Owner: Brookfield Office Properties
Tenant: Macquarie Group
Property Services: Brookfield Office Properties
Construction Contractor/Developer: Brookfield Multiplex
Architect: Fitzpatrick + Partners
Structural Engineers: Arup & Robert Bird Group
Services Engineer: Lincolne Scott
Interior Design: Clive Wilkinson Architects, Woods Bagot
Sustainability: Built Ecology unit at Lincolne Scott, Brookfield Multiplex and Brookfield Office Properties

7.83 To reduce solar gain, the curved roof on top of the Gauge in Melbourne forms double eaves that shade the north-facing glass. A horizontal louver system shades the west façade. Photo: Lend Lease.

THE GAUGE, Melbourne

The Gauge is a 111,535-sq-ft (10,362-sq-m) commercial office building located in Victoria Harbour, Melbourne. Completed in April 2008, the project was the first in the country to receive the 6-Star Green Star Office "As Built" certification. Designed and developed by Lend Lease, the building's sustainability agenda focused on Australia's primary environmental challenges: GHG emissions and water supply. At the same time, the Gauge is an office building that encourages employee innovation and creativity.

The Gauge is located in the Docklands, a trendy urban area that blends residential, office, and retail and community spaces. Formerly an industrial port area, the location's history inspired building design features such as the ground-level "Y" columns and the atrium, which emulate steelwork of industrial structures, cranes, rail lines, and ships.

The Gauge's interior design reflects the famous Melbourne Hoddle Grid system. Designed in 1837, the urban grid system contains wide streets for traffic and narrow lanes that offer rear access to properties. Today the narrow lanes are pedestrian-only enclaves lined with shops, restaurants, and bars. This grid system encourages residents to flow and fuse together, and the recent "laneway" culture explosion is celebrated worldwide as an example of urban living. The Gauge uses the successful Melbourne design to inform the building layout.

7.84 The narrow floor plate (21 × 70 m) and floor-to-ceiling, high-performance glazing maximize natural light to the workspaces. Photo: Lend Lease.

The Hoddle Grid system shows in the clear flow of fit-out from front of house to back of house, from southern façade to northern façade. It's clear and concise, and there are no barriers to easy movement through the building.

Aiming beyond the well-worn dictum, "form follows function," the project objective was to make the highest level of sustainability mainstream in new buildings in Australia. For the Gauge, "sustainable form follows sustainable function," and this is evidenced by extensive daylighting, high quality indoor air, and efficient and flexible workspaces.

The building recycles wastewater on site and generates most of its own power. The building's demand on water and energy is 30 percent less than a typical 5-Star Green Star Building and 50 percent less than industry standard buildings.

Perhaps the most visually apparent features are two full-height atriums and curved roof profile. The atriums draw heated air away from the floor plates and up to the roof where it leaves the building. This "stack effect" provides natural air movement throughout the building, thereby reducing fan energy. Along with the two atriums, the narrow floor plate (70 × 230 ft/21 × 70 m) and floor-to-ceiling high-performance glazing maximize natural light to the workspaces.

The façade design incorporates shading for solar control, including double eaves to shade the north-facing glass and a horizontal louver system that shades the west façade. Along with high performance low-e insulating glass, these shading devices reduce peak cooling loads.

Energy

A gas-fired cogeneration unit located on the roof provides electricity to the base building systems (and emits fewer GHG emissions than coal-fired power generation). Waste heat from the cogeneration system preheats the incoming air supply in winter months and provides heating for service hot water.

On the demand side, the building is performing close to anticipated performance. However, on the supply side, the cogeneration system isn't operating as designed, owing to constraints applied by the local electric utility during the commissioning phase. The cogeneration system is tied to the municipal grid, but the utility company set a minimum quantity for utility-supplied energy to the building, to prevent net export of electricity from the building. This requirement reduces electric power from the cogeneration system and increases the electricity imported into the building.[79]

The office areas throughout the building are conditioned using passive chilled beams and a low-volume, primary air distribution system. The beams offer radiant space cooling, reducing the need for air movement by fans to provide cooling, increasing energy efficiency. The chilled beam system contributes to the building's high IAQ. The ventilated air moves from workspaces into the atriums and out the roof as it heats up during the day. The beam configuration is set up in two zones. The perimeter zone addresses the additional heating issues due to proximity to the façade and the associated solar gain, while the interior zone cools the workspaces and meeting rooms. The system is a single-pass ventilation system, so that it reduces significantly air's average "age" through effective distribution and zero recirculation, which maximizes IAQ.

TABLE 7.40

Energy use, 2011

	Annual use	Intensity
Total (gas and electric)		**238 kWh/sq m**
Imported electricity (house services)	277,274 kWh	26.8
Imported electricity (tenants)	1,050,825	101.6
Imported electricity (total)	1,328,099	128.4
Cogeneration electricity (supplied to house services)	(240,973	(23.3)
Cogeneration energy demand (natural gas)	2,449,882 MJ	236.4 MJ/sq m 65.7 kWh/sq m
Other natural gas demand (heating)	1,634,241 MJ	157.7 MJ/sq m 43.8 kWh/sq m

TABLE 7.41

Water use, 2011

	Annual use	Intensity
Total (office and retail)	**4,800 kl**	**463 l/sq m**
Potable water	4,000	386
Indoor potable water	(2,700)	(260)
Cooling tower potable water	(1,300)	(125)
Outdoor potable water	0	0
Treated water (from black water system)	800	77

Water

The Gauge's on-site wastewater recycling system is integrated with the base building plumbing design and has the capacity to treat 2,642 gallons (10 kl) per day. The treated water is reused for toilet flushing. The system was designed to recycle 660,400 gallons (2,500 kl) or 96 percent per year. The Gauge was designed to use 65 percent less potable water than an average building in Melbourne.[80] For example, rainwater that lands on site is captured and used for irrigating adjacent parkland.

Sustainability Features

Additional sustainability features are listed below.

- 90 percent of the net lettable area is designed for individual control of thermal comfort (air supply, temperature).
- The base building achieves at least a predicted 5-star NABERS rating, with an additional 20 percent CO_2 reduction.
- All refrigerants have zero ozone-depleting potential (ODP).
- Base building and tenancy electrical sub-metering assist in monitoring and managing electricity consumption.
- Single-tube 35W T5 fittings are provided for tenancy lighting. This energy-efficient lighting system reduces air-conditioning loads and electricity use.
- Concrete with recycled polystyrene and stack pallet woodchips was used in lieu of aggregate, the first time this product was used in an "in-situ" application.
- The interiors feature FSC-certified wood materials and second-hand furniture.

"Ultimately, we aspire to generate zero-net carbon, water and waste in the buildings we develop," said Steve McCann, Group Chief Executive Officer and Managing Director for Lend Lease. "The Gauge is an important step toward achieving that aim."[81]

The name "The Gauge" reflects a benchmark or tool for measurement, and, with the 6-Star Green Star Office "As Built" rating, it now becomes the yardstick for industry to gauge its progress on environmental sustainability in new commercial developments. As one of the world's greenest buildings, the Gauge can now be looked to as a meter for assessing sustainability progress in other new commercial offices.

At a glance

Name: The Gauge

Location: Melbourne, Australia

Size: 111,536 sq ft (10,366 sq m)

Completed: April 2008

Cost: Not publicly available, but similar to typical "non-green," Grade A office developments

Distinction: 6-Star Green Star Office "Design" (Score: 79) and 6-Star Green Star Office "As Built" (Score: 77)

Program: Commercial office building

Project team

Owner: Australian Prime Property Fund

Developer: Lend Lease

Architect: Lend Lease

Structural Engineer: Lend Lease

MEP Engineer: Lend Lease and Cundall

General Contractor: Lend Lease

WORKPLACE6, Sydney

Workplace6 is a six-story, 193,759-sq-ft (18,000-sq-m) building in Sydney's central business district, located in the Pyrmont area, an increasingly attractive destination for businesses seeking cost-effective office space.

As part of the third stage of Sydney's Darling Island Master Plan, the landowner, Sydney Harbour Foreshore Authority, let the contract for a landmark building in environmental design and construction. Construction began in April 2007 and was completed in November 2008 at a total construction cost of AUD$56 million. GPT Wholesale Office Fund acquired the building in December 2007; it was last valued at AUD$160 million in December 2011. Today, Google and Accenture lease the entire 174,375 sq ft (16,200 sq m) of office space, with the award-winning Doltone House eatery occupying 19,375 sq ft (1,800-sq-m) of a ground floor devoted to restaurants, convention space, and function centers.

Workplace6 was the first project in New South Wales to receive a 6-Star Green Star Office "Design" v2 rating. In May 2009, the project was additionally awarded a 6-Star Green Star Office "As Built" v2 rating for the completed building. Workplace6 acquired 83 points; a minimum of 75 points is required to achieve a 6-Star rating.

Even with some of the largest commercial floor plates in Sydney (over 38,950 sq ft/3,620 sq m), Workplace6 was designed for maximum daylighting. An open central atrium surrounds an internal recycled-timber staircase. The atrium allows light to reach the center zone of each floor with light shelves directing natural light into the internal space. No point on the floor plate is more than 39 ft (12 m) away from an external window or the atrium. Intelligent façade design and sun-shading devices reduce heat load on the building, thereby reducing cooling load.[82]

Operable windows allow for fresh air and access to winter gardens. Occupant comfort is enhanced by chilled beams, which allow

7.85 *Facing Page*: The heat from Workplace6 is rejected to Sydney Harbour through a series of plate heat exchangers in the building basement. This method saves 8 million liters of water annually from evaporation in the cooling towers. Photo: The GPT Group.

7.86 *Below*: Workplace6 houses 16,200 sq m of office space in six stories and 1,800 sq m of retail space on the building's ground floor. Photo: The GPT Group.

TABLE 7.42

Energy and water use, 2011

	Annual use	Intensity
Electricity	1,361,777 kWh	74.8 kWh/sq m
Gas	900 GJ	49 MJ 13.7 kWh
Total energy use		**88.5 kWh**
Total energy use (with tenant electricity use at 33% of base building)		**114 kWh**
Potable water	21,000	117

temperature control zones of 735 sq ft (70 sq m) or less for perimeter areas, and 1,076 sq ft (100 sq m) or less for central areas. Fresh air is supplied to each floor at 50 percent greater than the minimum required under Australia building standards.

A 575-kVA gas-fired generator produces enough electricity to reduce the building's peak load by at least 25 percent. The generator's waste heat is used to run an absorption chiller, further limiting the energy demands of the building and contributing to carbon footprint reductions of up to 70 percent compared with a typical office building.[83]

In lieu of cooling towers, the building's waste heat is rejected into the harbor through a series of plate heat exchangers in the building basement. Using harbor water for the heat exchange eliminates the need for anti-microbial chemicals used in cooling towers. In this way, the building also saves 2.1 million gallons (8 million liters) a year of water that would otherwise have been required for evaporation in a cooling tower.[84] Forty roof-mounted solar thermal panels supply the building's service hot water needs.

A blackwater-treatment system collects sewage from the building along with sewage extracted from the adjacent sewer main, a process known as "sewer mining." The 10,600-gallon-per-day (40.1 kl) system consists of a membrane bioreactor (MBR) and activated carbon treatment with anoxic zone (for denitrification), UV disinfection, and chlorine residual injection. The reclaimed water is used on site for toilet flushing and landscape irrigation.[85] Not only does the building use 60 percent less potable water compared to a conventional building, but it also generates enough treated wastewater to irrigate two adjacent parks.[86]

Workplace6 also incorporates a unique education aspect into the design and management of the AUD$1 million blackwater system. The glass-front building allows the public to view the wastewater treatment system inside, and information screens tell viewers about the treatment process and end-uses of the recycled water.[87]

More of Workplace6's environmental features are listed below.

- Use of PVC was reduced by 60 percent.
- Recycled FSC-rated timber was used throughout the building.
- A mold-prevention system in the ductwork preserves a healthy work environment for tenants.
- Low-flow urinals, low-flow taps, and low-flush toilets further reduce water consumption.
- Zero-ozone-depletion refrigerants were selected, and a refrigerant leak detection and recovery system was installed.

As the first 6-Star Green Star commercial office building in New South Wales, Workplace6 sets a world-class example in environmental performance without compromising occupant comfort and productivity. Adjacent parks, showers, changing rooms, lockers, bicycle racks, and city and harbor views also make this building appealing to tenants.

Demonstrating that demanding design targets can be translated into superior, measured, performance, Workplace6 is one of few buildings to have achieved both 5.5-star NABERS energy and 5.0-star water ratings (the highest possible ratings).

At a glance
Name: Workplace6
Location: Sydney, New South Wales, Australia
Size: 193,750 sq ft (18,000 sq m)
Completed: February 2009
Building Cost: AUD$56 million
Distinction: 6-Star Green Star Office "Design" (Score: 83), 6-Star Green Star Office "As Built" (Score: 82)
Program: Commercial office, ground floor retail, underground parking

Project team
Owner: CPT Group
Developer: Citta Property Group
Design and Construct Main Contractor, Sustainability Consultant: Buildcorp
Architect: Nettleton Tribe
Structural Engineer: TLB
Environmental Modeling: Waterman AWH
Commissioning: Thwaite Consulting

7.87 Floating above a landscaped garden, the horizontal skyscraper, Vanke Center, is as long as New York's Empire State Building is tall. Photo: Henderson Land Development Company Ltd.

VANKE CENTER, Shenzhen

Hovering over a tropical garden, this "horizontal skyscraper"—as long as New York's iconic Empire State Building is tall—is a hybrid building that includes apartments, a hotel, and offices for the headquarters for China Vanke Co. Ltd. A conference center, spa, and parking are located under the expansive green, tropical landscape, characterized by mounds containing restaurants and a 500-seat auditorium.[88]

The building appears as if it were once floating on a higher sea that has now subsided, leaving the structure propped up high and dry on eight legs. The decision to float one large structure right under the 115-ft (35-m) height limit, replacing several smaller structures each catering to a specific program, generated the largest possible green space, one that is open to the public on the ground level.[89]

Suspended on eight cores, as far as 165 ft (50 m) apart, the building's structure combines cable-stay bridge technology with a high-strength concrete frame. The first structure of this type, its tension cables carry 3,280 tons (2,976 metric tons), a record load.[90]

The underside of the floating structure is its main elevation—six stories off the ground—from which "Shenzhen windows" offer 360-degree views over the lush tropical landscape below. A public path beginning at the "dragon's head" connects the hotel and the apartment zones up to the office wings.[91]

As a tropical design strategy, the building and the landscape integrate several original sustainable aspects. Cooling ponds fed by a graywater system create an interior microclimate. The building has a green roof with solar panels, and the interior features locally sourced materials such as bamboo. Porous louvers protect the glass façade against the sun and wind. It is among the first LEED Platinum certified buildings in Southern China.[92]

7.88 The building serves as the new headquarters for Vanke, one of China's largest property developers, and is a symbol of the firm's vision to promote sustainable and socially responsive urbanization. Photo: Henderson Land Development Company Ltd.

The designers, Steven Holl Architects, paid careful attention to using renewable and healthy materials in the China Vanke Co.'s corporate headquarters.

- Bamboo: This rapidly renewable material, readily available in China, is used for doors, floors, and furniture throughout the building, replacing materials made from non-renewable raw materials or exotic tropical hardwoods.[93]
- Green carpet: InterfaceFLOR carpet tiles are used throughout the open office area. This carpet is a cradle-to-cradle product: not only is it produced from recycled materials but also the manufacturer agrees to collect the carpet at the end of its useful life and recycle it into other carpet or products.[94]
- Nontoxic paint: All paint finishes, as well as the millwork and adhesives, have low toxicity or are free of VOCs such as phenols and formaldehyde.[95]
- Greenscreen shading: The project uses Greenscreen solar shading fabrics from Nysan, a PVC-free product that contains no VOCs.[96]

The building sits on reclaimed land that integrates with the municipal stormwater-management system. The lagoon functions as a bioswale or stormwater retention pond connected to several adjacent creeks. The landscape water-edge approach in part incorporates redesigning the existing municipal hardscape bulkhead into a soft-edge planted estuary. As a restorative ecology, the Vanke Center landscape works to maintain native ecosystems and to minimize run-off, erosion, and environmental damage.[97]

The project is both a building and a landscape, delicately intertwining sophisticated engineering and the natural environment. By raising the building above the ground plane, the project creates an open, publicly accessible park with new social space in an otherwise closed and privatized community.[98]

The site area is approximately 645,835 sq ft (60,000 sq m), with plantings totaling 484,376 sq ft (45,000 sq m). Adding the planted roof area of the main building (approximately 161,459 sq ft/15,000 sq m), the total planted area is roughly equal to the site area prior to development.[99]

In addition to the planted areas, the project installed permeable pavement measures, such as local river stones, crushed gravels, open-joint stone pavers, grasscrete, and compressed sand pavers. These measures retain substantial rainfall before it flows into the secondary gutters, which redirect overflow into ponds and wetlands planted with marsh grasses and lotus. These systems function collectively as a bioswale that filters, aerates, and irrigates the landscape so that the project exterior will not require potable water.[100]

To conserve potable water, the project installed low-flow, high-efficiency plumbing fixtures and waterless urinals throughout. Graywater is recycled and used in dual-flush toilets.[101]

TABLE 7.43

Actual vs. projected energy and water use (electricity, twelve months ending September 2010)[a]

	Annual use	Intensity
Actual	**1,980,000 kWh**	**139 kWh/sq m**
Projected (LEED energy model)	1,345,171 kWh	94.5 kWh/sq m
Photovoltaic power production	266,700 kWh	18.7 kWh/sq m
Water use (projected)	3,396 kl	240 l/sq m (5.9 g/sq ft)

a Steven Holl Architects, "Vanke Center Electricity Consumption Report," supplied by Julia van den Hout via email, January 5, 2012.

Energy Efficiency

The team analyzed each of twenty-six building faces, assessing solar heat gain throughout the year, and fine-tuned the louver design based on those findings. Some louvers are fixed horizontally, some have differently sized apertures, and some are dynamically controlled by sensors, opening and closing according to the solar angle.[102]

The full-height glass curtain wall brings daylight deep into all interior spaces, and high-performance glass coatings (double silver, low-e) are used throughout the project. With higher visible light transmittance, these coatings ensure better natural lighting and, at the same time, with their extremely low solar heat transmittance, reduce cooling loads.[103]

In addition to the high-performance coatings, perforated aluminum louvers in a secondary layer create a double-skin façade. The interstitial cavity created by these two layers creates a convective stack effect, drawing cool air in through the building's underside and sending hot air out at the top near the roof. The perforated louvers provide extensive primary sun protection in their closed condition. They reduce solar heat gain by up to 70 percent yet still provide 15 percent visible light transmittance.[104]

Given tropical sunlight's intensity, field measurements calculated that 15 percent light transmittance in closed mode provides sufficient natural lighting to perform routine office functions without the need for additional artificial lighting in most spaces.[105]

In the office portion, a series of interior and exterior sensors, which balance ambient light levels, solar heat gain, and ambient temperatures for maximum energy efficiency, coordinate the operation of the exterior louvers, interior shades, air-conditioning, and lighting systems. There are individual controls for lighting and shade operation in most offices. Individual task/spotlights are provided for off-hour, additional use.[106]

Indoor Environmental Quality

The upper building's shallow floor plate resembles a branching pattern lifted high off the ground to allow for unimpeded views to the ocean, mountains, and surrounding landscape. Prevailing ocean (day) and mountain (evening) breezes circulate underneath and through the building. Exceptionally large (2-m wide) operable windows provide natural ventilation and generous cross breezes for the interiors during the cooler months.[107]

From November to March, outdoor conditions in Shenzhen are calm, and window ventilation can take over most ventilation in the office building (and completely in the condominium section). During this season, mechanical ventilation systems can be switched off at least 60 percent of the time, reducing electric energy consumption annually by 5 kWh/sq m.[108]

Sky gardens, sunken courtyards, balconies at the end of each floor, and terraces throughout the building all serve to create micro-climates that bring the landscape further indoors and create passively cooled zones.[109]

Renewable Energy/Green Power

Photovoltaic panels comprising 15,065 sq ft (1,400 sq m) installed on the roof provide 12.5 percent of electric energy demand for Vanke Headquarters.[110]

At a glance

Building Type: Corporate Headquarters Office
Size: 153,268 sq ft (14,239 sq m)
Stories: 6
Completed: 2009
Latitude: 22°55′ N
Climate: Hot and humid
Distinction: LEED-NC Platinum

Project team

Owner: Vanke Real Estate Co., Ltd.
Architect, Interior Design, Landscape: Steven Holl Architects
Associate Architects, Structural Engineer, Mechanical Engineer: CCDI (China Construction Design International)
Climate Engineer: Transsolar
Structural Engineer: China Academy of Building Research
General Contractor: CSCEC (The First Construction Engineer Limited Company of China Construction)

SUZLON ONE EARTH, Pune, Maharashtra

Suzlon One Earth is a 816,000-sq-ft (75,808-sq-m), three-story commercial office building in Pune, western India. The project serves as the corporate headquarters for Suzlon Energy Ltd., one of Asia's largest wind-turbine manufacturers. Certified at LEED Platinum, Suzlon One Earth also earned the highest rating, 5 stars, from India's national green building rating system, Green Rating for Integrated Habitat Assessment (GRIHA).

Suzlon One Earth, the global headquarters of Suzlon Group, the world's fifth-largest wind-energy company, was conceptualized and managed by Synefra E & C Limited. This project was envisioned by Suzlon Group's CMD, Mr. Tulsi Tanti, who wanted a campus that represented his company's mission, "Powering a Greener Tomorrow." The challenge for creating a unique workplace was taken up by architect Dr. J. R. Tanti of Synefra, to create a campus driven by two major goals: sustainability and an inspiring place to work.

The campus-like setting draws inspiration from large Indian historical towns and temple complexes. Combining open and closed spaces, strong horizontal elements, and accent features that emphasize quadrants, the project's components work together to give the structure scale and proportion. Following the precedents of historic towns and temples, the campus contains water bodies and open courtyards. This corporate campus is a counterblast to the prevailing glass-box architecture occurring across India.

The design process started by creating a central gathering space, or Brahmasthan, with the sky as the ceiling. The architect conceived it as an "office in a garden" that gives an exclusive and unique feel to the campus. It is a pedestrian-friendly, human-scale, and convivial space. The ultimate goal was to raise the imagination from life's day-to-day trivia into a special realm of creativity and inspiration.

Within the campus are five "lounges," comprising office buildings and a learning center. The lounges are named after the five natural elements—water, wind, sky, fire, and earth—that connect the exterior spaces with interior ones. The Suzlon Excellence Academy serves as the corporate learning center and houses a wind-energy museum along with classrooms, a multimedia room, theater, library, and business halls. Inspired by a traditional Indian town square, the interior central space of the Excellence Academy is designed like a courtyard with a central water body shaded by building-integrated PV panels.

7.89 *Facing Page:* The One Earth campus, located on 10 acres of land in Hadapsar, Pune, serves as the corporate headquarters for Suzlon, a wind power company. Photo: Suzlon One Earth.

7.90 *Left*: The Brahmasthan central gathering space uses the sky as a ceiling. Photo: Suzlon One Earth.

7.91 *Below Left*: Within the campus are five "lounges," named after the five natural elements—water, wind, sky, fire, and earth—that connect the exterior spaces with interior ones. Photo: Suzlon One Earth.

Daylight and views to the outdoors service 90 percent of workstations. Aluminum louvers used on the building façade act as a protective skin, yet allow daylight penetration. LED lighting and solar water heating contribute to the building's energy savings. The campus is equipped for maximum rainwater harvesting, and it also recycles 100 percent of graywater, which is then used for toilet flushing, landscape irrigation, and cooling system make-up.

Glass exhaust chimneys with tropical plants act as visual connectors between all floors and allow aeration of the basement parking area. The tubes heat up in the sunlight, and, as the warm air begins to rise, the chimneys suck air out of the basement and the upper floors. A waterfall and the crescent-shaped cafeteria in the central courtyard provide a focus for the complex. This central garden plaza encourages communication, interaction, and innovation among the 2,300 (design capacity) occupants and provides a memorable visual aesthetic for visitors.

About 6 to 8 percent of the building's annual energy requirement is generated on site through hybrid solar-wind resources, and the

TABLE 7.44

Water use, 2010

	Annual use	Intensity
Total consumption	56,000 kl	739 l/sq m
Total recycled water including harvested rainwater	33,000 kl	435 l/sq m
Net consumption	**23,000 kl**	**304 l/sq m**

TABLE 7.45

Energy use, 2010

	Annual use	Intensity
Electricity	4.5 million kWh	5.5 kWh/sq ft 59 kWh/sq m
Renewable energy generated on site	0.125 million kWh	1.65 kWh/sq m

balance of energy requirements is generated off-site; hence it is 100 percent powered by renewable energy.

Sustainability features at Suzlon One Earth are listed below.

- A stormwater and rainwater management system channels all rainwater into a controlled flow, preventing erosion.
- The air-conditioning and cooling systems contain no CFCs, HCFCs or Halon (ozone-destroying chemicals).
- Energy-efficient air-conditioning systems are flexible and vary the amount of cooling delivered according to requirements.
- Sensors and modulating dampers in all densely occupied spaces monitor CO_2 levels. The sensors provide additional inflow of fresh air as soon as the CO_2 differential between inside and outside air rises above a specified limit.
- Exterior louvers provide efficient screening without hindering views, reducing heat gain and aiding efficient cooling.
- Daylight sensors in the workstation areas minimize use of artificial lighting. Occupancy sensors control task lighting in unoccupied workstations, saving about 20 percent of energy costs.
- Jet fans installed in the basements intermittently push out stale air and bring in fresh air, saving 50 percent energy as compared to ducted basement ventilation system.
- Interlocking concrete paver blocks on road surfaces enable water infiltration and reduce stormwater run-off.
- LED exterior street lighting is completely powered by on-site renewable energy-based systems, reducing about 25 percent of total lighting load.[111]

"I believe that Suzlon One Earth—named as a tribute to Earth's unique existence as a self-replenishing ecosystem—will be an inspiration to others that it is possible, if we are really determined, to create a sustainable world for our future," said Mr. Tanti, chairman of Suzlon Group.[112] "Suzlon One Earth is conceptualized and created as a self-sustaining ecosystem wherein it maintains its own water, energy usage and maintains its waste making it an ecosystem in itself," expressed Dr. Tanti of Synefra.[113]

Summary: Annual Savings by System

- Energy savings: 47 percent
- Water savings: 60 percent
- Water recycling: 85 percent

At a glance
Name: Suzlon One Earth
Location: Pune, Maharashtra, India
Size: 816,000 sq ft (75,809 sq m)
Completion: 2009
Distinction: LEED-NC Platinum, GRIHA 5 Star
Program: Commercial Office Space

Project team
Owner: Suzlon Energy Ltd.
Project conceived, managed and executed by Synefra E & C Ltd., Pune
Principal Architects: Christopher Charles Benninger Architects, Pune
Project Design Coordinators: Tao Architecture, Pune
Landscape Architects: Ravi & Varsha Gavandi, Pune
Interior Architect: Space Matrix, Singapore, in association with Tao Architecture
Communication Consultant: Elephant Design, Pune
Contractors: Vascon Engineers, Pune

JAPAN

EPSON INNOVATION CENTER, Nagano Prefecture

Seiko Epson Corporation, one of the world's leading manufacturers of computer printers and information and imaging-related equipment, is headquartered in Nagano Prefecture in mountainous central Japan. Seiko Epson started in 1942 as a manufacturer of watch parts, but when Seiko was selected to be the official timekeeper for the 1964 Summer Olympics in Tokyo, a printing timer was required to time events, and an electronic printer was developed. In 2006, Epson inaugurated its new "Innovation Center," a research facility in Nagano, designed by Tokyo's Nikken Sekkei architects.[114]

7.92 The Epson Innovation Center achieved an "S" award, the highest rating, from the CASBEE system. Photo: Rococo Produce, Inc.

Located at an altitude of 2,300 ft (700 m), with seven stories and a penthouse, the building takes advantage of the natural environment with a large atrium that motivates researchers to communicate and collaborate with one another. The facility contains the C-Cube building, which was designed for collaboration with the outside world, and the "Innovation Center A," which was designed to promote closer relationships among researchers. The latter building can be extended to connect with the C-Cube building in the future. Deep eaves and clear glass give the facility a fresh and sharp look. The atmosphere inside is unusually comfortable with warm wooden interiors and soft light from overhead lamps.

What makes the building green (it was rated "S" [Superior] in the CASBEE system) are features such as a two-way sock filter system, a green roof, low-e glass, daylight blind controls, and individual lighting-equipment controls. Natural ventilation through the windows has an automatic opening–closing control. Natural daylight also enters the building through light shelves and light ducts. Ground heat is used via a cooling/heating trench system. Photovoltaic power generation and a vacuum-collector type solar water-heating system harvest the sun. There is a heat-recovery system for the cooling water. The rainwater and also the water from air-conditioning condensate are recycled. Wastewater from experiments is also treated on site for reuse.

A natural ventilation system uses cool mountain weather for space conditioning. Operable windows automatically open and close according to the inside and outside temperatures and humidity; they can be forced closed based on high outside wind velocity or rainfall. The system functions annually for 970 hours, almost half the working year. Since this project is an experimental (laboratory) facility, it requires a large outside air supply.

A large-scale cooling and heating system involves a 3,300-ft (1,000-m) trench for incoming outside air, which cools in summer and heats in winter. Heat exchangers extract energy from the cooling water for a highly efficient refrigeration system to deal with dehumidification and to reheat loads both in summer and intermediate seasons. Except during severe winter weather, the set temperature of warm water is low, and the heat-recovery system is used as much as possible.

The site is located in an area where annual sunshine hours are plentiful. For the daylighting unit to employ this natural feature, a solar-tracking light tube system was developed. This system tracks the sun with a biaxial-controlled lens and introduces outside light into a room on the northern side with a secondary mirror.

At a glance

Owner: Seiko Epson Corporation
Architect: Nikken Sekkei, Tokyo
Rating: CASBEE "S"
Site: Hirooka, Shiojiri, Nagano Prefecture
Completion: 2006
Site Area: 2.95 ha, or about 7.3 acres (29,525 sq m)
Gross Floor Area: 574,500 sq ft (53,372 sq m)

TABLE 7.46

Energy and water use, 2006[a]

	Intensity
Carbon emissions	69.9 kg CO_2e/sq m
Electricity (calculated)	168 kWh/sq m[b]
Water	580 l/sq m[c]

a www.ibec.or.jp/CASBEE/english/SB08_pdf/Nikken_Epson_Innovation_Center.pdf, accessed January 27, 2012.

b www.sunearthtools.com/dp/tools/CO2-emissions-calculator.php, accessed January 27, 2012.

c Includes cooling tower and laboratory.

HONDA, Wako, Saitama Prefecture

The automobile R&D center in Wako centralizes Honda's design-related aspects of car development. New car designs developed here undergo comprehensive development at the automobile R&D center in Tochigi before they evolve into products. The Honda Building in Wako is designed as a "base for creation." Its aim is to create a campus-like environment for "co-creation" and "speed." The "Midori-no-oka" (green hill) inherits an existing engine plant's image, with a parking area under an artificially created ground level.

A huge working space measuring 110 m × 73 m (86,400 sq ft/8,030 sq m) creates an office for co-creation for all employees to work together and experience a sense of community. The large floor area reduces the building height to six stories, with a one-story penthouse, and reduces the visual effect of such a large building on the environment. The minimized external skin also contributes to a reduced environmental load and lower initial and running costs. All workspaces are located in a bright, thermally stable environment created by atriums and top lights. The perimeter-less working spaces have atriums, machine rooms, lavatory, staircases, and other amenities installed along the circumference.[115]

To make the building more environmentally friendly, the owner, architect, and constructor worked together to reduce $LCCO_2$ (life-cycle carbon dioxide) emissions and achieve zero emissions. The double-skin façade has low-e glass for openings and aluminum vertical louvers on the eastern and western walls to protect against sunlight. The blinds and roll screens are automatically controlled by sunlight tracking and luminance sensors. Air-conditioning around individual desks is zoned for use after normal business hours. Lighting is controlled by occupancy and luminance sensors and remote-controllable by sensor. The fresh-air ventilation rate is 1.2 times the ventilation standard for offices in Japan.

The building's earthquake-resistance performance is 30 percent higher than the value specified in the Japanese Building Standard, through the installation of buckling-restraint braces and toggle mechanism dampers. There is an emergency power generation, to guarantee uninterrupted power supply during grid outages.

The landscaping design supports the architecture's goals: Most existing trees were preserved. The exterior green coverage ratio is 48 percent, and the area ratio of roof greening is 29 percent. Shading is provided by green space, pillars and eaves, and the project reduced

7.93 Honda's Automobile R&D Center in Wako provides 8,030 sq m of space for creative design work. Photo: Kume Sekkei.

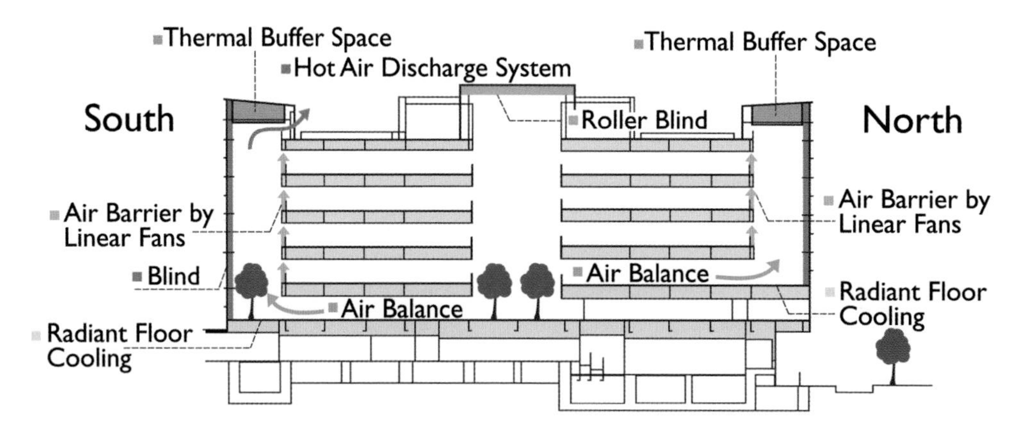

7.94 Honda Wako summer ventilation mode, showing the cooling effects of the atrium. © Kume Sekkei.

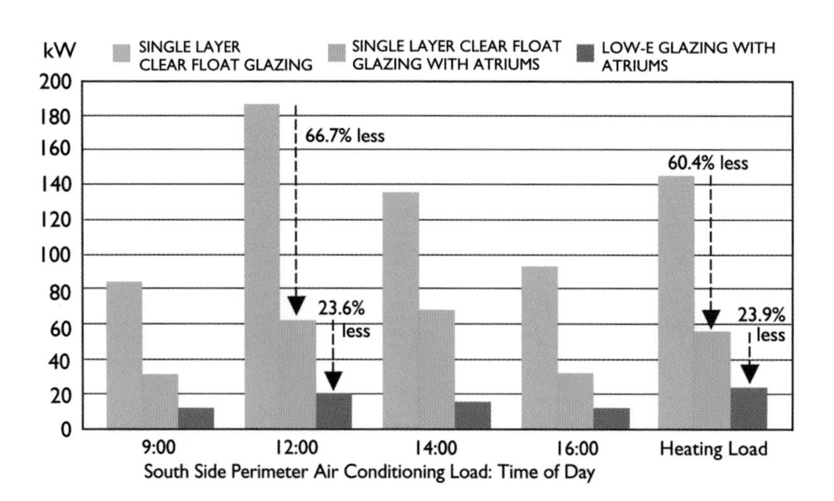

7.95 Honda Wako air-conditioning load, showing reductions from various design approaches. Source: www.aivc.org/members area/medias/pdf/Conf/2008/Paper_136.pdf.

asphalt and concrete use from typical conditions. In addition to the large-scale greening there are water-permeable pavements, to use rainwater to recharge local groundwater.

Renewable energy generated annually is 3.6 kWh/sq m. Compared with typical Japanese "coefficient of energy consumption" values, energy consumption is reduced by 23 percent. Compared with all Japanese office buildings larger than 430,556 sq ft (40,000 sq m), energy consumption is reduced 15–20 percent.[116] A building energy-management system was included with the project. After construction completion, engineers conducted a thermal environment measurement to verify energy use and commissioned all equipment.

There is a toilet-flushing sound simulator, and water-saving toilets were installed. Well water, rainwater, and air-conditioning condensate are used for toilet flushing. The wastewater from the kitchens is recycled. Nitrogen-gas fire-extinguishing equipment was used with an ODP (ozone depletion potential) of zero. All thermal insulating materials have an ODP of zero and also have a low "global warming potential." Composters were installed, and compost made from kitchen garbage is sold to neighboring farmers.

Thermal buffer spaces in the south and north atriums have three environmental adjustment systems, as shown in Figure 7.94. One discharges hot air near the ceiling in summer. Another prevents cold drafts along the windows in winter. The third provides natural ventilation in spring and autumn, with remote operation and outdoor climate sensors to reduce cooling load.

To ensure the thermal buffer effect, airflow from linear fans installed in the floor facing south and north atriums (between the office spaces and atriums) blocks thermal effects from the atriums. If the temperature at the top of the south atrium exceeds a set value, exhaust air fans open to discharge hot air. The second- and third-floor return-air supply volume balances the hot-air discharge volume.

Natural ventilation and night purge (ventilation) operates by opening windows at the bottom and top of the atriums, providing cooler temperatures the following morning. Motorized ventilation openings are installed at the bottom of the south and north atriums, and, at the top of each atrium, "Natural Ventilation Recommended" is displayed on the central supervisory board only when weather conditions are suitable for natural ventilation. The operations manager decides when to operate the natural ventilation system.

TABLE 7.47

Energy and water use, 2005–2006[a]

	Annual use	Intensity
Electricity	8,116,743 kWh	156 kWh/sq m
Photovoltaic generation	69,187	1.3
Natural gas	331,898 cu m (3,852,107 kWh)	73.9
Total energy	**12,038,037 kWh**	**231 kWh/sq m**
	Water use	Intensity
City water	37,132 kl	714 l/sq m

a www.aivc.org/members_area/medias/pdf/Conf/2008/Paper_136.pdf, accessed January 27, 2012.

Cold air near the window is collected from the suction openings at the bottom of the atriums before it flows into the office space. Figure 7.95 shows how much this approach reduced projected air-conditioning loads and contributed to building energy efficiency.[117]

At a glance
CASBEE Rank: S (Superior)[118]
Completion: March 2005
Site Area: 24 acres (97,700 sq m)
Total Floor Area: 561,200 sq ft (52,138 sq m)

Project team
Owner: Honda Motor Co., Ltd.
Architect: Kume Sekkei
Contractors: Takenaka Corporation, Shinryo Corporation, Kandenko

KANSAI ELECTRIC POWER COMPANY HEADQUARTERS, Osaka

Comprising Kobe, Osaka, and Kyoto, the Kansai region is the second most important region of Japan after Tokyo's Kanto area. Kansai is largely powered by an electric utility company known as Kansai Electric Power Company (KEPCO) or Kanden. It runs 164 plants and is thus a big player in Japan's energy market. It is no surprise then that the company decided to make its new headquarters a showcase for environmentally friendly design. This tower in central Osaka was designed by architects Nikken Sekkei as Phase 1 of the "Nakanoshima 3-Chome Joint Development Project." The 1,146,000-sq-ft (106,484-sq-m) building is rated "S" in the CASBEE system with an excellent BEE score of 4.0 (see Chapter 3).[119] The headquarters building contains forty-one floors above ground, plus a penthouse and with five floors below ground. The site comprises about 5.2 acres (2.1 hectares).

The building is situated on a river island in central Osaka. The cool air above the river is used for natural ventilation. At nighttime, the top of the tower is lit up like a lighthouse. The floor plan of the tower is a simple rectangular box, with the rectangular core not occupying a central position, but pushed to one of the long façades. The design is based on three concepts: (1) the "eaves" (utilizing columns and beams to block direct solar radiation), (2) district heating and cooling utilizing the river water, and (3) a new air-conditioning and lighting system that enables personal control. Nikken Sekkei made a comparative study on life-cycle cost and life-cycle CO_2 emissions. The study on initial cost and operating cost was done for all new technologies proposed and the design adopted only those economically advantageous.

The task and ambient air-conditioning system provides office workers with separate controls for their personal workspaces and the room's overall environment. The indoor environment level secures comfort for workers' task zones with underfloor cool air outlets and ambient ceiling diffusers. The underfloor air diffusers allow changes in air direction and volume. Task air-conditioning can effectively heat or cool task zones without creating perceptible drafts.

The district heating and cooling system utilizes river water as a thermal source. River water has smaller temperature changes throughout the year than air, increasing the water-based heat pump system's efficiency, resulting in 14 percent less energy consumption. In addition, the system uses a large-scale ice thermal-energy-storage tank, which is in turn located in the foundation pits. At night electricity is used to make ice for daytime air-conditioning, to reduce electricity use during the day.[120]

The "eco-frame," a set of columns and beams, jutting out by 6 ft (1.8 m) from the window, blocks the direct solar radiation from 10 a.m. to 2 p.m., the peak demand period for cooling in summer. The cooling load in the perimeter zone is greatly reduced (by two-thirds of the perimeter annual load for a standard Japanese building), so that air-conditioning in the perimeter zone is unnecessary. By the shape of the eco-frame's ventilation inlet there is less effect from strong wind or rain. In this way, ventilation can be accomplished by wind pressure, leading the river wind inside from the ventilation inlet under the eaves. Opening and closing the ventilator is automatic to meet target performance levels (reducing 24 percent of cooling load). The design of ventilation inlets into the room directs the current along the ceiling to send ventilation air deep into the room.

Skylights take in as much light as possible while blocking direct solar radiation, reducing energy needed for illumination. The ceiling near the window is bent up to maximize window height up to the lower part of the eco-frame. Also, there are window shades that rise up from the bottom, automatically controlled according to an annual schedule based on sun position and direct solar radiation intensity.

Solar panels are installed on the south-facing eco-frames on each floor, making effective use of space, resulting in 13 kWh/sq m of annual renewable (natural) energy generation, about 4 percent of annual energy use.

In 2006, energy use was 338 kWh/sq m and water use was 462 l/sq m. To provide 27 percent of annual water requirements, the project recycles rainwater and domestic wastewater.

At a glance
Location: Osaka
Client: Kanden (Kansai Electric Power Co.)
Architect: Nikken Sekkei, Tokyo
Completion: 2004
Gross Area: 1,140,975 sq ft (106,000 sq m)
Net Conditioned Area: 645,835 sq ft (60,000 sq m)
Rating: CASBEE "S"

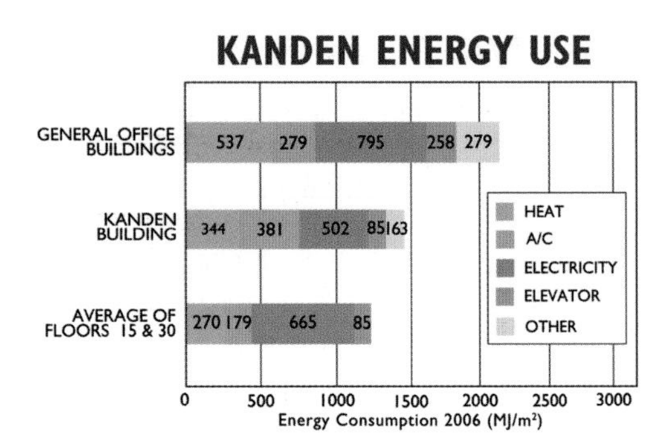

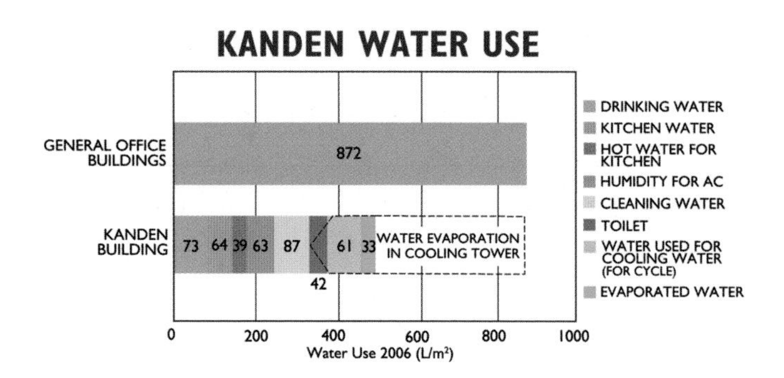

7.96 *Below*: The 106,484-sq-m Kansai Electric Power Company headquarters building in Osaka is rated "S" in the CASBEE system with an excellent BEE score of 4.0. Photo: Photo Bureau.

7.97 *Facing Page, Left*: Kanden energy use. Courtesy of Kansai Electric Power Co.

7.98 *Facing Page, Right*: Kanden water use. Courtesy of Kansai Electric Power Co.

KEIO UNIVERSITY HIYOSHI CAMPUS FOURTH BUILDING, Yokohama

In 2009, Keio University inaugurated the 198,050-sq-ft (18,399-sq-m) Fourth Building on the Hiyoshi Campus in Yokohama as part of the university's 150-year celebration. The two main project goals were: (1) the facilities would cater to 10,000 students at peak times, and (2) it should serve the university for at least fifty years.

The large roof and louvers facing the street connect the building with its environment while students pass through the entryway and atrium. The interior and exterior common spaces incorporate systems that utilize renewable energy sources and capitalize on the site's approximately nine-meter (nearly 30-ft) difference in elevation between lowest and highest points to provide a diverse space for students. The combination of atrium, rooftop courtyard, and innovative classroom layout protects thirty-five large and small learning spaces from noise and afternoon sun, providing a constant flow of fresh air through the atrium to the classrooms.

The lower part of the atrium is continuously open, and the operable skylight provides continuous ventilation. The atrium, a large-scale common area, is an indoor–outdoor space designed to maintain a comfortable environment while minimizing the use of fossil fuels. The use of stack effect ventilation and wind-driven ventilation provides a continuous flow of air through the atrium. During winter, by closing the skylight ventilation window, the interior temperature reaches 9–18°F (5–10°C) above the outside temperature. The design team conducted a series of thermal environment simulations to determine the size of the ventilation window aperture. The team also measured the brightness levels in a part of the campus where there is a row of ginkgo trees and utilized this data in simulations conducted to determine the size of the skylight and the lighting system, with the aim of attaining a similar level of brightness.[121]

Along the building's western road frontage, the campus previously was divided by a 26-ft-high (8-m) concrete retaining wall. Removing this wall from above the adjoining main road created a 590-ft-long (180-m) open space that has become a scenic plus for the town.

The building design incorporated a variety of innovations with the aim of reducing noise and excess solar gain while enhancing the sidewalk's attractiveness. A 16-ft-wide (5-m) space bordering the road is open to the local community as a walkway lined with newly planted trees. The design of the exterior wall along that section of the building uses waste concrete from the previous building. In addition to giving the wall a more elegant appearance, this design utilizes recycled materials, and the porous characteristics of the wall prevent heat buildup from the late afternoon sun.[122]

While fulfilling the role of providing a pleasant approach to the building, the approach avenue was designed to act as a buffer. The building's large roof and vertical double louvers abate the late afternoon sun and road noise while providing privacy. Similar to the atrium, the building conducted an array of simulations for such aspects as brightness level to determine the louver's best shape and pitch.[123]

Additional high performance features include:[124]

- water-conservation fixtures such as automatic faucets, low-flow faucets, and user sensor systems

7.99 *Left*: The atrium, a large-scale common area, is an indoor–outdoor space designed to maintain a comfortable environment while minimizing use of fossil fuels. Photo: Koushi Miwa.

7.100 *Far Left*: Keio University inaugurated the 18,399 sq m (198,050 sq ft) Fourth Building on the Hiyoshi Campus in Yokohama as part of the university's 150-year celebration. Photo: Koushi Miwa.

- rainwater is captured and used for toilet and urinal flushing
- reduction of outdoor air thermal load through the use of heat recovery ventilation
- use of recycled lumber and concrete
- insulation materials with zero global-warming potential and zero ozone-depletion potential.

Energy Use Intensity

The annual EUI in 2011 at Keio University's Fourth Building on the Hiyoshi Campus was 158 kWh/sq m.

At a glance

Name: Keio University Hiyoshi Campus Fourth Building
Location: Yokohama, Japan
Total Floor Area: 198,050 sq ft (18,399 sq m)
Distinction: CASBEE S

Project team

Owner: Keio University
Designer: Kajima Design
Contractor: Kajima Corporation Yokohama Office

NISSAN GLOBAL HEADQUARTERS, Yokohama

The Nissan Motor Corporation is Japan's second-largest automotive company. At Nissan, more than 248,000 employees produce 4 million vehicles a year. After forty-one years in Tokyo, the headquarters was moved back to Yokohama in August 2009.

Nissan Motor Corporation selected a team with an architect and two major contractors to design and construct its new head office. An international competition between four teams was held. In addition to design and technology, the energetic response of the winning team led to its selection. Architect Yoshio Taniguchi and Takenaka Corporation designed the building, and Shimizu Corporation undertook the construction. Nissan relocated most of its head-office functions and personnel to Yokohama from Tokyo in 2010. At least 2,000 of Nissan's 3,000 employees based at the Tokyo head office moved to the 845,000-sq-ft (78,500-sq-m) Yokohama office.[125]

The company decided to build an environmentally friendly building. The tower consists of steel-framed reinforced concrete and steel, comprising twenty-two floors above ground and two floors below.

Construction was completed in April 2009, the 150th anniversary of the Port of Yokohama's opening. The site is located at the northwestern edge of Yokohama's new waterfront, the Minato Mirai 21 area.

The building comprises the headquarters office in the upper section and a gallery hall in the lower section in the shape of a gate, partly making up a wide and open arc-shaped gallery space. In the upper section, some exterior walls are also arc-shaped, exhibiting the same curvature as that of the gallery space, and are covered with louvers.[126]

Two-level atriums with stairs were installed in both the northern and southern floor areas. An atrium that rises through to the upper section and stairs were installed in the center of the standard floors, functioning as the workspace skeleton, both for getting around and for visual effect, designed to enhance communication.

Nissan's new headquarters reduces CO_2 emissions and conserves energy by harnessing renewable energy resources. As a result, the building received the highest S rating from Japan's CASBEE system in 2008. In May of the same year, the building was also awarded the "Cool City" designation by Japan's Ministry of the Environment.

Natural light is maximized with a curtain-wall exterior; the building also utilizes sunlight channeled by condensing lenses in five sets that track the sun automatically and direct it into the central channel of the building. Window louvers control sunlight, contributing not only to natural lighting but also to air-conditioning energy savings. Super-insulated glass and louvers regulate interior temperatures. Air-conditioning energy consumption is controlled by dampers installed in the exterior wall, which automatically detect wind speed and humidity and allow air to flow into the building.

An additional energy-saving feature uses the ascending air current generated by the building's central channel, reducing energy required for ventilation fans. Rainwater and miscellaneous drainage, including that from the kitchen, are processed and used for toilet flushing and

7.101 *Facing Page*: Nissan Motor Corporation's headquarters building in Yokohama consists of steel-framed reinforced concrete and steel, containing twenty-two floors above grade and two floors below ground. Photo: Nissan Motor Co. Ltd.

7.102 *Above*: The building comprises offices in the upper section and a gallery hall in the lower section in the shape of a gate, partly making up a wide and open arc-shaped gallery space. Photo: Nissan Motor Co. Ltd.

plant irrigation. With the green roof system on the gallery, the green space makes up 11 percent of total site.

The Nissan Global Headquarters will emit only 10,200 tons per year of CO_2, 3,800 fewer tons than its former headquarters in Tokyo. The building uses only electricity for water or space heating. Air-conditioning and heating are provided through a system managed by local government where super-cooled water and steam are piped from a central source to several office buildings in the vicinity of Minato Mirai, including Nissan's headquarters.

Nissan began generating power from solar cells in April 2011. The new solar-power charging system in the building enables Nissan to charge 1,800 Leaf electric vehicles per year without any CO_2 emissions.

Energy Use
10,200 metric tons/year CO_2; 0.13 tons/sq m, 313 kWh/sq m[127]

Water Use
260 l/sq m/year (2011)

At a glance
Name: Nissan Global Headquarters
Location: Yokohama, Japan
Size: 845,000 sq ft (78,500 sq m)
Completion: 2009
Distinction: CASBEE "S"[128]
Program: Corporate office

Project team
Owner: Nissan
Architect: Yoshio Taniguchi and Takenaka Corporation
Engineer(s): Takenaka Corporation
Contractor: Shimizu Corporation

SCHOOL OF ART, DESIGN AND MEDIA,
Nanyang Technological University

Completed in 2006, the School of Art, Design and Media at Nanyang Technological University (NTU-ADM) is Singapore's first professional art school. The university, which is the island's largest on-campus academic facility, is located on a 500-acre (200-hectare) campus in southwestern Singapore.

NTU-ADM received a Green Mark Platinum rating, the highest possible award from Singapore's nationally accepted benchmark for designing, constructing, and operating high-performance buildings.

"The BCA Green Mark Platinum Award is an important recognition of NTU-ADM's commitment toward sustainability," said Chan Keng Luck, Executive Director of the Office of Facilities Planning and Management. "The University has already secured more than

7.103 *Facing Page:* Designed to be a "non-building building," the NTU-ADM building merges and almost disappears into the surrounding landscape and minimizes the loss of green space. Photo: CPG Consultants, Singapore.

7.104 *Below*: Turf-covered curved arms form an arc creating a sunken entry courtyard. Photo: CPG Consultants, Singapore.

S$830 million in sustainability research. In addition, the NTU Campus Master Plan, which will guide the physical development of our campus over the next 15–25 years, is also based on sustainability principles. In fact, in the upcoming new academic year, all first-year undergraduates will take a compulsory course in environmental sustainability."[129]

Designed by Singapore-based CPG Consultants Pte. Ltd., the team created a "non-building building" to preserve open space on the campus, which is known for its garden and park-like setting. With its sloping green roofs, NTU-ADM merges and almost disappears into the surrounding landscape and minimizes loss of green space. Two curved arms with grass roofs interlock with a third, smaller arc, creating a sunken entry courtyard. "Instead of imposing a building onto the landscape, we let the landscape play a critical role in molding the building," stated Lim Choon Keang, Senior Vice President (Architecture) of CPG Consultants.[130]

The 215,000-sq-ft (19,975-sq-m), five-story structure houses a 450-seat auditorium, a library, more than two dozen studios and laboratories, two galleries, two lecture halls, and classrooms along with many other breakout spaces.

"The building design challenges the traditional linear system of education with a clear teacher–student arrangement," according to CPG Consultants. "Here, we create different types of spaces, from the formal auditorium seating to the more informal studios, lobbies, passageways, and breakout lounges. There are also cozy outdoor corners, a sunken plaza formed by the building's embracing arms, and turf roofs. Together, these provide varied spaces for students to interact, explore, and learn as well as display their creative works."[131]

Accessible by stairs and illuminated at dark, the green roof is an outdoor gathering place for students throughout the day. The roof was perhaps the project's most challenging aspect. "It took tremendous site coordination, [a complicated] scaffolding system, and accurate setting-out for such curvilinear structures," according to CPG Consultants[132]

The roof is irrigated with harvested rainwater; a moisture-retention mat installed below the soil ensures that the roots are constantly moist. "Inventing a turf system suitable to the local tropical climate was a challenge, requiring a good understanding of turf growth and a precise installation of irrigation and water drainage," said CPG Consultants.[133]

Additional high performance features include:[134]

- air-conditioning plant system with 0.67 kW/ton efficiency
- motion sensors for all restrooms and corridors
- CO_2 sensors installed at all air handling units to modulate fresh air intake
- harvested rainwater used in the cooling tower for make-up water
- building orientation with its long axis façades facing north and south minimizes solar gain in this tropical climate, for a project at 2° N latitude
- high-efficiency discharge lights throughout the building.

"The university is indeed proud of its new iconic building which not only caught the attention of the university fraternity but also that of the local media," according to NTU. "More importantly, the architectural design and spaces complement the aspirations of the school; that is to become the foremost art, design, and media school in the region."[135]

Average EUI
134.8 kWh/sq m/year

At a glance
Name: School of Art, Design and Media, Nanyang Technological University
Location: Singapore
Size: 215,000 sq ft (19,975 sq m)
Completed: July 2006, opened April 2009
Cost: S$36 million
Distinction: Green Mark Platinum from Building and Construction Authority (BCA), Singapore
Program: Academic building with gallery, auditorium, library, studios, and classrooms

Project team
Owner: Nanyang Technological University
Architect, Interior Designer, Engineer, Landscape Architect, Environmental Consultant: CPG Consultants Pte. Ltd.
Contractor: Teambuild Construction

7.105 The Zero Energy Building, the Building and Construction Authority's flagship project, is the first zero-net energy building in Singapore. Photo: Building and Construction Authority of Singapore.

ZERO ENERGY BUILDING, BUILDING AND CONSTRUCTION AUTHORITY, BRADDELL ROAD CAMPUS

In October 2009, Singapore's Building and Construction Authority (BCA), opened the Zero Energy Building (ZEB) located at the BCA Academy. Formerly a workshop, the renovated 48,438-sq-ft (4,500-sq-m) ZEB now houses corporate offices and academic classrooms and is a true net-zero energy building. Yudelson visited this building in 2010 and saw first-hand not only the measures taken to reduce energy use but also the main lobby's continuous display of energy supply and demand, making this a very transparent ZEB.

BCA is an agency under the Singapore Government's Ministry of National Development, charged with developing green technologies to make 80 percent of Singaporean buildings green by 2030. ZEB is BCA's flagship project and the first net-zero energy building in Singapore.[136] It received the Singapore Green Mark Platinum certification.

Zero energy refers to energy self-sufficiency—a building that produces as much energy as it uses. In Singapore, an island country devoid of natural resources, "the success of ZEB in achieving this target is exciting and has tremendous implications on the way energy is used in Singapore for specific types of buildings," according to the BCA.[137]

ZEB was conceived with two primary objectives:

1 to serve as a laboratory for integrating green building technologies in existing buildings
2 to be a hub to study energy efficiency and green buildings.[138]

The technologies currently undergoing testing at ZEB will have potential applications for many existing buildings that will be retrofitted over the next twenty years to meet national energy use goal.

TABLE 7.48

Energy use, 2011

	Annual use	Intensity
Electricity consumption	183 MWh	41 kWh/sq m
Renewable energy production	203 MWh	45 kWh/sq m
Carbon emissions from imported energy, 2009	0.48 kg CO_2/kWh	N/A

TABLE 7.49

Energy end-use requirements

Air-conditioning	104 MWh/year
Building internal lighting	24
Building internal plug loads	28
Common area lighting and power	27
Total	**183 MWh** **40.7 kWh/sq m**

"Besides bringing our vision into fruition, it is something that we strongly believed in and set out to do, and for this reason the ZEB places Singapore favorably on the world green building map," said Dr. John Keung, BCA's CEO.[139]

To meet the zero-energy goal, the design team adopted an integrated design approach that focused on two general principles to reduce energy consumption: passive and active design. The first step was to incorporate passive design solutions that utilize natural resources to minimize the amount of power required from the grid. The next step was to incorporate active solutions: energy-efficient equipment and solar-power systems.[140]

Passive Solutions

Three passive design strategies informed the energy efficiency strategy at ZEB:

1 minimize heat transmittance into the building
2 bring daylighting deep into the space
3 use natural ventilation to reduce the air-conditioning load.[141]

Improved glazing is a primary strategy to control heat transference. At ZEB, four different types of glazing were installed, allowing researchers to study the performance of each type:

1 Electro-chromic glass is glazing that changes opacity depending on solar intensity.
2 Building-integrated PV glass provides both shading and power generation at the same time.
3 Double-glazed units (DGU) with internal operable glass were studied for their impact on views, shading, and heat absorption.
4 Clear DGU glass was used as a reference for comparison. Double-glazing surrounds all air-conditioned areas, with single glazing installed in the classrooms and school hall.[142]

Mirror ducts, light shelves, and light pipes are three daylighting strategies used at ZEB. Mirror ducts capture zenith daylight (which is brighter than horizontal daylight) through external collectors. Light harvested from mirror ducts is usually glare-free, and the technology involves no mechanical parts and requires no power.[143]

Light shelves are highly reflective surfaces that reflect daylight deeper into the building. Externally mounted on the façade, they also provide shading against direct sunlight.[144] Light pipes protrude from a building's roof, directing sunlight into interior rooms. They are more energy-efficient than skylights because less energy escapes from a reduced surface area.[145]

The roof-mounted solar panels assist in ZEB's ventilation system. Heat builds up in the 12-in (300-mm) gap between the solar panels and the metal roof, creating a negative pressure area as warmed air rises. Due to the buoyancy effect, when heat is removed from the gap, warm air from inside the building is drawn up toward ceiling vents and out through the four solar chimneys.[146]

Active Solutions and Systems

Obviously it is not possible to eliminate electricity use entirely. To achieve the goal of net-zero energy use on an annual basis, active solutions are required. In ZEB, lighting sensors represent a key active solution. Occupancy sensors control how much artificial lighting is used. Lights are activated only when someone enters a room; additionally, light intensity is adjusted according to daylighting levels.[147]

To achieve net-zero energy power consumption, the building produces electricity on site. Photovoltaic panels comprising about 16,575 sq ft (1,540 sq m), mounted on the roof and façade, connect to the grid power supply and, in the first year of operation, generated about 203,000 kWh a year to offset building energy use. Over the course of a year, the solar array generates more than the energy required by ZEB. Additional non-grid-tied PV panels supply power for specific functions such as the visitor center's phone-charging kiosk.[148]

"The project's main target was to demonstrate that a zero-energy building is possible even in the tropics, where high air-conditioning loads make up more than 50 percent of a building's electricity consumption," said Stephen Wittkopf, Associate Professor and Director at the Solar Energy Research Institute of Singapore. "After almost one year of analytical energy monitoring, we are happy to confirm that we achieved this target. The building-integrated photovoltaic systems generated a surplus of electricity which is fed back into the BCA premises grid."[149]

Because an important goal is to serve as a test bed for green building technologies, the ZEB building's performance is carefully monitored,

TABLE 7.50

Water use, 2011

Indoor potable water	194.5 kl
Outdoor potable water	159 kl
Cooling tower potable water	88.5 kl
Total	**442 kl; 98 l/sq m**

7.106 Roof-mounted solar panels are not only a source of energy but also aid in the Zero Energy Building's ventilation system, along with four solar chimneys. Photo: Building and Construction Authority of Singapore.

and it is performing better than predicted! Initial modeling estimated energy usage to be 207,000 kWh, whereas the building's annual actual usage is 183,000 kWh. BCA estimates that ZEB's CO_2 emissions reductions are close to 200 tons of CO_2 equivalent annually.[150] In all, the building will save S$84,000 (based on electricity rate of 21.69 Singapore cents/kWh) a year compared to typical office building in Singapore.[151]

At a glance

Name: Zero Energy Building
Location: Braddell Road Campus, Singapore
Size: 48,438 sq ft (4,500 sq m)
Completed: October 2009
Cost: S$11 million, S$227/sq ft (US$8.8 million; $182/sq ft; $1,955/sq m)
Distinction: Green Mark Platinum, BCA, Singapore
Program: Government office and academic facilities

Project team

Owner: Building and Construction Authority (BCA), Singapore
Architect: DP Architects Pte. Ltd.
Project Manager: Beca Carter Hollings & Ferner (S.E. Asia) Pte. Ltd.
Mechanical, Electrical, Civil Engineer: Beca Carter Hollings & Ferner SEA Pte. Ltd.
Quantity Surveyor: Langdon & Seah Singapore Pte. Ltd.
Principal Investigators for Green Building Technologies: Associate Professor LEE Siew Eang (energy efficiency), Associate Professor Wong Nyuk Hien (greenery and natural ventilation), Associate Professor Stephen Wittkopf (building integrated PV and daylighting)
Contractor: ACP Construction Pte. Ltd.

TAIWAN

MAGIC SCHOOL OF GREEN TECHNOLOGY, National Cheng Kung University, Tainan City

The Y. S. Sun Green Building Research Center, also known as the Magic School of Green Technology (MSGT), is Taiwan's first zero-carbon building. The project was the first building in Asia to achieve the highest ratings from Taiwan's Energy, Ecology, Waste Reduction and Health (EEWH) system, as well as from the US Green Building Council's LEED rating system.[152]

The three-story, 48,096-sq-ft (4,469-sq-m) building serves as the National Cheng Kung University's (NCKU) international conference center. Designed by Professor Lin Hsien-Te and Joe Shih Architects along with NCKU's architecture department, the building's exterior aesthetic was influenced by Noah's Ark and a Star Wars spaceship. A leaf-shaped, mobile PV "blade" with a huge model ladybug adorns the roof. The vent tower is shaped like a ship's bridge, while the railing, handrails, and balconies reflect the nautical theme.[153]

Fourteen small wind turbines are encased in an orange scaffolding-like frame tower that projects outward from the roof line, and three solar chimneys that rise from the building's top.[154] The design team's aim was "to build an economical, pragmatic Noah's Ark for the entire human race rather than an ark for the wealthy who can afford a billion-euro fare as in the movie *2012*."[155]

Aesthetics aside, the efficacy of the design and systems were thoroughly researched by four senior professors and twelve NCKU PhD and master's degree students, making it perhaps the most extensively researched green building project in Asia.[156] After just under a year of operation, the MSGT is showing an EUI of 40.43 kWh/sq m/year, considerably less than Taiwan's medium-rise office buildings which consume 125 kWh/sq m/year on average.[157]

The team evaluated thirteen techniques and strategies to maximize energy efficiency. The technologies were divided into three categories:

1 energy saving from design
2 energy saving from MEP equipment
3 renewable energy.

The first category includes energy-saving strategies that cost little or nothing and were achieved simply through architectural design. These strategies yielded 41 percent total energy saving, compared with a conventional design. The second category includes efficient equipment, resulting in 19.1 percent total energy savings. The third category accounts for 5 percent in energy savings through the use of renewable energy systems, such as solar and wind power. The overarching principle is, according to Lin, "the more simple and natural the technique, the more effective it is."[158] Table 7.51 shows the cumulative energy savings from each strategy.

The team found that window design is the most important building block in an energy-saving building envelope plan. Window-to-wall ratio directly affects air-conditioning consumption in Taiwan's subtropical climate. Figuring out the glazing-to-wall ratio was the first step in the energy-saving design, and the team settled on about 25 percent

TABLE 7.51

Benefit analysis of energy-saving techniques[a]

Energy efficiency measure/ technique	Incremental energy efficiency (%)	Cumulative energy efficiency (%)
Operable windows	11.4	11.4
Sunshading	4.9	16.3
Rooftop garden	0.2	16.5
Fan-forced ventilation	5.5	22.0
Buoyancy ventilation	5.4	27.4
Air-conditioning size reduction	4.9	32.3
Lighting reduction	8.7	41.0
Air-conditioning efficiency increase	5.2	46.2
Lighting efficiency increase and control	7.2	53.4
Heat exchanger of fresh air	1.2	54.6
Power equipment efficiency/control	1.0	55.6
High-efficiency transformer	4.5	60.1
Renewable energy	5.0	65.1

a Yu-Chung Wang, et al., "Energy-Saving Techniques of Full-Scale Green Building Analysis Research: Taiwan's First Zero-Carbon Green Building," supplied via email by Hsien-te Lin, August 27, 2011.

7.107 The Magic School of Green Technology is Taiwan's first zero-carbon building. Photo: © Lin Hsien-Te.

glazing, with shading on the south-facing windows. The team's research revealed that in tropical climates, sun-shading devices will block 68 percent of incoming solar radiation annually, if positioned at a 45-degree angle on south-facing glazing.[159]

"Glass is the genesis of contemporary architecture, but it's also a big killer of energy," said Lin. "In subtropical and tropical regions especially, glass curtain wall designers really waste energy."[160]

A major breakthrough on this project was effective use of natural buoyancy (stack-effect) ventilation, which is typically not utilized in tropical climates because the warm season is so long. Using clear glass positioned in front of a black enamel finish for maximum solar gain, the team discovered that the temperature difference between the chimneys and the building interior creates a massive channeling airflow during most of the year. The chimney design lengthens the period in which buoyancy ventilation can be effective and therefore decreases the annual air-conditioning load by 30 percent.[161] Only when outdoor air temperatures reach 84°F (29°C) is the air-conditioning system turned on.[162]

"We designed a natural ventilation system so that the building's 300-seat auditorium does not need air-conditioning at least four months of the year," said Lin. "From what I've seen so far, the results have been really good, and we might be able to do even better than that."[163]

The auditorium's ventilation system is based on the ancient "kiln ventilation system." A low-velocity wind stream similar to the workings of a kiln moves from the bottom to the top of the hall across all 300 auditorium seats, leaving the hall comfortable and well ventilated in the winter without using any electricity.[164] Simulations using

7.108 Fourteen small wind turbines are encased in an orange scaffolding-like frame tower that projects from the roof, and three solar chimneys rise from the top of the building. Photo: © Lin Hsien-Te.

computational fluid dynamics (CFD) and a 1:20 scale physical model showed that a draft just below 1.6 ft (0.5 m) per second exchanges the auditorium air five to eight times each hour, keeping it comfortable enough to avoid air-conditioning use, even during Taiwan's humid spring and fall months.[165] The system cost NT$200,000 (US$6,500) with a three-year payback and delivered superior energy efficiency compared to most existing energy-saving air-conditioning systems.[166]

Ventilation for the office spaces is assisted by an atrium, which initiates a cross flow from exterior windows through atrium-facing windows, then out the atrium and up into the chimneys where it exits the building.[167]

Operating Data

Annual energy use (actual): 40.43 kWh/sq m. (Total Energy Use: 123,296 kWh in 3,055 sq m floor area not including the 15,220 sq ft [1,414 sq m] basement parking area. Table 7.52 shows that measured energy use for the first nine months is somewhat better than predicted, giving confidence in the predicted results.) Tables 7.53 and 7.54 show how this project accumulated the points to achieve LEED Platinum and the highest (Diamond) rating in Taiwan's EWHH rating system, respectively.

The Inside Story: An Interview with Professor Lin Hsien-Te[168]

Q: Why was net-zero energy the goal for this project?

A: The net-zero-energy design is the top goal of sustainable architecture. The construction budget of the MSGT was donated from thirty-four Taiwanese companies to [NCKU] to build an education center for environmental education. For my department, the top architecture department in Taiwan, it was our best chance to demonstrate our academic research achievement through this project.

Q: What compromises were made in order to achieve net-zero energy?

A: Energy-saving design is my professional field, and I confirmed that the Magic School can meet the ambitious target of 65 percent energy saving. This means consuming only 43 kWh/sq m/year of electricity comparing to 123 kWh/sq m/year, the average electricity usage of the same-scale office building in Taiwan. However, we are not satisfied

TABLE 7.52

Differences between eQUEST simulation prediction and actual energy consumption, 2011

	Jan	Feb.	Mar.	Apr.	May	Jun.	Jul.	Aug.	Sep.	Oct.	Nov.	Dec.
eQUEST simulation prediction (kWh)	5,180	5,810	7,990	9,830	10,610	12,930	12,440	13,820	13,230	12,840	11,020	9,620
Actual energy consumption (kWh)	5,099	5,745	7,322	9,318	11,241	12,181	11,613	13,286	12,532	12,991	11,732	10,236
Differences (%)	1.6%	1.1%	8.4%	5.2%	5.9%	5.8%	6.6%	3.8%	5.3%	1.2%	6.5%	6.4%

TABLE 7.53

LEED evaluation

LEED-NC Version 2.2 categories	Points
Sustainable sites	11
Water efficiency	8
Energy and atmosphere	14
Materials and resource	6
Indoor environmental quality	12
Innovation and design process	5
Total (required for Platinum Rating: 52)	**56**

TABLE 7.54

Taiwan's EEWH system evaluation for MSGT

EEWH-2010 categories		Points
Ecology	1. Biodiversity	3.88
	2. Greenery	4.93
	3. Soil water content	4.01
Energy	4. Energy conservation	19.35
Waste	5. CO_2 emission reduction	5.21
	6. Waste reduction	5.82
Health	7. Indoor environmental quality	7.86
	8. Water conservation	8.50
	9. Sewer and garbage treatment	2.0
Total (required for Diamond Rating: 53.0)		**61.6**

with the efficiency of 65 percent energy conservation; we want to pursue mankind's highest ideals of zero-carbon architecture. The President of NCKU helped us to find the secret of carbon neutral, which is by way of forestation to increase photosynthesis to absorb CO_2 emissions from the building to achieve the goal of zero-carbon architecture. The NCKU set aside 0.2 hectares (about 0.5 acres) of green space beside the MSGT, as well as the 4.5 hectares (about 11 acres) of wasteland on the campus to be used for permanent forestation, helping to successfully reach our zero-carbon architecture ideals.

Q: How were you able to control costs?

A: Because two-thirds of the total budget was donated through my relationships, the University let me control all of this project's design, analysis, and experiments.

At a glance

Name: National Cheng Kung University, Magic School of Green Technology (Y. S. Sun Green Building Research Center)

Location: Tainan City, Taiwan

Size: 51,660 sq ft (4,800 sq m)

Completion: January 2011

Cost: NT$180 million (US$6.0 million) (including landscape construction)

Distinction: LEED-NC Platinum, EEWH Diamond

Program: Academic research offices, meeting rooms, 300-seat conference hall, and museum.

Project team

Owner: National Cheng Kung University

Consultant Professor Team: Lin Hsien-Te (energy), Chou Rong-Hwa (CFD), Lai Rong-Ping (acoustic)

Architect: Lin Hsien-Te & Joe Shih Architects

MEP Engineers: Wang Yu-Chung, Tayang Energy Technology Co., Ltd

8

Lessons from the Case Studies

In this chapter, we look at the water and energy use of the forty-nine high-performance buildings profiled in Chapter 7. In Chapter 2, we introduced some expected energy performance results, shown in Table 8.1. Of course, energy performance will vary by building type (e.g., research laboratories and healthcare facilities typically use three to five times [or more] the energy used in office buildings), but it's important to set some markers in the ground. The best marker is energy- and water-use intensity, measured per unit building area.[1] Based on the case-study data, Table 8.1 is a guide for future projects.

From the discussion in Chapter 2, you may recall that ultimately, to measure carbon-emission reductions, we need to be concerned with the *source* energy use (i.e. the energy consumed and carbon emitted at the power plant). Since about 70 percent of large nonresidential building energy use comes from electricity, it's source energy that will ultimately drive carbon-neutral design considerations.[2] So the power source also matters; in countries where most power comes from hydroelectric plants, the ratio of source to site energy could be nearly one to one. In regions where coal-fired electricity is the norm, the ratio can be as high as three to one. So designers also need to take into account regional differences in power supplies in determining what really constitutes a "zero-carbon" building. By producing on-site solar power equivalent to a building's annual energy use, one can get pretty close to a zero-carbon building (excluding the carbon content of the building materials).

TYPICAL BUILDING ENERGY USES

Reviewing estimates of building electrical energy requirements, organized by end uses, is a very practical way to look at low-energy building design. Figure 8.1 shows the split between various energy uses at a large office building, One Shelley Street, in Sydney, Australia. You can see that lighting is 22 percent, air movement and space conditioning total nearly 40 percent, with the remaining energy in other uses. Trying to design a low-energy building requires considering all uses, including perhaps 25 to 33 percent devoted to miscellaneous uses and "plug/process loads" from all types of equipment.[3]

To these totals must be added an additional energy demand for direct thermal applications (typically representing 25 to 30 percent of total building energy consumption) such as water heating, and even cooking, a demand that will vary greatly by building type.

Examining a high-performance new building in China, the World Financial Center in Beijing (profiled in Chapter 9), one can see that the projected distribution of energy end uses shows dramatically different characteristics. Table 8.2 shows that the largest single energy use is plug loads.

In this high-performance building in a temperate climate, the largest end uses are, in order: plug loads, ventilation fans, space heating, interior lighting, water heating, and space cooling. These together account for more than 77 percent of the total projected energy use. In this climate, heating is relatively more important than in Sydney. Interestingly, plug loads are significantly impacted by occupant behavior, and many building science researchers are beginning

TABLE 8.1

Energy and water use goals for high-performance office buildings

	Energy intensity	Water intensity[a]
Europe	100–200 kWh/sq m/year	200–300 l/sq m/year
Americas	10–20 kWh/sq ft/year, 34,000–68,000 BTU/sq ft/year	5–10 g/sq ft/year
Asia Pacific	100–200 kWh/sq m/year	300–600 l/sq m/year

a Water use intensity is heavily dependent on whether the building uses a cooling tower for air-conditioning

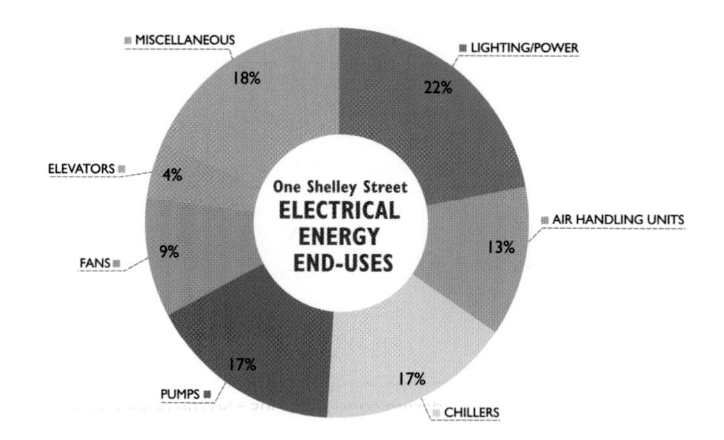

8.1 Distribution of electrical energy end uses at One Shelley Street, Sydney, Australia. Source: AECOM, 1 Shelley Street Energy Monitoring Report, October 2011, p. 30.

TABLE 8.2

Projected annual energy end uses for World Financial Center, Beijing, China

End use	Energy use (kWh)	Percentage of total load (with space heating)	Percentage of electrical load only
Interior lighting	2,956,491 kWh	13.9	16.3
Exterior lighting	216,075	1.0	1.2
Space cooling	1,341,909	6.0	7.4
Space heating (steam) @ 10,553 million BTU	3,092,001	14.6	–
Pumps	768,438	3.6	4.2
Heat rejection	226,700	1.1	1.2
Fans – interior	3,339,364	15.7	18.3
Fans – parking garage	903,701	4.3	5.0
Service water heating	1,378,486	6.5	7.6
Receptacle equipment (plug loads)	4,847,612	22.8	26.6
Elevators and escalators	2,206,647	10.5	12.2
Total	**21,247,424 kWh**	**100.0**	**100.0**

to study how to persuade occupants to become more engaged in reducing building energy use.

One can also look at the difference between the lower-rise Sydney (ten stories) building and the higher-rise (twenty-two-story) Beijing building, with elevators representing a more important load in the Beijing building, and pumps a much smaller load, whereas in Sydney the building employs direct cooling from Sydney Harbour, requiring considerable pumping energy.

ENERGY USE IN CASE-STUDY PROJECTS

Figure 8.2 shows the measured site energy use intensity for case-study buildings, organized by region. Operating data is from the individual case studies in Chapter 7. There was simply neither data nor time to calculate the primary (source) energy use for each building, but this can be done by interested researchers. The reader can also readily see from Figure 8.2 that certain building types such as research laboratories and healthcare facilities have much higher energy use intensities than office or academic buildings.

What one can see in Table 8.3 and Figure 8.2, is that most projects' site energy use exceeded 100 kWh/sq m/year, although about 12 percent were able to reduce that number to 50 or 60, or even lower.[4] To reach a truly "stretch" goal of 100 kWh/sq m/year of primary (source) energy use would require most projects, with such technologies as ground-source heat pumps or free cooling from a nearby cold-water body, to reduce site energy use to nearly 50 kWh/sq m/year (EUI of 16 kBtu/sq ft/year), an achievable number in theory, but not yet widespread in practice. Of course, with on-site solar-power generation (or in the case of one building, a neighboring forest set aside for permanent conservation and carbon-fixing), it's possible to have a zero-carbon building with an EUI of 30–35 Btu/sq ft/year, as we saw for the NREL RSF I building in Colorado and the Zero Energy Building in Singapore.

So, for designers, there are now clear targets: achieve at least the median energy use of similar LEED Platinum, BREEAM Excellent/Outstanding, 6-Star Green Star buildings in your region. Of course, many projects now aim at the low end of the energy-use range and have a clear goal to match the "best in class" results already obtained in that region.

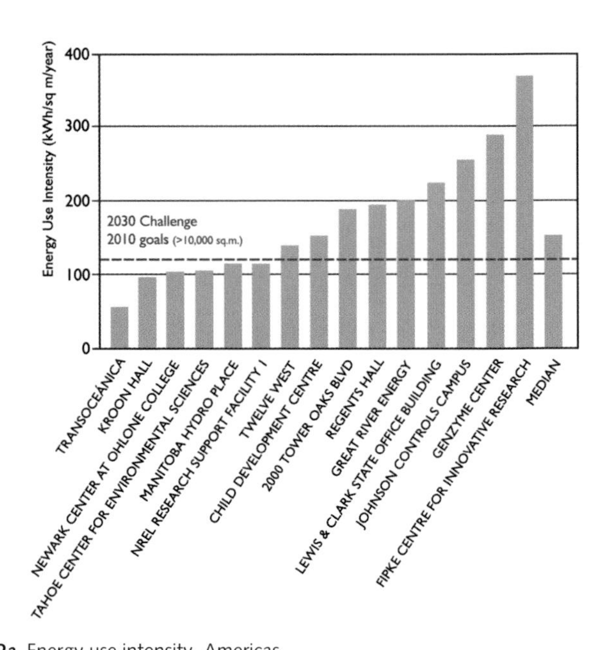

8.2a Energy use intensity, Americas.

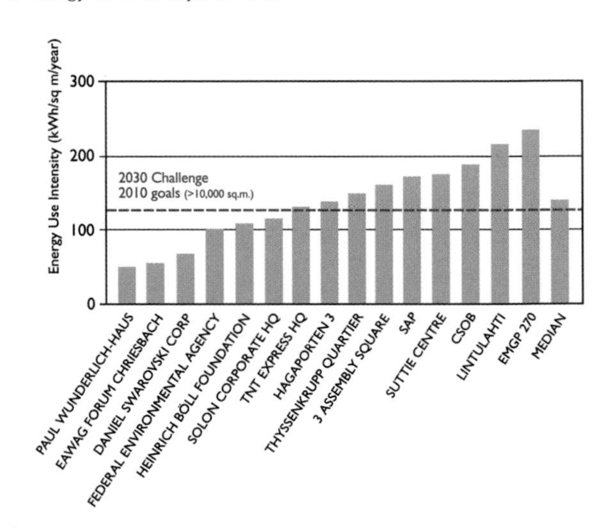

8.2b Energy use intensity, Europe.

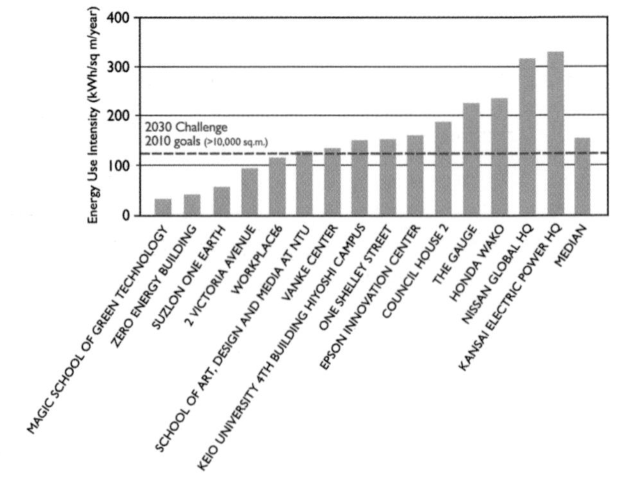

8.2c Energy use intensity, Asia Pacific.

TABLE 8.3

Median energy use intensity, by region

Americas	193/156 kWh/sq m/year	19 examples; or 15 examples, excluding four very energy-intensive lab/research and hospital projects
Europe	135 kWh/sq m/year	15 examples
Asia Pacific	158 kWh/sq m/year	15 examples

TABLE 8.4

2030 Challenge target for 2010: 60 percent reduction from US national average[a]

Building type	Energy use intensity (1,000s of Btu/sq ft/year)	Energy use intensity (kWh/sq m/ year)
Education	30	95
Healthcare: inpatient	91	287
Office, 10,000–100,000 sq ft	36	113
Office, > 100,000 sq ft	42	132

a AIA 2030 Commitment Reporting Tool, www.aia.org/about/initiatives/AIAB079458, accessed February 4, 2012.

Beyond actual results, it's useful to look at what projects should achieve to meet the 2030 Challenge goals introduced in Chapter 1. Table 8.4 shows what these goals would be for 2010, representing a 60 percent reduction in energy use from US national averages in 2005. Recall that by 2015 new buildings should be performing 16 percent lower than these levels, to meet the 2030 Challenge goal of a 70 percent reduction (by 2015). One can see that the median energy use of the world's greenest buildings barely misses the 2010 large office target in Europe, exceeds it by about 20 percent in Asia Pacific, and misses the target by 18 percent in the Americas region, demonstrating that in some places the best buildings are on a path toward carbon-neutral energy use by 2030, but that in other places, designers, builders and operators still have a way to go.

WATER USE IN COMMERCIAL AND INSTITUTIONAL BUILDINGS

Water use in buildings in the commercial, industrial, and institutional (CII) sectors accounts for the majority of urban water use. We know that as the world's population continues to grow, water resources will come under increasing pressure and that high-performance green buildings should do much better in reducing potable water consumption.

Australian experience during the country's 1995–2009 drought showed how a developed country contended successfully with difficulties in preparing for present and future water supply.[5] With a metropolitan area of 4 million inhabitants, Sydney is home to Australia's first major response to continuing drought: major conservation programs, water reuse, public education, and a new desalination plant to provide new water for major cities. In Sydney, there is growing public acceptance for water conservation and reuse of treated municipal wastewater, a feature in several of the Australian buildings profiled in Chapter 7, along with two of the newer buildings profiled in Chapter 9. Because Sydney temperatures can reach more than 100°F (38°C) in summer, and many office buildings require cooling much of the year, almost 20 percent of water use derives from cooling towers, a level susceptible to reduction through improved technology, reusing rainwater, graywater, and blackwater, and more efficient operations. These facts suggest priorities for reducing water use in new high-performance buildings, by focusing first on a total water systems analysis and then by supplying as much of the demand as possible with non-potable water.[6]

HOW MUCH WATER SHOULD A BUILDING USE?

To find out how much water a commercial office building should use, we examined data from three countries: Australia, Germany, and the USA, as shown in Table 8.5. Australian data come from a study conducted in 2006 by the Australian Government; US data are representative from public and private offices; German data are from unpublished studies supplied by Transsolar, a German climate engineering firm.[7] While not definitive, the data represent both average use and "best practices." Increased water use can result from buildings in hot climates that require significantly more water for operating cooling towers. Interestingly, German data are quite a bit lower than either Australian or US data, reflecting perhaps a milder climate as well as more water-efficient building operations. From these data, building managers can get a better idea about establishing best practice goals, ranging from 5 to 10 gallons per year per sq ft (200 to 400 liters per sq m) for buildings without irrigation or cooling towers, up to 15 to 25 gallons per sq ft (600 to 1,000 liters per sq m) for buildings in hot climates with site irrigation and cooling towers. For benchmarking purposes, as with energy use, it's better to focus on absolute water use rather than just on relative improvement (e.g., saving 20 percent compared with a reference or "code" building).

WATER USE IN CASE-STUDY PROJECTS

Figure 8.3 shows the water use in the case-study buildings in each region. Interestingly, fewer projects measured (or reported to us) the water demand, but the actual use was very close to the numbers shown in Table 8.5. We believe that the same methods applied to zero-net-energy buildings can be applied to generate zero-net-water buildings; this goal is aspired to, for example, by the Bullitt Foundation office building in Seattle, Washington, profiled in Chapter 9.

TABLE 8.5

Office building annual water use in three countries[a]

Country/use	Australia[b]	USA	Germany[c]
Average private office: no leaks, with cooling towers	1,010–1,125 l/sq m (24.8–27.6 g/sq ft)		
Average public building	3,340 l/sq m (82.0 g/sq f)		
"Best practices": private office with cooling towers	500–770 l/sq m (12.3–18.9 g/sq f)		
"Best practices": private office no cooling towers[d]	400 l/sq m (9.8 g/sq f)		
"Best practices": public building	2,000 l/sq m (49.2 g/sq f)		
NABERS[e] 5-star (highest level)	350 l/sq m (8.6 g/sq f)		
1,500 buildings, both private offices and public[f]			150–200 l/sq m (3.7–4.9 g/sq f)
Large insurance company (6 offices): office only[g]			150–200 l/sq m (3.7–4.9 g/sq f)
Large insurance company: office with cooling tower and irrigation			106 l/person/day 800–1,200 l/sq m (19.5–29.5 g/sq f)
Large office building, Nashville, TN[h]		24.7 g/sq f (2006) 17.7 g/sq f (2009)	
Large office buildings, Portland, OR[i]		14.0 g/sq f (2007) 26.5 g/sq ft (2009)	
Federal buildings in NE, TN, CA, and CO[j]		3.6–16.2 g/sq f (2007)	

a Jerry Yudelson, 2010. *Dry Run: Preventing the Next Urban Water Crisis*, Gabriola Island, BC: New Society Publishers, p. 60.
b "Water Efficiency Guide: Office and Public Buildings," Australian Government Department of the Environment and Heritage, October 2006, p. 2.
c Personal communication, Thomas Auer, Transsolar Climate Engineering, Stuttgart.
d "Best Practice Guidelines for Water Conservation in Commercial Office Buildings and Shopping Centres," Sydney Water, 2007, p. 130.
e NABERS is the National Australian Built Environment Rating System.
f AGES GmbH, "Energie und Wasserverbrauchskennwerte (2005) in der Bundesrepublik Deutschland, February 2007, pp. 29–30, available from www.ages-gmbh.de, copyright by ages-GmbH, Kosterstrasse 3, 48143 Münster, Germany, project leader Carl Zeine.
g 15 to 30 liters/day/worker x 225 working days/year divided by 20 to 30 sq m per person average office space, per Thomas Auer.
h Data from Jeffrey Martin, Caterpillar Financial, January 2010. Building is 323,000 sq ft. A new ozone cleaning system for cooling tower installed in 2008 reduced water use by nearly 30 percent in 2009 from 2006 levels.
i Data from Byron Courts, Melvin Mark Companies, Portland, OR, December 2009. First building is 360,000 sq ft, housing federal office workers. Second building is 250,000 office building. Other office buildings in Portland operated by the same company show water use in this range.
j Kim Fowler and Emily Rauch, "Assessing Green Building Performance: A Post-Occupancy Evaluation of 12 GSA Buildings," 2008, GSA/Pacific Northwest National Laboratory, Richland, WA, Report PNNL-17393, www.gsa.gov/Portal/gsa/ep/contentView.do?programId=13852&channelId=-26364&ooid=28927&contentId=28929&pageTypeId=17109&contentType=GSA_BASIC&programPage=%2Fep%2Fprogram%2FgsaBasic.jsp&P=, accessed February 7, 2010. Buildings range from 68,000 to 327,7000 gross square feet. Usage depends somewhat on cooling towers and outdoor irrigation.

Table 8.6 shows the median water intensity for case-study buildings in three major regions. The water-intensity figures are based on about half the reported results for energy intensity and should be combined with the figures in Table 8.5 to set goals for each new project.

So, one can see that, for design purposes, there are now clear targets to help a project achieve the median result of other LEED Platinum and similar buildings; of course, some projects will want to match the "best in class" results shown in Table 8.5. In Europe and the Americas there is much more focus on rainwater harvesting in high-performance green buildings, as well as a growing movement to treat and reuse building-generated graywater and blackwater. Total potable water use depends on the amount of water used in cooling towers and whether there is recycled or reclaimed water reused in the building. In more humid or tropical regions, one would expect considerably more water use for cooling purposes.

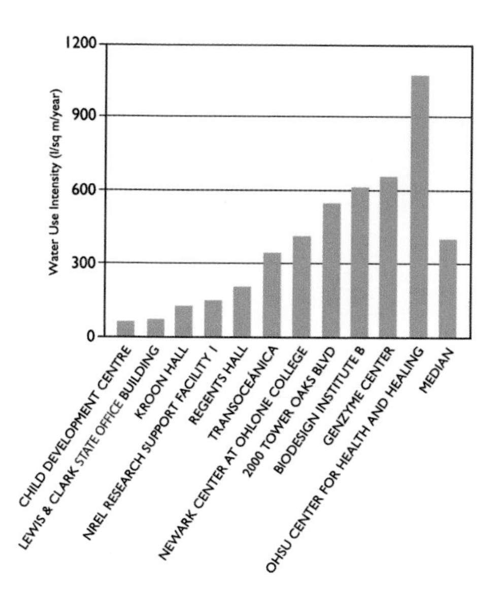

8.3a Water use intensity, Americas.

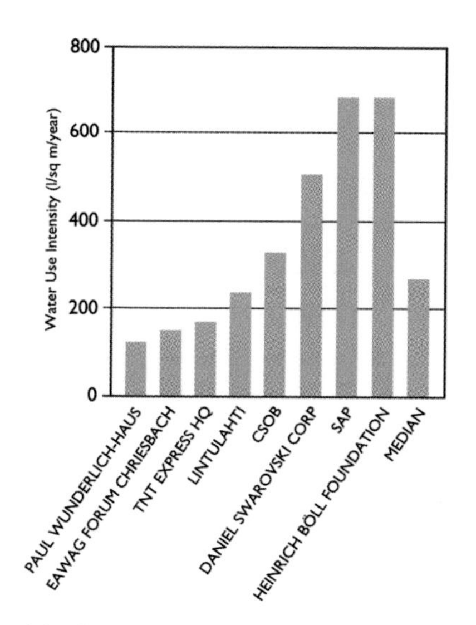

8.3b Water use intensity, Europe.

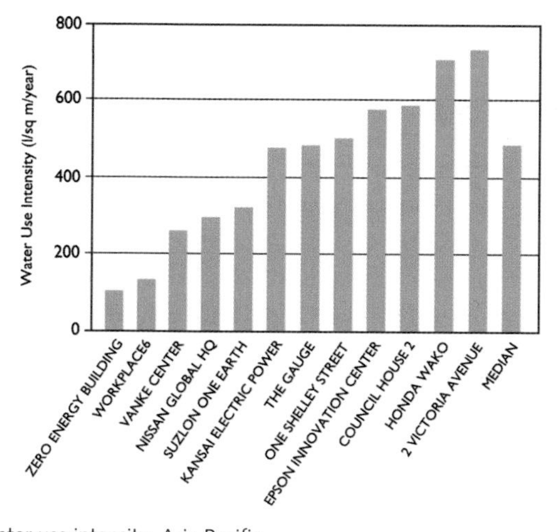

8.3c Water use intensity, Asia Pacific.

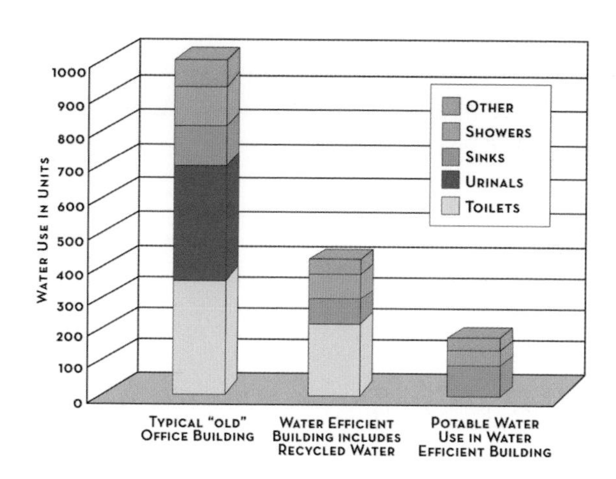

8.4 Potable water use in water-efficient buildings can be reduced more than 80 percent with efficient fixtures and widespread use of recycled or reclaimed water. Source: Guenter Hauber-Davidson, "Towards a Greater Sustainable Water Supply for Our Office Buildings through Grey Water Recycling," PowerPoint® Presentation, March 2007, p. 6.

TABLE 8.6

Median water use intensity, by region

Americas	375 l/sq m/year	11 examples
Europe	273 l/sq m/year	8 examples
Asia Pacific	463 l/sq m/year	12 examples

WATER EFFICIENCY TECHNOLOGIES

Water use in the CII sector can be cut substantially, to everyone's economic benefit. Figure 8.4 shows what might be accomplished in office buildings with the widespread use not only of conservation measures but also of recycled and reclaimed water, a total savings approaching 80 percent. There are many measures that will accomplish this goal, but, in our view, we can expect water price increases to drive demand for new technologies in green buildings regardless of other driving forces. This is a phenomenon we are seeing worldwide, as older infrastructure needs to be replaced to meet growing urban water demands. Rules help, too: for example, the US Green Building Council's LEED 2009 rating system has already sparked a significant reduction in water use from office buildings, schools, colleges, hotels, and retail enterprises, with its prerequisite of a minimum 20 percent water-use reduction, since the green certification has clear marketing and branding benefits for existing buildings.

8.5 Students view the enthalpy wheels at the Ohlone College's Newark Center, an attempt to "lift the veil" and expose key energy efficiency systems to the public. Photo: © Robert Canfield Photography.

OCCUPANCY EFFECTS ON BUILDING PERFORMANCE, CONTRIBUTED BY MARK FRANKEL[8]

Architects and engineers strive to create energy-efficient buildings by controlling physical features such as insulation, windows, and HVAC systems. To deliver great energy performance in buildings, however, building operations and occupant behavior have to be addressed, and the management and technology tools to do that are just starting to emerge.

New Buildings Institute and Ecotope, Inc., recently analyzed the relative energy impact of a series of typical design features, compared to a set of operations and maintenance practices and occupant habits also affecting building energy use.[9] The study found that the impact on building energy use from poor (but not atypical) operations and maintenance practices can increase energy use by more than 50 percent in some climates. Occupant behavior can increase energy use by a significant 80 percent over the predicted use, based on anticipated behavior during the design process. In most cases, the magnitude of these ranges is larger than the total savings effect of all the building's physical efficiency features.

Post-construction impacts are, by nature, more likely to fall short of the anticipated outcome than to improve it, because the design community, energy modelers, and energy codes all tend to work from a best-case scenario when imagining future maintenance and occupant activities. It's no surprise that owners and occupants play a major role in building energy use and that these actions take place outside the design team's control or influence. Now the study reveals just how significant that energy use is.

As the role of post-construction characteristics becomes more widely recognized in the marketplace, there are likely to be significant changes to design practice and to building codes and incentive programs. The design community will have to more effectively communicate the role of operations and occupants in building performance, and features such as better metering and occupant feedback systems will become design imperatives.

The New Buildings Institute and Ecotope study also has significant implications for energy modeling practice, which still struggles to predict building energy use—a situation that will change if the energy modeler can realistically foresee how the building will really be used and maintained.[10] In addition, building owners and developers have to recognize that the aggressive goals set for energy code upgrades will be impossible to meet without directly addressing post-construction energy-use patterns, which have so far been well outside the scope of code language and enforcement procedures. In response, codes will evolve not only to include more features that allow for better building operation, such as commissioning, metering, and feedback systems, but may also start to incorporate energy-performance outcome targets into the code-enforcement process.

Perhaps nothing will more effectively drive us to recognize the role of building operations and occupants in building energy use than the proliferating [energy performance] disclosure ordinances now being adopted around the USA. These ordinances will bring a much more intense, market-based focus on the issues really driving building energy performance. In the meantime, the findings of this study can help the building community better align their priorities with those building features and operational characteristics that have the greatest effect on building energy-use outcome.

WHY DON'T BUILDINGS PERFORM BETTER?

A central conundrum in building performance evaluation is why buildings don't actually perform better right "out of the box," but the fact is that they don't. Some part owes to actions of building occupants that go against what the designers intended. Another part owes to poor design thinking or to engineers who don't design the actual system beyond a list of input and output points, a control diagram and sequence of operations, leaving the rest of the controls to the controls contractor. But perhaps the most important reason is that building designs are needlessly complex, as Adrian Leaman argues in Chapter 5, well beyond the capabilities of the controls industry and building operators to deal with. This situation argues persuasively in favor of "passive" design strategies already adopted by many projects profiled in the case studies.

A well-known green building engineer from the USA has a particular view about this issue. Peter Rumsey is Managing Director at Integral Group and widely recognized as a national leader in sustainable and resource-efficient building design and innovation. In the following section, he presents his views about how high-performance design is hindered by the reliance on controls contractors to do the detailed programming for innovative building systems and technologies.

OUT-OF-CONTROL CONTROLS, CONTRIBUTED BY PETER RUMSEY[11]

Imagine buying a new high-end car that doesn't work. You have it inspected by a specialist to diagnose problems that take weeks to fix. Finally you regain possession after most, but not all, problems have been repaired and you are told you need a service contract. You wonder why you bothered buying a new car! Car buyers wouldn't put up with this scenario, yet the building sector tolerates a similar situation with commissioning building controls systems. The bottom line is this: Owners shouldn't have to commission new buildings. The controls industry business model includes selling inadequate software and installing sensors that don't work effectively. This industry needs a makeover.

Simply stated: Controls don't deliver on the promise of optimizing building performance. Nighttime commercial building energy use is 20 to 40 percent of daytime levels, but with lights off, empty buildings should obviously use much less. The Center for the Built Environment at the University of California, Berkeley, reported that only 11 percent of buildings meet ASHRAE comfort criteria (i.e. that 80 percent of occupants be comfortable at any given time). A study funded by the California Energy Commission found that over 50 percent of airside economizer dampers were not working as intended, owing to factors including bad sensors and bad control logic. The Lawrence Berkeley National Laboratory determined that 90 percent of buildings have HVAC controls and systems that don't work properly during the first year of occupancy.

While statistics and macro-statistics do bear out the problem with controls, direct experience provides more compelling examples of problems. For an engineer who has been working in buildings for his whole career, the list of horror stories is long. Building facility maintenance engineers know all too well the case of out-of-control variable air volume (VAV) boxes. It is common to see temperature sensors, air dampers, and reheat coils all doing something that is beyond possibility. I have seen room sensors read 30 degrees or lower when the temperature is in the 70s. I have seen VAV dampers running at "120 percent" and reheat valves "fully open" when no heat is produced.

The simple errors in controls systems are so prevalent that, when our firm starts looking at the system after installation, we have an entry-level engineer run through the control screens and find the glaring problems. On the more complicated systems such as boilers or chilled-water production, the controls problems are even more prevalent. [In our practice], we often observe control valves, variable-speed pumps and variable-speed fans that oscillate wildly. Figure 8.6 shows a trend log of the hot-water supply to a building. The period of the 20°F to 30°F oscillations shown is five minutes. This caused the heating zones downstream of this supply to hunt continuously for the right setting and not be able to maintain comfort. And all this is on a fairly ordinary building!

On innovative and high-performance buildings where nonstandard mechanical systems are used, the problems tend to be exacerbated. In our experience, the next generation of mechanical systems such as radiant heating and cooling and chilled beams are no more complicated than traditional systems. However, due to their differences, control contractors and installers tend to have more problems implementing them.

A recent LEED Platinum office building that we designed is a perfect example. The building was not comfortable for several months after people were already in the building and using it. The contractors, especially the controls contractor, convinced the owner that the systems and controls were built as designed and that it was the engineer's design that was at fault, i.e. that not enough cooling was installed. After weeks of diagnostics, we found close to 200 problems with the system installation. In one case we couldn't understand why, when a valve was supposedly opened, we saw no evidence of flow. It was only after one of the designers opened the protective housing and found that the valve motor had fallen off of the valve that we realized the problem. Then it turned out that due to incorrect implementation of the controls sequence the radiant slab went into the cooling mode when it was supposed to be in the heating mode. To prove that there was adequate heat in the design, we manually opened the valves and turned on the boilers. We did this during the coldest part of the winter and occupants began to complain that the building was overheating. To our dismay we found that the project manager for the controls contractor, after having worked on the project for a year, still did not understand the concept of radiant heating and radiant heat transfer and how it could work from overhead. Happily, in the end, the building now works exceptionally well and the occupants are comfortable. But this only came after months of exhaustively proving to the controls contractor that each of the nearly 200 problems related to incorrect implementation of the control logic or broken controls equipment not to design errors.

Extrapolating to all office buildings, we find that controls commonly function off of design intent. Green and innovative low-energy buildings fare even worse: Preprogrammed ("canned") controls solutions don't mesh well with nonstandard techniques. It's hard to pinpoint the source of this breakdown, but in my experience software implementation problems are usually key. System performance varies with the quality of the installer and programmer; bad code compounds poor implementation. Control loops that don't work correctly cause valves, dampers, fans, and pumps to cycle uncontrollably for years at a time. Faulty sensors are another factor. The controls contractors we work with are often installers with electrical or programming backgrounds, not well versed in HVAC systems. They lack inter-disciplinary knowledge—like thermodynamics and electronics—that could improve things.

Don't blame building operator error or insufficient training for failures. Controls need a more user-friendly interface that points out problems and opportunities. The system has to work; operators don't

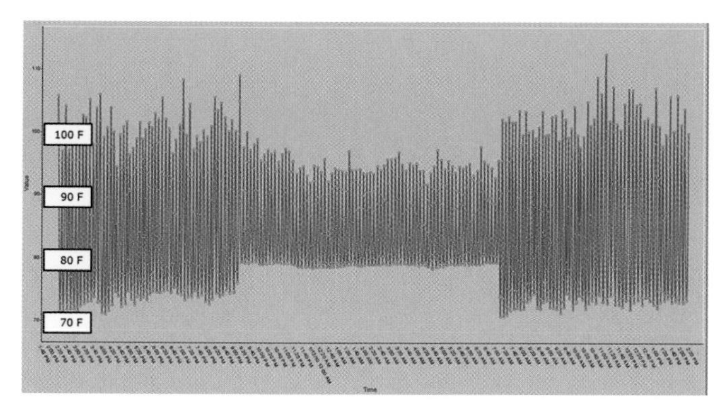

8.6 This trend log of hot water supply to a building shows a 20–30 degree oscillation inside of 5 minutes, so that heating zones downstream of this supply search continuously for the right setting and are unable to maintain comfort. Courtesy of: Integral Group.

have time to debug it. Controls should be like smart phones: reliable, intuitive, easy to use, automatically diagnosing problems and self-healing them. In the rare event that my iPhone crashes, I don't have to hack its source code. Perhaps some day artificial intelligence innovation will yield controls breakthroughs.

I look forward to the day when commissioning is no longer necessary, when I won't have to explain to owners why they must pay to verify that the system they just purchased is working. We need a better "controls paradigm," where a project's success no longer hinges on who installs the system or which software is used. In the venture capital world investors seek disruptive technologies that will transform an industry. The controls industry is ripe for disruption. Controls should work properly the first time and consistently deliver comfort and energy savings. Building owners and occupants deserve no less.

HOW CAN WE GET BETTER RESULTS FROM INNOVATIVE DESIGN?

An alternative (and more positive viewpoint) comes from an engineer, Steve Carroll, experienced in building commissioning.[12] In his view, commissioning is a quality assurance process that starts in the pre-design phase and continues all the way through the first year of occupancy. If controls contractors are not brought on board during the pre-design phase, they cannot be effective partners in the commissioning process.

Commissioning is performed by a third-party entity not by someone who is involved with the design and construction. The importance of this service is that commissioning agents work directly for the owners, analyze deviations from design intent and required performance, state what is wrong and how to fix it, without a financial benefit whether the owner decides to follow their recommendations. Just as with fixing a car, buildings will only work well when the owner hires a trusted mechanic (commissioning agent) and follows his recommendations.

What do these issues portend for the practical world of architecture and engineering? How does one navigate all the competing interests to get to a great sustainable building? What we're seeing is the emergence of a new type of engineer, one fully versed in all aspects of integrated building design, the "ecological engineer." Here's what Steven A. Straus, an engineer and the CEO of a leading US practitioner of sustainable engineering design, Glumac, whose project Twelve West is profiled in Chapter 7, had to say about this.[13]

Many building projects have ambitious goals but fall short on delivering energy efficiency, comfort, and rate of return on the investment. Creating great buildings is challenging, with so many competing interests. Developments are often led by a project manager who is rated solely on achieving the project's goals within a set budget and schedule, regardless of future maintenance and operating costs or sustainable features.

[In today's world], there is art in the architecture of the building, but to the ecological engineer, there is science as well. It is extraordinarily complex to predict the comfort or illumination of a space. Historically, it has not been cost-effective to conduct detailed analyses of building systems. However, new software technology has become available, including the ability to study energy performance, air flows with computational fluid dynamics, and daylighting design alternatives at very early project stages. These technologies allow us to provide a far more detailed examination of building designs than was available ten years ago. More importantly, commissioning has gained acceptance over the past decade, which provides feedback to designers about what is working and what is not, to ensure that new and complex systems are properly installed and operating.

The theme "green buildings that work" pervades the work and ethos of this ecological engineer. Some building performance results in our study of the world's greenest buildings demonstrate that engineers are in fact learning more about low-energy-use sustainable design with each passing year. Other results demonstrate that project constraints can still increase energy and water use to more conventional levels. In this chapter, we addressed some of the larger remaining challenges in sustainable design: changing user behavior and getting better construction quality (especially with building controls), issues which continue to bedevil those of us anxious to see the promise of the world's greenest buildings fulfilled on every project.

Part III

Looking Ahead

Chapters 9–11

9

Projects to Watch

In the course of our research, we came across a few LEED Platinum, 6-Star Green Star, and DGNB Gold certified projects that had all the attributes of the world's greenest buildings presented in Chapter 7 and met all of our other selection criteria but lacked one full year of operating data at the time this research concluded in late 2011. We decided to present eight of them in the hope that you would find these projects, their environmental design strategies and integration of world-class architecture, green building features, and low-energy design to be interesting and thought-provoking.

We expect that a subsequent edition of this book would find them in the top rank for performance and that even in a few years such a collection would show a huge number of the world's greenest buildings to be in China. We also believe that the next edition of this book would include far more projects, especially in Europe, where third-party rating systems are finally gaining acceptance, as is complete disclosure of operating data.

The projects are listed, as before, in terms of the three major regions of the world where green building is taking place at its most advanced level: Asia Pacific, North America, and Europe. Figure 9.1 shows the projected energy performance of these projects.

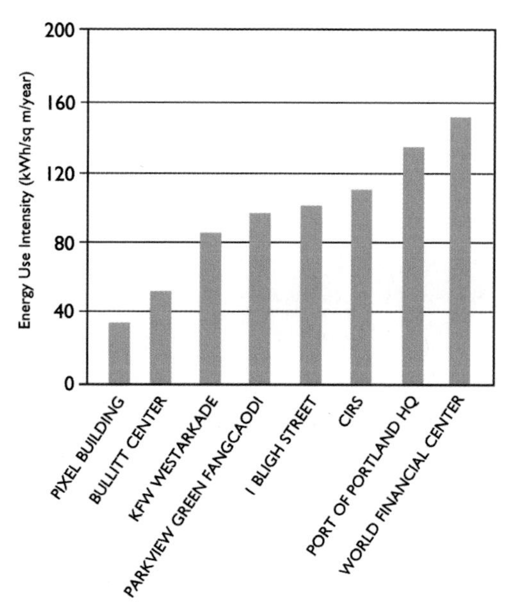

9.1 Projects to Watch energy use intensity.

ASIA PACIFIC

9.2 On the twenty-eighth floor of 1 Bligh in Sydney there is a large rooftop terrace protected from wind by a 12-m-high glazed screen. Photo: H. G. Esch, Hennef. Courtesy of ingenhoven architects + architectus.

1 Bligh, Sydney, Australia

In Sydney's Central Business District, the new office tower 1 Bligh, designed by ingenhoven architects of Düsseldorf, Germany and Architectus of Sydney, was inaugurated on August 30, 2011. It is the first high-rise office building in Australia with a double façade and earned a 6-Star/World Leadership certification from Australia's Green Star standard for sustainable design. It is the first office tower in Sydney to receive this rating from the GBCA.

The twenty-eight-story building's shape was derived from considering various view corridors. The transparent, elliptical office building offers unobstructed views of the world-famous Harbour Bridge. A public plaza with a grand stair complements Farrer Place on the opposite corner to form an attractive urban space. The foyer is publicly accessible during daytime. At the base of the tower there are two bistros and a kindergarten. The ground floor has an open louver-glass façade. An elevator transfer-level on the fifteenth floor offers a large outdoor terrace. On the twenty-eighth floor there is a large rooftop terrace protected by a 39-ft (12-m) glazed screen. Making a green commute easy, there are 300 secure bike racks and showers.

The tower offers 461,000 sq ft (42,800 sq m) of floor space with few columns, creating a highly flexible floor area. The outer row of columns is set in from the façade, leaving the façade column-free. As of April 2012, when Yudelson toured this building, it had announced leases totaling 85 percent of total leasable floor area,

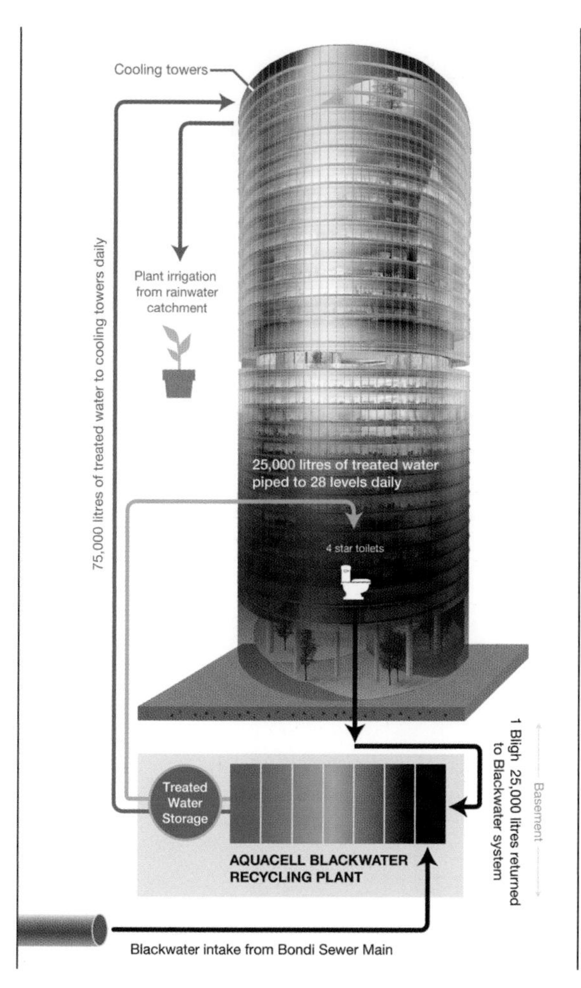

9.3 The filtration plant in the basement cleans 75,000 liters (19,813 gallons) of wastewater per day from the nearby public sewer, a process known as "sewer mining." Courtesy of Aquacell Water Recycling (www.acquacell.com).

although only a handful of floors were occupied at that time, most by a major law firm.

The energy system is used for combined cooling, heating, and power generation (a process known as tri-generation). A 5,382-sq-ft (500-sq-m) vacuum-tube collector-solar array on the roof cools the building by means of a heat exchanger and absorption cooling system.[1] Exhaust air from the offices is brought to the atrium and exhausted through it. Thus, the energy in the conditioned air is not wasted but is used for heating and cooling this space. The suspended ceilings are 30 percent perforated and are used for thermal activation, employing the building's mass and chilled beams.

Because water is particularly scarce (and thus valuable) in Australia, 1 Bligh has its own filtration plant in the basement, which can clean more water than just the wastewater produced in the building. In fact, 90 percent of the water demand for the building comes from recycling (Figure 9.3). For this reason, 19,813 gallons (75 kl) per day of wastewater from the public sewage system are cleaned and used in the building, a process known as "sewer mining," which is gaining

TABLE 9.1

Projected energy and water use[a]

	Annual use	Intensity
Electricity	1,360,287 kWh	115.5 MJ/sq m
Gas	11,173,498 MJ	263.5 MJ/sq m
Diesel	3,000 liters	2 MJ/sq m
Total energy use	**16,155,341 MJ**	**381 MJ/sq m** **106 kWh/sq m**

	Annual net water use	Water use intensity
Amenity water demand	14,817 kl	0.37 kl/sq m
Cooling tower water demand	16,537	0.41
Landscape water demand	804	0.02
Rain water supply (to irrigation)	755	0.018
Blackwater supply	20,000	0.49
Net potable water use	**11,403 kl**	**280 l/sq m**

a Figures for energy and water consumption for all case study projects were provided by the project owner, architect, engineer, or consultant, unless otherwise noted.

popularity in Australia's largest office buildings. Graywater from the washbasins is recycled and used for toilet flushing. Rainwater is collected and used for irrigation. Water-conserving fixtures are used throughout the building.

The full-height atrium is Australia's tallest and creates the central circulation and communications area. It offers daylight and fresh air intake as well as fascinating views. The atrium allows for a continuous airflow and acts as a thermal buffer. Eight glass elevators travel up and down in the atrium, turning the trip to one's desk into an exciting spatial experience. Naturally ventilated balconies in the atrium offer spots for breaks and conversations. To conserve energy for cooling or heating air in the atrium, it is separated from the offices with a glass wall.

To keep heat out, the space between the two layers of the façade contains a flexible sun screen that functions as glare protection. Made of low-iron glass, the outer façade protects the sun screen. Only 10 percent of the time will the lowered louvers have to tilt by more than 30 degrees. The lamellas (shutters) are fully horizontal most of the time, so they don't obstruct the views. They are centrally controlled but can be regulated individually as well.

Cantilevered brise-soleil elements protect the outer façades from overheating. Flexible floorplans allow for varied layouts with a maximum four tenants per floor: Along the façade, the floor plans can be subdivided easily into single offices easily, as necessary. The project's owners, DEXUS Property Group, DWPF, and Cbus Property, large real-estate funds, specified the sustainable concept, not only because it

9.4 The tower offers 42,000 sq m (452,000 sq ft) of floor space with few columns, creating a highly flexible floor area. Photo: H. G. Esch, Hennef. Courtesy of ingenhoven architects + architectus.

demonstrates a new environmental awareness important to tenants in Australia but also because the company believes the building will be "future-proof," command higher rents, and have lower operating costs.

At a glance

Construction: 2008–2011
Floor Area: 460,695 sq ft (42,800 sq m)
Floors: 28
Architects: ingenhoven + architectus
Owner: DEXUS Property Group, DEXUS Wholesale Property Fund, Cbus Property
Rating: 6-Star Green Star, "World Leadership" Rating (GBCA)

PIXEL, Melbourne, Australia

At only 10,764 sq ft (1,000 sq m), the Pixel building in Melbourne claims to be "the smallest building with the biggest expectations" and is by far the smallest building featured in this book.[2] However, it is a noteworthy project because it received a perfect Green Star score—100 points—with an extra 5 points awarded for innovation.[3] The Pixel project also received 105 points (LEED Platinum) (out of 110 possible), making it the highest-scoring building in the world under the LEED rating system. The project also is on track to achieve the highest rating, Outstanding, from BREEAM.[4]

The building's most dramatic feature is its colorful façade (Figure 9.5). The multicolored fixed louvers wrap around all four sides to create a "pixilated" sun shading system.

Pixel aims to produce all of its power needs on-site. Three 1.5-kW wind turbines, combined with 6.5 kW of rooftop PV panels, mounted on a tracking device to improve output by 40 percent, are projected to generate more electricity than the building requires.[5]

Another of Pixel's innovative features is vacuum-toilet technology. Similar to airplane toilets, the system reduces water consumption to a minimum and helps Pixel to maintain water self-sufficiency.

9.5 The multicolored fixed louvers on the Pixel building wrap around all four sides to create a "pixilated" sun shading system. Photo: Grocon.

TABLE 9.2

Projected annual energy end-use summary

	Electricity (kWh)	Natural Gas (kWh)
Common area light and power	1,121	–
Lifts	567	–
Domestic hot water	–	0
Space heating	–	4,725
Space cooling	–	24,058
HVAC fans	3,833	–
HVAC pumps	423	–
Condenser fans	958	
Hydraulic pumps	237	
Miscellaneous loads, controls, etc.	150	
Total energy use	7,289	28,783
Energy use intensity	6.4 kWh/sq m	25.3 kWh/sq m (31.7 kWh/sq m, overall)
Fixed solar PV	3,509	
Tracking solar PV	6,853	
Wind turbines	15,282	
Total renewables	25,644	
Net energy use	(18,355)	28,783
Total energy use intensity	(16.1 kWh/sq m)	25.3 kWh/sq m
Net energy use intensity		9.2 kWh/sq m

If Melbourne maintains its ten-year average rainfall levels, Pixel is predicted to be net-zero, self-sustainable for water supply, using only harvested rainwater, except for drinking water.[6]

Another innovative feature is the anaerobic digester, which processes the building's sewage flows. Located on the ground level, the system extracts methane from the building's blackwater waste. Tanks in series hold toilet and kitchen waste, and the digester harvests methane gas, which replaces natural gas for heating water.[7]

Other high-performance features utilized in the Pixel building include:[8]

- 100-percent fresh-air distribution
- night purge cooling
- gas-fired absorption chiller
- "Pixelcrete," concrete with reclaimed and recycled aggregates
- daylighting and glare control
- living (green) roof
- rainwater, graywater, and blackwater harvesting and reuse.

"Our objectives were to provide an example of the sustainable office of the future and to set a benchmark that exceeds all current-day sustainable office developments," said Shane Esmore, with energy consultants Umow Lai.[9] The annual gross energy-use intensity is projected to be 31.7 kWh/sq m, with a net intensity (after renewable energy contribution) of 9.2 kWh/sq m.

As of April 2012, when Yudelson toured this project, it had only a handful of occupants, on the ground floor. The developer plans to place a team in the remaining floors in the building, to serve the project management needs of adjacent residential towers just beginning construction. Until the project is actually fully occupied and operating for a year, the projected energy and water performance will be difficult to verify. Nonetheless, the project is noteworthy for its "world's-best" achievements in design and the use of a full palette of green building measures in a commercial environment.

At a glance

Name: Pixel

Location: Carlton, Victoria, Australia

Size: 12,230 sq ft (1,136 sq m)

Distinction: 6-Star Green Star Office "Design," LEED Platinum, and BREEAM Outstanding (expected)

Program: Corporate office

Project team

Owner: Developer, Builder: Grocon

Architect: Studio505

Building Services Engineer: ESD

Energy Engineer: Umow Lai & Associates

Structural Engineer: Van Der Meer Consulting

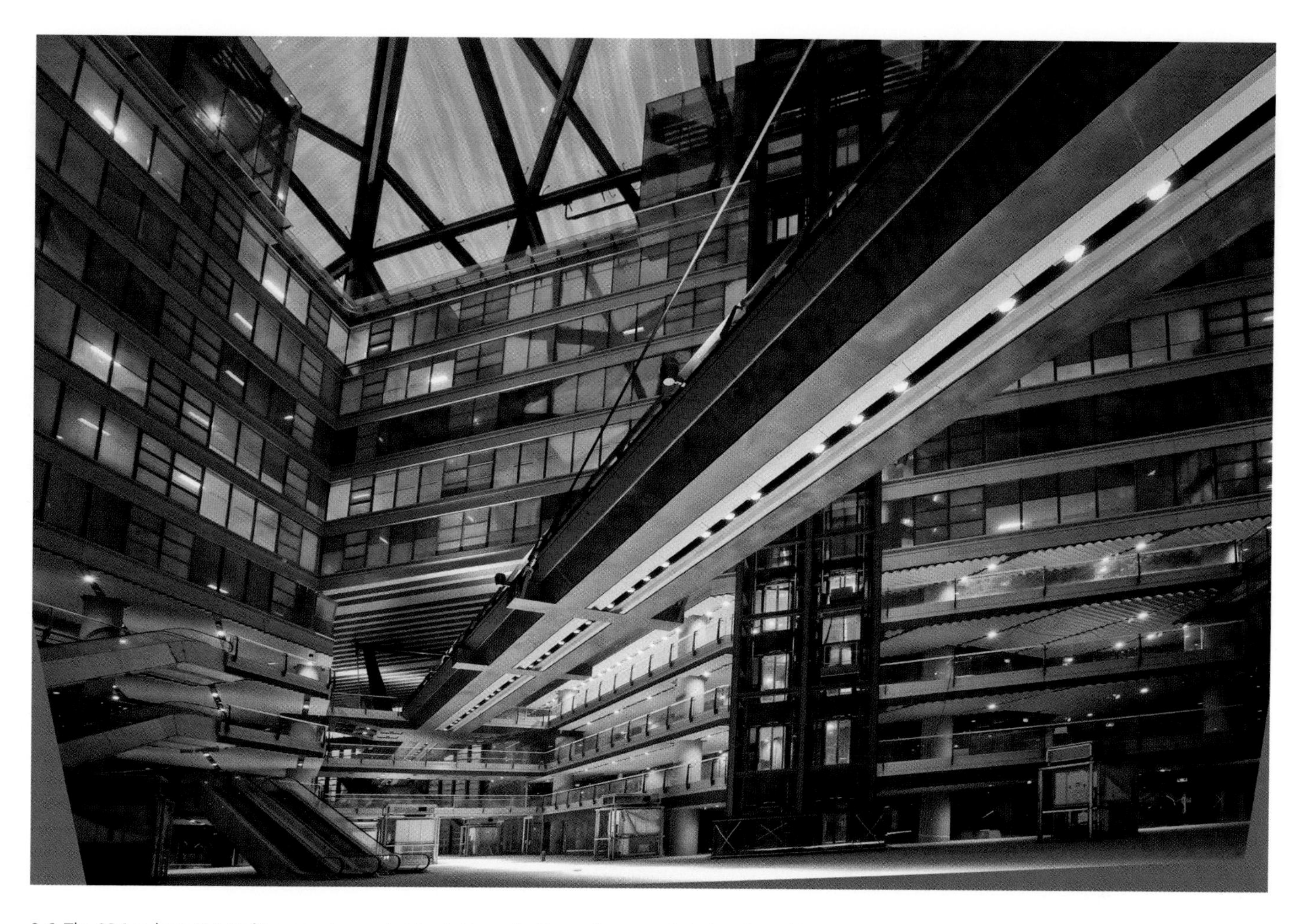

9.6 The 236-m-long (2,540-ft) suspension pedestrian bridge cuts diagonally across Parkview Green FangCaoDi in Beijing. Photo: Parkview Green FangCaoDi.

PARKVIEW GREEN FANGCAODI, Beijing, China

Parkview Green FangCaoDi is a 2,153,000 sq ft (200,000 sq m) mixed-use building in Beijing, China. This LEED-CS Platinum (precertified) development comprises four buildings (two eighteen-story towers and two nine-story towers) enclosed in an "environmental shield." Rising up from a public courtyard, the towers include a 100-room boutique hotel, nearly 538,000 sq ft (50,000 sq m) of luxury retail and restaurants, and 861,000 sq ft (80,000 sq m) of office space. At 2,540 ft (236 m) long, Asia's longest suspension pedestrian bridge cuts diagonally across the building so that occupants can see the four towers rising above and the open courtyard below.

The "environmental shield" encloses the entire development and creates a microclimate inside the building. Made of glass walls and an ETFE (ethylene tetrafluoroethylene copolymer) membrane system roof, the shield tempers Beijing's extreme climate and is controlled by an automated BMS.[10]

ETFE is a very lightweight polymer foil that is approximately 1 percent the weight of glass. ETFE requires much less structural support than a normal roof, reducing steel use and ultimately construction costs. It is anti-static, which makes it essentially self-cleaning. The sealing process is virtually leakproof (unlike a glass roof, which needs gaps to allow for thermal expansion), and it is 100 percent recyclable. The ETFE membrane allows 95 percent of external light to enter the building; as a result, the entire building interior is exposed to natural light.[11]

Designed by Integrated Design Associates and Arup, this glass and ETFE envelope creates a microclimate with various zones and is designed to control temperature and humidity within the development. The double-skin glass creates an air chamber that stores thermal energy and reduces the building's overall energy use. It also functions as a natural ventilation system that circulates fresh air into office and atrium spaces, allowing the building to "breathe." During Beijing's hot summers, the external shield opens at the base of the building, drawing in fresh air that then circulates throughout the office interior and atrium as natural ventilation before exhausting as warm air from vents at the roof of the environmental shield. Chilled ceilings and triple-glazed windows with integrated venetian blinds support the system in maintaining comfortable temperatures within the offices.[12]

In the winter months, fresh air continues to be drawn into the

9.7 The glass and ETFE envelope creates several microclimates and is designed to control temperature and humidity within the development. Photo: Parkview Green FangCaoDi.

TABLE 9.3

Projected energy and water use

	Annual use	Intensity
Energy use	17,800,000 kWh	89 kWh/sq m
Water use	42,200 kl	211 l/sq m

building, but the atrium vent is closed, trapping air in the outer shell where it is heated by the sun and used to heat the office areas. Temperatures in the office spaces are regulated with radiant chilled ceiling panels, which are controlled at around 61°F (16°C) and serve to keep the office environment cool in summer. In the spring and autumn, the building's energy requirement is low, and natural ventilation largely controls the internal atmosphere.[13]

ETFE "pillows" are connected together by a gutter structure designed to collect rainwater. The gutters channel the water into an underground tank where it is recycled for use throughout the building.[14] Water-use reduction strategies in the building include electronic flow-control faucets and water-saving urinals, along with low-flow toilets and showers. Recycled rainwater collected from the roof and paved areas provides irrigation water for landscaping.[15] With a low projected water use, 56 gallons (211 liters) per square meter annually, the building saves 48 percent on water usage, compared with the LEED water-use baseline.[16]

Parkview Green FangCaoDi predicts energy use to be 89 kWh per sq m/year, 44 percent less than the LEED baseline and about 50 percent less than a comparable building.[17]

At a glance

Name: Parkview Green FangCaoDi
Location: Beijing, China
Size: 2,153,000 sq ft (200,000 sq m)
Completion: 2011
Distinction: LEED-CS Platinum Precertification
Program: Mixed use—retail, office, hotel

Project team

Owner: Beijing Chyau Fwu Properties Co. Ltd.
Architect: Integrated Design Associates, Beijing Institute of Architectural Design and Research
Engineering: Arup & Partners Hong Kong Ltd.
Contractor: China Jiansu International Construction

9.8 The 140,452 sq m World Financial Center in Beijing comprises two twenty-four-floor "jewel box" towers connected by a two-story atrium. Photo: Henderson Land Development Company Ltd.

WORLD FINANCIAL CENTER, Beijing, China

Located in Beijing's Central Business District, the World Financial Center (WFC) comprises two twenty-four-floor towers connected by a two-story atrium. The WFC contains more than 1.5 million sq ft (140,452 sq m) of office and public space. The building achieved Platinum ratings in both the LEED-CS and HK-BEAM (Hong Kong Building Environmental Assessment Method) green building rating systems.

The WFC's design recalls twin jewel boxes, symbols of prestige. The glass façade extends beyond the highest occupied level and folds back to create a crystalline effect that also conceals the roof-mounted mechanical equipment. The crystal theme was carried inside the building by using jewel-like materials throughout the common areas, lobbies, and restrooms. A 13 × 151 ft (4 × 46 m) crystal wall designed by German artist Michael Hammers is located along the main wall in the ground-floor lobby. The art piece was constructed from 1,200 glass pyramid-shaped boxes, each with different dimensions. Crystal chandeliers at the entrance to each tower are the "jewels within the jewel boxes."[18]

"The aim of the project team . . . was to create a quality building that would transcend time and would be a benchmark for commercial buildings in Mainland China for years to come," according to Henderson Land Group.[19] WFC was designed for world-renowned banks, financial firms, and multinational companies and meets their stringent demands in the areas of power supply, security, intelligent facilities, floor area, and property management. Each floor contains about 47,361 sq ft (4,400 sq m) of column-free space. WFC contains special trading floors for financial institutions that have 10-ft (3.3-m) ceilings, 12-in (300-mm) raised floors and additional reliable electrical and air-conditioning capacity.[20]

9.9 The World Financial Center was designed for world-renowned banks, financial firms, and multinational companies and meets their stringent demands in the areas of power supply, security, intelligent facilities, floor area, and property management.
Photo: Henderson Land Development Company Ltd.

Basement parking accommodates more than 1,200 vehicles and 2,000 bicycles, with the lowest garage floors doubling as a national defense air-raid shelter. Public open space of nearly 3 acres (1.2 ha) surrounds the building.[21]

Absorption chillers using steam supplied from the municipal network are used in the chiller group to reduce refrigerant use and also to increase the chilled water system's reliability. Adequate humidity is a critical design concern in Beijing's dry winter climate, and steam, reused from power stations' energy waste, is used for humidity control in the ventilation system. Heating is provided through radiators which are integrated within the raised floor system and located along the building's perimeter. The perimeter ducts with air-handling units are interlinked and supplement the cold-air supply during summer when air-conditioning loads are high, improving summer performance with no extra energy usage.[22]

The team completed a life-cycle assessment (LCA) for WFC; the assessment looked at ten environmental impacts from the whole life-cycle perspective, including:

- raw material extraction
- building material manufacturing
- transportation
- construction
- building operation
- repair and maintenance
- disposal.[23]

Other high-performance solutions include:[24]

- window-to-wall ratio: 69 percent
- dual-panel metal-frame, low-e glass windows with thermal break
- HVAC system: variable air volume (VAV) plus baseboard radiators for offices
- outside air quantity based on demand-control ventilation (DCV) sensors
- air-side heat recovery: 70 percent efficiency energy wheel.

"As a developer, our vision was to create the first environmentally sustainable, Grade A office building in Beijing," said David Dumigan, General Manager, Henderson Land Group. "It was the objective of the project team to create the most technologically advanced, energy efficient, and sustainable building in the region."[25]

TABLE 9.4

Projected energy use

	Annual use	Intensity (conditioned area)
Electricity	18,155,423 kWh	12.0 kWh/sq ft
Steam (10.6 MMBtu)	3,092,001	2.5
Total	**21,247,424 kWh**	**14.5 kWh/sq ft, 156 kWh/sq m**
Projected savings	25% vs. code	

At a glance
Name: World Financial Center
Location: Beijing, China
Project Area: 1,870,202 sq ft (173,747 sq m)
Conditioned Area: 1,511,818 sq ft (140,452 sq m)
Office Area (twenty floors, Floors 3–22): 1,358,780 sq ft/126,234 sq m
Unconditioned Area (garage): 358,384 sq ft/32,552 sq m
Distinction: LEED-CS Platinum and Hong Kong HK-BEAM Platinum
Program: Corporate office

Project team
Developer: Henderson Land Group
Architect: Cesar Pelli

NORTH AMERICA

CENTRE FOR INTERACTIVE RESEARCH ON SUSTAINABILITY, University of British Columbia, Vancouver, British Columbia, Canada

Located on the campus of the University of British Columbia (UBC) in Vancouver, the 61,085-sq-ft (5,675-sq-m) Centre for Interactive Research on Sustainability (CIRS) opened in November 2011. CIRS aims to become an internationally recognized research institution whose mission is to accelerate adoption of sustainable building and urban development practices. The vision behind the building is a "living lab" where researchers from leading academic institutions perform interactive research on and assessment of building systems and technologies, accelerating the path to sustainability.

"With the world's urban population projected to jump by 2 billion people in twenty years, universities have a crucial role to play in accelerating solutions for the sustainability challenges facing society," said UBC President Stephen Toope. "CIRS is a flagship project in UBC's

9.10 The Centre for Interactive Research on Sustainability (CIRS) is LEED Platinum certified and also designed to meet the Living Building Challenge requirements. Photo: Perkins+Will Canada Architects Co.

9.11 CIRS is constructed primarily of FSC-certified wood and beetle-killed wood (currently BC's largest source of carbon emissions). Its wood structure locks in more than 500 tons of carbon. Photo: Perkins+Will Canada Architects Co.

TABLE 9.5

Projected energy and water use[a]

	Annual use/ production	Intensity
Electricity	610,550 kWh	71 kWh/sq m
Earth and ocean sciences pre-heat system	N/A	40
Total energy use	**N/A**	**111 kWh/sq m**
Onsite solar thermal	14,300 kWh	2.6
Onsite solar PV	24,430 kWh	4.4
Net energy output (returned to UBC for use in other buildings)	(622,000 kWh)	(113 kWh/sq m)

	Annual use	Intensity
Water demand	730,000 l	129 l/sq m
Rainwater harvested	1,226 kl	216 l/sq m
Graywater/blackwater harvested	N/A	

a Information from CIRS Technical Manual, http://cirs.ubc.ca/building/building-manual, accessed January 22, 2012.

'living laboratory' concept, where researchers, students, operational staff, and partners develop sustainability innovations on campus to be shared with society."[26]

Designed in collaboration with Perkins+Will Canada architects, CIRS has capacity for housing more than 200 people from several academic disciplines, including applied science, psychology, geography, forestry, and business, along with operational units such as the UBC Sustainability Initiative, which works collaboratively to integrate the university's academic and operational efforts on sustainability.[27]

LEED Platinum-certified and designed to meet the Living Building Challenge (which will be submitted for at the end of 2012, following the first full year of operations), CIRS is a net-zero energy, net-zero water, net-zero carbon (construction and operations) building. It is organized around a pair of four-story office, classroom, and lab blocks linked by an atrium.

CIRS sources energy from the ground and scavenges heat from neighboring buildings, generates electricity from the sun with a 25-kW PV array, obtains ventilation from the wind, and harvests its water

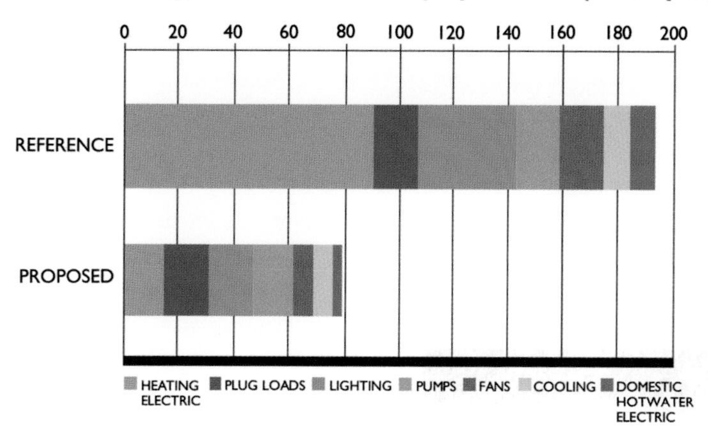

9.12 CIRS energy use projections. Source: Perkins+Will Canada Architects Co.

from the rain. Utilizing new technologies, CIRS also returns energy and water back to neighboring buildings and the environment.[28] As shown in Figure 9.12, CIRS is highly energy-efficient, using 63 percent less energy than required by Canada's Model National Energy Code for a typical British Columbia building. Careful attention to controlling energy end-uses resulted in the estimates shown in Figure 9.12. Notice that energy use for space heating and cooling has been reduced 79 percent in CIRS compared with a standard, or reference, building. At CIRS, all of the energy supplied from the campus grid is electric, owing to low prices in British Columbia for hydroelectricity.

By capturing energy from the sun, the ground, and the nearby Earth and Ocean Sciences building, CIRS heats itself and is projected to return 622,000 kWh of surplus energy back to the campus each year. CIRS operations require no fossil fuel; the surplus energy CIRS generates returns to nearby buildings.

By capturing and treating rainwater and by treating site-generated blackwater, CIRS harvests enough water for its 200 occupants, plus hundreds of auditorium and café users. Water that can't be reused on site is discharged to the ground to recharge the local aquifer.[29]

CIRS was constructed, using both certified and beetle-killed wood (dying forests are BC's largest source of carbon emissions). Its wood structure locks in more than 500 metric tons of carbon, offsetting GHG emissions resulting from using other non-renewable construction materials in the building such as cement, steel, and aluminum.[30]

At a glance

Name: The Centre for Interactive Research on Sustainability, University of British Columbia
Location: Vancouver, British Columbia, Canada
Completed: September 2011
Size: 61,085 sq ft (5,675 sq m)
Budget: CDN$37 million
Program: University laboratories, classrooms, office space
Sustainability Targets: LEED Platinum, Living Building Challenge

Project team

Owner: University of British Columbia
Architect: Perkins+Will Canada
Mechanical and Electrical: Stantec Consulting
Structural: Fast + Epp
Civil Engineer: Core Group Consultants

THE BULLITT CENTER, Seattle, Washington, USA

Currently under construction and scheduled for occupancy in 2013, the Bullitt Center is a six-story, 50,000-sq-ft (4,700-sq-m) building in Seattle designed by the Miller Hull Partnership. The building is a project of the Bullitt Foundation, whose mission is "to safeguard the natural environment by promoting responsible human activities and sustainable communities in the Pacific Northwest."[32] In addition to meeting criteria for both LEED Platinum and the 2030 Challenge, the Bullitt Center will be the first speculative large commercial office building to meet the Living Building Challenge's goals. "We set out to build the greenest office building, by far, in the world," said Denis Hayes, President and CEO of the Bullitt Foundation.[33]

"I think this is the most important building being built in the country today," said Jason McLennan, CEO of the Cascadia Green Building Council, the organization responsible for the Living Building Challenge.[34] The challenge is performance based, and each project is evaluated one year after building occupancy to ensure it meets the zero-net energy and water performance requirements. Certification requires projects to meet twenty imperatives such as:

- 100 percent of energy demands met with on-site renewable energy generation
- 100 percent of water needs met by on-site rainwater collection
- 100 percent on-site waste management
- operable windows and natural daylighting in all occupied spaces
- nontoxic, locally sourced construction materials.

By meeting 100 percent of its annual power needs on site with solar energy, the project requires no fossil-fuel combustion and therefore will produce no air pollution. Human waste will be treated on site, reducing downstream impacts of increased density. All graywater will be treated by an intensive green roof and infiltrated at rates to emulate the site's predevelopment hydrology. Every workstation in the building will have access to natural daylight and operable windows, and indoor air quality will be monitored and verified. Required stairways (e.g., for fire egress) have been pushed to the exterior, toward the best views from the site, encouraging occupants to use them instead of elevators when going from floor to floor.

9.13 In addition to meeting the criteria for both LEED Platinum and the 2030 Challenge, the Bullitt Center will be the first speculative large commercial office building to meet the Living Building Challenge's goals. Photo: Miller Hull Partnership.

TABLE 9.6

Projected energy and water use

	Annual use	Intensity
Electricity consumption	230,000 kWh	16 kBtu/sq ft; 48.9 kWh/sq m
PV power production (242-kW PV system)	230,000 kWh	48.9 kWh/sq m
Water consumption	470,000 g/year FTEs 113,000 g/year visitors	9.4 g/sq ft FTE 2.7 g/sq ft visitors 12.1 g/sq ft (total); 493 l/sq m
Onsite water recovery: rainwater	Rainwater system sized to provide water for all potable and non-potable uses. During the winter and spring, cistern is expected to overflow to the public storm drains.	
Onsite water recovery: graywater	All graywater is treated on site in a constructed wetland and infiltrated in an onsite drain field.	

To balance the solar energy available on the site with the building's demands, the design team incorporated such solutions as high-performance envelope, geothermal heat exchanger, maximized daylighting, exhaust-air heat recovery, hydronic radiant heating, night-flush ventilation, and engaging the building occupants' behavior to further reduce energy loads. Additional strategies such as an expanded "seasonally appropriate" comfort range, extensive plug load analysis and elimination of "phantom loads," combined to reduce the projected energy demand by 82 percent compared to the typical office building in Seattle.

The project is also leading to changes in city, county, and state laws that act as barriers to sustainability. Seattle recently passed a Living Building Ordinance that allows city agencies to waive or modify certain development standards that would hinder green building innovation. "Without that cooperation from the city government, we could have never done it," said Craig Curtis, a partner with the Miller Hull Partnership.

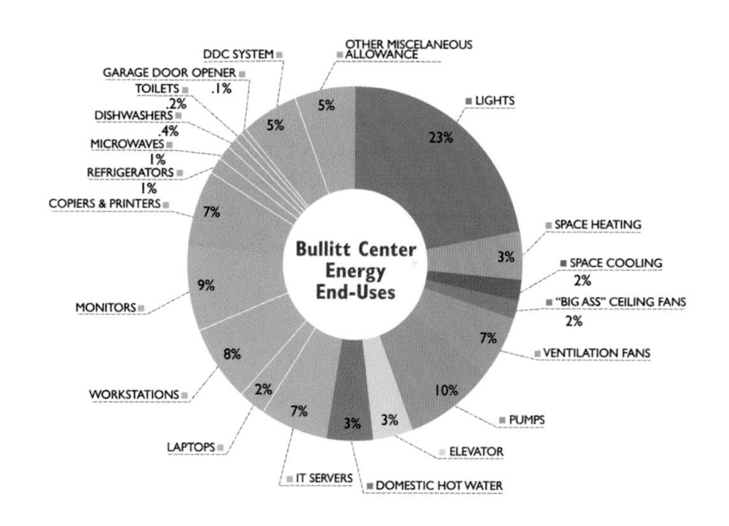

9.14 Bullitt Center energy projections.
Source: Miller Hull Partnership.

At a glance

Name: The Bullitt Center
Location: Seattle, Washington
Size: 50,000 sq ft (4,700 sq m)
Total Budget: $30 million
Construction Budget: $18 million
Program: Speculative office building with some corporate tenants
Sustainability Targets: LEED Platinum, Living Building Challenge

Project team

Owner: Bullitt Foundation
Architect: The Miller Hull Partnership
Developer: Point32
Mechanical, Electrical, Plumbing Engineer: PAE Consulting Engineers
Graywater and Wastewater: 2020 Engineering
General Contractor: Schuchart
Photovoltaic System Designer: Solar Design Associates
Structural Engineer: DCI Engineers

PORT OF PORTLAND HEADQUARTERS, Portland, Oregon, USA

The Port of Portland Headquarters is a ten-story, 1.4 million sq ft (130,000 sq m), LEED Platinum building located at the entrance to Portland International Airport. Perched atop a seven-story 3,500-space public parking garage, 450 Port employees are served by 205,500 sq ft (19,092 sq m) of office space.[35] (See Figure 9.16.)

"LEED Platinum certification affirms the goal we set out at the beginning of the project: that the building reflects this region's commitment to sustainability. This includes considering how our choices affect the environment, the economy, and the community we serve," said Bill Wyatt, Port Executive Director.[36]

The building gathers the Port's aviation, marine, and real-estate departments together under one roof. In an effort to encourage communication, interaction, and awareness of activities within the building, the Port chose an open floor plan.

"Key design goals included iconic architecture representing the Port's role within the community and enhancing employee experience and collaboration," said Doug Sams, project manager with ZGF Architects. "The facility's north façade includes a dominant curving lapped-glass curtain wall, reminiscent of the prow of a ship or the wing of a plane. Inside the open office environment there are very few enclosed offices, but several collaboration spaces for informal meetings and staff interaction."[37]

The most innovative feature in the building is the Living Machine, a wastewater treatment and reuse system. Natural processes that simulate a tidal wetland ecosystem recycle both graywater and blackwater for re-use in and around the building. The system greets visitors at the building's main entrance (Figure 9.16) inside the first floor lobby, looking like a conventional, yet lush tropical planter, "but it actually contains a functional ecosystem, employing enhanced natural recycling," said Worrell Water Technologies' Will Kirksey.[38]

Located in the building's entrance lobby, the system comprises ten wetland tanks that successively process the wastewater. Each contains gravel and plants and uses naturally occurring bacteria to consume and convert the organic matter. The tidal action introduces oxygen, which helps microorganisms do most of the work. At the end of the cycle, the water is sterilized by ultraviolet light and ready to be used again for flushing toilets and as makeup water in the cooling tower.[39]

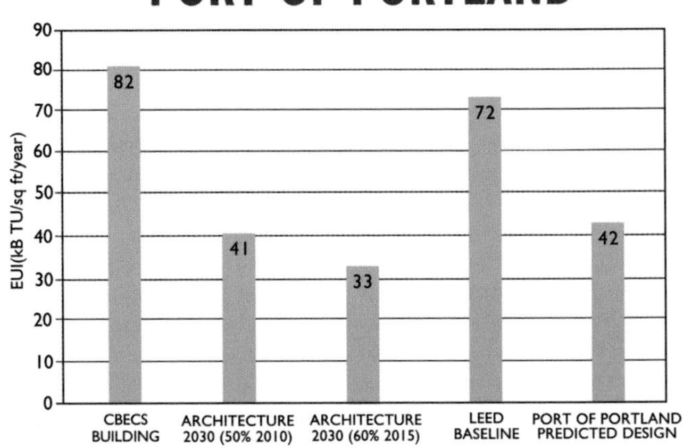

9.15 Port of Portland energy use compensations. Source: Data supplied by Brad Wilson, PAE Consulting Engineers Inc., January 24, 2012.

Heating and cooling for the building come from renewable sources, including 200 geo-exchange boreholes, each 340 ft (100 m) deep, which provide most of the building's heat. These boreholes are also used to cool the building twice as efficiently as conventional chillers. Depending on the season, chilled or hot water from heat pumps is then pumped to 56,000 sq ft (5,200 sq m) of radiant heating and cooling panels located in ceilings of occupied spaces.[40]

Additional high-performance features of the Port of Portland building include:

- radiant ceiling panels heat and cool all office spaces, with warm or chilled water as necessary to maintain comfort conditions in each space, while using far less energy than required by a forced-air HVAC system
- a dedicated outside air system (DOAS) that provides fresh air to maintain proper indoor air quality (IAQ) in all occupied spaces and recovers energy from the building exhaust air to preheat the incoming fresh air
- daylight and views provided via an open floor plan and large windows that visually connect the interior spaces of the building to the external environment

9.16 *Left*: Located at the entrance to Portland International Airport, the Port of Portland Headquarters is a ten-story LEED Platinum building with a 3,500-space public parking garage and 205,500 sq ft (19,092 sq m) of office space. Photo: Loren Nelson.

9.17 *Below*: Completely odor-free, the Living Machine adds a warm touch of nature to the Port's entrance lobby. Photo: Living Machine® Systems, L3C.

TABLE 9.7

Projected energy and water use[a]

Office building	Intensity	Intensity	Projected savings vs. baseline (code)
Electricity[b]	132 kWh/sq m	42 kBtu/sq ft	41.7%
Potable water (net)	0.89 g/sq ft	36 l/sq m	79.6%

a Much of the area of the project is in the large parking garage. As of January 2012, the system's measurement and verification system, which would distinguish between energy uses in the office portion of the project and the parking garage, was still not working properly, hence actual operating data were not available. Personal communication, Brad Wilson, PAE Consulting Engineers, January 24, 2012.

b There is no natural-gas use in the project, so electricity is the only fuel source.

- an effective lighting system incorporating energy-efficient luminaires, automatic daylight-based dimming systems in perimeter areas, and occupancy sensor controls
- 66 percent lower lighting power density in the garage than a code building
- water-efficient plumbing fixtures and an on-site wastewater recovery system that provide 80 percent potable water savings compared to standard buildings, with 352,000 gallons per year (1,330 kl) savings from low-flow fixtures and 360,000 gallons per year (1,360 kl) savings from graywater and blackwater reused on site
- green roof areas with plantings specially selected to avoid attracting birds, which are hazardous to air traffic.[41]

The building was designed to use 80 percent less water and 42 percent less energy than a standard office building. The office space requires no fossil fuel to maintain a comfortable indoor temperature, and all other energy used in the building comes from 100 percent renewable energy sources through a multi-year green power purchase contract.[42]

"We are committed to incorporating green building techniques into all of our projects, and the headquarters building is the most ambitious one yet," said Wyatt.[43]

At a glance

Name: Port of Portland Headquarters and public parking garage
Location: Portland, Oregon
Completed: May 2010
Construction Cost, headquarters: $78.7 million
Construction Cost, parking garage/pedestrian tunnel: $156 million
Size: 205,500 sq ft (19,902 sq m) of office space; 1.2 million sq ft (111,484 sq m) of public parking
Distinction: LEED Platinum
Program: Municipal Office

Project team

Owner: Port of Portland, Oregon
Architect and Interior Design: ZGF Architects LLP
MEP Engineer: PAE Consulting Engineers
Lighting: Luma Lighting Design
Structural Engineer: KPFF Consulting Engineers
General Contractor: Hoffman Construction

EUROPE

KfW WESTARKADE, Frankfurt, Germany

This bank is blue, purple, pink, and red—yet it claims to be a green building. And it is! It is not often that a mid-size bank building has good reason to claim that. But the new headquarters for the KfW Bank in Frankfurt, designed by Sauerbruch Hutton Architects, does. The KfW Bank was founded in 1948, largely with money from the European Recovery Program or "Marshall Plan," to get Germany's economy back on its feet after World War II. Today it is owned by the Federal Government of Germany and the Länder (states) and is one of Germany's ten largest banks.

KfW is headquartered in Frankfurt and employs 3,500 people. When the need arose for a new building just outside the existing bank headquarters in downtown Frankfurt, the decision was made to have Sauerbruch Hutton design a new building, known as the "Westarkade." At only fifteen stories high, it is tiny compared to Frankfurt's sprawling high-rise bank towers all around. But the new

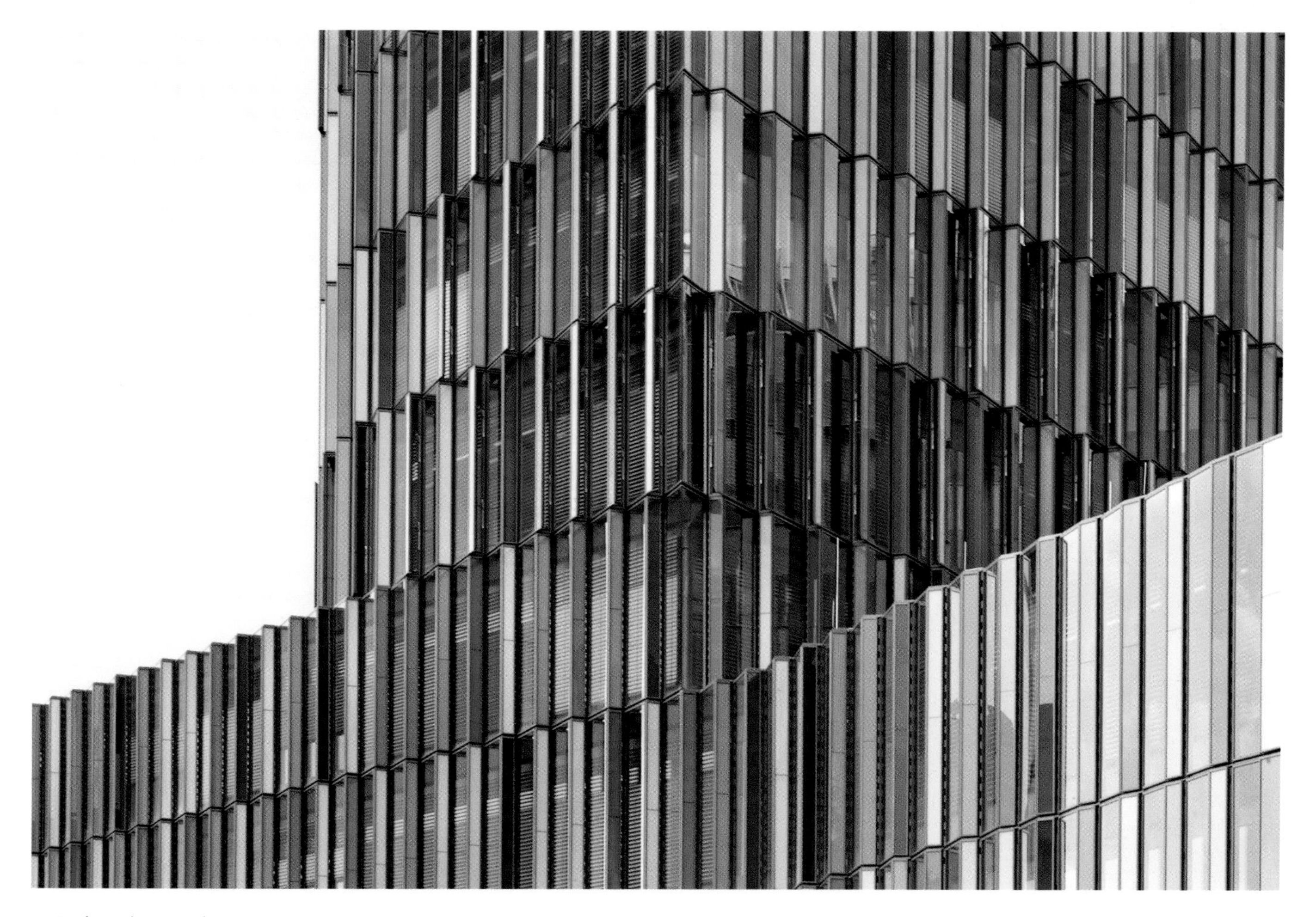

9.18 Through a complex computer-controlled system and operable windows, the façade at the KfW Westarkade in Frankfurt negates the effects of varying wind pressures around the building, allowing it to be naturally ventilated. Photo: Jan Bitter © Sauerbruch Hutton.

building's energy performance outshines the taller headquarters of its nearby private-sector peers. With projected annual *primary* energy consumption at less than 100 kWh/sq m/year, the Westarkade is designed to be one of the world's most energy-efficient office towers. It contains a conference center and offices for some 700 bank employees.

Situated in the affluent West End neighborhood, the building fits into the ensemble of disparate existing buildings from the same bank remarkably well and without obstructing too many views from the existing offices. Along the street it acts like a narrow slab, while creating a nice backdrop to the neighboring Palmengarten, a public botanical garden. At its base, the tower is widened to help form a typical European perimeter block edge connecting to the eave heights of neighboring bank buildings. At the rear, there is a nice little park. Corridors in the new building are connected to the existing bank buildings next door on several levels. The new tower forms an extension to the KfW Banking Group's headquarters, completing an ensemble of buildings from the 1970s, 1980s, and 1990s, integrating well into the cluster of existing office towers. The base's flowing form defines the street edge, where the façade is set back at ground level to create a protective arcade. The building's organic shape results from considering the prevailing wind direction and the sun's daily and yearly path.

The design uses several methods to achieve its ambitious low-energy goals such as thermally activating the slabs, utilizing geothermal heating and cooling, and reusing excess heat from a data-processing center. The architects predict annual site energy consumption of only 89 kWh/sq m/year. Monitoring studies by the University of Karlsruhe will reveal if these amazing numbers really have been met. The simulation was done following the German EnEV 2004, Germany's rigid law for building insulation. This law results in rather thick façades: For the new KfW building, they are made of parapets with 10 in (25.4 cm) of concrete, 2 in (5.1 cm) of rock wool, and another 3 in (7.6 cm) for the outer façade.

Forced ventilation through raised floor air distribution will only be used when outside temperatures are below 50°F (10°C) or above 77°F (25°C). Incoming fresh air is preconditioned using a geothermal heat exchanger. Heat from the exhaust air is recycled through a heat-recovery system. Air diffusers in the raised floor are placed along the façade to avoid unpleasant drafts from the colder air at the windows. The interior areas are both heated and cooled using thermal activation of the slabs.

Structurally the building is a simple reinforced-concrete skeleton with a curtain wall. This façade holds a special clue, however: It is called a pressure-ring façade, because it is designed to control natural ventilation effectively, to avoid possible updrafts or heat loss. The façade is designed to allow maximum natural daylight into the building. But that alone would not be enough. The double-layer, dynamically operated "pressure-ring-façade," developed together with the climate engineering firm, Transsolar, assures natural ventilation regardless of weather, type of insulation, or sun screening.

This façade is the first of its kind. It negates the effects of varying pressure around the building and thereby allows it to be ventilated naturally. A complex computer-controlled system of flaps in the outer façade balances pressures throughout and means that windows in the inner façade can be opened without adversely affecting the office's comfort. The façade has automatically operating inner louvers that guarantee an even and slow air flow between the two layers of glass. Depending on the wind speeds on any given day, the louvers' settings can be readjusted every fifteen minutes and in 15-degree intervals until fully perpendicular to the glass. The louvers are operated using weather data from Frankfurt Airport. This system allows completely natural ventilation of the offices in spring and fall. In winter, the air is preheated geothermally, while in summer it is pre-cooled geothermally.

So the curvy geometry, a signature element of any Sauerbruch Hutton project, in this case has some practical reasons as well: It is designed to be aerodynamic, so that the air flow within the façade takes place without any unwanted heat loss.

Sauerbruch wouldn't be Sauerbruch if they did not use some of their signature color concepts in the façade as well. For each project since the GSW Tower in Berlin (Figure 5.3), which you will find in many books on sustainable design as a prime example of an environmentally friendly, non-air-conditioned office tower, Louisa Hutton creates a "family of colors" with great sensitivity. Colorful printed glass, one of the practice's main research interests, was also used to animate this bank's façades. Along the short sides, the prefabricated, L-shaped façade panels have green tones, while different shades of blue dominate the elevation toward the bank's other towers nearby. Taken together, the combination of great urban design, a showcase sustainable design concept, and a sensitively colorful design make the KfW Bank in Frankfurt a new benchmark in "green" design in Europe, even if the building is largely blue, purple, pink, and red.[44]

At a glance
Owner: KfW Bankengruppe, Frankfurt
Architect: Sauerbruch Hutton, Berlin
Engineers: Transsolar Energietechnik (energy concept); ZWP Ingenieur-AG, Köln (mechanical); Reuter Rührgartner (electrical); Werner Sobek (structural/façade)
Size: 419,640 sq ft (39,000 sq m)
Completed: May 2010
Annual Carbon Footprint (predicted): 9 lbs CO_2/sq ft (43 kg CO_2/sq m)
Height: 184 ft (85 m)
Gross Floor Area: 195,000 sq ft (18,116 sq m)
Distinction: Council on Tall Buildings and Urban Habitat – Best Tall Building 2011 – Europe

TABLE 9.8
Projected energy use

	Intensity
Electricity	89 kWh/sq m

10
Sustainable Cities

(How) Can Sustainable Urban Development Be Quantified?

Beyond getting individual buildings to work well, there is a larger issue of placing them in sustainable cities. In this section, Ulf Meyer relates his experience teaching sustainable urban design and challenging students to come up with metrics for sustainable cities.

Nowadays, everything and everyone wants to be sustainable. Just like the inflation of labels such as "organic" or "eco" a few years ago, which soon adorned conventional products and processes, the same is now happening to the "sustainable" label. It threatens to become a victim of its own success. The label has become so popular that it will soon cease to mean much. Because there are no strict, clear, and universal rules for sustainability for building and construction (or any other service or product), rating systems for sustainable construction must therefore take the bull by its horns and consider ever-larger contexts and processes.

For the world of architecture and building this is a welcome development: The "right" building in the "wrong" urban context does not help the world. If, for example, an "ecological" office building, equipped with all the tricks and treats of environmentally friendly design is built on the extreme outskirts of the city and hundreds of its users have to go there by car every day, the site of the building forces a larger energy consumption than the building itself could ever save. The analysis and rating of a larger context is therefore quite useful for buildings. In the past fifty years alone the urban population has increased by 50 percent worldwide. However, people's use of resources increased during the same time by about 1,000 percent.[1] The resulting danger is imminent, making urban development the new arena for sustainable construction.

The global rating systems for sustainable construction have names such as "LEED," "BREEAM," or "CASBEE." The largest system of its kind, the American LEED rating, has already detected the trend to look at greater contexts and relationships. After LEED for new buildings of all types, LEED for renovations and existing buildings followed, and, since 2009, there also is a LEED for Neighborhoods program. This does not consider the performance of individual buildings, but considers them as one part of a whole town. The next logical step will be the consideration and comparison of entire cities (Figure 10.1).

Indeed, headlines like "Portland Beats Seattle as the 'Greenest' City in the US" and "Energy Consumption Per Capita Decreased by 14 Percent" could be quite conceivable in just a few years. Which mayors would not like to adorn themselves with the fact that their city is among the "Top 10 Greenest Cities in the Country"? So how do you measure the environmental performance of whole cities? What criteria should be used for evaluation?

I gave this task to my students in a seminar at Kansas State University in 2009 and received amazing and thought-provoking answers. It was a special and great enrichment of the seminar to have students from different parts of the world present—even in remote and rural Kansas. I asked my students to start thinking about some basic parameters of sustainable urban design such as "high density and urban mix/little sprawl" or "well-developed and affordable public transport network" and to propose what else could be measured as part of a possible LEED for Cities system?

10.1 Australia's largest city, Sydney, is dense but very livable. Photo: H. G. Esch, Hennef. Courtesy of ingenhoven architects + architectus.

For example, could simple units be used such as number of inhabitants per square mile of urban area or number of subway kilometers per 100,000 population? The students were each asked to develop a point system and to rate their hometown with the system to evaluate whether the result represents an accurate assessment of the city or if it was too strict or too generous.

First, the seminar looked at the Ecological Footprint analysis by Bill Rees, which expresses the consumption of fossil fuels (and their residues) as a surface that is needed to ensure that the city functions.[2] While this metaphor nicely shows that the environmental effects of cities go far beyond their borders, it is not good for the comparison of different cities.

In his book *Taking Sustainable Cities Seriously*, Kent Portney examined twenty-four American cities on the basis of thirty-four criteria and expressed the result of his findings in a single figure with a hit list of the most sustainable cities (as is always popular in America).[3] The system mainly looked at "smart growth," public transport, the prevention and reduction of pollution, and direct energy-saving measures.

Mr. Al-Tashkandi, a graduate student from Riyadh, Saudi Arabia, took Herbert Girardet's principles for sustainable urban development as the basis for his proposal, as defined by Girardet in *Creating Sustainable Cities*. For Girardet, a sustainable city is "organized in such a way that all its citizens can satisfy their needs and welfare and enjoy nature without contributing to the destruction of or to endanger the lives of others, now or in the future."[4] This was a good starting point for factors such as air and water quality, healthy food, quality living and good education, a vibrant cultural scene, a good health system, and a thriving job market. In addition, for Girardet, public safety, equal opportunities, and civil rights must be guaranteed in any sustainable city. This view of sustainability is too broad for a simple rating matrix. In *Cities for a Small Planet*, British architect Richard Rogers took this interpretation of a sustainable city even further and considered concepts such as justice, beauty, creativity, ecology, mobility, compactness, and poly-centrality.[5]

My student Al-Tashkandi selected six indicators with several sub-items for which points are awarded in each case. The highest possible score is 100, with zero the lowest. Only cities with more than 76 points in his system are models, while cities with 51–75 points are merely sustainable. The six indicators are:

1 **Resource protection**: Independence from fossil fuels with wind and solar energy, water recycling in buildings, and waste reduction ("reduce, reuse, recycle").
2 **Health**: Containment of direct pollution from emissions, organic food production.
3 **Transport**: Subway and commuter rail networks, bus and taxi traffic, as well as unmotorized traffic (pleasant walking and cycling).
4 **Sustainable architecture**: Low-resource consumption for all new buildings and stringent requirements for any modifications, use of recycled materials, and healthy indoor conditions.
5 **Open spaces and land use**: Strengthening both the built (parks, squares, avenues, gardens and school playgrounds) and the green spaces and natural ecosystems (biodiversity, urban heat island effect), urban density and mixed use, establishment of UGBs (urban growth boundaries).
6 **Sustainable living and economies**: Factors such as quality of life, rent levels, historical richness of the city, development of local culture, preservation of the specific identity, and heritage conservation.

With this relatively handy system, Mr. Al-Tashkandi proposed a useful rating system and rated his native Riyadh as arguably one of the most unsustainable cities in the world.

Mr. Chakraborty, a graduate student from Kolkata, India, surprised the seminar with his great enthusiasm for his hometown, which in the West is often portrayed as an oversized slum and the poorhouse of South Asia. Chakraborty developed a system that underscored his positive assessment of his native city in terms of sustainability. He started with Douglas Farr's work, for whom the trend for sustainable urban development in the USA is based on three pillars: (1) smart growth, (2) New Urbanism, and (3) green building.[6]

From the objectives of these three movements, Chakraborty named fifteen measurement criteria: seven quantitative (10 points each) and eight qualitative (5 points each), for a total of 110 points in a complex matrix (that cannot be shown here). Kolkata got 60 percent of the points. The city's biggest weaknesses are the lack of citizen participation, the reliability and predictability of policy decisions, and low-quality architecture and urban planning. But when it came to mixed-use and urban density, and especially environmentally sustainable transport, however, Kolkata was hard to beat: The American students were surprised!

Given that the world's cities have different topographic, climatic, cultural, and economic conditions, and access to resources, it is difficult to develop a unified sustainability rating system for all cities in the world. After all, what Susan Maxman said about sustainable architecture is even truer for urban planning: "There is no recipe for sustainability. It is a mindset and approach—and should not need any labels."[7]

11 Afterword

A Challenge to Building Teams

We've come to the end of a long journey, trying to identify the world's greenest buildings. We hope you will be surprised, delighted, and informed at finding many projects about which you knew nothing before we started this trip together. Certainly, we were! What's our conclusion? It's easy. There is a long way to go before we can say that most new buildings meet our three basic criteria for the world's greenest buildings:

1. high level of sustainability in design, construction, and operations, documented through reputable third-party evaluations
2. low levels of energy and water use, moving toward zero-net energy and zero-net water requirements of the Architecture 2030 and Living Building Challenges
3. great architecture that delights the soul, fosters healthy, comfortable, and productive environments at affordable costs, and integrates well into the urban fabric.

Where are we now? We are amazed at how few of the most highly rated green (and publicized) buildings in the world could (or would) meet our most basic criterion: full disclosure of operating results. We think this is a scandal, one for which architects, engineers, building owners, and developers should apologize. There is no inherent difficulty in publishing energy-use data, with appropriate analysis of particular circumstances. Without data, architects and engineers are lost at sea trying to meet the most basic tenet of evidence-based design. Where, indeed, is the evidence on which to base future designs? The fact is that most building projects are "black holes" into which light and information disappear, never again to emerge.

What can be done? With more than fifty-five case studies, we show that integrated design, a commitment to low-energy goals, and use of post-occupancy evaluations can go a long way toward creating "Max Green" buildings. We show how designers who aim at openness, transparency, connectedness, and sustainable outcomes can also create great architecture. What we need from design and construction professions, building owners, and managers, as well as the global property industry, is a fully realized commitment to openness, transparency, and "full frontal sustainability" that they claim to embrace in their other activities, honestly disclosing energy and water use in building operations and investigating why results deviate from expectations.

Consider this: There is no other multi-billion-dollar industry in the world that does not inspect its products with diligence before they leave the factory, identify defects and fix them before they go into use, and try to make them better over time, via continuous improvement. Can you imagine Boeing or Airbus producing airplanes without carefully inspecting whether they will fly as designed before they leave the factory? Yet a $100-million building typically will get far less formal and continuing scrutiny after it's built than a $50 million aircraft, if it has any at all.

Getting to carbon-neutral buildings by 2030 is not a game, and there are fewer than twenty years to build a base of trained professionals, design methods, construction techniques, building management, and energy-efficiency products and systems to reach that outcome. Currently we are on a path to not reach that goal (Figure 11.1). With large projects taking three to five years from startup to realization, sometimes even longer, there are only five complete cycles of new buildings before 2030 from which to gather information. The case for full disclosure of actual information on new building performance, using established international protocols, couldn't be more urgent.

So, here is a special plea from us to all of our friends and colleagues in the design professions: make a commitment to evaluate *all* of your future projects for energy and water use (and as many past ones as you can), put that commitment as a standard requirement into your contracts with owners and developers, set aside the fees required to do this, and then publish the results widely. If we all share information, we will be amazed at how fast building science will progress and how relevant the skills of architects and engineers will be to the sustainable future we all envision.

Thank you for reading this far! We'd love to hear from you about your reaction to this book and about how you are implementing this commitment in your own work.

Jerry Yudelson, jerry@greenbuildconsult.com
Ulf Meyer, ulfmeyerb@aol.com

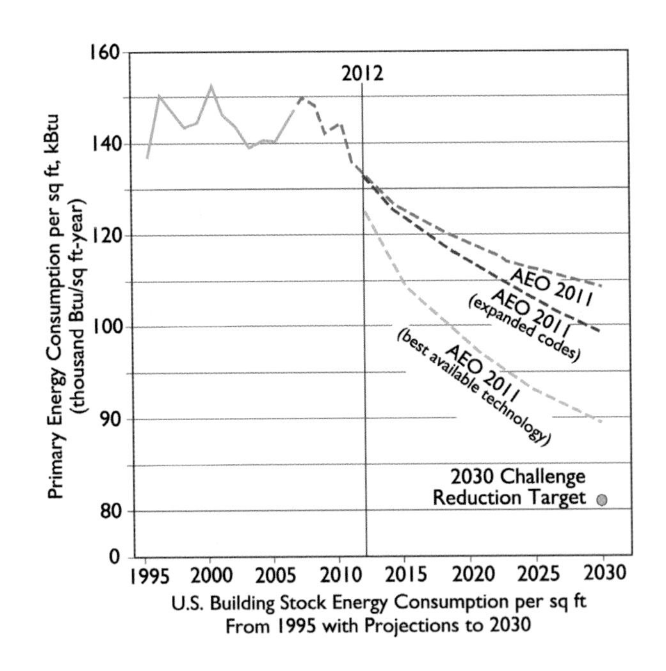

11.1 Glide path to a sustainable future: we're not yet on the right slope in cutting building energy use. AEO is the Annual Energy Outlook of the US Department of Energy.

Appendix A
Interviews

Below is a list of people we interviewed specifically for this book. Many others are quoted in the book, but these people generously gave of their time to provide specific interviews.

John Andary, Integral Group, USA

Jeff Baker, National Renewable Energy Laboratory, USA

Stefan Behnisch, Behnisch Architekten, Germany

Alan Brewster, School of Forestry and Environmental Studies, Yale University, USA

Merritt Bucholz, Bucholz McEvoy Architects, Ireland

Craig Curtis, Miller Hull Partnership, USA

Andy Frichtl, Interface Engineering, USA

Lin Hsien-Te, National Cheng Kung University, Taiwan

Christoph Ingenhoven, Ingenhoven Architects, Germany

Stephen R. Kellert, School of Forestry and Environmental Studies, Yale University, USA

Adrian Leaman, Building Use Studies, Usable Building Trust, UK

Matthias Sauerbruch, Sauerbruch Hutton, Germany

Dave Shelton, Design Sense, USA

Paul Stoller, Atelier Ten, USA

Appendix B
English/Metric Terminology

ENERGY USE

USA and Canada: BTU/sq ft/year, or 1,000 BTU/sq ft/year (kBTU/sq ft/year)

Rest of World: kWh/sq m/year

Conversion: 31,729 BTU/sq ft/year = 100 kWh/sq m/annum

Other conversions: 1 MJ of energy = 0.277 kWh; 1 cubic meter of natural gas = 11.13 kWh (depending on the calorific value of the gas)

WATER USE

USA and Canada: gallons/sq ft/year

Rest of World: liters/sq m/annum, or kl/sq m/annum

Conversion: 10 gallons/sq ft/year = 407 liters/sq m/annum = 0.407 kL/sq m/annum

BUILDING AREA

USA and Canada: sq ft

Rest of World: sq m

Conversion: 10 sq m = 107.6 sq ft

SITE AREA

USA and Canada: acres = 43,560 sq ft

Rest of World: hectares = 10,000 sq m

Conversion: 2.47 acres = 1 hectare

BUILDING VENTILATION RATES

USA and Canada: cubic feet per minute (CFM)

Rest of World: liters per hour (LPH)

Conversion: 1 cubic meter = 35.3 cubic feet = 1,000 liters; 10 CFM = 17.0 LPH; 1 LPH = 0.59 CFM

Notes

Foreword

1 www.usgbc.org/leed
2 www.2030.org
3 www.ilbi.org
4 http://ec.europa.eu/energy/efficiency/buildings/buildings_en.htm, accessed January 28, 2011.

Preface

1 Many great architectural projects with LEED Platinum or similar ratings were not willing to share operating data and thus had to be eliminated from further consideration. This situation illustrates why green building rating schemes worldwide must *require* online posting of operating data, on a continuing basis, as a condition for certification in the future, regardless of owners' privacy or competitive concerns.

1 Green Buildings and the Carbon Challenge

1 See www.unep.org/sbci/pdfs/SBCI-BCCSummary.pdf, accessed January 15, 2012, s. 1, p. 7.
2 See www.esrl.noaa.gov/gmd/ccgg/trends, accessed January 15, 2012.
3 See www.architecture2030.org, accessed January 15, 2012.
4 For a method to help set targets for a specific project you are undertaking, check the estimating and evaluation tool offered by the global design firm Perkins+Will (see http://2030e2.perkins will.com, accessed January 15, 2012). The company says, "2030e2 results are contingent on the Baseline kBtu (site energy use baseline, in 1000s of Btu per sq ft/year; 31,720 kBtu/sq ft/year is equivalent to about 100 kWh/sq m/year of building energy use) being properly established. At this time, data for establishing baselines is limited in availability and will require further development by the community. The 2030e2 results are goals and should not be used as predictions of how a specific design will perform."

2 The Issue of Building Performance

1 See, for example, www.architecture2030.org, accessed September 20, 2010.
2 See David J. C. MacKay, 2010, *Sustainable Energy—Without the Hot Air*, Chapter 1, www.withouthotair.com, accessed September 20, 2010. This is the best work we know of at present for getting it right about energy conservation opportunities and the potential contribution of renewables, in this case on the scale of the UK.
3 See www.mckinsey.com/clientservice/ccsi/greenhousegas.asp, accessed September 20, 2010.
4 See, for example, Jerry Yudelson, 2009, *Sustainable Retail Development: New Success Strategies*, Berlin and New York: Springer, pp. 189–205, for a discussion of eight of the world's leading rating systems, including LEED.
5 See "Energy Performance of LEED for New Construction Buildings," by Cathy Turner and Mark Frankel, www.newbuildings.org, March 2008, p. 4, accessed September 20, 2010.
6 See http://architecture2030.org/2030_challenge/the_2030_challenge, accessed September 20, 2010.
7 William McDonough and Michael Braungart, "Why Being 'Less Bad' Is No Good," *The Globalist*, June 21, 2010, www.theglobalist.com/StoryId.aspx?StoryId=8521, accessed February 11, 2012.
8 Greg Kats, 2010, *Greening Our Built World: Costs, Benefits and Strategies*, Washington, DC: Island Press.

9 "Site" vs. "Source" energy is a critical concept for building teams. Consider energy use at the building site. Since about two-thirds of the energy for buildings is delivered as electricity (heating and hot-water needs often are produced on site from oil or gas), we need to consider carbon emissions at the power plant. Taking a conservative multiplier of 3.0, we have annual *source* energy use of about 150,000 Btu/sq ft (470 kWh/sq m), even with best practice at about 50,000 Btu (EUI = 50). Consider building energy use, the only thing that makes *ultimate* sense is to describe source energy use of the base building. Using on-site renewables is certainly one way to reduce both site and source energy use. Best German Practice data is based on the project booklet "KfW Westarkade, Frankfurt am Main," edited by Professor Matthias Sauerbruch, Sauerbruch Hutton, July 2010.

10 Personal conversation, Thomas Auer, Transsolar, Stuttgart, Germany, June 2010.

11 Personal communication, Steven A. Straus, Glumac Engineers, July 2010.

12 Jerry Yudelson, 2009, *Green Building Trends: Europe*, Washington, DC: Island Press.

13 This discussion is ongoing in the building community since 2009. See, for example, Charles Eley, et al., "Rethinking Percent Savings: The Problem with Percent Savings and the New Scale for a Zero Net-Energy Future," Architectural Energy Corporation, July 2009, www.newbuildings.org/sites/default/files/Rethinking_Percent_Savings.pdf, accessed July 2, 2012.

14 For LEED 2009 requirements for new construction projects, see www.usgbc.org/DisplayPage.aspx?CMSPageID=220, accessed September 20, 2010.

15 Eley, et al., "Rethinking Percent Savings," op. cit., Executive Summary.

16 As we continue to reduce base building energy use, embodied energy will become an even larger component of total building energy use.

17 See, for example, the description in Chapter 7 of Oregon Health and Science University's Center for Health and Healing, in Portland, Oregon, a project designed in 2003, completed in 2006 and, for several years, the largest LEED Platinum project in the USA, www.betterbricks.com/casestudies.aspx?ID=1184. The project had a site EUI of 156 kBTU/sq ft/year, very good (at the time) for a complex medical building. In this project, MEP costs were cut by 10 percent (from the general contractor's original MEP budget for conventional systems) or more than $3 million in a $145 million project. The key: an involved (and very savvy) owner, a set of strong performance goals, and an integrated design approach by the design team.

18 Jerry Yudelson, 2008, *Green Building through Integrated Design*, New York: McGraw-Hill.

19 See, for example, www.aia.org/contractdocs/AIAS077630, accessed September 20, 2010.

3 Worldwide Green Building Rating Systems

1 United Nations, 1987, "Report of the World Commission on Environment and Development: Our Common Future" (also known as the Brundtland Report), http://conspect.nl/pdf/Our_Common_Future-Brundtland_Report_1987.pdf, accessed July 2, 2012.

2 UL Environment: ULE 880—Sustainability for Manufacturing Organizations, www.ulenvironment.com/ulenvironment/eng/pages/offerings/standards/organizations, accessed January 28, 2012.

3 See www.breeam.org/page.jsp?id=66, accessed November 5, 2011.

4 See www.breeam.org/filelibrary/Technical%20Manuals/SD5073_BREEAM_2011_New_Construction_Technical_Guide_ISSUE_2_0.pdf, accessed November 5, 2011.

5 See www.breeam.org/podpage.jsp?id=362, accessed November 5, 2011.

6 In December, 2011, Certivéa announced plans to offer an international HQE certification in 2012, www.certivea.com/assets/download/en/CP_Certivea_Developpement_Offre_Internationale.pdf, accessed January 28, 2012.

7 Rob Watson, 2011, "Green Building Market and Impact Report," p. 20, www.greenbiz.com/research/report/2011/11/07/green-building-market-and-impact-report-2011, accessed January 28, 2012.

8 Watson, "Green Building Market and Impact Report," p. 13.

9 So that we could include a wider geographic range of projects, we present also two Gold projects (CSOB in Prague and Transoceánica in Santiago, Chile) and one nonrated project (SAP in Ireland) with excellent energy performance.

10 See www.ibec.or.jp/CASBEE/english/overviewE.htm, accessed November 5, 2011.

11 www.ibec.or.jp/CASBEE/english/methodE.htm, accessed July 2, 2012.

12 See www.gbca.org.au/green-star/green-star-overview, accessed October 22, 2011.

13 See www.gbca.org.au/green-star/what-is-green-star/background/2140.htm, accessed October 22, 2011.

4 The Business Case for High-Performance Green Buildings

1 Yudelson has coined the acronym ZONE for ZerO Net Energy and believes it to be superior to the terms Zero Net Energy (ZNE) or Zero Energy Building (ZEB) now in use in the USA.

2 See http://ilbi.org/lbc/v2–0, accessed January 2, 2011.

3 Personal communication, Thomas Auer, Transsolar, December 2010, based on Transsolar's experience with several buildings in Germany.

4 100 kWh/sq m/yr @ 3,414 Btu/kWh and 1 sq m/10.76 sq ft, giving a total source EUI of about 31. Ratio of site to source energy use is about 2.5 kWh/kWh for fossil-fuel-fired US electric power, resulting in a site EUI goal of 13. This will vary by region, of course, with those areas having more hydroelectric power having a lower site-to-source ratio.

5 See Jerry Yudelson, 2009, *Green Building Trends: Europe*, Washington, DC: Island Press.
6 HOK and the Weidt Group, 2010, "The Path to Net Zero Co_2urt: Where Form Follows Performance," www.netzerocourt.com, accessed January 2, 2011.
7 Alex Wilson, 2005, "Making the Case for Green Building," *Environmental Building News,* 14 (4), www.buildinggreen.com/articles/IssueTOC.cfm?Volume=14&Issue=4, accessed January 2, 2011.
8 Lawrence Berkeley National Laboratory, 2004, "The Cost-Effectiveness of Commercial-Buildings Commissioning," http://eetd.lbl.gov/emills/PUBS/Cx-Costs-Benefits.html. This research reviewed 224 studies of the benefits of building commissioning and concluded that based on energy savings alone, such investments have a payback within five years.
9 See www.esl.tamu.edu/continuous-commissioning, accessed January 15, 2012.
10 See the studies cited on www.nilskok.com, accessed January 15, 2012.
11 See http://greenedgellc.com/posts/global-real-estate-sustainability-benchmark-gresb, accessed January 15, 2012.
12 World Business Council for Sustainable Development, May 2009, "Energy Efficiency in Buildings: Transforming the Market," http://62.50.73.69/transformingthemarket.pdf, accessed May 1, 2009.

5 Integrated Sustainable Design for High-Performance Buildings

1 Jerry Yudelson, 2008, *Green Building through Integrated Design*, New York: McGraw-Hill, Chapters 1 and 3.
2 Yudelson, *Green Building through Integrated Design*, pp. 45–46.
3 Interview with Gretel Hakanson, September 2011, edited.
4 Interview conducted by Ulf Meyer, September 2011, edited.
5 Interview conducted by Ulf Meyer, September 2011, edited.
6 See www.ctbuh.org/LinkClick.aspx?fileticket=lljgfExE83U%3d&tabid=2244&language=en-US, accessed January 18, 2012.
7 Yudelson, *Green Building through Integrated Design*, p. 57.
8 Yudelson, *Green Building through Integrated Design*, pp. 63–64.
9 Interviewed by Gretel Hakanson, November 30, 2011. Transcript edited for publication.
10 See subsequent interview with the energy engineer, John Andary, later in this chapter.
11 Interview with Gretel Hakanson, December 20, 2011. Transcript edited for publication.
12 Interview with Gretel Hakanson, December 1, 2011. Transcript edited for publication. John Andary was with Stantec Consulting at the time of the project.
13 David Cook, personal communication, February 1, 2012.
14 Jerry Yudelson, 2009, *Green Building Trends: Europe*, Washington, DC: Island Press, pp. 30, 124–125.
15 Interview with Gretel Hakanson, September 19, 2011. Transcript edited for publication. Adrian Leaman is Principal of Building Use Studies and Secretary of the Usable Buildings Trust, in the UK, www.usablebuildings.co.uk.
16 See www.usablebuildings.co.uk/Probe/ProbePDFs/BRI1.pdf, accessed January 19, 2012.
17 Yudelson, *Green Building through Integrated Design*, p. 249.

6 Introduction to the Case Studies

1 In one case, Transoceánica in Santiago, Chile, we relaxed one criterion to LEED Gold, so that we could include at least one South American project. In the case of some European projects, we asked for a legitimate third-party certification because at the time these buildings were designed and built, neither LEED nor BREEAM was in widespread use.

7 Case Studies

The Americas

1 See www.dovetailinc.org/files/u1/GreenBuildingGreenGlobes.pdf, accessed January 23, 2012.
2 Jones Lange LaSalle, "UBC-O Green Globes Report," February 2011.
3 See www.solaripedia.com/13/207/fipke_centre_awarded_five_green_globes.html, accessed January 23, 2012.
4 Ibid.
5 See http://ubco.tv/frontend2.php?cm=movies/76FipkeOpening.flv, accessed January 23, 2012.
6 See http://agoracom.com/ir/Cantex/forums/off-topic/topics/292344-fipke-centre-for-innovative-research/messages/1014492, accessed January 23, 2012.
7 See www.pec.ucalgary.ca/news/uofcpublications/oncampus/biweekly/oct26-07/cdc-leed, accessed April 11, 2011.
8 Bradley Fehr, 2007, "University of Calgary Child Development Centre Opens," *Journal of Commerce*, November 12, www.joconl.com/article/id25047, accessed April 11, 2011.
9 See www.pec.ucalgary.ca/news/uofcpublications/oncampus/biweekly/oct26-07/cdc-leed, accessed April 11, 2011.
10 Personal communication, Jim Love, University of Calgary, June 20, 2011.
11 See www.ilgbc.org/download/files/Child%20Development%20Center.pdf, accessed May 2, 2011.
12 See www.ilgbc.org/download/files/Child%20Development%20Center.pdf, accessed May 2, 2011.
13 Judy MacDougall, 2008, "Far More Than Child's Play," *Construction Canada,* September, p. 102, www.kenilworth.com/publications/cc/de/200809/98.html, accessed May 2, 2011.

14 Based on average nighttime temperatures in December, January, and February.
15 Nico Saieh, December 24, 2009, "Manitoba Hydro/KPMB Architects," www.archdaily.com/44596/manitoba-hydro-kpmb-architects, accessed May 2, 2010.
16 Bruce Kuwabara, Thomas Auer, Tom Gouldsborough, Tom Akerstream, Glenn Klym, "Manitoba Hydro Place: Integrated Design Process Exemplar," http://manitobahydroplace.com/site_documents/PLEA ManitobaHydroAbstract%20FINAL.pdf, accessed January 27, 2012.
17 Ibid.
18 Charles Linn, 2010, "Manitoba Hydro Place," *GreenSource,* March/April, http://greensource.construction.com/green_building_projects/2010/1003_ManitobaHydroPlace.asp, accessed May 2, 2011.
19 "College Walks Tall After Green Accolade," CTV News, www.ctv.ca/generic/generated/static/business/article1998125.html, accessed May 2, 2011.
20 Linn, "Manitoba Hydro Place," op. cit.
21 Saieh, "Manitoba Hydro/KPMB Architects," op. cit.
22 Kuwabara et al., "Manitoba Hydro Place," op. cit.
23 Ibid.
24 Ibid.
25 Linn, "Manitoba Hydro Place," op. cit.
26 2030 Challenge Case Study. Document provided by Julie Epp, February 28, 2011.
27 Kuwabara et al., "Manitoba Hydro Place," op. cit.
28 Ibid.
29 Ibid.
30 Linn, "Manitoba Hydro Place," op. cit.
31 There were no Platinum projects in South America that met all of our criteria, so we chose this project to represent what is a growing, but still early stage movement on that continent.
32 See www.cooper.edu/cubuilds/green.html, accessed May 23, 2011.
33 See www.arcspace.com/architects/morphosis/cooperunion/cooperunion.html, accessed May 20, 2011.
34 "The Inner Sanctum," 2009, *World Architecture News*, September 30, www.worldarchitecturenews.com/index.php?fuseaction=wanappln.projectview&upload_id=12454, accessed May 20, 2011.
35 Nico Saieh, "The Cooper Union for the Advancement of Science and Art/Morphosis Architects," November 12, 2009, www.archdaily.com/40471/the-cooper-union-for-the-advancement-of-science-and-art-morphosis-architects, accessed May 20, 2011.
36 "The Inner Sanctum," op. cit.
37 See www.architecture-page.com/go/projects/new-academic-building-cooper-union__2, accessed May 20, 2011.
38 See http://morphopedia.com/projects/cooper-union, accessed May 20, 2011.
39 Ibid.
40 See www.cooper.edu/cubuilds/donors.html, accessed May 25, 2011.
41 For Maharishi Vastu architecture, see www.maharishivastu.org/principles-of-maharishi-vastu-architecture, accessed October 1, 2011.
42 Jerry Yudelson, 2007, *Green Building A to Z*, Gabriola Island, BC: New Society Publishers, pp. 176–177.
43 John D. Macomber and Griffin H. James, 2010, "Design Creates Fortune: 2000 Tower Oaks Boulevard," Harvard Business School, May 4. Available at: http://hbr.org/product/design-creates-fortune-2000-tower-oakes-boulevard/an/210070-PDF-ENG.
44 Anuradha Kher, "MHN Interview with Jeffrey S. Abramson: Vedic Architecture Change Way People Feel, Work," May 5, 2010, www.multihousingnews.com/2010/05/05/mhn-interview-with-jeffrey-s-abramson-vedic-architecture-can-change-the-way-people-feel-and-work-2, accessed October 1, 2011.
45 Elizabeth Sherrod, 2009, "A Cosmic Force," *Development,* summer, pp. 24–25, www.naiop.org/developmentmag/strategicallygreen/index.cfm?content=200902.cfm, accessed October 1, 2011.
46 Yudelson, *Green Building A to Z*, op. cit.
47 See www.maharishivastu.org/principles-of-maharishi-vastu-architecture, accessed October 1, 2011.
48 Macomber and James, "Design Creates Fortune," op. cit.
49 Ibid.
50 Kher, "MHN Interview with Jeffrey S. Abramson," op. cit.
51 Macomber and James, "Design Creates Fortune," op. cit.
52 Ibid.
53 Yudelson, *Green Building A to Z*, op. cit.
54 The Tower Companies, "2000 Tower Oaks Blvd. Base Building LEED Platinum Certified," www.toweroaks.com/files/Tower_Oaks_Base_Building_PDF.pdf, accessed October 1, 2011.
55 Macomber and James, "Design Creates Fortune," op. cit.
56 Personal communication, Elizabeth Oliver-Farrow, President and CEO of the Oliver Group, September 28, 2011.
57 The Tower Companies, "2000 Tower Oaks Blvd. Base Building LEED Platinum Certified."
58 Macomber and James, "Design Creates Fortune," op. cit.
59 Personal communication, Trudi Hummel, Principal, Gould Evans, March 2008.
60 "Biodesign Institute at ASU Earns Arizona's Top Rating from US Green Building Council," August 1, 2007, www.biodesign.asu.edu/news/biodesign-institute-at-asu-earns-arizonas-top-rating-from-us-green-building-council, accessed March 5, 2011.
61 Ibid.
62 Ibid.
63 Personal communication, John Dimmel, architect and designer, Gould Evans, March 2008.

64 Personal communication, Larry Lord, Principal at Lord, Aeck & Sargent, March 2008.
65 Personal communication, Mike McLeod, Directory of Facility Services, Biodesign Institute, Arizona State University, March 2008.
66 "ASU's Biodesign Institute LEEDs the Way in Rooftop Solar Energy," May 4, 2009, www.biodesign.asu.edu/news/asus-biodesign-institute-leeds-the-way-in-rooftop-solar-energy, accessed March 5, 2011.
67 "Biodesign Institute at ASU Earns Arizona's Top Rating," op. cit.
68 Personal communication, Tamara Shroll, Project Designer, Gould Evans, March 2008.
69 "Biodesign Institute at ASU," op. cit.
70 Mike McLeod, personal communication, July 30, 2012.
71 Ibid.
72 Shelley Seale, "Cutting Edge Children's Treatments, Medical Research and LEED Certification Put Seton Healthcare Family on the Map," October 10, 2010, Culture Map Austin, http://austin.culturemap.com/newsdetail/10–10–11–10–21-cutting-edge-childrens-treatments-medical-research-put-seton-on-the-map, accessed December 23, 2011.
73 "Dell Children's Medical Center of Central Texas is World's First Platinum LEED Hospital," January 9, 2009, http://impactnews.com/healthcare/news/3775-dell-childrens-medical-center-of-central-texas-is-worlds-first-platinum-leed-hospital, accessed December 23, 2011.
74 Eileen Schwartz, 2007, "Green Guidelines Take Root in Austin," *Texas Construction*, February, http://texas.construction.com/features/archive/0702_cover.asp, accessed December 23, 2011.
75 Sue Durio, "Dell Children's Medical Center: Taking Green Building to Highest Level," April 2006, Texas Hospitals, www.intertechflooring.com/w_TH_DellChildrens.pdf, accessed December 23, 2011.
76 "Dell Children's Medical Center Video (text version)," www1.eere.energy.gov/buildings/alliances/hea_dell_leed_text.html, accessed December 23, 2011.
77 Ibid.
78 Josephine Minutillo, 2008, "Design Professionals Follow the Physician's Precept," *Architectural Record*, August, http://continuingeducation.construction.com/article.php?L=5&C=434&P=2, accessed December 23, 2011.
79 "Dell Children's Medical Center Video," op. cit.
80 Durio, "Dell Children's Medical Center," op. cit.
81 Minutillo, "Design Professionals Follow the Physician's Precept," op. cit.
82 Dell Children's Medical Center, www.dellchildrens.net/about_us/about_our_green_building/leeds_interactive_slideshow/#slide_1, accessed December 23, 2011.
83 Durio, "Dell Children's Medical Center," op. cit.
84 Karlsberger, 2010, "Dell Children's Medical Center Becomes First Hospital in the World to Achieve LEED Platinum," April 26, www.karlsberger.com/dell-childrens-medical-center-becomes-first-hospital-in-the-world-to-achieve-leed-platinum, accessed December 23, 2011.
85 Siemens, 2009, "Dell Children's Become World's First LEED Platinum Hospital with Assist from Siemens," November 11, www.buildingtechnologies.siemens.com/bt/us/Press/press_release/2009_press_releases/Pages/DellChildrensBecomeWorldFirstLeedPlatinumHospitalWithAssistFromSiemens.aspx, accessed December 20, 2011.
86 Schwartz, "Green Guidelines Take Root in Austin," op. cit.
87 Ibid.
88 See www.genzymecenter.com, accessed June 27, 2011.
89 "Genzyme Center Earns Highest Environmental Rating from US Green Building Council," September 8, 2005, www.prnewswire.com/news-releases/genzyme-center-earns-highest-environmental-rating-from-us-green-building-council-54806287.html, accessed June 29, 2012.
90 Dara Olmstead and Dona Neely, "Genzyme Center," September 27, 2005, Tufts Climate Initiative and Tufts University Department of Urban and Environmental Policy and Planning, www.solaripedia.com/files/704.pdf, accessed June 27, 2011.
91 Ibid.
92 Behnisch Architekten, Genzyme Case Study, www.solaripedia.com/files/707.pdf, accessed June 27, 2011.
93 Mimi Zeiger, 2006, "Bright Green Machine," *Architecture*, August, www.solaripedia.com/files/703.pdf, accessed June 27, 2011.
94 See www.genzymecenter.com, accessed June 27, 2011.
95 Olmstead and Neely, "Genzyme Center," op. cit.
96 See www.aiatopten.org/hpb/materials.cfm?ProjectID=274, accessed June 28, 2011.
97 Olmstead and Neely, "Genzyme Center," op. cit.
98 Tony McLaughlin, 2002, "Genzyme Center: Environmental Design Narrative," Summer, published by Buro Happold.
99 Ibid.
100 Email communication with Abigal DiMatteo, Genzyme Center, March 2, 2011.
101 Olmstead and Neely, "Genzyme Center," op. cit.
102 Ibid.
103 Ibid.
104 Ibid.
105 Behnisch Architekten, Genzyme Case Study. Available at: http://behnisch.com/content/02.projects/104/104.pdf .
106 Olmstead and Neely, "Genzyme Center," op. cit.
107 Zeiger, "Bright Green Machine," op. cit.
108 Olmstead and Neely, "Genzyme Center," op. cit.
109 Ibid.
110 Ibid.
111 Ibid.
112 McLaughlin, "Genzyme Center," op. cit.
113 Olmstead and Neely, "Genzyme Center," op. cit.
114 Jack Murphy, 2004, "Genzyme Center," Cambridge: Community Development Department, July.

115 Ibid.
116 Olmstead and Neely, "Genzyme Center," op. cit.
117 See www.solaripedia.com/files/702.pdf, accessed June 27, 2011.
118 Great River Energy, 2009, "A White Paper on Building for Platinum LEED Certification," March.
119 Ibid.
120 Ibid.
121 Ibid.
122 Ibid.
123 Ibid.
124 Ibid.
125 Ibid.
126 Ibid.
127 Ibid.
128 Ibid.
129 Ibid.
130 Ibid.
131 Ibid.
132 See www.solaripedia.com/13/277/great_river_energy_hq_powers_on.html, accessed August 8, 2011.
133 Great River Energy, "A White Paper on Building," op. cit.
134 Candace Roulo, 2009, "Electric Utility Leads by Example: Headquarters Is Platinum LEED Certified," *Contractor Magazine*, May 8, http://contractormag.com/green-contracting/electric-utility-headquarters-leed-0508, accessed August 8, 2011.
135 See www.solaripedia.com/13/277/great_river_energy_hq_powers_on.html, accessed August 8, 2011.
136 Doug Pierce and Randy Olson, 2011, "Evolving," *High Performance Buildings*, summer, www.hpbmagazine.org/images/stories/articles/GreatRiver.pdf, accessed August 9, 2011.
137 Pierce and Olson, "Evolving," op. cit.
138 Roulo, "Electric Utility Leads by Example," op. cit.
139 Ibid.
140 Pierce and Olson, "Evolving," op. cit.
141 Ibid.
142 Ibid.
143 Great River Energy, "A White Paper on Building," op. cit.
144 Johnson Controls, "Case Study: Johnson Controls Headquarters Glendale, Wisconsin." Furnished by Steve Thomas, Manager, Global Energy and Sustainability Communications, June 2, 2011.
145 Ibid.
146 Candace Roulo, 2010, "Johnson Controls' Geothermal System Delivers 30% Reduction in Energy Consumption," *Contractor*, December 2, http://contractormag.com/green-contracting/johnson-controls-geo-system-1234, accessed August 24, 2011.
147 "System Integration Improves Corporate Campus," *Consulting-Specifying Engineer*, March 7, 2011, www.csemag.com/search/search-single-display/system-integration-improves-corporate-campus/3b196e132c.html, accessed August 24, 2011.
148 Johnson Controls, "Case Study," op. cit.
149 "System Integration Improves Corporate Campus," op. cit.
150 Ibid.
151 Ibid.
152 Ibid.
153 Johnson Controls, "Case Study," op. cit.
154 "System Integration Improves Corporate Campus," op. cit.
155 Ibid.
156 Personal communication, Paul Stoller, Director, Atelier Ten, June 8, 2011.
157 Kroon Hall Project Description, supplied by Paul Stoller.
158 Personal communication, Paul Stoller, Director, Atelier Ten, June 8, 2011.
159 Personal communication, Alan Brewster, former Deputy Dean, Yale University School of Forestry and Environmental Studies, August 30, 2011.
160 Personal communication, Paul Stoller, Director, Atelier Ten, June 8, 2011.
161 Kroon Hall Project Description, supplied by Paul Stoller.
162 Personal communication, Paul Stoller, Director, Atelier Ten, June 8, 2011.
163 Ibid.
164 Joann Gonchar, 2009, "Kroon Hall, Yale University," *GreenSource*, http://greensource.construction.com/green_building_projects/2009/0909_Kroon-Hall.asp, accessed September 13, 2010.
165 Personal communication, Paul Stoller, Director, Atelier Ten, June 8, 2011.
166 See http://environment.yale.edu/kroon/design.php, accessed September 12, 2011.
167 Personal communication, Stephen Kellert, Tweedy Ordway Professor Emeritus of Social Ecology and Senior Research Scholar at the Yale University School of Forestry and Environmental Studies, May 18, 2010.
168 Ibid.
169 Ibid.
170 Ibid.
171 Personal communication, Alan Brewster, former Deputy Dean, Yale University School of Forestry and Environmental Studies, August 30, 2011.
172 Personal communication, Laura Lesniewski, BNIM, April 21, 2008.
173 Personal communication, Erin Gehle, April 21, 2008.
174 Missouri Department of Natural Resources, "Gold to Platinum," www.dnr.mo.gov/greenbldg/docs/gold-to-platinum.pdf, accessed October 18, 2011.
175 Rocky Mountain Institute, "State of Missouri Department of Natural Resources Lewis & Clark State Office Building," http://bet.rmi.org/files/case-studies/mo-dnr/State_of_Missouri.pdf, accessed October 18, 2011.

176 Ibid.
177 "HVAC and Associated Systems," www.dnr.mo.gov/greenbldg/docs/hvac-systems.pdf, accessed October 31, 2011.
178 Personal communication, Erin Gehle, BNIM, October 10, 2011.
179 Missouri Department of Natural Resources, "Gold to Platinum," op. cit.
180 Rocky Mountain Institute, "State of Missouri Department of Natural Resources Lewis & Clark State Office Building," op. cit.
181 See www.bnim.com/work/lewis-and-clark-state-office-building-missouri-department-natural-resources, accessed October 31, 2011.
182 "Getting to Net Zero Today through a Performance-Based Design/Build Process," webinar, March 8, 2010, www1.eere.energy.gov/buildings/rsf_webinar_text_version.html, accessed October 8, 2011.
183 Heather Lammers, "NREL Solar Technology Will Warm Air at 'Home,'" July 30, 2010, www.nrel.gov/news/features/feature_detail.cfm/feature_id=1522, accessed December 22, 2011.
184 Jeff Erlichman, 2011, "How a Federal Data Center Cut Its Energy Needs by 80 Percent," AOL Government, August 9, http://gov.aol.com/2011/08/09/how-a-federal-data-center-cut-its-energy-needs-by-80-percent, accessed October 17, 2011.
185 Heather Lammers, 2011, "Solar System Tops Off Efficient NREL Building," September 20, www.nrel.gov/news/features/feature_detail.cfm/feature_id=1516, accessed December 22, 2011.
186 Katie Weeks, 2011, "AIA COTE 2011 Top Ten Green Projects: Research Support Facility, National Renewable Energy Laboratory," *EcoStructure*, April 12, www.eco-structure.com/awards/aia-cote-2011-top-ten-green-projects-research-sup.aspx, accessed October 8, 2011. Shanti Pless.
187 "NREL's Research Support Facility: An Energy Performance Update, October 2011, www.nrel.gov/sustainable_nrel/pdfs/rsf_operations_10–2011.pdf, accessed October 8, 2011.
188 www.oneworkplace.com/images/dynamic/case_studies/ohlone_college_case_study.pdf, accessed February 23, 2011.
189 Personal communication, Doug Treadway, President, Ohlone College, February 25, 2008.
190 Guy Esberg, 2010, "Dispelling the Cost Myth," *High Performing Buildings,* winter, pp. 30–42.
191 "Sustainable Architecture for a College of the Future," www.ohlone.edu/org/pio/docs/newark/newarkcenter-presspacketinsert-sustainable architecture.pdf, accessed March 1, 2011.
192 David Sokol, 2010, "Going for a Spin: Enthalpy Wheels Flood the Ohlone College Newark Center for Health Sciences and Technology with Fresh Air," *GreenSource*, March, http://greensource.construction.com/features/Solutions/2010/March/1003_Ohlone_College_Newark_Center.asp, accessed February 23, 2011.
193 Sokol, "Going for a Spin," op. cit.
194 "Ohlone College NC: Narrative for ASHRAE 2009 Technology Award Application," supplied by Marco Alves, PAE Consulting Engineers.
195 "Ohlone College New Campus Is the 'Greenest College in the World!,'" August 28, 2008, www.ohlone.edu/org/president/pressreleases/2008 2009/20080828greenestcollege.html, accessed February 23, 2011.
196 Michael Lucas, PE, is now the principal in charge of PAE Engineers, San Francisco office.
197 Sokol, "Going for a Spin," op. cit.
198 Personal communication, Michael Lucas, Principal, Alfa Tech, March 21, 2008.
199 "Ohlone College New Campus Is the 'Greenest College in the World!,'" op. cit.
200 "Ohlone College NC," op. cit.
201 Ibid.
202 Ibid.
203 Ibid.
204 Steelcase, "Green Campus Grows Innovated Learning Environments," op. cit.
205 Dennis Wilde, 2009, "Rx For Platinum," *High Performing Buildings,* winter, www.hpbmagazine.com/images/stories/articles/Winter2009 OHSU.pdf, accessed September 27, 2011.
206 Wilde, "Rx For Platinum," op. cit.
207 RMI, "Oregon Health & Science University Center for Health and Healing," http://bet.rmi.org/files/case-studies/ohsu/Oregon_Health_Science_University.pdf, accessed September 27, 2011.
208 Wilde, "Rx For Platinum," op. cit.
209 Better Bricks, "OHSU Center for Health and Healing: A Post-Occupancy Evaluation," www.betterbricks.com/sites/default/files/casestudies/pdf/bb_casestudy_ohsu-chh.pdf, accessed February 16, 2011.
210 RMI, "Oregon Health & Science University Center for Health and Healing," op. cit.
211 Wilde, "Rx For Platinum," op. cit.
212 Ibid.
213 Better Bricks, "OHSU Center for Health and Healing," op. cit.
214 RMI, "Oregon Health & Science University Center for Health and Healing," op. cit.
215 Ibid.
216 Ibid.
217 Ibid.
218 Wilde, "Rx For Platinum," op. cit.
219 Ibid.
220 Ibid.
221 Ibid.
222 Interface Engineering, 2005, "Engineering a Sustainable World," October, http://interfaceengineering.com/sustainable-engineering/energy-strategies, accessed September 27, 2011.
223 Wilde, "Rx For Platinum," op. cit.
224 Better Bricks, "OHSU Center for Health and Healing," op. cit.

225 Christina Williams, 2011, "OHSU Buildings Earns Second LEED Platinum," September 23, http://sustainablebusinessoregon.com/articles/2011/09/ohsu-building-earns-second-leed-platinum.html, accessed September 27, 2011.
226 "OHSU Center for Health and Healing Post Occupancy Evaluation," December 2010; supplied by Dennis Wilde via email, February 2011.
227 RMI, "Oregon Health & Science University Center for Health and Healing," op. cit.
228 Better Bricks, "OHSU Center for Health and Healing," op. cit.
229 Ibid.
230 Ibid.
231 RMI, "Oregon Health & Science University Center for Health and Healing," op. cit.
232 Ibid.
233 Interface Engineering, "Engineering a Sustainable World," op. cit.
234 Wilde, "Rx For Platinum," op. cit.
235 Ibid.
236 Better Bricks, "OHSU Center for Health and Healing," op. cit.
237 Interface Engineering, "Engineering a Sustainable World," op. cit.
238 RMI, "Oregon Health & Science University Center for Health and Healing," op. cit.
239 Ibid.
240 Wilde, "Rx For Platinum," op. cit.
241 RMI, "Oregon Health & Science University Center for Health and Healing," op. cit.
242 Ibid.
243 Ibid.
244 Wilde, "Rx For Platinum," op. cit.
245 Ibid.
246 Ibid.
247 RMI, "Oregon Health & Science University Center for Health and Healing," op. cit.
248 Email interview with Andy Frichtl, December 2011.
249 McQuay International, "Designed for LEED Platinum Certification Regents Hall at St. Olaf College Combines Sustainable Design, Interdisciplinary Science Education," www.mcquay.com/mcquaybiz/DocumentStorage/AirHandlers-Indoor/CaseStudies/St_Olaf_Science_Bldg.pdf, accessed November 3, 2011.
250 See www.stolaf.edu/regentshall/green.html, accessed January 23, 2012.
251 "Regents Tour," PDF supplied by Peter Sandberg.
252 McQuay International, "Designed for LEED Platinum Certification," op. cit.
253 Regents Tour, op. cit.
254 Ibid.
255 Ibid.
256 McQuay International, "Designed for LEED Platinum Certification," op. cit.
257 Regents Tour, op. cit.
258 See www.stolaf.edu/regentshall/green.html, accessed January 23, 2012.
259 Regents Tour, op. cit.
260 Ibid.
261 McQuay International, "Designed for LEED Platinum Certification," op. cit.
262 Leo Poppoff, 2006, "New Era for Tahoe Science," *Tahoe Quarterly*, Fall, pp. 44–46. Available at: http://www.collaborativedesignstudio.com/publications/newEra.pdf.
263 Collaborative Design Studio, Tahoe Center for Environmental Sciences Project Profile, furnished by Todd Lankenau.
264 Heather Livingston, 2006, "Tahoe Science Lab Goes for Platinum-LEED," *AIArchitect,* 13 (October 27). Available at: http://info.aia.org/aiarchitect/thisweek06/1027/1027n_tahoe.cfm .
265 "Innovative Mechanical Designs in the Sierras," June 12, 2009, www.energydesignresources.com/resources/publications/case-studies/case-studies-tahoe-center-for-environmental-sciences.aspx, accessed August 22, 2011.
266 Ibid.
267 Kate Gawlik, "Active and Passive," *Eco-Structure,* November 2006.
268 Livingston, "Tahoe Science Lab Goes for Platinum-LEED," op. cit.
269 Gawlik, "Active and Passive," op. cit.
270 Ibid.
271 Personal communication, Todd Lankenau, Principal and Managing Partner, Collaborative Design Studio, March 2008.
272 "Innovative Mechanical Designs in the Sierras," op. cit.
273 Personal communication, Todd Lankenau, Principal and Managing Partner, Collaborative Design Studio, March 2008.
274 Ibid.
275 Ibid.
276 "Innovative Mechanical Designs in the Sierras," op. cit.
277 Eva Hagberg, 2010, "Twelve West," *Metropolis Magazine*, February, www.metropolismag.com/story/20100217/twelve-west/1, accessed July 1, 2011.
278 Nadav Malin, 2010, "Case Study: Twelve West," *GreenSource,* July/August, http://greensource.construction.com/green_building_projects/2010/1007_twelve-west.asp, accessed July 1, 2011.
279 David R. Macaulay, 2011, *The Ecological Engineer: Glumac*, Portland, OR: Ecotone, p. 264.
280 Hagberg, "Twelve West," op. cit.
281 Macaulay, *The Ecological Engineer*, op. cit., p. 268.
282 AIA Case Study, www.aiatopten.org/hpb/overview.cfm?ProjectID=1725, accessed July 1, 2011.
283 Hagberg, "Twelve West," op. cit.

284 See www.archinnovations.com/featured-projects/mixed-use/zgf-architects-twelve-west-in-portland-or, accessed July 2, 2011.
285 Ibid.
286 Macaulay, *The Ecological Engineer*, op. cit., p. 267.
287 Ibid.
288 Malin, "Case Study: Twelve West," op. cit.
289 Ibid.
290 Macaulay, *The Ecological Engineer*, op. cit., p.268.
291 Ibid.
292 AIA Case Study, op. cit.
293 Macaulay, *The Ecological Engineer*, op. cit., p. 272.
294 Ibid.
295 Macaulay, *The Ecological Engineer*, op. cit., p. 267.
296 Hagberg, "Twelve West," op. cit.
297 AIA Case Study, op. cit.
298 Hagberg, "Twelve West," op. cit.
299 AIA Case Study, op. cit.
300 Malin, "Case Study: Twelve West," op. cit.
301 AIA Case Study, op. cit.
302 Malin, "Case Study: Twelve West," op. cit.
303 AIA Case Study, op. cit.
304 Hagberg, "Twelve West," op. cit.
305 Personal communication, Mitchell Dec, Glumac, December 2010.
306 Macaulay, *The Ecological Engineer*, op. cit., p. 272.
307 AIA Case Study, op. cit.
308 Ibid.

Europe

1 "CSOB's Eco-Building in Radlice Is Open," www.csob.cz/en/CSOB/Media-service/press-releases/Stranky/PR070423b.aspx, accessed January 6, 2012.
2 See http://skanska-sustainability-case-studies.com/pdfs/30/30_CSOB_v001.pdf, accessed May 30, 2011
3 Julian Parsley and Anna Serra, 2009, "Prague's Gold Standard," summer, *High Performing Buildings*. Summer, pp. 28–39
4 See http://skanska-sustainability-case-studies.com/pdfs/30/30_CSOB_v001.pdf, accessed May 30, 2011.
5 See www.csreurope.org/solutions.php?action=show_solution&solution_id=458, accessed May 30, 2011.
6 "The Building of the Year 2007: Another Award for CSOB's New Headquarters," press release provided by Jan Solnicka, CSOB.
7 See http://skanska-sustainability-case-studies.com/pdfs/30/30_CSOB_v001.pdf, accessed May 30, 2011.
8 Ibid.
9 See www.csreurope.org/solutions.php?action=show_solution&solution_id=458, accessed May 30, 2011.
10 See http://skanska-sustainability-case-studies.com/pdfs/30/30_CSOB_v001.pdf, accessed May 30, 2011.
11 Ibid.
12 Parsley and Serra, "Prague's Gold Standard," op. cit.
13 Ibid.
14 Ibid.
15 Ibid.
16 Ibid.
17 Ibid.
18 See http://skanska-sustainability-case-studies.com/pdfs/30/30_CSOB_v001.pdf, accessed May 30, 2011.
19 Ibid.
20 See http://skanska-sustainability-case-studies.com/pdfs/30/30_CSOB_v001.pdf, accessed May 30, 2011.
21 Ibid.
22 Ibid.
23 Ibid.
24 Ibid.
25 Ibid.
26 Frank Hovorka, 2008, "Coloring Paris," *High Performing Buildings*, summer, www.hpbmagazine.com/images/stories/articles/Coloring%20Paris%20Nights.pdf, accessed November 9, 2011.
27 See www.brenac-gonzalez.fr/fr/projet/emgp-batiment-270-bureaux-hqe, accessed November 15, 2011.
28 Hovorka, "Coloring Paris," op. cit.
29 See www.novethic.fr/novethic/planete/environnement/immobilier/le_270_immeuble_bureau_certifie_haute_qualite_environnementale/95034.jsp, accessed November 15, 2011.
30 Hovorka, "Coloring Paris," op. cit.
31 Jean Carassus, "Are 'Green' Office Buildings Keeping Their Promises?" March 2011. Available at: http://www.certivea.com/assets/download/en/JCarassus_Report.pdf.
32 Ibid.
33 Susanne Stephens, 2006, "Sauerbruch Hutton Architects Brings Pizzazz to Sustainability in the Federal Environmental Agency," *Architectural Record*, August, pp. 82–89, http://archrecord.construction.com/projects/portfolio/archives/0608fedAgency.asp, accessed June 9, 2011.
34 See www.umweltbundesamt.de/uba-info-e/index.htm, accessed June 9, 2011.
35 Ibid.
36 Ibid.
37 "Federal Environmental Agency Dessau," Case Study, www.sauerbruchhutton.de/images/environmental_agency_en.pdf, accessed June 4, 2011.

38 "New Building for the German Federal Environmental Agency," www.enob.info/en/pdf/new-buildings/project/details/new-building-for-the-german-federal-environment-agency-in-dessau, accessed June 4, 2011.
39 "Federal Environmental Agency Dessau," op. cit.
40 "New Building for the German Federal Environmental Agency," op. cit.
41 Ibid.
42 Ibid.
43 See www.umweltbundesamt.de/uba-info-e/besucher/index.htm, accessed June 9, 2011.
44 "New Building for the German Federal Environmental Agency," op. cit.
45 Ibid.
46 Ibid.
47 Ibid.
48 Bundesinstitut für Bau-, Stadt- und Raumforschung (BBSR), April 10, 2009, "Abschlussbericht: Part A and Part C," 117–07–10–04–2009.
49 See www.boell.de/stiftung/neubau/neubau-3615.html, accessed January 22, 2012.
50 In late 2011, Solon filed for bankruptcy protection, and, as of this writing, the long-term viability of the project is uncertain.
51 See www.gap-arch.de; www.paul-wunderlichhaus.de, accessed January 22, 2012.
52 Personal communication, Merritt Bucholz, architect, Bucholz McEvoy Architects, August 30, 2011.
53 Merritt Bucholz and Wolfgang Kessling, 2008, "SAP Building Galway," *Xia International,* January, pp. 14–21.
54 Ibid.
55 John Hearne, "A Breath of Fresh Air," *Constructireland,* http://constructireland.ie/Articles/Design-Approaches/Naturally-ventilated-call-centre-combines-sustainability-with-striking-aesthetic.html, accessed September 28, 2011.
56 Bucholz and Kessling, "SAP Building Galway," op. cit.
57 Personal communication, Merritt Bucholz, architect, Bucholz McEvoy Architects, August 30, 2011.
58 Bucholz and Kessling, "SAP Building Galway," op. cit.
59 Ibid.
60 Personal communication, Merritt Bucholz, architect, Bucholz McEvoy Architects, August 30, 2011.
61 Hearne, "A Breath of Fresh Air," op. cit.
62 Interview with Gretel Hakanson and Merritt Bucholz, Bucholz McEvoy Architects, August 30, 2011. Transcript edited for publication.
63 Personal communication, Merritt Bucholz, architect, Bucholz McEvoy Architects, August 30, 2011.
64 Hearne, "A Breath of Fresh Air," op. cit.
65 Ibid.
66 Ibid.
67 See www.ovg.nl/images/uploads/files/OVG_boekje_TNT_ENG_LR.pdf, accessed February 15, 2012.
68 See www.ovg.nl/images/uploads/files/OVG_boekje_TNT_ENG_LR.pdf, accessed February 15, 2012.
69 Maija Virta (ed.), in "HVAC in Sustainable Office Buildings," REHVA Guidebook No. 16, Brussels, 2012, p. 88.
70 Gross floor area of office space is 185,610 sq ft (17,250 sq m); parking space is 77,575 sq ft (7,210 sq m). However, parking garage lighting is only about 2.5 percent of total energy use. Other parking garage energy use would be primarily from ventilation fans.
71 Solar thermal system output is very small, at 3,982 kWh/year (0.22 percent of total energy use), from 4.8 sq m of panels.
72 www.skanska.com/upload/Projects/Files/Hagaporten.pdf, accessed November 28, 2011.
73 Ibid.
74 Ibid.
75 Ibid.
76 Ibid.
77 Ibid.
78 Ibid.
79 Ibid.
80 Ibid.
81 Maija Virta (ed.), in "HVAC in Sustainable Office Buildings," REHVA Guidebook No. 16, Brussels, 2012, p. 93.
82 Ibid.
83 Ibid.
84 Ibid.
85 Ibid.
86 Skanska, "Hagaporten 3 Energy Use," PDF supplied by Jonas Gräslund, September 23, 2011.
87 Daniel Wentz, "Research Center in Switzerland," Holcim Foundation, www.holcimfoundation.org/T981/Planet-CH.htm, accessed June 9, 2011.
88 Ibid.
89 See www.eawag.ch/about/nachhaltig/fc/index_EN, accessed June 9, 2011.
90 See www.bgp.ch/English/PR.asp?ID_UT=5&Offset=2&ID=1, accessed June 14, 2011.
91 Wentz, "Research Center in Switzerland," op. cit.
92 Ibid.
93 Ibid.
94 See www.bgp.ch/English/PR.asp?ID_UT=5&Offset=2&ID=1, accessed June 14, 2011.
95 Wentz, "Research Center in Switzerland," op. cit.
96 Current figures are 5,000 watts in Switzerland; 6,000 in western Europe; and 12,000 in the USA.

97 Jerry Yudelson, 2009, *Green Building Trends: Europe*, Washington, DC: Island Press, pp. 37–38.
98 See www.coltgroup.com/projects/offices/empa-forum, accessed June 14, 2011.
99 Wentz, "Research Center in Switzerland," op. cit.
100 Ibid.
101 Ibid.
102 B. Lehmann, H. Güttinger, V. Dorer, S. van Velsen, A. Thiemann, and Th. Franka, 2010, "Eawag Forum Chriesbach: Simulation and Measurement of Energy Performance and Comfort in a Sustainable Office Building," *Energy and Buildings*, 42: 1958–1967, www.elsevier.com/locate/enbuild, accessed January 26, 2011.
103 Ibid.
104 See www.eawag.ch/about/nachhaltig/fc/energie/index_EN, accessed June 9, 2011.
105 Lehmann et al., "Eawag Forum Chriesbach," op. cit.
106 See www.eawag.ch/about/nachhaltig/fc/energie/index_EN, accessed June 9, 2011.
107 Lehmann et al., "Eawag Forum Chriesbach," op. cit.
108 Stefan Mennel, Urs-Peter Menti, Gregor Notter, 2007, "MINERGIE-P: A Building Standard of the Future," *Proceedings of Clima 2007 WellBeing Indoors*, www.rehva.eu/projects/clima2007/SPs/B01D1349.pdf, accessed June 15, 2011.
109 See www.eawag.ch/about/nachhaltig/fc/wasser/index_EN, accessed June 9, 2011.
110 Ibid.
111 Ibid.
112 Conversion rate on January 25, 2012.
113 Ibid.
114 Ulf Meyer, originally published 2010 as "Eine 'brand-architecture' der besonderen Art," *Greenbuilding*, December, http://greenbuilding-planning.schiele-schoen.de/zeitschrift/allgemein/archiv/preview.asp?f=gb21012022.pdf&s=15881, accessed January 21, 2011. Edited for publication.
115 See www.breeam.org/page.jsp?id=66, accessed November 15, 2011.
116 Scott Brownrigg, RIBA Awards 2010, February 2010. Available at: www.architecture.com/RegionsAndInternational/UKNationsAndRegions/Wales/Awards/RIBA%20Awards.aspx .
117 "BREEAM Awards Wales 2009," www.breeam.org/filelibrary/BREEAM%20Awards/BREEAM_Awards_Wales_2009_Case_Studies.pdf, accessed November 15, 2011.
118 "BREEAM Awards Wales 2009," op. cit.
119 BCO Submission, 3 Assembly Square Cardiff Waterside, November 2009.
120 Brownrigg, RIBA Awards 2010, op. cit.
121 Ibid.
122 BCO Submission, op. cit.
123 Ibid.
124 Ibid.
125 "BREEAM Awards Wales 2009," op. cit.
126 Ibid.
127 Ibid.
128 "M&A Solicitors to Lay Down the Law As First Tenant at 3 Assembly Square," November 22, 2009, http://investincardiff.com/News/MA-Solicitors-to-lay-down-the-law-as-first-tenant-at-3-Assembly-Square.html, accessed November 15, 2011.
129 Knight Frank, "Energy Performance Analysis," op. cit., p. 4.
130 Ibid.
131 "Innovative Medical Building Wins Environmental Award," September 22, 2008, www.abdn.ac.uk/~wox004/release.php?id=1512, accessed December 16, 2011.
132 John Miller, Bennetts Associates Architects, "Suttie Centre for Teaching and Learning: Sustainability Report," March 2010.
133 Penny Lewis, 2010, "The Suttie Centre: Developing the Evidence Base," *Architecture Today*, February 5, www.architecturetoday.co.uk/?p=11461, accessed December 16, 2011.
134 Ibid.
135 www.clinicalservicesjournal.com/Story.aspx?Story=4570, accessed December 16, 2011.
136 Lewis, "The Suttie Centre," op. cit.
137 Miller, "Suttie Centre for Teaching and Learning," op. cit.
138 Ibid.
139 "Perfect Prescription for Sustainability," op. cit.
140 "Innovative Medical Building Wins Environmental Award," op. cit.
141 See http://departments.oxy.edu/physics/csp6/CSP6_Handouts/Energy Conversion_CarbonTrust.pdf, accessed January 27, 2012, ratio of 0.43 kg-CO_2e/kWh.

Asia Pacific Region

1 Bassett, "Durack II: Design Intent Manual for Stockland Investments," June 15, 2009, supplied by Greg Johnson, National Environment Manager, February 15, 2011.
2 Ibid.
3 Ibid.
4 See www.nabers.com.au, accessed March 14, 2011.
5 Stockland, 2009, "Energy Efficient Tenancy Fitout Durack II: Design Intent Manual for Stockland Investments," June 15, supplied by Greg Johnson, National Environment Manager, February 15, 2011. See www.nabers.com.au, accessed March 14, 2011; "Design Guidelines," May 5, 2009, supplied by Greg Johnson, National Environment Manager, February 15, 2011.
6 Bassett, "Durack II," op. cit.

7 Personal communication, Greg Johnson, National Environmental Manager, Stockland, February 15, 2011.
8 Bassett, "Durack II," op. cit.
9 Ibid.
10 Will Jones, 2008, "Council House 2, Melbourne: Australia's Greenest Office Building," *Building,* January 29, www.building.co.uk/council-house-2-melbourne-australia%E2%80%99s-greenest-office-building/3104100.article, accessed January 17, 2011.
11 Ibid.
12 City of Melbourne, www.melbourne.vic.gov.au/Environment/CH2/Design Delivery/Documents/Design_Environmental_Design_Schematic.pdf, accessed January 17, 2011.
13 City of Melbourne, www.melbourne.vic.gov.au/Environment/CH2/Design Delivery/Documents/CH2_Snapshot4.pdf, accessed January 17, 2011.
14 City of Melbourne, www.melbourne.vic.gov.au/Environment/CH2/Design Delivery/Documents/CH2_Snapshot4.pdf, accessed January 17, 2011.
15 City of Melbourne, www.melbourne.vic.gov.au/Environment/CH2/Design Delivery/Documents/CH2_Snapshot3.pdf, accessed January 17, 2011.
16 Ibid.
17 Ibid.
18 Ibid.
19 City of Melbourne, www.melbourne.vic.gov.au/Environment/CH2/Design Delivery/Documents/CH2_Snapshot11.pdf, accessed January 17, 2011.
20 CH2 Virtual Tour with Project Director, Rob Adams, www.youtube.com/watch?gl=AU&hl=en-GB&v=vJVOwnbAZ6M, accessed January 17, 2011.
21 City of Melbourne, www.melbourne.vic.gov.au/Environment/CH2/Design Delivery/Documents/CH2_Snapshot3.pdf, accessed January 17, 2011.
22 City of Melbourne, www.melbourne.vic.gov.au/Environment/CH2/Design Delivery/Documents/CH2_Snapshot5.pdf, accessed January 17, 2011.
23 Ibid.
24 Ibid.
25 City of Melbourne, www.melbourne.vic.gov.au/Environment/CH2/Design Delivery/Documents/CH2_Snapshot3.pdf, accessed January 17, 2011.
26 Ibid.
27 City of Melbourne, www.melbourne.vic.gov.au/Environment/CH2/Design Delivery/Documents/CH2_Snapshot5.pdf, accessed January 17, 2011.
28 City of Melbourne, www.melbourne.vic.gov.au/Environment/CH2/Design Delivery/Documents/CH2_Snapshot6.pdf, accessed January 17, 2011.
29 Ibid.
30 Ibid.
31 City of Melbourne, www.melbourne.vic.gov.au/Environment/CH2/Design Delivery/Documents/CH2_Snapshot15.pdf, accessed January 17, 2011.
32 Ibid.
33 City of Melbourne, www.melbourne.vic.gov.au/Environment/CH2/Design Delivery/Documents/CH2_Snapshot5.pdf, accessed January 17, 2011.
34 City of Melbourne, www.melbourne.vic.gov.au/Environment/CH2/Design Delivery/Documents/CH2_Snapshot15.pdf, accessed January 17, 2011.
35 Yudelson, *Green Building A to Z*, op. cit.
36 Ibid.
37 Ibid.
38 Email communication with Paul Di Nello, City of Melbourne, December 23, 2010.
39 Jones, "Council House 2, Melbourne," op. cit.
40 Note that this is a Southern Hemisphere building, so orientations are reversed between south and north, compared with the Northern Hemisphere.
41 City of Melbourne, www.melbourne.vic.gov.au/Environment/CH2/Design Delivery/Documents/CH2_Snapshot14.pdf, accessed January 17, 2011.
42 CH2 Virtual Tour, op. cit.
43 Ibid.
44 Ibid.
45 Jones, "Council House 2, Melbourne," op. cit.
46 City of Melbourne, www.melbourne.vic.gov.au/Environment/CH2/Design Delivery/Documents/CH2_Snapshot8.pdf, accessed January 17, 2011.
47 Ibid.
48 Ibid.
49 Ibid.
50 City of Melbourne, www.melbourne.vic.gov.au/Environment/CH2/Design Delivery/Documents/CH2_Snapshot5.pdf, accessed January 17, 2011.
51 Jones, "Council House 2, Melbourne," op. cit.
52 Ibid.
53 City of Melbourne, www.melbourne.vic.gov.au/Environment/CH2/Design Delivery/Documents/CH2_Snapshot5.pdf, accessed January 17, 2011.
54 Jones, "Council House 2, Melbourne," op. cit.
55 Peter St. Clair, "Human Health, Comfort and Productivity in Commercial Office Buildings: An Evaluation of 30 The Bond and Council House 2," www.peterstclair.com/pdf/Human-Health-Comfort-Productivity-The-Bond-Council-House-2_LR.pdf, accessed January 17, 2011.
56 Russell Fortmeyer, 2009, "Case Study: Council House 2," *GreenSource,* http://greensource.construction.com/projects/2009/05_Council-House.asp, accessed January 17, 2011.
57 City of Melbourne, www.melbourne.vic.gov.au/Environment/CH2/Design Delivery/Documents/CH2_Snapshot20.pdf, accessed January 17, 2011.
58 St. Clair, "Human Health, Comfort and Productivity," op. cit.
59 Green Building Council of Australia, www.gbca.org.au/project-directory.asp#505, accessed December 29, 2011.
60 Email communication with Paul Di Nello, City of Melbourne, December 23, 2010.
61 Adrian Leaman, et al., "Occupant survey of CH2," January 16, 2008. Supplied via email by Adrian Leaman.

62 Email communication with Paul Di Nello, City of Melbourne, December 23, 2010.
63 CH2 Virtual Tour, op. cit.
64 See www.clivewilkinson.com/feature/mac_description17.html, accessed November 9, 2011.
65 Andrew Metcalf, 2009, "The Diagonal Principle," *Architectural Review*, April, pp. 77–85.
66 "One Shelley Street, Macquarie Group," November 24, 2010, http://designbuildsource.com.au/one-shelley-street-macquarie-group, accessed November 9, 2011.
67 Ibid.
68 See www.contemporist.com/2010/03/28/one-shelley-street-office-interior-by-clive-wilkinson-architects, accessed November 7, 2011.
69 "One Shelley Street, Macquarie Group," November 24, 2010, http://designbuildsource.com.au/one-shelley-street-macquarie-group, accessed November 9, 2011.
70 Philips, "One Shelley Street: Office Lighting Gets Six Stars," www.lighting.philips.com/main/subsites/dynalite/projects/office/one_shelley_street.wpd, accessed November 7, 2011.
71 "One Shelley Street, Sydney," *Mondo*, May 2010, www.mondoarc.com/projects/commercial/458219/one_shelley_street_sydney.html, accessed November 7, 2011.
72 Ibid.
73 See www.brookfieldmultiplex.com/newsfeed/view/6_star_green_star_rating_for_one_shelley_street_2011_09_01, accessed November 7, 2011.
74 Advanced Environmental, 2008, "King Street Wharf: 1 Shelley Street Building Users' Guide," December 16.
75 Brookfield Multiplex, "Building Outperformance Research Fact Sheet." supplied by Yvette Elvy, Brookfield Asset Management.
76 AECOM, "Energy Monitoring Report," October 2011, p. 35.
77 See, for example, Jerry Yudelson, 2010, *Dry Run: Preventing the Next Urban Water Crisis*, Gabriola Island, BC: New Society Publishers, p. 60.
78 Brookfield Multiplex, 2009 "API NSW Excellent in Property Awards: Estate Master Property Development Award One Shelley Street, Sydney NSW." Supplied via email by Yvette Elvy.
79 Personal communication, Jon Collinge, Senior Sustainability Manager, Lend Lease, December 21, 2010.
80 See www.wjpsolutions.com.au/docs/CASE%20STUDY_THE%20GAUGE.pdf, accessed April 6, 2011.
81 See www.wjpsolutions.com.au/docs/CASE%20STUDY_THE%20GAUGE.pdf, accessed April 6, 2011.
82 Ibid.
83 See www.gbca.org.au/green-star/green-building-case-studies/workplace6/2918.htm, accessed April 6, 2011.
84 Ibid.
85 Water Environment Research Foundation, "Case Study: Workplace6 Recycled Water Factory," www.werf.org/AM/Template.cfm?Section=Home&TEMPLATE=/CM/ContentDisplay.cfm&CONTENTID=13311, accessed January 23, 2012.
86 See www.gbca.org.au/green-star/green-building-case-studies/workplace6/2918.htm, op. cit.
87 Water Environment Research Foundation, "Case Study," op. cit. NABERS is the National Australian Built Environment Rating Scheme, equivalent roughly to the US Energy Star and the EU's Energy Performance in Buildings Directive, www.nabers.com.au.
88 www.newyork-architects.com/en/projects/detail_thickbox/32401/plang:en-gb?iframe=true&width=850&height=99, accessed January 11, 2012.
89 Ibid.
90 Ibid.
91 Ibid.
92 Ibid.
93 Julia van den Hout, "Horizontal Skyscraper: Vanke Center—Green Sheet," supplied via email, January 5, 2012.
94 Ibid.
95 Ibid.
96 Ibid.
97 Ibid.
98 Ibid.
99 Ibid.
100 Ibid.
101 Ibid.
102 Ibid.
103 Ibid.
104 Ibid.
105 Ibid.
106 Ibid.
107 Ibid.
108 Ibid.
109 Ibid.
110 Ibid.
111 See www.suzlon.com/careers/l3.aspx?l1=8&l2=39&l3=81, accessed November 22, 2011.
112 "Suzlon Global Headquarters 'One Earth' Receives 'LEED Platinum' Certification," April 29, 2010.
113 Personal communication, Anjali Dwivedi, January 20, 2012.
114 See www.ibec.or.jp/jsbd/Q/features.htm, accessed January 27, 2012.
115 See www.ibec.or.jp/jsbd/W/features.htm, accessed January 27, 2012.
116 See www.inive.org/Ibase_Search/search-detail-airbase-001.asp?ID=17883, accessed January 27, 2012.
117 See www.ibec.or.jp/jsbd/W/tech.htm, accessed December 28, 2011.

118 See www.ibec.or.jp/CASBEE/accredited_pdf/0029.pdf, accessed January 27, 2012.
119 See www.ibec.or.jp/CASBEE/accredited_pdf/0016.pdf, accessed January 27, 2012.
120 See www.ibec.or.jp/jsbd/A/features.htm, accessed January 27, 2012.
121 See www.ibec.or.jp/jsbd/AQ/index.htm, accessed February 10, 2012.
122 See www.ibec.or.jp/jsbd/AQ/tech.htm, accessed February 10, 2012.
123 Ibid.
124 See www.ibec.or.jp/jsbd/AQ/features.htm, accessed February 10, 2012.
125 See www.ibec.or.jp/jsbd/AS/features.htm, accessed January 27, 2012.
126 www.takenaka.co.jp/takenaka_e/majorworks_e/topics/2009/aut/02.html, accessed June 29, 2012.
127 See www.sunearthtools.com/dp/tools/CO2-emissions-calculator.php, accessed January 27, 2012.
128 See www.ibec.or.jp/CASBEE/accredited_pdf/0029.pdf, accessed January 27, 2012.
129 Nanyang Technological University, 2011, "NTU Wins Platinum Award from BCA for Sustainable Design," May 19, http://news.ntu.edu.sg/pages/newsdetail.aspx?URL=See http://news.ntu.edu.sg/news/Pages/NR2011_May19.aspx&Guid=a8e4c01d-3d26–484f-86ed-1a25cee9dbcf&Category=News+Releases, accessed September 15, 2011.
130 CPG Consultants, "Architect's Narrative," supplied by CPG Consultants Pte Ltd, December 18, 2011.
131 Ibid.
132 Aric Chen, 2009, "View from the Roof," *GreenSource*, May/June, http://greensource.construction.com/projects/2009/05_Nanyang-Technological-University.asp, accessed December 26, 2011.
133 Ibid.
134 BCA Green Mark, www.greenmark.sg/property-detail.php?id=464, accessed December 26, 2011; and NTU, www.ntu.edu.sg/fpm/usefulinfo/green Website/Pages/NewBuildings.aspx, accessed December 26, 2011.
135 NTU, "Educator's Narrative," supplied by CPG Consultants Pte Ltd, December 18, 2011.
136 Juniper Foo, 2009, "Singapore Showcases Its First Zero Energy Building," October 27, http://asia.cnet.com/crave/singapore-showcases-its-first-zero-energy-building-62109198.htm, accessed September 2, 2011.
137 Building and Construction Authority (BCA), www.bca.gov.sg/zeb/whatiszeb.html, accessed September 10, 2011.
138 Green Mark, www.greenmark.sg/about_proj_zero.html, accessed September 2, 2011.
139 Eugene Tay, 2010, "Singapore's Zero Energy Building (ZEB) On Track to Meet Net Zero Power Consumption," *Green Business Times*, September 15, www.greenbusinesstimes.com/2010/09/15/singapores-zero-energy-building-zeb-on-track-to-meet-net-zero-power-consumption, accessed September 2, 2011.
140 Personal communication, Alice Swee Lee Goh, Senior Executive Research Office, Centre for Sustainable Buildings and Construction—Building and Construction Authority, August 4, 2011.
141 Green Mark, www.greenmark.sg/about_proj_zero.html, accessed September 2, 2011.
142 See www.bca.gov.sg, accessed September 10, 2011.
143 BCA, www.bca.gov.sg/zeb/daylightsystems.html, accessed September 10, 2011.
144 Ibid.
145 Ibid.
146 Ibid.
147 Green Mark, www.greenmark.sg/about_proj_zero.html, accessed September 2, 2011.
148 Zero Energy Building, www.bca.gov.sg/zeb/poweredbysun.html, accessed September 2, 2011.
149 Tay, "Singapore's Zero Energy Building," op. cit.
150 Personal communication, Alice Swee Lee Goh, Senior Executive Research Office, Centre for Sustainable Buildings and Construction—Building and Construction Authority, August 4, 2011.
151 Zero Energy Building, www.bca.gov.sg/zeb/poweredbysun.html, accessed September 2, 2011.
152 "National Cheng Kung University's Y. S. Sun Green Building Research Center Ranked World's No. 1 in Green Architecture," August 17, 2011, http://chicago.taiwantrade.com.tw/news/detail.jsp?id=6093&lang=en_US, accessed October 5, 2011.
153 Hsien-te Lin, "The First Zero-Carbon Architecture in Taiwan," supplied via email by Hsien-te Lin on August 27, 2011.
154 "Green Architecture: Y. S. Sun Green Building Research Center," January 24, 2011, www.robaid.com/tech/green-architecture-y-s-sun-green-building-research-center.htm, accessed October 5, 2011.
155 Lin, "The First Zero-Carbon Architecture in Taiwan," op. cit.
156 Personal communication, Hsien-Te Lin, Professor of the Department of Architecture at National Chung Kung University, March 2, 2011.
157 "National Cheng Kung University's Y. S. Sun Green Building Research Center Ranked World's No. 1," op. cit.
158 Lin, "The First Zero-Carbon Architecture in Taiwan," op. cit.
159 Wang et al., "Energy-Saving Techniques," op. cit.
160 Discovery Channel, www.youtube.com/watch?v=e8xMeXkBN-M, accessed October 5, 2011.
161 Wang et al., "Energy-Saving Techniques," op. cit.
162 Discovery Channel, www.youtube.com/watch?v=e8xMeXkBN-M, accessed October 5, 2011.
163 Luke Sabatier, 2011, "Quirky but Efficient, Taiwan's First Carbon Neutral Building Opens," *Focus Taiwan*, January 13, http://focustaiwan.tw/Show News/WebNews_Detail.aspx?Type=aALL&ID=201101130012, accessed October 5, 2011.

164 Lin, "The First Zero-Carbon Architecture in Taiwan," op. cit.
165 Sabatier, "Quirky but Efficient," op. cit.
166 Lin, "The First Zero-Carbon Architecture in Taiwan," op. cit.
167 Sabatier, "Quirky but Efficient," op. cit.
168 Interview via email with Gretel Hakanson, by Professor Lin Hsien-Te, Magic School of Green Technology, Taiwan.

8 Lessons from the Case Studies

1 For office buildings, some might argue that the benchmark should be energy and water use per occupant, but since most office buildings aim at nearly 100 percent occupancy, we choose to use energy use per unit area as the basic measure of efficiency.
2 In addition, building materials have their own embodied energy, called "gray energy" in Germany, which adds about 20 percent to the energy use of a building over its lifetime. In researching the case study for Forum Chriesbach in Chapter 7, we found one of the few instances where buildings had actually calculated gray energy.
3 US average energy use in buildings can be found in a 2003 survey, the most recent available, www.eia.gov/emeu/cbecs/, accessed January 19, 2012.
4 European results need to be interpreted with some caution because they often include only "regulated" use: heating, cooling, hot water, and lighting, which can understand total energy use by one-third or more.
5 Yudelson, 2010, *Dry Run: Preventing the Next Urban Water Crisis*, Gabriola Island, British Columbia: New Society Publishers, pp. 57 ff.
6 Yudelson, *Dry Run*, pp. 105–108.
7 Personal communication, Thomas Auer, Transsolar, December 2009.
8 Contributed by Mark Frankel, Technical Director, New Buildings Institute, from *GreenSource* magazine, Nov/Dec 2011. Reprinted with permission. http://greensource.construction.com/opinion/2011/1111-The-Next-Frontier-in-Green-Building.asp, accessed January 20, 2012.
9 http://newbuildings.org/sensitivity-analysis, accessed February 12, 2012.
10 As John Andary's story in Chapter 5 showed, it's possible to get excellent results with very early stage modeling that informs the building designers about daylighting and glazing.
11 Contributed by Peter Rumsey, and updated from "Out of Control Controls," *GreenSource* magazine, Sept/Oct 2011, p. 132, http://greensource.construction.com/opinion/2011/1109_Out-of-Control.asp, accessed January 20, 2012. Reprinted with Permission.
12 Steve Carroll is a principal and leads the commissioning practice at Glumac engineers, Los Angeles, California.
13 Steven A. Straus, Glumac, quoted in David R. Macaulay's *The Ecological Engineer: Glumac*, 2011, pp. 13–14.

9 Projects to Watch

1 See www.thefifthestate.com.au/archives/2189, accessed January 29, 2012.
2 See www.archdaily.com/190779/pixel-studio505, accessed January 27, 2012.
3 See www.gbca.org.au/green-star/pixel/13600.htm, accessed January 26, 2012.
4 Ibid.
5 Ibid.
6 See www.archdaily.com/190779/pixel-studio505, accessed January 27, 2012.
7 See www.gbca.org.au/green-star/pixel/13600.htm, accessed January 26, 2012.
8 www.pixelbuilding.com.au/FactSheet.pdf, accessed January 27, 2012.
9 See www.gbca.org.au/green-star/pixel/13600.htm, accessed January 26, 2012 and http://greensource.construction.com/green_building_projects/2012/1207-pixel.asp, accessed July 24, 2012.
10 "Parkview Green FangCaoDi Named the Best Green Building in Asia," November 12, 2010, http://en.prnasia.com/pr/2010/11/12/100230612.shtml, accessed December 5, 2011.
11 See www.parkviewgreen.com, accessed December 5, 2011.
12 Ibid.
13 Ibid.
14 www.parkviewgreen.com/en/download/Parkview%20Green%20brochure_pdf.pdf, accessed December 5, 2011.
15 www.parkviewgreen.com, accessed December 5, 2011.
16 Personal communication with Will Tseng, PR and Communications Manager, Parkview Green, November 27, 2011.
17 See www.parkviewgreen.com, accessed December 5, 2011.
18 "Quality Transcends Time," *Building Journal*, November 2010, www.building.hk/feature/2010_1206wfc.pdf, accessed January 23, 2012.
19 Ibid.
20 Ibid.
21 Ibid.
22 Ibid.
23 Ibid.
24 Ibid.
25 Ibid.
26 "UBC Opens North America's 'Greenest' Building to Advance Sustainability Research and Innovation," November 3, 2011, www.publicaffairs.ubc.ca/2011/11/03/ubc-opens-north-america%E2%80%99s-%E2%80%98greenest%E2%80%99-building-to-advance-sustainability-research-and-innovation, accessed November 9, 2011.
27 Ibid.
28 See http://sustain.ubc.ca/hubs/cirs/building/building-overview, accessed November 9, 2011.

29 "UBC Opens North America's 'Greenest' Building," op. cit.
30 Ibid.
31 Information from CIRS Technical Manual, http://cirs.ubc.ca/building/building-manual, accessed January 22, 2012.
32 See http://bullitt.org/who-we-are/mission-et-cetera, accessed November 9, 2011.
33 Ibid.
34 Eric Pryne, "Ultra-Green Office Building Breaking Ground," *Seattle Times*, August 27, 2011, http://seattletimes.nwsource.com/html/business technology/2016016390_bullitt28.html, accessed November 9, 2011.
35 Randy Gragg, "The Fifth-Annual Smart Environments Awards: Port of Portland Headquarters," February 14, 2011, *Metropolis Magazine*, www.metropolismag.com/story/20110214/the-fifth-annual-smart-environments-awards-port-of-portland-headquarters.
36 "Port of Portland HQ Goes LEED Platinum," June 14, 2011, www.portof portland.com/NewsRelease.aspx?newsContent=A_2011614171049RCHQ LEED35.ascx&topic=Corporate%20News%20Release, accessed January 11, 2012.
37 Ibid.
38 Living Machine Systems, "Port of Portland Headquarters Receives LEED Platinum," August 1, 2011, http://livingmachines.com/News/News-Releases/Port-of-Portland-Headquarters-Receives-LEED%C2%AE-Plati.aspx, accessed July 3, 2012.
39 "ACEC Engineering Excellence Awards 2011," supplied by McKenzie R. Volz via email on January 9, 2012.
40 Ibid.
41 Ibid.
42 "Port of Portland HQ Goes LEED Platinum," op. cit.
43 Jim Redden, "Airport Building Pushes Green Limits," *Portland Tribune*, May 14, 2009, www.portlandtribune.com/sustainable/story.php?story_id=124216043275524500.
44 Case study text adapted from Ulf Meyer, "Case Study: KfW Westarkade, Frankfurt, Germany," http://greensource.construction.com/green_building_projects/2011/1105_KFW_Westarkade.asp, accessed January 24, 2012.

10 Sustainable Cities

1 Jonathan Chapman, 2005, *Emotionally Durable Design: Objects, Experiences and Empathy*, London: Routledge.
2 William Rees and Mathis Wackernagel, 1998, *Our Ecological Footprint: Reducing Human Impact on the Earth*, Gabriola Island, BC: New Society Publishers.
3 Kevin Portney, 2003, *Taking Sustainable Cities Seriously: Economic Development, the Environment, and Quality of Life in American Cities*, Cambridge, MA: MIT Press.
4 Herbert Girardet, 1999, *Creating Sustainable Cities*, White River Jct., VT: Chelsea Green.
5 Richard Rogers, 1998, *Cities for a Small Planet*, London and New York: Basic Books.
6 Douglas Farr, 2008, *Sustainable Urbanism: Urban Design with Nature*, New York: John Wiley & Sons.
7 S. Guy and G. Farmer, 2001, "Reinterpreting Sustainable Architecture: The Place of Technology," *Journal of Architectural Education*, 54 (3): 140–148.

Bibliography

ASHRAE, USGBC and CIBSE (2010) 'Performance Measurement Protocols for Commercial Buildings', www.ashrae.org/standards-research–technology/special–project-activities (accessed July 3, 2012).

Calthorpe, Peter (2011) *Urbanism in the Age of Climate Change*, Washington, DC: Island Press.

Farr, Douglas (2007) *Sustainable Urbanism: Urban Design with Nature*, New York: John Wiley & Sons.

Frankel, Mark (2011) "The Next Frontier in Green Building," *GreenSource*, November–December 2011, http://greensource.construction.com/opinion/2011/1111-The-Next-Frontier-in-Green-Building.asp (accessed January 20, 2012).

Girardet, Herbert (1999) *Creating Sustainable Cities*, White River Jct., VT: Chelsea Green.

Guy, S. and Farmer, G. (2001) "Reinterpreting Sustainable Architecture: The Place of Technology," *Journal of Architectural Education*, 54 (3): 140–148.

Kats, Greg (2010) *Greening Our Built World: Costs, Benefits and Strategies*, Washington, DC: Island Press.

Macaulay, David R. (2011) *The Ecological Engineer: Glumac*, Portland, OR: Ecotone.

Meyer, Ulf (2010) "Eine 'brand-architecture' der besonderen Art," *greenbuilding*, December, http://greenbuilding-planning.schiele-schoen.de/zeitschrift/allgemein/archiv/preview.asp?f=gb21012022.pdf&s=15881 (accessed January 21, 2011).

—— (2011) "KfW Westarkade: Colors 'n' Curves: A New Bank Headquarters in Frankfurt May Well Be the World's Most Energy-Efficient Office Tower," *GreenSource*, May–June. http://greensource.construction.com/green_building_projects/2011/1105_KFW_Westarkade.asp (accessed January 21, 2012).

Portney, Kevin (2003) *Taking Sustainable Cities Seriously: Economic Development, the Environment, and Quality of Life in American Cities*, Cambridge, MA: MIT Press.

Rees, William and Wackernagel, Mathis (1998) *Our Ecological Footprint: Reducing Human Impact on the Earth*, Gabriola Island, BC: New Society Publishers.

Rogers, Richard (1998) *Cities for a Small Planet*, London and New York: Basic Books.

Rumsey, Peter (2011) "Out of Control Controls," *GreenSource*, September–October, p. 132, http://greensource.construction.com/opinion/2011/1109_Out-of-Control.asp (accessed January 20, 2012).

Watson, Rob (2011) "Green Building Market and Impact Report," www.greenbiz.com/research/report/2011/11/07/green-building-market-and-impact-report-2011 (accessed January 28, 2012).

Yudelson, Jerry (2008) *Green Building through Integrated Design*, New York: McGraw-Hill.

—— (2009a) *Greening Existing Buildings*, New York: McGraw-Hill.

—— (2009b) *Green Building Trends: Europe*, Washington, DC: Island Press.

—— (2010) *Dry Run: Preventing the Next Urban Water Crisis*, Gabriola Island, BC: New Society Publishers.

Index